Michael   O'Neill.
1946.

The GUINNESS Book of
Rail
Facts and Feats

A 'Unit-train' of empty coal cars traversing the Rockies on the Canadian Pacific Railway (Canadian Pacific Limited)

The GUINNESS Book of
Rail
Facts and Feats
Second Edition

by
John Marshall

GUINNESS SUPERLATIVES LIMITED

2 CECIL COURT, LONDON ROAD, ENFIELD, MIDDLESEX

First published in 1971
Second edition 1975

© 1975 Guinness Superlatives Ltd

Published in Great Britain by
Guinness Superlatives Ltd, 2 Cecil Court,
London Road, Enfield, Middlesex

SBN 900424 33 8

Set in 'Monophoto' Baskerville Series 169,
printed and bound in Great Britain by
Jarrold and Sons Ltd, Norwich

Contents

Introduction

In compiling this book I have used sources which I consider to be reliable and I have carefully checked anything doubtful. Source references, however, are omitted because to name them for each statement would greatly increase the size of the book without adding to its value. Principal sources were: *The Railway Directory and Year Book*; *Jane's World Railways*; Bradshaw's *Railway Manual* (1851–1923); Minutes of Proceedings of the Institution of Civil Engineers; files of *The Engineer*; *Engineering*; *Railway Magazine*; *Railway Gazette*; *Modern Railways*; and *Trains*; *The Dictionary of National Biography*; *Dictionary of American Biography*; *Webster's Biographical Dictionary*; and *Modern English Biography* (Boase); and numerous railway books, British and foreign, biographies, atlases and maps; and not least, my own notes collected over a period of nearly 40 years. *Early Wooden Railways* by M. J. T. Lewis (1970) is a piece of sound scholarship useful for pre-locomotive history. Individual books of particular value for locomotive history were: *A Century of Locomotive Building* by J. G. H. Warren (1923, 1970); *Articulated Locomotives* by Lionel Wiener (1930, 1970); *The Steam Locomotive in America* by Alfred W. Bruce (1952) and, the best of all, *American Locomotives, an Engineering History 1830–1880* by John H. White Jr (1968). The Bruce and also *The British Steam Locomotive 1825–1925* by E. L. Ahrons (1927, 1961), while sound on mechanical details, are not entirely reliable as histories.

I am grateful to many readers of the first edition who wrote to me to point out errors and to make suggestions. In particular I should mention Hugh Hyland of Sydney, Australia; Raymond F. Corley, O. S. A. Lavallée and Fritz Lehmann of Canada; Dr Bernard L. Albert and A. Barlow of New York and John H. White of the Smithsonian Institution, Washington, for valuable material on railways in Australia and North America. Ken Mills and Brian Fawcett helped with South American material. I am greatly indebted to R. H. N. Hardy for his unfailing kindness and interest, to G. Harrop for reading and correcting the proofs, and to my sons Andrew and Simon whose critical appraisal of every detail has been most valuable. My wife Ann, besides living uncomplainingly in the midst of a welter of papers, books and photographs, has relieved me of much of the inevitable drudgery in the final preparation of the book.

Besides those who helped by supplying photographs (all acknowledged under the captions) I am grateful to the following for information in addition to those mentioned in the first edition: Tønnes Bekker-Nielsen of Denmark; K. W. Foster; J. R. Glastonbury of the Australian Railway Historical Society; Ian G. Henderson; George Kraus of the Southern Pacific; P. G. Laws; W. I. O. Moffat, chief engineer of Cowans Sheldon, Carlisle; Peter Phillips; Dr P. Ransome-Wallis; L. Stanton, Chile; H. R. Stones; Norman Webster; and Harry de Winter of Amsterdam. Organisations to which I owe my gratitude are: Austrian Federal Railways; Danish State Railways; Norwegian State Railways; Altoona Area Public Library, Pennsylvania; Baltimore & Ohio Railway; Burlington Northern; Chicago, Milwaukee, St. Paul & Pacific; Louisville & Nashville Railway; and the Union Pacific Railroad companies.

My colleagues K. B. Smith and K. Jowett have kindly lent stamps from their collections, and Mr Smith supplied all the information which I have used in the section on stamps.

Once more I must thank the staff of the Social Sciences Library, Manchester Public Libraries, and in particular Mr Harry Horton whose vast knowledge of books has been of inestimable value.

Again no attempt has been made to compile a bibliography. For books on British railway subjects the reader should consult *A Bibliography of British Railway History* compiled by George Ottley (Allen & Unwin 1965). However, in the last ten years numerous important books (and even more unimportant ones) have appeared in Britain and North America, and I can only repeat the warning that not all railway books are of reliable authenticity, and that discrimination is needed in their use.

J. M., Bolton, Lancashire, 1975

Section 1
THE BEGINNINGS

The principle of a railway, a track which guides vehicles travelling along it, dates back to Babylonian times, about 2245 BC. Parallel lines of stone blocks with grooves in the centres, with a gauge of about 5 ft (1·524 m), can still be found.

The ancient Greeks used grooved stone wagon-ways with a gauge of 5 ft 4 in (1·626 m). Remains of these can be found all over Greece, principally between Athens and Piraeus.

The oldest known illustration of anything resembling a railway is a window high up in the Minster of Freiburg-im-Breisgau, Germany, dating from about 1350. It was presented by Johann Snewlin der Gresser who owned the Schauins-land Mines, and shows a miner pushing a box-like vehicle.

One of the earliest illustrations of a mine railway is found in a book published by Johan Haselberger of Reichenau in Lower Austria about 1519 with a title beginning *Der Ursprung gemeynner Berckrecht wie die lange Zeit von den Alten erhalten worde*. . . . It shows a man pushing a small truck along a wooden railway.

A Flemish painting, dated 1544, entitled *Les Travaux de la Mine*, on a wood panel 42 × 22 in (106·7 × 55·9 cm) was discovered about 1940. It shows a miner pushing a four-wheeled truck along a railway out of a mine. The painter probably obtained his information from the above book.

The earliest record of a railway in the generally accepted sense is an illustration of a narrow-gauge mine railway at Leberthal in Alsace in *Cosmographiae Universalis* by Sebastian Münster (1489–1552), dated 1550.

Rail wagons were described and illustrated by Georg Bauer (1494?–1555), in English George Farmer, who called himself Georgius Agricola, in *De Re Metallica*, first published in 1556.

A mine wagon with flanged wooden wheels, some wooden track with a gauge of 480 mm (1 ft 6⅞ in), and a switch or point with one blade, as used in gold-mines at Siebenbürgen in Transylvania, is stored in the Verkehrs und Bau-

museum, Berlin. They are said to date from the late sixteenth century which, if correct (and this is doubtful) would establish that railways were in general use in central Europe in the Late Middle Ages. Transylvania is now part of Romania.

The first recorded 'railway' in Britain was a line about 2 miles (3·219 km) long, made of baulks of timber, from coal-pits at Strelley to Wollaton near Nottingham. It was built by Huntingdon Beaumont between October 1603 and October 1604. Beaumont then established the wagonways on Tyneside, between 1605 and 1608.

Flanged wooden wheels were used on English wagonways from about 1660 or earlier. They were generally turned with the grain lengthways, that is parallel to the axle. Elm was preferred, but beech, oak and ash and even softwood were used. One example discovered at Broseley, near Ironbridge in Shropshire, probably dates from this period. It measures 9½ in (241 mm) diameter over the flange and 8 in (203 mm) over the tread which is 3¾ in (95 mm) 'wide' (along the grain).

The idea for the flanged wheel was a direct outcome of the guide-pin (*Leitnagel*), allowing a much wider gauge to be used with corresponding greater

Mine truck as illustrated by Georg Bauer, 1556. Note the guide-pin (Leitnagel) *which ran between the wooden rails and kept the wagon on the track* (*The Science Museum, London*)

stability and carrying capacity. For the guide-pin (see Georg Bauer's illustration on p. 9) the rails had to be close together and on this narrow gauge wagons were small and easily upset.

The first recorded use of the word 'railway' was in 1681 at Pensnett about $2\frac{1}{2}$ miles (4·023 km) north-east of Stourbridge, in Staffordshire, England (now West Midlands).

'Railroad' was first used at Rowton on the Tarbatch Dingle line near Coalport on the River Severn in Shropshire in 1702. The two words were then used indiscriminately in Britain until about 1850 after which 'railway' became standard. In North America this was reversed and 'railroad' became the more widely used.

The word 'waggonway' was first recorded at Broxley in Shropshire in 1631. It became widely used on Tyneside where it lasted until about 1800.

The earliest discovered record of the word 'tramroad' was in the Minutes of the Brecon & Abergavenny Canal Company, in South Wales, on 17 October 1798. This referred to the L-shaped iron rails or plates and was generally used in this connection. 'Tramway' generally denoted a light railway or mineral railway.

The word 'tram' is believed to derive from a Swedish dialect word *tromm* meaning a log, and probably originated with the old wooden railways or with the frame on which baskets of coal were carried.

Strips of wrought iron on the tops of wooden rails to protect them from wear were introduced in Britain by or before 1716.

The most famous of the early British wagonways was the Tanfield Wagonway in County Durham. The first section was built in 1725 and it was extended in 1726. It was a double-track wooden railway with a gauge of 4 ft (1·219 m). It was converted to iron rails in 1839. The Tanfield, or Causey ('courseway'), Arch built in 1727 by master-mason Ralph Wood, has a span of 105 ft (32 m) and is probably **the world's oldest major railway bridge**. It is a semi-elliptical arch with a rise of 35 ft (10·668 m), 22 ft $7\frac{1}{2}$ in wide (6·895 m) and the deck is 80 ft (24·384 m) above the stream. It remained the largest arch in Great Britain until surpassed by the span of 140 ft (42·672 m) over the Taff at Pontypridd, Wales, built by William Edwards in 1755. It carried traffic until the 1770s or later.

The Tanfield line, but not the arch, remained in use until 18 May 1964. The arch still carries a footpath across the gorge.

The use of 'check rails' on curves is known to date from 1729, and may be earlier, when they were recorded as used on a wagonway at Ravensworth in County Durham. The back of the wheel flange on the inside of the curve bears against the check rail and so prevents the outer flange from mounting the running tail. Check rails are also used on bridges and viaducts to prevent derailments.

Cast-iron flanged wheels were made at Coalbrookdale in Shropshire, England, from 1729.

The first railway in Scotland was the Tranent-Cockenzie Wagonway, about 10 miles (16 km) east of Edinburgh, laid down with wooden rails in 1722. Part of the line was used on 21 September 1745 in the course of a battle with the Young Pretender, Prince Charles Edward. Iron rails were used from 1815. It continued in use as a horse tramway until after 1880 when part of it was converted into a steam colliery railway.

A wooden wagonway was constructed by Ralph Allen (1694–1764), the Post Office reformer, at Prior Park, Bath, England, in 1731 to convey stone from quarries to the town. The well-known

Tanfield Arch, built in 1727 for the Tanfield Wagonway, the oldest railway bridge in the world (John Marshall)

engraving shown below by Anthony Walker, published in 1752, was the first illustration of an English railway. This was the first railway in Britain on which the use of flanged wheels is positively recorded.

Ralph Allen's wooden wagonway at Prior Park, Bath, from an engraving by Anthony Walker published in 1752; the first illustration of an English railway

The first railway authorised by Parliament in Britain was the line from a colliery at Middleton into Leeds, Yorkshire, constructed under an Act granted to Charles Brandling, Lord of the Manor of Middleton, on 9 June 1758. It was described in the Act as a 'wagonway' and was **the first on which steam locomotives were commercially used**. The first two engines, built by Matthew Murray of Leeds (see p. 31) to an order by John Blenkinsop, first ran on 12 August 1812. Because Blenkinsop believed that smooth wheels

would not grip the rails, it was propelled by a toothed wheel engaging on a rack on one of the rails. Two more similar engines were built in 1813. The rack engines continued in service until 1835. The wheels of one are preserved on a section of the original track in York Railway Museum.

A portion of the Middleton Railway is still active, preserved by the Middleton Railway Trust, founded in 1959 with the co-operation of the National Trust. Steam locomotives are still at work after 163 years, a world record.

The 'standard gauge' of 4 ft 8½ in (1·435 m) was first established on the Willington Colliery wagonway system near Newcastle upon Tyne, England. Killingworth Colliery, where George Stephenson began his railway work, was part of this system. The first section of 3 miles (4·828 km), from Killingworth Moor to Willington Quay on the Tyne, was built in 1764–65. It had wooden rails.

Cast-iron bars on the tops of wooden rails were first recorded in use at Coalbrookdale, Shropshire, in 1767. They served a double function: to protect the rails from wear; and to act as a store for stocks of pig-iron during a period of low prices and at the same time to enable the furnaces to remain in operation. They were 5 ft (1·524 m) long, 4 in (10·2 cm) wide and 1¼ in (32 mm) thick. The men who fixed these were known as 'platelayers', a term still in use today for permanent-way men.

John Blenkinsop's locomotive, built by Matthew Murray in 1812 for the Middleton Colliery Railway, Leeds (The Science Museum, London)

The first use of a railway as a canal feeder was from Caldon Low Quarries in Staffordshire to Froghall Wharf for which the Trent & Mersey Canal Company obtained an Act on 13 May 1776, the second British Railway Act. The canal was authorised in 1776 and completed at the same time as the railway in 1777. The course of the railway can still be traced.

Iron-flanged rails or 'plates' were introduced in England by John Curr of Durham, while he was viewer of the Duke of Norfolk's collieries at Sheffield in 1787. They were first used only underground in Sheffield Park Colliery. The 'L'-shaped rails, laid on wooden sleepers to a gauge of 2 ft (610 mm) were 6 ft (1·829 m) long and weighed 47–50 lb (21–22 kg) each. Their first use on surface lines was in 1788 on the Ketley inclined plane in Shropshire. They were cast at Ketley Ironworks and were laid on longitudinal timber bearers, 14 in (356 mm) square. The rails were 6 ft (1·829 m) long, 8 in (203 mm) wide, 2 in (50 mm) thick and the flange was 3 in (76 mm) high.

The flanged iron plates cast at Coalbrookdale rapidly replaced the cast-iron bars on wooden rails for flanged wheels used around Coalbrookdale since 1767.

Flanged rails were inefficient compared with edge rails and their use was restricted to mineral lines on which wagons were pulled by horses. Their most concentrated use was probably in South Wales, in the Forest of Dean in Gloucestershire and around Coalbrookdale. **The world's first steam locomotive,** Richard Trevithick's of 1803 (see pp. 32 and 115) was designed to run on flanged rails but proved too heavy for them. On the Peak Forest Tramroad in Derbyshire they continued in use until the 1920s and in the Forest of Dean until 1952.

The principal advantage of a 'plateway' was that flat-wheeled wagons could make part of their journey by road and part by rail. It was the first 'road-rail' device. Flanged rails formed a side track in the evolution of railways and were not in the direct line of development.

The oldest surviving railway wagon in Britain is a quarry truck of 1797 from the Peak Forest Canal Company, Derbyshire. It can be seen at the York Railway Museum. It ran on flanged rails.

Cast-iron edge rails for flanged wheels were first used in South Wales about 1790. They were 6 ft (1·829 m) long, 3 in (76 mm) wide at the bottom, 2½ in (64 mm) at the top and about 2 in (50 mm) thick.

'Fish-bellied' cast-iron rails were designed by William Jessop (see p. 31) in 1792 and were laid in 1793–94 on the railway from Nanpantan to Loughborough in Leicestershire. They had a broad head on a thin web, deepest in the centre (see illustration below). One end had a flat foot which was nailed into a peg in a stone block. The other end had a round lug which fitted into a slot in the foot of the next rail. These were the true ancestors of the modern rail.

Cast-iron fish-bellied rail of about 1830 in the Cromford Workshop of the Cromford & High Peak Railway, Derbyshire, England (John Marshall)

The first malleable iron edge rails were used at Walbottle Colliery near Newcastle upon Tyne in England in 1805. They were faulty, however, and were replaced by cast-iron 'fish-bellied' rails.

Wrought-iron rails were first used on the Brampton Railway in Cumberland, between 1808 and 1812 when about 3½ miles (5·632 km) were relaid with wrought-iron bars on stone block sleepers. About 2 miles (3·219 km) were laid with cast-iron rails.

The Brampton Railway was built as a wooden railway, begun in 1775 and completed in 1799. In 1836 the company bought the Stephensons' *Rocket* from the Liverpool & Manchester Railway (see p. 14) and used it until 1840.

An improved method of rolling wrought-iron rails was patented by John Birkinshaw at the Bedlington Ironworks, Northumberland, on 23 October 1820. They had a swelled upper edge and were in 18 ft (5·486 m) lengths. The patent even included welding the rail ends.

The first recorded use of flanged wheels in eastern Europe was in 1794 at the Oraviga Mines in the Banat, Hungary. They were wooden rollers 8 or 9 in (200–230 mm) diameter with flanges about 14 in (355 mm) diameter between the rails. The rollers were turned with the grain across them and frequently split. They lasted, at best, about a year. The use of flanged wooden wheels in the Banat and Transylvania dates from about 1774, possibly even earlier.

The oldest wagon with flanged wheels in Britain, also at York Railway Museum, is from the Belvoir Castle Railway in Leicestershire. This was a 4 ft 4½ in (1·333 m) gauge railway with 'fish-bellied' cast-iron rails 3 ft (914 mm) long, laid in 1815 by the Butterley Company of Derbyshire, to carry supplies from the Grantham Canal up to Belvoir Castle. Wagons were pulled by horses, until the line closed in 1918. It was dismantled in 1940, but parts near Belvoir Castle remain *in situ*.

A wagon of the Stratford & Moreton Railway on the original rails at Stratford-upon-Avon. The railway was opened in 1826 and used until 1881 (John Marshall)

The first public goods railway in the world to be sanctioned by Parliament was the Surrey Iron Railway, on 21 May 1801. It was 4 ft (1·219 m) gauge and opened from Wandsworth to Croydon on 26 July 1803 and was extended by the Croydon, Merstham & Godstone Railway, incorporated by Act of Parliament on 17 May 1803, and opened from Croydon to Merstham on 24 July 1805.

The first railway to carry fare-paying passengers was the Oystermouth Railway, also known as the 'Swansea and Mumbles Railway', incorporated by Act of Parliament on 29 June 1804. It was opened about April 1806 and carried passengers from 25 March 1807. Horse-traction was used at first, and even sail-power was tried.

From about 1826 horse-buses began plying along a turnpike road beside the railway and completely stole the passenger traffic; probably the first instance in the world of a railway succumbing to road competition!

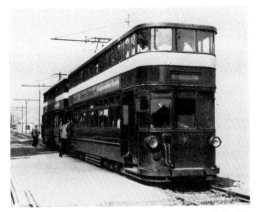

Cars of the Swansea & Mumbles Railway at Mumbles (John Marshall)

Passenger traffic was resumed in 1860 after the track was relaid. Steam-power was introduced on 16 August 1877 and lasted for 52 years until, on 2 March 1929, electric double-decked cars were put in service. They were the largest electric tramway cars in Britain, seating 106 passengers.

For goods traffic a petrol locomotive was obtained in 1929 and a diesel in 1936, making in all seven forms of motive power on one short railway.

For the second time, on 5 January 1960, the railway succumbed to a bus service. This time, however, it was dismantled.

It was the first railway in the world to celebrate 150 years of passenger services.

The first 'proper' railway in Scotland was the Kilmarnock & Troon Railway, incorporated on 27 May 1808 and opened for horse-drawn traffic on 6 July 1812. Steam-traction was introduced in 1817.

The oldest portion of the former Midland Railway, England, and one which still survives, was the Mansfield & Pinxton Railway in Nottinghamshire, incorporated on 16 June 1817 and opened on 13 April 1819. It was taken over by the M.R. in 1848, completely rebuilt, and reopened for steam-traction on 9 October 1849.

The first public railway to use steam from the beginning was the Stockton & Darlington Railway, opened on 27 September 1825. Steam locomotives were used at first only for goods trains.

The steam locomotive first established itself as a reliable form of motive power at the Rainhill Trials on the Liverpool & Manchester

Railway from 6 to 14 October 1829. The locomotives entered included *Rocket* (George and Robert Stephenson), *Sanspareil* (Timothy Hackworth) and *Novelty* (Braithwaite and Ericsson). The £500 prize was awarded to the *Rocket* on the last day.

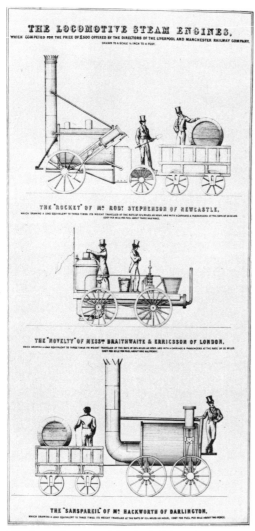

The locomotives entered in the Rainhill Trials on the Liverpool & Manchester Railway in October 1829 (The Science Museum, London)

The Canterbury & Whitstable Railway was opened on 3 May 1830. Stephenson's locomotive *Invicta* was driven by Edward Fletcher, later to be locomotive engineer of the North Eastern Railway (see p. 44). It inaugurated the

George Stephenson's Invicta *built in 1830 for the Canterbury & Whitstable Railway (The Science Museum, London)*

first regular steam passenger service over a mile of the line between Bogshole Farm and South Street, Canterbury.

The world's first 'modern' railway was the Liverpool & Manchester. The first of its several Acts received the Royal Assent on 5 May 1826 and the entire railway was opened on 15 September 1830.

It was the first public railway to be operated entirely by locomotives, except for winding engines at Edge Hill, Liverpool, for working traffic to and from the docks, Crown Street, and later Lime Street Station. It was the first to have double track throughout and the first to operate passenger trains to a time-table with freight trains fitted into 'paths' in between. It was also the first to operate all the traffic itself with its own vehicles and locomotives.

It is still a busy main line today, with 15 to 20 passenger trains each way between Liverpool and Manchester daily.

The first railway amalgamation to be authorised by Act of Parliament was the formation of the North Union Railway on 22 May 1834, uniting the Wigan Branch Railway with the Wigan & Preston Railway.

Sankey Viaduct on the Liverpool & Manchester Railway, built in 1829 (John Marshall)

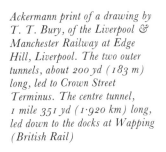

Ackermann print of a drawing by T. T. Bury, of the Liverpool & Manchester Railway at Edge Hill, Liverpool. The two outer tunnels, about 200 yd (183 m) long, led to Crown Street Terminus. The centre tunnel, 1 mile 351 yd (1·920 km) long, led down to the docks at Wapping (British Rail)

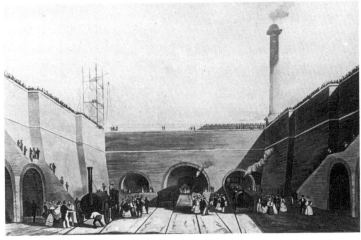

EARLY RAILROADS IN THE U.S.A.

The first railroad in North America was a short length of wooden track laid on Beacon Hill, Boston, Massachusetts, in 1795 to carry building material for the State House. A railway was laid on the same hill in 1807 to carry bricks. It was operated by Silas Whitney.

In 1811 a railway was built at Falling Creek near Richmond, Virginia, to serve a powder-mill. Another was built at Bear Creek Furnace, near Pittsburgh, Pennsylvania in 1818.

The first American railroad charter was obtained on 6 February 1815 by Colonel John Stevens of Hoboken, New Jersey, to build and operate a railroad between the Delaware and Raritan rivers near Trenton and New Brunswick.

Lack of financial backing prevented construction. (See p. 31.)

The first steam locomotive in North America was built by John Stevens in February 1825 and was tested on a circular track at his home at Hoboken. It had four flat-tyred wheels guided by four vertical rollers running against the insides of the rails, and it was propelled by a central toothed rack.

John Stevens was granted another railroad charter on 21 March 1823 for a steam-powered railroad from Philadelphia to Columbia, Pennsylvania. The company was incorporated under the title of the 'Pennsylvania Railroad' which established that name as the oldest among the numerous railroad companies of the U.S.A. It was 1829, however, before any part of the railroad was opened, and the whole line was not opened until 16 April 1834.

The Delaware & Hudson Canal Company

obtained one of the first U.S.A. railroad charters on 23 April 1823, for a line from Carbondale to the canal at Honesdale in the Lackawanna Valley. The railroad was built by John Bloomfield Jervis (1795–1885) and was opened on 9 October 1829, with a gauge of 4 ft 3 in (1·295 m).

For this railroad a steam locomotive named

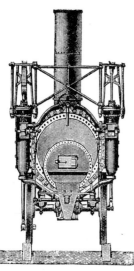

Drawing of Stourbridge Lion *built by Foster, Rastrick & Company in 1829* (The Engineer)

Stourbridge Lion was obtained from Foster, Rastrick & Company, Stourbridge, England, and it was tried on the line on 8 August 1829, driven by Horatio Allen (see p. 40). However, it was too heavy for the wooden rails covered with iron strips, and for many years afterwards the line was worked as a gravity railroad. It later became part of the present Delaware & Hudson system.

The *Stourbridge Lion* weighed 8 tons and measured 15 ft (4·572 m) high and 7 ft 7 in (2·311 m) wide. It ran only a few trial trips. About 1845 the boiler and one cylinder were sold to a foundry for use as a stationary engine and the boiler worked until 1871. This and a few other parts are preserved in the Smithsonian Institution, Washington D.C. A full-size operating replica built by the Delaware & Hudson Railroad in 1932 is exhibited at Honesdale, Pennsylvania.

The first railway corporation in the U.S.A. to build and operate a railroad was the Granite City Railway Company, incorporated in Massachusetts on 4 March 1826.

The first railroad in the U.S.A. to offer a regular service as a public carrier was the Baltimore & Ohio Railroad. This was chartered on 28 February 1827. The first stone was laid on 4 July (Independence Day) 1828, and the first 13 miles (21 km) between Baltimore and Ellicott's Mills, Maryland, were opened for passenger and freight traffic on 24 May 1830. The first fare-paying passengers were carried on 7 January 1830 from Pratt Street, Baltimore, to the Carrollton Viaduct. Horse-traction was used until July 1834. This line was closed to passengers on 31 December 1949.

The first steam locomotive on the Baltimore & Ohio Railroad, *Tom Thumb*, was built in 1829 by Peter Cooper (1791–1883) and was first run on 25 August 1830 from Baltimore to Ellicott's Mills and back. It developed only 1·43 hp which, however, was more than three times that of the Stephensons' *Rocket*. It had a vertical boiler.

The first Baltimore & Ohio rails were 6 in (150 mm) square wood baulks topped by iron strips. Mount Clare Station, Baltimore, was completed on 24 May 1830 and is the oldest surviving railroad station in the U.S.A. (see photograph p. 206).

On 30 June 1831 the Baltimore & Ohio became the first railroad in the U.S.A. to carry troops.

Tom Thumb, *the first steam locomotive on the Baltimore & Ohio Railroad, built in 1829 (Smithsonian Institution, Washington)*

The first U.S. President to travel by train was Andrew Jackson, on the Baltimore & Ohio Railroad from Ellicott's Mills to Baltimore on 6 June 1833.

The first train into Washington was run by the Baltimore & Ohio on 24 August 1835. In 1842, shortly after Charles Dickens had travelled on it, the railroad was extended to Cumberland, Maryland.

Washington became linked with New York in January 1838 by a chain of railways with ferries across major rivers and stage-coaches between stations in cities.

The first regular steam railroad in the U.S.A. was the South Carolina Railroad, opened on 15 January 1831. It now forms part of the Southern Railway system.

The first successful steam locomotive to be built in the U.S.A., *Best Friend of Charleston,* was built by West Point Foundry, New York, for the South Carolina Railroad in 1830 and was first tested with passengers on 14 December. It entered service on Christmas Day. It had a vertical boiler, weighed under 4 tons and developed about 6 hp.

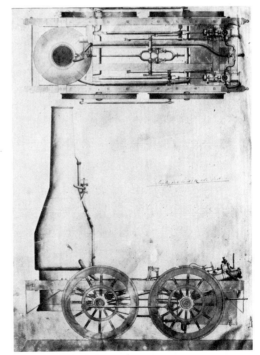

The Best Friend of Charleston *built in New York in 1830 for the South Carolina Railroad (The Science Museum, London)*

The original drawing of the inside-cylinder 0-4-0 De Witt Clinton, *the third steam locomotive in the U.S.A. and the one which pulled the first train in New York State on the Mohawk & Hudson Railroad from Albany to Schenectady on 9 August 1831 (The Science Museum, London)*

The Best Friend of Charleston had the distinction of **the first locomotive boiler explosion** in the U.S.A. On 17 June 1831, while it was being turned on the 'revolving platform' the Negro fireman held down the safety-valve to stop the steam escaping. In a few minutes the boiler blew up, injuring the fireman and several others including Mr Darrell, the engineer.

West Point, *the second locomotive of the South Carolina Railroad, built at West Point Foundry, New York, in 1831 (The Science Museum, London)*

The first steam train in New York State was pulled by the *De Witt Clinton* on the Mohawk & Hudson Railroad from Albany to Schenectady on 9 August 1831. This engine was also built at the West Point Foundry. It was a 0–4–0 with cylinders $5\frac{1}{2} \times 16$ in (140×460 mm), and 54 in ($1·371$ m) wheels, and weighed 4 tons.

One of the earliest constituents of the Pennsylvania Railroad, the Newcastle & Frenchtown Turnpike & Railroad Company, was opened in July 1831; it was 16·19 miles (27·842 km) long. Steam-power was used from October 1832.

U.S. mail was first carried by rail on the South Carolina Railroad (now part of the Southern Railway) in November 1831, and on the Baltimore & Ohio in January 1832. (See p. 171.)

The first American railroad tunnel was Staple Bend Tunnel, 901 ft (275 m) long, 4 miles (6·437 km) east of Johnstown, Pennsylvania, on the Allegheny Portage Railroad opened on 7 October 1834. Work on the tunnel began in 1829 and it was built by J. & E. Appleton at a cost of $37 498.84. It is 20 ft (6·096 m) wide, 19 ft (5·791 m) high, and it is lined with cut stone for 150 ft (45·72 m) at each end.

This section of the Pennsylvania Railroad, linking canals between Johnstown and Hollidaysburg, formed part of the route between Philadelphia and Pittsburgh. It was abandoned when the Pennsylvania Railroad opened its new route across the mountains, including the famous Horseshoe Bend, on 15 February 1854.

Charles Dickens travelled over the Portage

Crests of various British railway companies

Railroad in 1842 and described the journey in his *American Notes*.

By 1835 over 200 railway charters had been granted in eleven States and over 1000 miles of railway were open. For the development of railway mileage in the U.S.A. see p. 108.

Staple Bend Tunnel, Pennsylvania, the first railroad tunnel in North America (United States Department of the Interior, National Park Service, Western Pennsylvania Group)

The first iron railway bridge in the U.S.A. was probably one on the Reading Railroad near Manayunk, Pennsylvania, first used on 4 May 1845.

The Great Lakes were first joined by rail to the Atlantic seaboard in December 1842 when, except for the crossing of the Hudson River at Albany, New York, there were continuous rails from Boston to Buffalo on Lake Erie.

The first unbroken line of rails between the Atlantic and the Great Lakes was the New York & Erie (now Erie Lackawanna), completed from Piermont, New York, on the Hudson River to Dunkirk, N.Y., on Lake Erie and formally opened to through traffic in May 1851.

The first locomotive in Chicago was the *Pioneer*, weighing 10 tons, built by Matthias Baldwin of Philadelphia. It arrived by sailing-ship on 10 October 1848 and made its first run out of Chicago, pulling two cars, on 25 October.

Chicago became linked by rail to the eastern cities on 24 January 1854, but several changes of trains were necessary.

The first locomotive west of the Mississippi, *The Pacific*, ran the 5 miles (8 km) from St Louis to Cheltenham on 9 December 1852.

The first railroad to reach the Mississippi was the Chicago & Rock Island (now Chicago, Rock Island & Pacific), completed to Rock Island, Illinois, on 22 February 1854, opening up through rail communication to the Eastern seaboard.

The first railroad bridge across the Mississippi, at Davenport, Iowa, was opened on 21 April 1856. It was partly burned down on 6 May after a collison by the steamer *Effie Afton*, but was rebuilt and reopened on 8 September 1856.

The first railroad in the Pacific coast region was opened on 22 February 1856, when the locomotives *Sacramento* and *Nevada*, which had arrived by sailing-ship round Cape Horn, ran from Sacramento to Folsom, California, 22 miles (35·406 km).

The first southern rail route between the Atlantic seaboard and the Mississippi, from Charleston to Memphis, was completed on 1 April 1857.

Rail traffic first reached the Missouri River at St Joseph on 14 February 1859. The first bridge across the Missouri, at Kansas City, was opened on 4 July (Independence Day) 1869, establishing a through route from Chicago.

The first locomotive in the Pacific Northwest, the *Oregon Pony*, arrived at Portland, Oregon, on 31 March 1862.

The first American transcontinental railroad, from the Missouri River to the Pacific, was authorised by an Act signed by President Lincoln on 1 July 1862 (see p. 75).

The first railroad bridge in the U.S.A. with an all-steel superstructure was completed in 1879 at Glasgow, Missouri, on the Chicago & Alton Railroad, now part of the Gulf, Mobile & Ohio.

EARLY RAILWAYS IN CANADA

The first railways in Canada were coal railways in Nova Scotia, at Pictou in 1827 and North Sydney in 1828. Both used horses. They were 4 ft 8½ in (1·435 m) gauge and were probably the first in North America to use iron rails, which were cast in 5 ft (1·524 m) lengths.

Canada's first steam railway was the Champlain & St Lawrence Railway, 16 miles (25·750 km) long, chartered in 1832 and opened from Laprairie on the St Lawrence to St John on the Richelieu on 21 July 1836, with a 5 ft 6 in (1·676 m) gauge. (See 'The Provincial Gauge', p. 22.) The first locomotive was built by Robert Stephenson & Company, Newcastle upon Tyne, and named *Dorchester*. It was ordered on 26 October 1835 and was delivered on 21 July 1836, when the railway opened.

The oldest charter of a constituent of Canadian Pacific was that incorporating the St Andrews & Quebec Railroad Company in March 1836, for a railway from St Andrews, New Brunswick, to Lower Canada.

The first coal-burning locomotives in Canada, *Samson* (illustrated below), *Hercules* and *John Buddle* worked on a 6 mile (9·656 km) railway built in 1839 to carry coal from the Albion Mines to Pictou Harbour, Nova Scotia. *Samson* is preserved at Halifax Station.

The Erie & Ontario Railway, built in 1839, was the first railway in Upper Canada. It ran round Niagara Falls from Queenston to Chippawa. The original gradients were too steep for locomotives, and horses were used. It was later rebuilt with easier grades and in 1854 was reopened with locomotive operation. It was thus the third railway in Upper Canada to use locomotives. The Great Western and the Ontario, Simcoe & Huron Union Railway, both opened in 1853, used steam locomotives from the start.

The Montreal & Lachine Railway was opened in 1847, using an 18 ton American locomotive which took 21 minutes to cover the 8 mile (13 km) journey. The gauge was officially 4 ft 9 in (1·448 m).

The first locomotive from Great Britain to be imported into Lower Canada was the *James Ferrier*, built at Dundee, Scotland. It made its first trip on the Montreal & Lachine Railway on 24 July 1848. This was one of very few North American lines to use the British-type compartment carriage for three classes of passengers.

The first international railway link in North America was opened from Laprairie, Quebec, to Rouses Point, New York, on 16 August 1851. By international agreement, **the first of its kind in the world,** rolling stock of a foreign railway was given free entry into Canada or the U.S.A. This arrangement still operates.

The first steam train in Upper Canada ran from Toronto to Aurora, 25 miles (15·5 km), on 16 May 1853. This was the first section of the Northern Railway from Toronto to Collingwood on Georgian Bay, Lake Huron, completed in 1855. It is now part of the Canadian National system.

Samson, built by Timothy Hackworth in 1839 for Nova Scotia, one of the three first coal-burning locomotives in Canada (The Science Museum, London)

Early Grand Trunk Railway train, Canada (Canadian National Railways)

The railways of Canada grew from 22 miles (35 km) in 1846 to 66 miles (106 km) in 1850 and to 2065 miles (3325 km) by 1860.

The 'Provincial Gauge', 5 ft 6 in (1·676 m), was adopted in Canada partly for strategic reasons, to hamper invasion. It was also claimed that changing trains at the breaks of gauge would give passengers 'healthful exercise'!

In 1851 the gauge of the St Lawrence & Atlantic Railway, required by Charter to be 4 ft 8½ in (1·435 m) was changed to 5 ft 6 in (1·676 m) to match the Champlain & St Lawrence Railway. It was opened in 1853. Neighbouring lines in the U.S.A. were standard (4 ft 8½ in, 1·435 m) gauge.

The Great Western Railway of Canada, begun at London, Ontario, in 1847, was forced to adopt a third rail. It was opened from Niagara to London in 1853. The Grand Trunk Railway, chartered in 1852, was also built to the 5 ft 6 in (1·676 m) gauge.

The broad gauge held out until 1871, by which time most Canadian and U.S.A. railways had adopted standard gauge. Conversion of the Grand Trunk system took until September 1874. The Intercolonial Railway between Halifax and St John, New Brunswick, was converted to standard gauge by 1875, and the connection from Halifax to Rivière du Loupe was opened on 1 July 1876, bringing the mileage of the Intercolonial to 700 (1127 km).

The first 3 ft 6 in (1·067 m) gauge line in Canada was the Toronto & Nipissing Railway in Ontario, opened on 12 July 1871.

The first locomotive to be built in Canada was named *Toronto*. It was built at the foundry of James Good, Toronto, and made its first run on 16 May 1853 on the Ontario, Simcoe & Huron Union Railway, later renamed the Northern Railway.

Through trains were inaugurated between Montreal and Toronto on 27 October 1856 by the Grand Trunk Railway, later part of the Canadian National Railways.

Canada's first railway tunnel was opened by the Brockville & Ottawa Railway on 31 December 1860. It is about a third of a mile (536 m) long, passing beneath the town of Brockville, and is still in use by Canadian Pacific Rail.

The first railway tunnel in Canada at Brockville, Ontario, opened in 1860 and still used by Canadian Pacific trains. The photograph, taken in September 1957, shows the south portal (R. F. Corley)

The first railway in British Columbia was built in 1861 at Seton Portage, 140 miles (225 km) north of Vancouver. It had wooden rails, and cars were drawn by mules.

FURTHER RAILWAY DEVELOPMENTS

The railway was introduced to France by an Englishman, William Wilkinson (*c.* 1744–1808), who built a line in 1778–79 at Indret at the mouth of the Loire to serve a new ordnance factory. It was used until about 1800.

The first recorded use of the French term 'chemin de fer' was in 1784 by a Frenchman named de Givry, reporting on a visit to Coalbrookdale in Shropshire, England.

The first public railway in France, from Saint Etienne to Andrézieux, was begun in 1824 and formally opened on 1 October 1828. The Concession had been granted on 26 February 1823. The railway was used unofficially from May 1827. Passenger traffic began on 1 March 1832, but horse-traction was used until 1 August 1844. Cast-iron 'fish-bellied' rails were used. It was extended from Saint-Etienne to the Loire in 1828 using wrought-iron rails.

On 7 June 1826 a Concession was granted for the Saint-Etienne–Lyon Railway and the section from Givors to Rive-de-Gier was opened on 25 June 1830.

It was on this line that Marc Séguin (see p. 35) tried out his locomotive on 7 November 1829. This was the first locomotive with a multi-tubular boiler.

The remainder of the railway was opened from Lyon to Givors on 3 April 1832, and from the Rive-de-Gier to Saint-Etienne for goods on 18 October 1832 and passengers on 25 February 1833.

In Austria-Hungary the first railway opened on 7 September 1827, from Budweiss (now Budejovice, Czechoslovakia) to Trojanov, with horse-traction. It was the first section of the Linz–Budweiss Railway. Locomotives were not used until 1872.

The first railway wholly in modern Austria was the Kaiser Ferdinand Nordbahn from Vienna to Floridsdorf and Deutsch Wagram, 17·7 km (11 miles) long, and opened on 6 January 1838. It was the first railway in Austria to use steam locomotives.

The first railway in Ireland was the Dublin & Kingstown (now Dun Laoghaire) Railway, opened on 17 December 1834. It was standard (4 ft 8½ in, 1·435 m) gauge but was converted to the Irish standard of 5 ft 3 in (1·600 m) in 1857. The first locomotive, the 2–2–0 *Hibernia*, was built by Sharp Roberts & Company, Manchester.

The first section of the Ulster Railway, from Belfast to Lisburn, was opened on 12 August 1839, and was extended to Armagh on 1 March 1848. The gauge was originally 6 ft 2 in (1·880 m).

A story, possibly apocryphal, relates how an army officer was asked to settle the Irish gauge question. He simply rounded off the gauges to 6 ft and 4 ft 6 in, added them together and divided by 2. The result, 5 ft 3 in (1·600 m), became the Irish standard gauge which also found its devious way into Brazil and Australia, by the employment of Irish engineers.

The Ulster Railway was converted to 5 ft 3 in (1600 m) gauge in 1847.

Dublin & Kingstown Railway 2–2–0 Hibernia *built by Sharp, Roberts & Company of Manchester in 1834 (The Science Museum, London)*

Dutton Viaduct carrying the Grand Junction Railway (later London & North Western) over the River Weaver in Cheshire. The railway was built by Joseph Locke and was opened in 1838 (John Marshall)

The first railway in Belgium, from Brussels Malines, 14·5 miles (23·35 km), was opened on 5 May 1835. It was built and worked, as part of a planned national system, by the Belgian Government and was thus **the first nationalised railway**. It was also **the first steam railway on the European continent**. The first two locomotives, inside-cylinder 2–2–2s, *La Flèche* and *Stephenson*, were built by Robert Stephenson & Company at Newcastle upon Tyne. The third, *Olifant*, was built at the same time by Cockerill, Seraing, and was **the first locomotive to be built on the Continent.**

The first railway in Germany, the Ludwigsbahn from Nuremberg to Fürth, was opened on 7 December 1835. Robert Stephenson & Company again built the first locomotive *Der Adler*, similar to the Belgian locomotives.

The first railway in Russia was the St Petersburg & Pavlovsk Railway, built to a gauge of 6 ft (1·829 m). The first portion, Pavlovsk to Tsarskoe Selo, was opened to horse-traction on 9 October 1836. The entire railway was opened on 30 October 1837. Robert Stephenson & Company built the first locomotive in 1836.

The first railway in London was the London & Greenwich Railway incorporated on 17 May 1833, and opened on 8 February 1836 from Spa Road to Deptford, extended to London Bridge on 14 December 1836 and to Greenwich on 24 December 1838. The railway, 3¾ miles (6·759 km) long, was almost entirely on a brick viaduct of 878 arches. **It was the first 'overhead railway'.**

The first British trunk railway was the Grand Junction Railway from Birmingham to Warrington, engineered by Joseph Locke (see p. 42) and opened on 4 July 1837. It became part of the London & North Western Railway on the formation of that company on 16 July 1846. It had already absorbed the Liverpool & Manchester Railway. With the opening, on 17 December 1846, of the Lancaster & Carlisle Railway, of which Locke was again engineer, it formed a section of the main line from London (Euston) to Carlisle.

The opening of the Caledonian Railway from Carlisle to Glasgow and Edinburgh, again engineered by Locke, on 15 February 1848 completed the West Coast Route from London to Scotland.

The first railway across England was the Newcastle & Carlisle Railway, opened on 18 June 1838. It became part of the North Eastern Railway on 17 July 1862.

The oldest main line into London, the London & Birmingham Railway, was opened from London (Euston) to Birmingham on 17 September 1838. With the Grand Junction and the Manchester & Birmingham railways it became a part of the London & North Western Railway on 16 July 1846.

Birmingham was bypassed by the opening of the 39¾ mile (64 km) Trent Valley line from Rugby to Stafford on 15 September 1847.

J. C. Bourne's lithograph of Camden Shed on the London & Birmingham Railway

The first main line to London south of the Thames was the London & Southampton Railway, another of Joseph Locke's works. It was opened from Nine Elms, London, to Woking on 21 May 1838 and was completed to Southampton on 11 May 1840. With the Act of Parliament authorising the branch to Gosport opposite Portsmouth on 4 June 1839 the name was changed to the 'London &

South Western Railway'. The Gosport branch opened on 7 February 1842. The L.S.W.R. was extended from Nine Elms to Waterloo on 11 July 1848.

The first section of the Great Western Railway, engineered by I. K. Brunel (see p. 43), was opened from London (Paddington) to Maidenhead on 4 June 1838. It had a nominal gauge of 7 ft (2·134 m). It was extended to Twyford on 1 June 1839, to Reading on 30 March 1840, and was completed to Bristol on 30 June 1841. Brunel was then only 35 years old. The present Paddington Station was designed by Brunel and opened on 16 January 1854. (See Frith's *The Railway Station*, p. 159).

Ten years after the Liverpool & Manchester was opened, in 1840, only two Acts authorised any new British railway construction, and these merely short branches in Scotland. In 1841 only one short branch, in Hertfordshire, was authorised. (But see entry 'Railway Mania' 1846, p. 25.)

The first railway in the Netherlands was opened from Amsterdam to Haarlem on 24 September 1839. The first locomotive, *Arend* (Eagle), was built by R. B. Longridge & Company at Bedlington, Northumberland (Works No. 119), and was scrapped in 1857. A full-size replica stands in the Netherlands Railway Museum, Utrecht.

The first Netherlands railway time-table was published on 14 April 1850.

The first railway in Italy, from Naples to Portici, opened on 4 October 1839.

The oldest principal section of the East Coast Route, the Great North of England Railway from York to Darlington, was opened on 4 January 1841 for goods trains and on 30 March for passengers (see p. 26).

The first trans-Pennine railway, the Manchester & Leeds, was opened throughout on 1 March 1841. On 9 July 1847 it became the Lancashire & Yorkshire Railway.

The first conference of railway managers was held in Birmingham, England, on 19 January 1841, to draw up a code of rules, signalling, etc.

The Railway Clearing House to settle rates for through traffic over different British railway companies' systems began operating on 2 January 1842. The Irish Railway Clearing House was established on 1 July 1848.

The Midland Railway was formed on 10 May 1844 by amalgamation of the North Midland (Derby–Leeds), Midland Counties (Derby–Rugby), and Birmingham & Derby Junction railways. Derby became and remained the headquarters of the Midland Railway until it became part of the London, Midland & Scottish Railway on 1 January 1923.

Switzerland's first railway, from Basel to St Ludwig, (now Saint-Louis, France), opened on 15 June 1844. The Zürich–Baden Railway, opened on 9 August 1847, was the first railway entirely in Switzerland.

The railway from Manchester to Sheffield, 41 miles (66 km), was opened throughout on 23 December 1845. It passed through Woodhead Tunnel, 3 miles 13 yd (4840 m), then the longest railway tunnel in Britain.

The western portals of the old Woodhead Tunnels, with a Great Central 'Sir Sam Fay' Class 4–6–0 leaving on an express to Manchester (L. Biltcliffe)

The year when the greatest number of railway Acts was passed was 1846, during the 'Railway Mania', when 272 Bills received the Royal Assent in Britain.

The first steam railway in Hungary from Pest to Vacz, 33 km (20·5 miles), was opened on 15 July 1846. An early line from Pest to Köbanya was opened in August 1827.

The oldest railway in modern Denmark is the Copenhagen–Røskilde Railway, opened on 26 June 1847. (The Altona–Keil Railway, opened in 1844, was afterwards annexed with its territory by Prussia.)

The first railway in Spain, 27 km (17 miles), from Barcelona to Mataró, was opened on 28 October 1848. The first locomotive was also named *Mataró*.

A through railway between London and Aberdeen was completed with the opening of the Scottish North Eastern (later Caledonian) Railway between Perth and Aberdeen on 1 April 1850.

The first section of the Great Northern Railway (England), from Louth to Grimsby, 14 miles (22·5 km), was opened on 1 March 1848.

The 'East Coast Route' from London (Euston) to Edinburgh via the Midlands was completed in 1848 with the opening, on 29 August, of a temporary bridge over the Tyne between Gateshead and Newcastle and, on 10 October, a temporary viaduct over the Tweed at Tweedmouth.

The Tyne bridge was replaced by Robert Stephenson's High Level Bridge, opened for rail traffic on the upper deck on 15 August 1849, and for road traffic below on 4 February 1850.

The Royal Border Bridge across the Tweed, also by Robert Stephenson, was opened on 29 August 1850.

The Great Northern Railway was opened from Werrington Junction, Peterborough, to Maiden Lane, London, 79 miles (127 km) on 7 August 1850. King's Cross became the terminus of the East Coast Route when the G.N.R. was extended from Maiden Lane on 14 October 1852. The 'Towns Line', Werrington Junction—Grantham—Retford, was opened on 1 August 1852.

The Chester & Holyhead Railway was completed with the opening of Robert Stephenson's tubular bridge over the Menai Strait on 18 March 1850. It formed the northern part of the main line between London and Dublin.

Robert Stephenson's Britannia Tubular Bridge across the Menai Straits, in 1947 (John Marshall)

The first railway in India, part of the Great Indian Peninsula Railway, was opened on 18 April 1853 from Bombay to Thana. The gauge of 5 ft 6 in (1.676 m) became the Indian standard.

The first railway in South America was opened on 3 November 1848. It ran from Georgetown to Plaisance, 5 miles (8 km), in British Guyana. It formed part of the standard gauge East Coast line, 61 miles (98 km), and was closed on 30 June 1972.

The High Level Bridge at Newcastle upon Tyne, designed by Robert Stephenson and built by Hawkes Crawshary & Company. The rails, on the upper deck, are 120 ft (36·5 m) above the water and the bridge is 1372 ft (418 m) long. It was opened in 1849 (John Marshall)

The first railway in Chile ran from the port of Caldera to Copiapo, 396 m (1300 ft) above sea-level, a distance of 80·5 km (50·25 miles). The company was formed locally in October 1849, and the line was opened in January 1852. Locomotive No. 1 *Copiapo*, illustrated, built by Norris Brothers of Philadelphia, U.S.A., in 1850 is **the oldest steam locomotive in South America.** It was standard gauge and worked until 1891. The railway was taken over by the Chilean government in 1911 and later converted to metre gauge.

The oldest steam locomotive in South America, Caldera & Copiapo Railway No. 1 built in 1850, now preserved at Copiapo, about 1000 km (621 miles) north of Santiago, Chile (Ricardo Kelly)

The first railway in Brazil was the 5 ft 6 in (1·676 m) gauge line, 10 miles (16 km) from Maua at the end of the Bay of Rio to the foot of the Petropolis Serra. It was opened on 30 April 1854, and was later converted to metre gauge. On its extension to Petropolis it climbed the Sierra de Estrella for 4 miles (6·437 km) with a Riggenbach rack. In 1897 it became part of the Leopoldina Railway.

From 1862 the Dom Pedro II Railway (later Central of Brazil) established 5 ft 3 in (1·600 m) as the Brazilian broad gauge.

The first railway in Argentina, from Parque to Floresta, was opened on 30 August 1857. It was built to 5 ft 6 in (1·676 m) gauge because its first locomotive, named *La Portena*, and built in 1856 by E. B. Wilson & Company,

Leeds, was originally intended for India, and this established the 5 ft 6 in (1.676 m) gauge in Argentina.

The first railway on the African continent was opened in January 1856 between Alexandria and Cairo, 129 miles (208 km), standard gauge.

The North Eastern Railway, England, was formed on 31 July 1854 by the amalgamation of the York, Newcastle & Berwick (which had absorbed the Great North of England Railway in 1846), York & North Midland, Leeds Northern and Malton & Driffield railways. The Stockton & Darlington was absorbed on 1 July 1863.

The first railway in Norway, from Christiania (later Oslo) to Eidsvoll, 67·6 km (42 miles), was opened on 1 September 1854.

The first railway in Portugal, from Lisbon to Carregado, 37 km (23 miles), was opened on 28 October 1856.

The oldest portions of the Swedish State Railways, from Gothenburg to Jonsered and Malmö to Lund, were opened on 1 December 1856.

The Isle of Wight off the south of England, measures only 20 miles (32 km) east to west and 13 miles (21 km) north to south, yet it once had 45·25 miles (73 km) of standard-gauge railway operated by seven separate companies.

The first railway in the Isle of Wight was the 4.5 mile (7·242 km) Cowes & Newport Railway, opened on 16 June 1862. The last steam trains ran on 31 December 1966.

All that is left on the island today is the short line from Ryde to Shanklin operated with former London Underground electric trains.

Train at Freshwater, Isle of Wight, on 3 June 1953, headed by Adams 0-4-4 tank No. W29 Alverstone (John Marshall)

The Royal Albert Bridge at Saltash near Plymouth, built by I. K. Brunel in 1859 and seen here on 25 April 1958 before the new suspension bridge was erected alongside. (British Rail)

The railway from London to Penzance was completed on 4 May 1859, following the opening of Brunel's Saltash Bridge on 2 May. The West Cornwall Railway, however, was standard gauge. It was rebuilt to 7 ft (2·134 m) gauge, and the first through passenger service between London and Penzance began on 1 March 1867.

EARLY AUSTRALIAN RAILWAYS

In Tasmania in 1836 a wooden railway 8 km (5 miles) long was laid across a peninsula. Passengers paid a shilling to ride in trucks pushed by convicts to avoid a stormy sea journey.

Australia's first steam-operated railway was the 4 km (2·5 miles) long 1·600 m (5 ft 3 in) gauge Melbourne & Hobson's Bay Railway, opened from Flinders Street, Melbourne, to Sandridge, Victoria, on 12 September 1854.

The first passenger railway, however, was the 11·265 km (7 mile) Port Elliot & Goolwa Railway in South Australia, also 1·600 m (5 ft 3 in) gauge, opened with horse-traction on 18 May 1854.

In 1857 an inclined tramway of iron rails was laid from Newcastle down to the waterfront to carry coal from mines.

The first railway in New South Wales was opened from Sydney to Paramatta Junction, now Granville, on 26 September 1855. It was built by the Sydney Railway Company, but was taken over by the New South Wales Government before opening.

The first locomotive in New South Wales was a 'Class 1' 0–4–2 No. 1, built by Robert Stephenson & Company at Newcastle upon Tyne, England, for the Sydney & Goulburn Railway in 1854, to a design by J. E. McConnell. It weighed 43 tons 5 cwt, and worked the first train from Sydney, where it is now preserved.

In South Australia the 1·600 m (5 ft 3 in) gauge railway from Adelaide to Port Adelaide, 12 km (7·5 miles), was opened on 21 April 1856. It was built and worked by the Government.

In Queensland the first railway, to a gauge of 1·067 m (3 ft 6 in), was opened in July 1865, between Ipswich and Grandchester, 33·297 km (20·69 miles), in the Southern Division.

The first locomotive in New South Wales, Australia, 'Class 1' 0–4–2 No. 1 built by Robert Stephenson & Company in 1854 for the Sydney & Goulburn Railway. It is shown on display in the forecourt of Sydney Station at the Centenary celebrations on 19 August 1955 (J. L. N. Southern)

On 14 June 1883 the railways of New South Wales and Victoria were joined at Albury, after the completion of the bridge over the Murray River.

The first 'proper' railway in Tasmania, to a gauge of 1·600 m (5 ft 3 in) as in South Australia, was opened in 1871 between Launceston and Deloraine, 72·4 km (45 miles). It was taken over by the Government in 1872 as was the later Launceston–Hobart line, opened in 1876. The lines were converted to 1·067 m (3 ft 6 in) gauge, standard in Tasmania, in 1888. The first 1·067 m (3 ft 6 in) gauge line was opened in 1885.

In Western Australia the first railway was a 1·067 m (3 ft·6 in) gauge private timber-carrying line from Yoganup to Lockville, 19 km (12 miles) opened on 6 June 1871. It was worked by horses until August when the locomotive *Ballaarat* arrived from Ballaarat, Victoria, where it was built.

The first railway in South Africa, from Durban to The Point, was opened by the Natal Railway on 26 June 1860. It was acquired by the Natal Government on 1 January 1877.

Cape Province's first railway was opened to Eerste River on 13 February 1862 and extended to Wellington in 1863.

The first railway in Pakistan was the 105 mile (169 km) line from Karachi to Kochi, opened on 13 May 1861.

New Zealand opened its first steam railway from Christchurch to Ferrymead with 1·600 m (5 ft 3 in) gauge on 1 December 1863.

The first station at Christchurch, New Zealand, on the 5 ft 3 in (1·6 m) gauge Christchurch–Ferrymead Railway about 1865. Pilgrim, New Zealand's first locomotive, is seen on the train in the background (High Commissioner for New Zealand)

The first railway in Sri Lanka (Ceylon), from Colombo to Ambepussa, was opened on 2 October 1865.

The first railway in Japan, from Yokohama to Sinagawa, was opened on 12 June 1872. It was completed to Tokyo on 14 October.

China had no railway until 1876 when a 2 ft 6 in (0·762 m) gauge line was opened from Shanghai to Woosung, about 20 miles (32 km). It was operated by two tiny 0–4–0 saddle tanks, built by Ransome & Rapier, England. The engineer was John Dixon (1835–91), nephew of John Dixon of the Stockton & Darlington Railway.

The Chinese were hostile and suspicious and, following a fatal accident, as soon as the redemption money was paid, in October 1877, the railway was bought by the Government and the entire outfit was torn up and dumped on Formosa.

The first permanent railway in China was the standard-gauge Tongshan–Hsukuchuang line, opened in 1880, extended to Lutai in 1886 and Tientsin in 1888. It now forms part of the Peking–Mukden section of the Chinese People's Republic Railways. Steam-traction was introduced in 1883.

After this, Chinese railway mileage grew rapidly. By 1900 it was 1458 (2346 km); in 1973 it was 23 900 (38 500 km).

Japanese railways in the ten years from 1880 to 1890, grew from 98 miles (158 km) to 1459 miles (2348 km). By 1974 the total was 16 953 miles (27 283 km), and it is still increasing.

The first railway in Burma was the metre-gauge line between Rangoon and Prome, opened on 1 May 1877.

ATMOSPHERIC RAILWAYS

The first application of atmospheric power on a railway was in 1698. Sir Humphrey Mackworth had a car equipped with a sail and used it with success on an early mineral railway at Neath, South Wales.

Sail-power was also tried on the Swansea & Mumbles Railway, Wales, on 17 April 1807, covering the 4·5 miles (7·242 km) line in 45 minutes.

A sail car was used for a time on the South Carolina Canal & Railroad in the U.S.A. after it was opened on 25 December 1830.

Sail-power was used as a matter of routine on the 2 mile (3·219 km) railway to Spurn Head Lighthouse, Yorkshire, England.

The idea of running trains powered by a piston driven by atmospheric pressure along a pipe exhausted ahead of the train by a pumping engine was conceived by Samuel Clegg and Jacob and Joseph Samuda; it was patented in 1839. It was first tried out at Wormwood Scrubs, London, in June 1840.

The first use of the system on a public railway was in Ireland. It was installed on the Kingstown–Dalkey line which formed a 1·75 mile (2·816 km) extension of the Dublin & Kingstown Railway. Experimental trains began running on 3 October 1843 and passengers were carried, without charge, from December. It was officially opened on 29 March 1844. After a succession of troubles it closed on 12 April 1854 for conversion to a locomotive line.

The system was next tried on the London & Croydon Railway, on which regular 'atmospheric trains' ran from 19 January 1846, although passengers had been carried free since 27 October 1845. It was abandoned on 4 May 1847.

The great engineer I. K. Brunel (see p. 43) became so enthusiastic that he decided to employ the system on the steeply graded South Devon Railway. It was introduced between Exeter and Teignmouth on 13 September 1847, and extended to Newton Abbot on 10 January 1848. After numerous exasperating failures, often caused by rats eating the leather flap which sealed the slot in the top of the tube, the system was abandoned on 10 September 1848.

In France atmospheric traction was tried on a 2·200 km (1 mile 646 yd) section of the Paris–Saint–Germain Railway from Bois du Vésinet to Saint-Germain on 14 August 1847. It was abandoned in favour of steam on 2 July 1860.

The last attempt at an atmospheric railway was in 1864, when an experimental line was built at the Crystal Palace, London. It consisted of a tubular tunnel, in which the car fitted like a piston and was forced along by air pressure.

Section 2
THE PIONEERS

William Jessop (1745–1814) was one of the leading early British civil engineers who, although mainly concerned with the construction of canals, was responsible for several important early railways. He was one of the founders of the Butterley Company in Derbyshire, close to the great tunnel on his Cromford Canal, a company which became responsible for many early iron railway bridges. He was the designer of the 'fish-bellied' cast-iron rail. After constructing several short lines of railway in connection with canals, he engineered the Surrey Iron Railway, the first public railway in Britain to be sanctioned by Parliament (1801). It was followed by a line from Croydon to Merstham in 1805. In this he was assisted by his son Josias Jessop, who later became engineer of the Cromford & High Peak Railway in Derbyshire.

John Stevens (1749–1838) was a pioneer of mechanical transport in the U.S.A. After graduating in 1766 he studied law for three years and then joined the army, serving under General Washington. In 1784 he bought a large estate in New Jersey, including most of what is now Hoboken. About 1788 he became interested in the work of Fitsch and Rumsey in the development of the steamboat and from then to the end of his life he devoted himself to the development of mechanical transport by land and water. In 1791 he became one of the first United States citizens to take out patents, for an improved boiler and a steamboat engine. In 1803 he patented a multi-tubular boiler, 26 years before the Stephensons' *Rocket*, and in 1804 built a steamboat with two screw-propellers. In 1809 his *Phoenix* became the first seagoing steamship in the world.

In 1810 he turned his attention to railways and pioneered some of the earliest in Pennsylvania. In 1825, at the age of 76, he designed and built a steam locomotive and a circular track on his estate at Hoboken (see p. 15). This was the first steam locomotive to be built in America.

Matthew Murray (1765–1826) was one of the earliest steam-locomotive engineers. After training as a blacksmith he worked on flax-spinning machinery until 1795, when he entered

William Jessop (The Science Museum, London)

into partnership with James Fenton and David Wood at Leeds. Murray took out a number of patents for steam-engines from 1799. In 1812 he was engaged by Blenkinsop to build engines for the rack railway from Middleton Colliery to Leeds and built his *Salamanca* and *Prince Regent*. They had two double-acting cylinders, and the piston-rods worked in vertical guides with connecting-rods to the spur-wheels, which drove the 3 ft 2 in (965 mm) diameter cog driving-wheels. Murray can claim to have built the first commercially successful locomotive.

Edward Pease (1767–1858), a promoter of early railways, friend and supporter of George and Robert Stephenson. In 1818 he first projected the Stockton & Darlington Railway and in 1821 became acquainted with George Stephenson whom he appointed engineer, also financing the construction of the first locomotive on the railway, *Locomotion*. The first rail of the S. & D. was laid in 1823

Edward Pease (The Science Museum, London)

and the railway was opened in 1825. Pease was a prominent Quaker and was active in efforts towards the abolition of slavery.

Richard Trevithick (1771–1833) was the first to use high-pressure steam in an engine instead of atmospheric pressure as in the condensing steam-engines of Newcomen and Watt. He was born in Cornwall, but details of his early career and training are scanty; he taught himself about engines by observing them at the Cornish tin-mines. About 1797 he built a steam-engine for Herland Mine and in 1800 built a double-acting high-pressure engine for Cook's Kitchen Mine.

In 1796 he experimented with model steam locomotives and by the end of 1801 he had completed the first steam locomotive to pull a passenger carriage on a road. In 1803 a steam road carriage was tested in London, reaching speeds of 8 or 9 m.p.h. (12 or 14 km/h).

His first steam rail locomotive was constructed in 1803 to haul iron from Penydarren to the Glamorganshire Canal in Wales, and it was set to work in February 1804, but with a weight of 5 tons it was too much for the cast-iron tramway rails then in use. In 1808 he again attempted to popularise the steam locomotive, by running one on a

circular track in London. The locomotive was a success, but the public was not sufficiently interested and after this he abandoned work on locomotives.

In 1809 he began a tunnel under the Thames, but the project failed. A steam threshing machine is recorded in 1811.

In 1816 he went to Peru to supervise the erection of his engines in mines, but in the insurrection in the 1820s he lost all his money. He was found, penniless, by Robert Stephenson who assisted his repatriation.

He took out his last patent, for the use of super-heated steam, in 1832 and the following year he died in poverty in Dartford, Kent.

Richard Trevithick (The Science Museum, London)

William Hedley (1779–1843) was closely associated with the early development of the steam locomotive. From 1805 he was colliery viewer at Wylam, Northumberland, and in 1811 with Jonathan Foster he helped Timothy Hackworth with the first locomotive to be built entirely at Wylam. He has been credited with the invention of the locomotive powered by smooth wheels, as opposed to the rack and with the first use of the steam-blast, using exhaust-steam to draw the fire. These features, however, had been used by Trevithick in 1804.

His first major work was the cast-iron road bridge over the Wye at Chepstow in Monmouthshire (1815–16). In 1817 he became managing partner in the firm of Foster, Rastrick & Company of Stourbridge, Worcestershire, which built several early locomotives. In 1826–27 he constructed the tramway from Stratford-on-Avon to Moreton-in-Marsh which was the first line to use Birkinshaw's wrought-iron rails.

Rastrick was appointed one of the judges at the Rainhill Trials. His greatest work was the London & Brighton Railway, 1837–40, one of the most magnificently engineered railways in the world, including the Merstham, Balcombe and Clayton tunnels and the tremendous Ouse Viaduct.

George Stephenson (1781–1848), perhaps the most famous name in the history of railways. He was the second son of Robert Stephenson, fireman at Wylam Colliery near Newcastle upon Tyne. He had almost no formal education, and gained his engineering experience working at various collieries, first as fireman and later as engineman, at the same time learning to read and write at a night school. In 1802 he married and the following year his only son Robert was born. His wife died of tuberculosis in 1806, and there followed a period of difficulty and hardship during which his father became incapable of further work and had to be supported as well as his mother. However, following his success in repairing a Newcomen pumping engine, he was appointed enginewright at Killingworth Colliery in 1812 at a salary of £100 a year.

His inventive genius was first applied to the production of a safety-lamp for miners. This was first tried on 21 October 1815. Unknown to each other, Sir Humphrey Davy had been working on the same problem and he produced a lamp on the same principle at about the same time.

Following attempts by Blackett and Hedley in 1812 to produce steam locomotives for Wylam Colliery, Stephenson turned his attention to this problem and built his first steam locomotive in 1813–14. It could pull 30 tons up a gradient of 1 in 450 at 4 m.p.h. (6·5 km/h). This was the first recorded example of a locomotive in which the blast of the exhaust-steam was used to create a draught for the fire.

Stephenson provided further locomotives for the 8 mile (13 km) long Hetton Colliery Railway in County Durham, opened in 1822. Shortly after this he was appointed by Edward Pease to construct the Stockton & Darlington Railway for which he built the first locomotive, *Locomotion*, in 1825. This engine can still be seen on Darlington Station.

John Urpeth Rastrick (The Science Museum, London)

John Urpeth Rastrick (1780–1856), like so many early British engineers, was a native of Northumberland. After training with his father he joined Hazeldine at Bridgnorth, Shropshire. In 1814 he took out a patent for a steam-engine and was soon experimenting with steam-traction on railways.

North end of Clayton Tunnel, 1 mile 507 yd (2·072 km) long, on Rastrick's London & Brighton Railway, with a Brighton–London electric express emerging, 12 August 1969 (John Marshall)

He was next appointed engineer to the Liverpool & Manchester Railway. Despite its progress of nearly a quarter of a century steam locomotion was still held in doubt. It was only after the Trials at Rainhill on the Liverpool & Manchester Railway in October 1829 in which the prize of £500 was won by the *Rocket*, specially constructed, mainly by his son Robert, that the proprietors became convinced of the advantage of steam locomotives.

Other railways to which George Stephenson was chief engineer were the Grand Junction (Birmingham–Warrington), Manchester & Leeds, North Midland (Derby–Leeds), York & North Midland (Normanton–York) besides many shorter lines such as the Whitby & Pickering, and the Leicester & Swannington.

During the construction of the North Midland Railway, Stephenson opened up lime-works at Ambergate, and collieries at Clay Cross near Chesterfield. It was near there, at Tapton House, that he spent his last years, taking up his hobby of horticulture. He died there on 12 August 1848 and was buried at Trinity Church, Chesterfield.

George Stephenson (British Rail)

John Blenkinsop (1783–1831) was born at Leeds, England. On 10 April 1811 he was granted a patent for a steam locomotive. The first engine to his order was built by Matthew Murray for the Middleton Colliery Railway, Leeds, in 1812. Its chief feature was a rack-wheel drive on to cogs on the side of one rail. At a test at Hunslet, Leeds, on 24 June 1812 it covered 1·5 miles (2·4 km) in 23 minutes. Other Blenkinsop engines were used at Orrell Colliery near Wigan and at Willington, Kenton and Coxlodge collieries near Newcastle upon Tyne. A set of Blenkinsop wheels with rack rails is preserved in the York Railway Museum.

William Cubitt (1785–1861) was trained as a millwright in Norfolk, England, in 1807 taking out a patent for self-regulating windmill-sails. In 1817 he invented the treadmill for using the labour of convicts in prison for grinding corn.

From 1826 to 1858 he practised as a civil engineer in London and was engaged in works on the Oxford and Liverpool Junction canals.

His principal work in railway engineering was the South Eastern Railway, which branched off from Rastrick's London & Brighton Railway at Redhill through the Weald of Kent to Folkestone. From here to Dover the line was carried through a succession of tunnels beneath the cliffs, and the work involved the blasting of Round Down Cliff with one 18000 lb (8165 kg) charge of gunpowder, exploded electrically on 26 January 1843.

In 1850–51 he superintended the erection of the Crystal Palace for the Great Exhibition in London, and in 1851 he was knighted at Windsor Castle. Other works included the floating landing-stages on the Mersey at Liverpool and the iron bridge over the Medway at Rochester.

Sir William Cubitt (The Science Museum, London)

Timothy Hackworth (1786–1850), one of the most important figures in the early development of the locomotive. He was the eldest son of John Hackworth, foreman smith at Wylam Colliery, Northumberland, and was trained in the same craft, first under his father who died in 1802, then under the supervision of Christopher Blackett, proprietor of the colliery. From 1816 to 1824 he was foreman smith at Walbottle Colliery near Newcastle upon Tyne; and after a short period supervising the Forth Street Works of Robert Stephenson & Company, while George Stephenson was away on the Liverpool & Manchester Railway and Robert in South America, he transferred to the Stockton & Darlington Railway and set up the Locomotive Works at New Shildon. Here he built the *Royal George* in 1827, the first six-coupled engine and the first in which the cylinders drove directly on to the wheels. In 1829 he built the *Sanspareil*, which he entered in the Rainhill Trials and which narrowly missed success. In 1838 he introduced his successful o–6–o type with inclined cylinders at the rear driving the front coupled wheels. One of these, the *Derwent*, is preserved on Darlington Station (see illustration). His last locomotive, the 2–2–2 *Sanspareil No 2*, was built in 1849.

Hackworth was also responsible for the first use of the following features on locomotives: the eight-wheeled bogie engine in 1813; side coupling-rods instead of chains (S. & D. *Locomotion* in 1825); spring-loaded safety-valve, instead of weights; self-lubricating bearings, with oil-reservoir; steam-dome on boiler to obtain dry steam; inside cylinders and crank-axle; valve gear reversed by single lever; 'lap' in slide-valves to permit expansive working.

Stockton & Darlington Railway o–6–o No. 25 Derwent designed by Hackworth and built in 1845 by W. & A. Kitching of the Hopetown Railway Foundry, Darlington

Marc Séguin (1786–1875), French engineer and scientist, the designer and builder of the first steam locomotive in France in 1829 for the Saint-Etienne–Lyon Railway. It was the first engine to incorporate a multi-tubular boiler which was patented by him in 1827. A forced draught was provided by two rotary fans on the tender, driven by the wheels. The engine weighed nearly 6 tons in working order and could haul 30 tons on a gradient of 1 in 167 at 4·5 m.p.h. (7·25 km/h).

Model of Marc Seguin's locomotive, the first in France (The Science Museum, London)

Robert Livingston Stevens (1787–1856), son of John Stevens (q.v.), American mechanical engineer and naval architect and pioneer of railroads and steam navigation. In 1830, on the establishment of the Camden & Amboy Railroad, he was elected president and chief engineer and he visited England, like Allen, Whistler and McNeill

Timothy Hackworth (The Science Museum, London)

before him, to study locomotives and railways. On the voyage he designed the flat-bottomed rail, now standard throughout the world, and had this rolled in England. At the same time he designed a fish-plate for joining rail ends, and the claw spike for holding rails to ties, or sleepers. In England he bought the Stephenson 'Planet'-type 0–4–0 named *Stevens* (later renamed *John Bull* and fitted it with the first American 'pilot'—see pp. 120 and 125), which was built in 1831. At the Hoboken shops, N.J., he devised a cut-off valve gear for locomotives, improved boilers and pioneered the burning of anthracite on locomotives.

Thomas Shaw Brandreth (1788–1873), mathematician, classical scholar and barrister-at-law, educated at Eton College and Cambridge University. His scientific bent resulted in a close friendship with George Stephenson and he was one of the original directors of the Liverpool & Manchester Railway until the end of 1830. He was active in the survey of the line, especially with John Dixon, across Chat Moss.

When Parliament laid down a speed limit of 10 m.p.h. (16 km/h) for steam locomotives, Brandreth invented a carriage in which a horse walked on a moving platform, so turning the wheels. It was named *Cycloped* and was entered in the Rainhill Trials, where it achieved a speed of 15 m.p.h. (24 km/h), but the success of the *Rocket* made it unnecessary. However, Brandeth's machine was used in Lombardy and in the U.S.A. in instances where the expense of a steam locomotive was not justified. (See p. 119.)

William Fairbairn (1789–1874), famous engineer, friend of George Stephenson, and builder of both bridges and locomotives for railways. He was born in Scotland, trained on Tyneside and in 1817 started a small engineering works in Manchester where he remained for the rest of his working life. His original partner, Lillie, was bought out, and later he was joined by his two sons.

Fairbairn & Sons built about 400 locomotives from 1839 to 1862. These included many bar-framed engines of Edward Bury's design. The most famous engines built by the firm were the 'Large Bloomers', 2–2–2s of McConnell design, for the Southern Division of the London & North Western Railway in 1852–54.

In 1845–49 Fairbairn devised the system of wrought-iron tubular girders used by Robert Stephenson at Conway and the Menai Strait in North Wales and at Montreal, Canada. Fairbairn built many other bridges using this type of girder, but of smaller section. In 1860 his firm rebuilt the

timber viaducts at Mottram and Dinting on the Sheffield–Manchester Railway without interrupting the passage of about 70 trains daily.

The firm was wound up about the time of his death in 1874.

Benjamin Hick (1790–1842) was trained as an engineer under Matthew Murray in the firm of Fenton, Murray & Jackson, Leeds, the first locomotive works in the world. In 1810 he moved to Bolton, Lancashire, where he went into partnership with the Rothwells at the Union Foundry, builders of many early locomotives.

In 1833 he left to form the Soho Foundry, Bolton, which under his son John in partnership with William Hargreaves became Hick, Hargreaves. This firm also built many locomotives from 1834 to 1855, including three Norris-type 4–2–0s for the Birmingham & Gloucester Railway, and two for the Saint-Etienne & Lyon Railway, France, in 1841.

Peter Rothwell (1792–1849) achieved distinction as a manufacturer of locomotives for many early railways. At an early age he joined his father at the Union Foundry, Bolton, of which he became manager, for a time being joined by Benjamin Hick. The first locomotive was a 2–2–0, the *Union*, built for the Bolton & Leigh Railway in 1831. It had a vertical boiler and horizontal cylinders fixed to the framing instead of the boiler, an innovation at the time.

Perhaps the most famous engines built by Rothwell were the 7 ft (2·134 m) gauge 4–2–4 tanks to Pearson's design for the Bristol & Exeter Railway in 1853–54, with 9 ft (2·743 m) driving-wheels. Many other broad-gauge engines were built for the Great Western Railway.

Other railways for which Rothwell built engines included the London & Birmingham, Midland Counties, Grand Junction, Liverpool & Manchester, London & Southampton, London & North Western, London & South Western and Eastern Counties.

The last engines were built by the firm in 1860, making a total of 200 engines in 30 years. The firm later became the Bolton Iron & Steel Company and for a time was managed by F. W. Webb, later the famous locomotive superintendent of the London & North Western Railway.

Thomas Edmondson (1792–1851) was the originator of the standard railway ticket. A native of Lancashire, he began in the cabinet-making trade. However, in 1836 he became a clerk on the Newcastle & Carlisle Railway where he quickly grew dissatisfied with the system of making out individual tickets for passengers. In 1837 he invented a machine for printing railway tickets on cards of standard size, numbered consecutively, and a press for stamping dates on the tickets. Almost identical date-presses are still in use today. The N. & C. was not interested in his invention, so Edmondson applied to the Manchester & Leeds Railway, where he was appointed at Manchester. His system was soon adopted for general use throughout Britain and in other parts of the world. He patented his invention, charging railways 10 shillings (50p) a mile per year for using it.

Thomas Rogers (1792–1856), American locomotive engineer and founder of the Rogers Locomotive Works in 1837. In 1849 he introduced the link motion (valve gear) in America, and was one of the first engineers to apply balance weights for rotating parts. In 1850 he introduced the 'wagon-top', or tapered, boiler to give a greater steam space over the firebox. This became a standard feature of early American locomotives.

His works continued until 1905, producing about 6300 engines, before being absorbed by the American Locomotive Company (ALCO).

Charles Blacker Vignoles (1793–1875) was one of the best known of the early railway civil engineers. He was born in Ireland and lost both his parents in infancy. The first part of his career was spent in the army until 1816, when he began as a surveyor.

His first principal railway work was on the lines forming the North Union Railway (Parkside–Wigan–Preston), after which he laid out the Dublin Kingstown line, the first railway in Ireland.

In 1837 he introduced the flat-bottomed rail section which bore his name and which is now standard throughout the world. During the 'Railway Mania' of 1846–48 he was engaged on many lines in Britain and Ireland. In 1847 he made the first of many visits to Russia, where he carried out many railway projects and in 1853–55 he was responsible for the first railway in western Switzerland. His last important line was from Warsaw to Tarespol in 1865.

Edward Bury (1794–1858) was an early locomotive engineer and originator of the bar-frame, universally used in American steam-locomotive practice. He was born in Salford, Lancashire, and set up his works in Liverpool before 1829. Here his works manager was James Kennedy, who later became a partner in the firm of Bury, Curtis & Kennedy. His first locomotive, apart from an early unsuccessful attempt, was the 0–4–0 *Liverpool* in 1830, the first engine with inside cylinders and bar-frames. It had 6 ft (1829 mm) diameter wheels, the largest up to that time. The upright cylindrical firebox with domed top became a standard feature of Bury's engines.

From 1837 he was locomotive superintendent on the London & Birmingham Railway at Wolverton, until succeeded by McConnell on 1 January 1847, when he was appointed to the Great Northern Railway as locomotive engineer. His work so impressed the management that in 1849 he was

The 4–2–0 Sandusky, *the first engine built by Thomas Rogers, in 1837 (The Science Museum, London)*

Edward Bury (The Science Museum, London)

appointed general manager. He resigned this post in 1850.

The Liverpool Works closed down in 1850. Two Bury engines survive today, the Furness Railway 0–4–0 No. 3 at the York Railway Museum, and the 2–2–2 No. 36 of the Great Southern & Western Railway at Cork (Kent) Station, Ireland.

Coppernob, Furness Railway 0–4–0 No. 3, built by Edward Bury in 1846 now in York Railway Museum. One of the two surviving Bury engines, photographed at Horwich Works in 1960 (John Marshall)

Nicholas Wood (1795–1865), as colliery viewer at Killingworth near Newcastle upon Tyne, became associated with George Stephenson and the earliest steam locomotives. One of three built by Stephenson and Wood for the Hetton Colliery, County Durham, in 1822 is preserved in the York Railway Museum. It worked (rebuilt) until 1912 and led the Railway Centenary Procession from Darlington to Stockton under its own steam in 1925. In 1825 Wood published an important treatise giving the results of his experiments in the use of fixed and locomotive engines for railways. In 1829 he was appointed one of the judges at the Rainhill Trials. He made great contributions to improvements in working and ventilation of coal-mines in the Newcastle area.

Nicholas Wood (The Science Museum, London)

Matthias W. Baldwin (1795–1866), founder of the famous Baldwin Locomotive Works in Philadelphia, U.S.A., the largest in the world.

He was born in Elizabethtown, New Jersey, and became first a watch-maker, then a tool-maker and then a machinist. This brought him into contact with stationary steam-engines and then locomotives. His first locomotive *Old Ironside* was built in 1832, and remained in service for over 20 years. His second locomotive, the 4–2–0 *E. L. Miller*, was a great advance and introduced many features which became standard American practice. In 1838 he instituted standardisation using templates and gauges, and by 1840 he was using metallic packing for glands. His first European engine was built for Austria in 1841. Horizontal cylinders in identical castings including half the smokebox saddle were introduced in 1858 and soon became standard in America. In England, nearly half a century later they were adopted by Churchward on the Great Western Railway.

When he died in 1866 his firm's annual output was 120 engines; also in that year the 2–8–0 was introduced, becoming the most numerous type in America. The last Baldwin steam-engine was built for India in 1955, bringing the total to about 75 000.

John Dixon (1796–1865) was the founder of the profession of civil engineer, and friend of George Stephenson. He assisted Stephenson in the survey of the Stockton & Darlington Railway in 1821. In 1827 he left the S. & D. and began the difficult task of surveying for the Liverpool & Manchester Railway across Chat Moss for which George Stephenson devised his famous method of 'floating' the line across the bog on a mattress of brushwood. Dixon returned to the S. & D. in 1845 and from then until his death, two years after the S. & D. had become part of the North Eastern Railway, he occupied the position of consulting engineer.

John Braithwaite (1797–1870) began training in his father's engineering works. Following the death of his father John in 1818 and his brother Francis in 1823, John Braithwaite carried on the business himself, taking up the manufacture of high-pressure steam-engines. In 1827 he became acquainted with the Stephensons and with Captain John Ericsson with whom he constructed a locomotive, *Novelty*, which was entered in the Rainhill Trials. It was the first engine to run a mile in under a minute. At the same time Braithwaite achieved distinction by manufacturing the first steam fire-engines. From 1834 he began to practice as a civil engineer, working with Vignoles on the 5 ft (1·524 m) gauge Eastern Counties Railway. With J. C. Robertson he was joint founder of the *Railway Times* in 1837, one of the earliest railway periodicals. In 1836–38 he and Ericsson fitted up a canal boat with a steam-engine and screw-propeller in which they made a circuit of canals between London and Manchester. In 1844–46 Braithwaite surveyed several railways in France.

William Bridges Adams (1797–1872), son of the Staffordshire coach-builder who invented the C spring. His early life was spent in Chile until 1837 when he returned to England. In 1838 he invented a rail-brake, acting on the sides of the rail, but the idea was first applied by J. B. Fell on the centre-rail on his Mont Cenis Railway in 1868.

In 1843 Adams established the Fairfield Engineering Works at Bow, London (now Bryant & May's Match Factory), and here in 1847 he built the very first railcar, the *Express*, for the Eastern Counties Railway. He also built the extraordinary 7 ft (1·134 m) gauge railcar *Fairfield* in 1848 for the Bristol & Exeter Railway. His 'light locomotive' idea was taken up by several other firms.

He invented the radial axlebox, first used on a 2–4–2 tank on the St Helens Railway in 1863. Perhaps his most famous invention was a rail fish-plate.

George Hudson (1800–71) was known as the 'Railway King'. He achieved considerable success as a draper in York, and at the age of 27 he received a bequest of £30 000 which he invested in North Midland Railway shares. He quickly rose to important positions in the town, becoming Lord Mayor of York in 1837. In that year he was appointed chairman of the York & North Midland Railway, opened in 1839, and he became closely acquainted with George Stephenson. He next became actively engaged in extending the railway from York to Newcastle upon Tyne. He was instrumental in the formation of the Midland Railway by amalgamation of several companies in 1844, and became chairman of the company.

John Braithwaite (The Science Museum, London)

During the rush of railway speculation in 1844 he was in control of 1016 miles (1635 km) of railway. This was the period of his greatest success, and despite his rough North Country accent and uncultivated manners his acquaintance was sought by the leading persons in the country, even the Prince Consort.

However, as his power increased his financial dealings became questionable and after paying dividends to the extent of £294000 out of Eastern Counties Railway capital his fall was rapid.

To his credit, however, it must be said that he was the first person in control of railways who attempted to guide their development according to an over-all plan, though his rule to 'mak' all t' railways cum t' York' did not always lead to the best routes being chosen. The railway which suffered his most powerful opposition, the Great Northern, was in the end the one which really put York 'on the railway map'.

George Hudson
(British Rail)

George Washington Whistler (1800–49) pioneered many of the earliest railways in the U.S.A. He began his career in the army, where he became friendly with William Gibbs McNeill (1801–53), whose sister became his second wife. In 1828 he and McNeill were sent to England to study locomotives and railway construction. On their return to the U.S.A. they built the Baltimore & Ohio and the Paterson & Hudson River railroads. In 1834 a son, James McNeill Whistler, was born in Lowell, Mass., destined to become the famous American

painter. After building the Western Railroad across the Berkshire Mountains from Worcester to Albany in 1841, Whistler was invited by Tsar Nicholas I to survey and build the railway from Moscow to St Petersburg. He went to Russia in 1842 and construction of the 420 mile (676 km) railway, one of the straightest in the world, began in 1844. He chose a gauge of 5 ft (1,524 m), standard on many early railways south of the Ohio River in the U.S.A. (see p. 108) and thus established the standard Russian gauge which was not, as is commonly assumed, adopted for strategic reasons. Construction became protracted, and in 1848 he succumbed to a cholera epidemic and died in St Petersburg on 7 April 1849.

George Bradshaw (1801–53) was born in Salford, Lancashire. On leaving school he was apprenticed to an engraver, and in 1821 he established an engraving business in Manchester where he specialised in the engraving of maps, his first being a map of his native county. In 1830 he produced the first of his maps of canals and inland navigations. In 1838, soon after the introduction of railways, he produced the first of his railway maps.

His famous railway time-table first appeared in 1839. In 1840 this became *Bradshaw's Railway Companion* with maps, price one shilling (5p), and in December 1841 *Bradshaw's Monthly Railway Guide*. Among other publications were *Bradshaw's Continental Railway Guide* from 1847 and *Bradshaw's General Railway Directory and Shareholders's Guide* from 1849.

While still a young man, Bradshaw joined the Society of Friends and was very prominent in philanthropic work. The last Bradshaw time-table was No. 1521 published in June 1961. An almost complete collection was handed over to Manchester Public Library. Blacklock's Printing Works, successor to Bradshaw & Blacklock, closed in 1971.

Horatio Allen (1802–90), American locomotive pioneer and civil engineer. After graduating with high honours in mathematics at Columbia College in 1823, he started a career in law but soon changed to engineering. He began with the Delaware & Hudson Canal Company; in 1824 he was appointed resident engineer of the Delaware & Susquehanna Canal and in 1825 resident engineer of the Delaware & Hudson Canal.

Early in 1826 he was sent to England to study the Stephenson locomotive and was appointed by the D. & H. to purchase rails for 16 miles (25·75 km) of line and also four locomotives. At Liverpool Allen met George Stephenson, then engineer of the Liverpool & Manchester railway. One engine was

ordered from Robert Stephenson & Company of Newcastle and three from Foster, Rastrick & Company of Stourbridge, Worcestershire. It was one of these, the *Stourbridge Lion*, which was the first locomotive to run in North America (see p. 16). The locomotives were received in New York in the winter of 1828–29, but it was not until August 1829 that they were taken to the railway at Honesdale, Pennsylvania.

In 1829 he was appointed chief engineer of the South Carolina Railroad (p. 17) for which, in 1832, he designed the world's first articulated locomotive, a 2–2–0 + 0–2–2 which was built by the West Point Foundry in New York City (see p. 137).

Later he became consulting engineer for the New York & Erie Railroad and for the Brooklyn Bridge. In 1844 he became a member of the firm of Stillman, Allen & Co, building marine engines. He retired in 1870 and devoted himself to a life of study and invention. He was credited with the invention of the bogie coach and an improved expansion valve gear.

Robert Stephenson (1803–59) ranks with Brunel, Locke and Vignoles as one of the greatest of early railway engineers. In 1814 his father, George, was able to send him to school in Newcastle upon Tyne. In 1823, when only 20, he was placed in charge of the locomotive works in Newcastle upon Tyne which his father had founded under the name of Robert Stephenson & Company.

In 1824 he visited South America for three years and there met Richard Trevithick, penniless, whom he helped to repatriate.

Under Robert Stephenson's direction the famous *Rocket* was built for the Rainhill Trials. He assisted

Robert Stephenson (The Science Museum, London)

Robert Stephenson's Victoria Tubular Bridge over the St Lawrence River at Montreal, Canada, as built in 1854–59 (Canadian National Railways)

his father on the Liverpool & Manchester, Leicester & Swannington and other railways and in 1833 was appointed engineer of the London & Birmingham Railway, completed in 1838.

It is for his great bridges, however, that he is best remembered. Famous examples are the High Level Bridge, Newcastle (1846–49), Royal Border Bridge over the Tweed at Berwick (1850), and his great bridges built on the tubular system devised in conjunction with William Fairbairn at Conway (1846–48) and the Menai Strait (1846–50, damaged by fire on 23 May 1970 and now rebuilt) and the Victoria Tubular Bridge over the St Lawrence at Montreal (1854–59).

Joseph Mitchell (1803–83), engineer of the Highland Railway, Scotland. He trained under Thomas Telford, later becoming engineer of roads and bridges in the Scottish Highlands. He also erected 40 churches in the Highlands. In 1844 he laid out the Scottish Central Railway (Perth–Falkirk) and in 1845 the Perth Inverness line of the H.R. This was considered impracticable at the time and it was not finished until 1863, to Forres, on the Inverness & Aberdeen Junction Railway, over the highest main-line summit in Britain, 1484 ft (452 m) at Druimuachdar. In the meantime he had surveyed most of the other H.R. lines, including that to Wick and Thurso. This was completed in 1874, seven years after Mitchell had retired following a paralytic disease. A member of the Institution of Civil Engineers from 1837, it was he who first established the Minutes of Proceedings of that Institution.

John Ericsson (1803–89), the famous inventor, was born in Sweden and, after spells in the army and navy, went to London in 1826. Here he continued his experiments towards an engine which would use heat more economically than a steam-engine. In 1828 he designed a steam fire-engine with a 12 in (304·8 mm) diameter cylinder and a boiler with forced draught, which was built by John Braithwaite. In 1829 he designed his only railway locomotive, also built by Braithwaite, the *Novelty*, which was entered for the Rainhill Trials. But for an unfortunate breakdown it might have won the prize. On 13 July 1836 he took out a patent for a screw-propeller and built a screw-vessel in 1837. Failing to interest anyone in his work in Britain he moved to America, where he remained until his death in New York.

Sylvester Marsh (1803–84), builder of the world's first mountain rack railway. He was born in White Mountain Village, New Hampshire,

U.S.A., and at the age of 19 he walked 150 miles (241 km) to Boston to find employment. In 1833 he moved to Chicago, then a settlement with a population of only 300, where he achieved success in the meat-canning industry. In 1855 he became interested in the idea of a cog railway to the summit of Mount Washington, close to his old home. After many attempts he obtained a concession and the assistance of financiers. Work began in 1866 and on 3 July 1869 the line was opened. It still operates (see p. 213). His ladder-type rack formed the prototype of that designed by Nikolaus Riggenbach.

Joseph Hamilton Beattie (1804–71) is famous for being the first to devise a means of burning coal on a locomotive without producing smoke, and for his feed-water heating apparatus. Details of his early career are obscure, but by 1839 he was assistant engineer on the London & Southampton Railway under Locke.

In 1850 he succeeded J. V. Gooch as locomotive superintendent on the London & South Western Railway (successor to the L. & S.) at Nine Elms, London.

The first locomotive to be fitted with his coal-burning firebox and feed-water heater was a 6 ft 6 in (1·981 m) single-wheeler named *The Duke* in 1853. The firebox was in two parts, one of which burnt coal and the other coke. It was the coke fire which burnt the smoke from the coal. This complicated arrangement was, however, made obsolete by the firebox with brick arch and baffle-plate in 1860.

The trouble with the feed-water heater was that injectors would not work, so that crosshead-driven boiler feed-pumps had to be used.

His 2–4–0 with outside cylinders achieved renown, two examples even being built for the East Lancashire Railway in 1857. Three examples of the tank version of this type built in 1874–75 and much rebuilt since, survived in use at Wadebridge, Cornwall, until 1962.

Joseph Locke (1805–60) was another of the principal early engineers. Born near Sheffield and educated at Barnsley Grammar School, he was articled to George Stephenson in 1823 and worked with him on the Liverpool & Manchester Railway. It was during the construction of the tunnel down to Liverpool Lime Street that Locke proved errors in Stephenson's survey which led to an estrangement.

Locke's principal works were the Grand Junction (Birmingham–Warrington–begun by Stephenson), 1835–37; the London–Southampton, 1836–40; the Sheffield–Manchester, 1838–40; the Lancaster–

Preston, 1837–40; the Greenock, 1837–41; the Paris–Rouen, 1841–43; the Rouen–Havre, 1843; the Barcelona–Mattaro, 1847–48; and the Dutch Rhenish Railway, 1856.

In 1840 Locke entered a partnership with John Edward Errington (1806–62) and together they constructed the Lancaster & Carlisle, 1843–46; the East Lancashire and the Scottish Central, 1845; the Caledonian (Carlisle–Glasgow and Edinburgh), 1848, and other Scottish lines.

Locke was noted for his avoidance of tunnels. For instance, there is no tunnel between Birmingham and Glasgow, despite the heavy climbs over Shap and Beattock. He was also noted for the low cost of his lines, some of which, however, proved expensive to operate because of the steep gradients.

Joseph Locke (The Science Museum, London)

Thomas Brassey (1805–70), one of the most famous railway contractors, born and educated in Cheshire and articled to a land surveyor at the age of 16. In 1834 he became acquainted with George Stephenson and through him obtained a contract for Penkridge Viaduct on the Grand Junction Railway. This was followed by other G. J. contracts under Locke.

Following his marriage in 1831, his wife persuaded him to take up a career as a railway contractor, and by 1850 he had works in progress throughout Britain and Europe. Other works were the Grand Trunk Railway, Canada, 1852–59; the Crimean Railway, with Peto and Betts, 1854; Australian railways, 1859–63; Argentinian railways, 1864; several Indian railways, 1858–65; and Moldavian railways, 1862–68.

He was remarkable for his punctuality and thoroughness in his contracts, his power of mental calculation, skill in organisation, his ability to delegate responsibility to his subordinates, and for his humane treatment of the navvies working under him. He was a man of unfailing courtesy and kindness, and scrupulous honesty.

Isambard Kingdom Brunel (1806–59) was the son of Marc Isambard Brunel (1769–1849), who was engineer of the Thames Tunnel, begun in 1825 and completed in 1843 and later adapted by John Hawkshaw as part of the East London Railway. I. K. Brunel worked with his father in the tunnel. His first major work was the Clifton Suspension Bridge, Bristol, although this was not completed until after his death. In March 1833, when only 27, he was appointed engineer to the Great Western Railway between London and Bristol, laying out the line with bold engineering works and to the unprecedented gauge of 7 ft (2·134 m). The

I. K. Brunel, beside the chains used in the launching of his great steamship Great Eastern *in 1858 (The Science Museum, London)*

Box Tunnel, 1·75 miles (2·8 km) long, was for long thought to be laid out on such a line that it was penetrated by the sun's rays only on 9 April – his birthday. However, it has now been positively established by observation that the dates are 15 to 17 April, at about 6.35–6.40 a.m. He continued as engineer of the Bristol & Exeter, the South Devon (where he experimented unsuccessfully with the atmospheric system of propulsion) and the Cornwall railways, also the line from Swindon to Gloucester and South Wales. For this he devised a combination of tubular, suspension and truss bridge to carry the line over the Wye at Chepstow and developed this design in his famous Saltash Bridge over the Tamar near Plymouth. This was completed just before his death in 1859. Besides railways, Brunel designed and built steamships, the most famous being the *Great Western* of 1838 and the *Great Britain* of 1845. His greatest ship, the *Great Eastern* was built for the Eastern Navigation Company in 1858. The anxieties connected with this broke his health and he died the following year.

George Parker Bidder (1806–70) is best remembered for his extraordinary calculating ability. In 1834 he became associated with Robert Stephenson of the London & Birmingham Railway. This brought him into Parliamentary work, where he achieved a reputation as a formidable opponent in committees, through his powers as a mental calculator. He was engaged in numerous railway works at home and abroad, but his most important construction work was the Victoria Docks, London. He was the originator of the railway swing-bridge, the first of which he designed and erected at Reedham on the Norwich & Lowestoft Railway, and was one of the founders of the Electric Telegraph Company. He was President of the Institution of Civil Engineers in 1860–62.

Edward Fletcher (1807–89) was a locomotive engineer. In 1825 he was appointed to Robert Stephenson & Company at Newcastle upon Tyne, where in 1829 he made much of the machinery for the *Rocket*. In 1830 he went to the Canterbury & Whitstable Railway, where he drove the locomotive *Invicta* on the opening day.

After working on the construction of the York & North Midland Railway from 1837, he became locomotive superintendent of the Newcastle & Darlington Railway and in 1854 assumed the same office on the newly formed North Eastern Railway at Gateshead, providing the company with a stud of simple, robust engines. When he retired, in 1882, he had completed 47 years in the service of the N.E.R. and its predecessors.

Thomas Cook (1808–92) founded the great English firm of Thomas Cook & Son Limited. He was born in Melbourne, Derbyshire, and after a succession of occupations he became interested in the Temperance Movement, and on 5 July 1841 he ran a Temperance excursion on the Midland Counties Railway. The success of this led to others and to the establishment of a business in Leicester which, in 1865, was transferred to London. In 1866 he arranged his first tours to the U.S.A. and from there followed many to other parts of the world, all at reduced rates. From 1948 control of Thomas Cook & Son was vested in the British Transport Commission. On 26 May 1972 it was sold for £22 500 000 to a consortium led by the Midland Bank.

Samuel Morton Peto (1809–89) stands second only to Brassey as one of the greatest of railway contractors. He inherited his father's firm of Grissell & Peto which was responsible for many important buildings in London, including Nelson's Column, 1843. His first major railway contracts were on the Great Western Railway in 1840 and the South Eastern Railway in 1844. In 1846 the firm of Grissell & Peto was dissolved, Peto retaining the railway contracts. These included works on the Chester & Holyhead, the London & South Western and, in partnership with E. L. Betts (1815–72), the Great Northern, the Oxford, Worcester & Wolverhampton, the Hereford & Gloucester, the Oxford & Birmingham, the South London & Crystal Palace and the Great Eastern railways in England; also railways in South America, Russia, North Africa and Norway. In conjunction with Thomas Brassey he constructed lines in Australia, the Grand Trunk Railway in Canada, including Robert Stephenson's Victoria Tubular Bridge at Montreal and in France. From 1847 to 1854 he sat in Parliament as Liberal Member for Norwich. He was knighted in 1855, following work on a railway in the Crimea. Like Brassey he was noted for his humane treatment of his workers.

Nathaniel Worsdell (1809–96) was the eldest son of Thomas Clarke Worsdell, builder of the tender for Stephenson's *Rocket*. In 1828 he began work on the Liverpool & Manchester Railway and with his father designed and built the earliest passenger coaches. In 1836 he succeeded his father as superintendent of the Carriage Department of the L. & M.

In 1837 he invented the apparatus for picking up and depositing mail-bags on railways which was patented in 1838, but he never received any remuneration for this. He is also credited with the invention of the screw-coupling, but using a single right-hand thread only.

The year his son Thomas William was born, 1838 (see p. 53), he built the *Experience* coach for the L. & M., consisting of three horse-carriage bodies on a railway-carriage frame, so establishing the design upon which future compartment coaches in Great Britain and Europe were based.

When the Locomotive and Carriage Departments were transferred from Liverpool to Crewe in 1843 he moved there and played an important part in the development of the new town. He retired in 1880.

He was a Quaker, like his father, and was renowned for his integrity. It was said of him that he would speak the truth if he had to die for it. His two brothers, Thomas and George, became noted railway engineers and of his five sons Thomas William and Wilson became locomotive engineers on the North Eastern Railway, Henry worked on railways in India, and Robert also on the N.E.R.

Henry Meiggs (1811–77) was engineer and contractor for what is surely the most wonderful railway in the world, the Central of Peru (see p.

Henry Meiggs in his last days, in 1877. In the background is the Rogers steam inspection coupé Favorita, *No. 24 on the Peru Central Railway. Above a train is climbing one of the famous zigzags (From a painting by Brian Fawcett)*

Railway engineering extraordinary, on the Peru Central Railway, beneath the south end of the Cacray zigzag where Meiggs made a tunnel for the river and took the railway through the old river bed (John Marshall)

69). He was born in New York State and was an outstanding mathematician. He had an astute business sense, an ability to select the right men to serve under him, and was a man of dauntless courage and optimism. After making several fortunes, not always honestly, and losing them, he settled in Chile in 1854, where he constructed the Santiago Railway. In 1867 he moved to Peru where he began work on the Oroya Railway from Lima to Oroya in the Andes, the highest railway in the world. He died before the railway was completed, but the rest of the route was fully worked out.

He had great generosity and was the first big contractor in North or South America to treat the imported Chinese coolies as humans.

John Hawkshaw (1811–91) was responsible for the greatest number of major engineering works of the foremost nineteenth-century engineers. He was born in Yorkshire and trained with C. Fowler and later with Alexander Nimmo.

He constructed a large portion of the Lancashire & Yorkshire Railway between 1845 and 1853, including some tremendous viaducts in Yorkshire, and was the first engineer to demonstrate conclusively that steam locomotives on smooth rails were capable of surmounting gradients steeper than 1 in 50 (2 per cent).

Other railway works included the Charing Cross and Canon Street railway bridges and stations, London; the East London Railway utilising Marc Brunel's Thames Tunnel; and the Severn Tunnel.

With Sir James Brunlees he was engineer to the original Channel Tunnel project from 1872 to 1886.

Abroad he reported on the Suez and Panama canal projects and from 1862 to 1876 was engineer to the Amsterdam Ship Canal.

His contributions to engineering literature were enormous and his various reports, articles and addresses make fascinating reading. He was knighted in 1873.

John Hawkshaw (Institution of Civil Engineers)

John Haswell (1812–97) was a Scottish engineer who settled in Vienna, having gone there originally to erect locomotives for one of Austria's first railways. In 1837 he planned and equipped a locomotive works, of which he became manager, in Vienna. Here he built some of the first locomotives on the European continent. He remained head of the works until 1882. In 1851 he produced the first eight-coupled engine in Europe, the *Vindebona*, for the Semmering Trials, and with his *Wien-Raab*, a large-boilered 0–8–0 with all parts accessible, in 1855, he established the pattern for European heavy freight engines for many years. He introduced the Stephenson Link Motion (see William Howe, below) into Europe, and his own inventions included a corrugated firebox and a rudimentary form of the Belpaire firebox, thermic syphons and counter-pressure braking. In 1861 he built one of the first four-cylinder engines in Europe. His works also produced the first railway carriages and post office carriages in Austria. For his services he received two orders of knighthood from the Emperor of Austria.

William Henry Barlow (1812–1902), civil engineer, trained at Woolwich Dockyard and London Docks. After six years on engineering works in Turkey he returned to England in 1838 and became assistant engineer on the Manchester & Birmingham Railway; in 1842 he became resident engineer on the Midland Counties Railway and in 1844 on the North Midland Railway. On the formation of the Midland Railway in 1844 he became chief civil engineer. In 1849 he patented the saddle-back form of rail which bore his name (it was much used on the Great Western Railway) and between 1844 and 1886 he took out many patents relating to permanent way. In 1862–69 he laid out the extension of the Midland Railway from Bedford to London and designed the great roof of St Pancras Station (opened on 1 October 1868).

With Sir John Hawkshaw in 1860 he completed the Clifton Suspension Bridge at Bristol, begun by I. K. Brunel. Barlow was closely connected with the Tay and Forth bridges.

William Howe (1814–79) was the inventor of the steam-engine valve gear known as 'Stephenson's Link Motion'. He was born in County Durham and trained under Hackworth at New Shildon, then at the Vulcan Foundry, Lancashire, and at Liverpool.

In 1840 he removed to Gateshead and joined Robert Stephenson & Company, and it was here in 1842 that he devised the reversing gear, using two eccentrics and a curved link. His original

model of this gear can be seen in the Science Museum, London (see illustration).

It was immediately adopted by Stephenson, who gave Howe full credit for the invention, and it was soon in universal use. It seems probable, however, that the gear was used at first as a reversing gear only, and that its use in expansive working by cutting off the steam to the cylinder before the end of the piston stroke was discovered later.

The original wooden model of William Howe's link motion (The Science Museum, London)

John Ramsbottom (1814–92) is best remembered as the inventor of the water-trough and the safety-valve named after him. About 1839 he entered the Locomotive Works of Sharp, Roberts &

John Ramsbottom (The Science Museum, London)

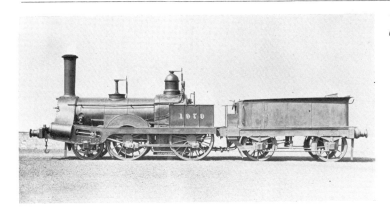

The Buddicom 'Crewe'-type locomotive (British Rail)

Company, Manchester, and in 1842 became locomotive superintendent of the Manchester & Birmingham Railway with his works at Longsight, Manchester.

In 1846 the M. & B. became a part of the newly formed London & North Western Railway, and in 1857 Ramsbottom succeeded Francis Trevithick as locomotive superintendent of the entire Northern Division of the L.N.W.R. at Crewe. He invented the water-trough in 1859, to enable locomotives to pick up water while in motion. In 1862, with the ending of locomotive work under McConnell at Wolverton, Crewe became the Locomotive Headquarters for the entire railway. Ramsbottom retired from the L.N.W.R. in 1871, but in 1883 he became connected with the Lancashire & Yorkshire Railway and was partly responsible for the establishment of the L.Y.R. Works at Horwich near Bolton.

William Barber Buddicom (1816–87) is best remembered for the famous Crewe-type engine about 1842, in which Alexander Allan also possibly had a share. The cylinders were mounted in an outside framing with the smokebox sheeting continued in a curve over the cylinders. The type was much used on the London & North Western, the Highland and the Caledonian railways.

He was born in Liverpool and from 1831 to 1836 served an apprenticeship with Mather, Dixon & Company, Liverpool. In 1836 he began work on the Liverpool & Manchester Railway for two years, then becoming resident engineer of the Glasgow, Paisley & Greenock Railway. In 1840 he was appointed locomotive superintendent of the Grand Junction Railway which had amalgamated with the L. & M., with his headquarters at Edge Hill, Liverpool. It was Buddicom who prepared the plans and estimates for the new works at Crewe, carried

out under his successor Francis Trevithick, (1812–77, son of Richard Trevithick).

In 1841 he went to France to superintend the construction of rolling stock for the Paris & Rouen Railway then being built by Thomas Brassey and MacKenzie and of which Joseph Locke was engineer. A company was formed under the name of Allcard, Buddicom & Company until 1851 when it became Buddicom & Company. When the Sotteville Works at Rouen were ready in 1842 Buddicom's firm entered into a contract for running the railway.

Thomas Russell Crampton (1816–88) must rank as one of the most courageous and original of early locomotive engineers. He was born at Broadstairs, Kent, and from 1839 to 1844 he worked under Marc Brunel, and afterwards with Daniel Gooch on the Great Western Railway at Swindon for a very short time. It was here that he conceived his famous design for a locomotive with a large low boiler and a pair of large driving-wheels behind the firebox.

In 1845 the first two of his engines of this type were built, and others followed for the London & North Western Railway and other lines. The biggest was the *Liverpool*, a 6-2-0 built by Bury, Curtis & Kennedy in 1848. It weighed 35 tons and had the largest boiler on any locomotive of that date. Its 8 ft (2·438 m) driving-wheels and general majestic appearance earned it a gold medal at the Great Exhibition of 1851.

The largest number of Crampton engines was in France, the first twelve being built for the Northern Railway of France in 1848–49 by Derosne, Cail & Cie. Hundreds more were built in France and Germany. One of the French Cramptons, *Le Continent* built in 1852 for the Paris–Strasbourg Railway, has been preserved for use on special trains.

Crampton steam locomotive Le Continent *of 1852 and carriages of the same period (French Railways Limited)*

Daniel Gooch (1816–89), the most distinguished member of a great family of engineers. He was born in Bedlington, Northumberland, the son of John Gooch, manager of Bedlington Ironworks, and Anna, daughter of Thomas Longridge of Newcastle upon Tyne. He was apprenticed at Robert Stephenson's Works at Newcastle, and after some experience with Tayleur at the Vulcan Foundry in Lancashire, and in Scotland, in 1837 he applied to I. K. Brunel for the post of locomotive superintendent of the Great Western Railway.

After some preliminary brushes with Brunel, whose misguided specifications for locomotives had resulted in some wretched specimens being obtained, Gooch ordered engines of his own design from Newcastle which at once achieved a reputation for speed and reliability. His 8 ft (2·438 m) single-wheeler design of 1847 remained in production until 1878, and examples survived to the end of the broad gauge in 1892.

Gooch took a leading part in the establishment of the new locomotive works at Swindon from 1843 and made an active contribution to the development of the new town.

In 1864 he resigned from the post of locomotive superintendent so as to lay the first Atlantic cable from Brunel's steamship *Great Eastern*. The first telegraph messages were sent across the Atlantic in 1866; and Gooch was made a baronet, the very first engineer to receive such an honour.

The same year he returned to the G.W.R. as chairman, remaining in this position until the last year of his life. During his chairmanship he guided the G.W.R. through difficult times, and in his last years threw all his energies into the Severn Tunnel project, which was completed in 1887.

His brothers Thomas Longridge (1808–82) and John Viret (1812–1900) were both distinguished

engineers. The first was resident engineer on the Manchester & Leeds Railway and the second was locomotive superintendent on the London & South Western and Eastern Counties railways.

Sir Daniel Gooch (British Rail)

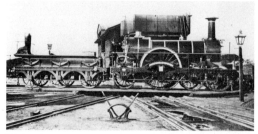

Lightning, *one of Daniel Gooch's 8 ft (2·438 m) single-wheelers (The Science Museum, London)*

James Brunlees (1816–92) was a civil engineer, responsible for some outstanding railway works. He learned surveying under Alexander Adie (1808–79) on the Bolton & Preston Railway and later with Locke and Errington on the Caledonian Railway. On the completion of the latter in 1844 he became acting engineer under Hawkshaw on lines forming the Lancashire & Yorkshire Railway until 1850.

He then became responsible for a succession of major railway projects: the Ulverston & Lancaster Railway, 1851, including viaducts across the Kent and Leven esturies; the São Paulo Railway, Brazil, with its amazing rope-worked inclines (see p. 67), 1856; the Fell Railway over Mont Cenis Pass (between France and Italy) (see p. 81), 1865; the Solway Junction Railway including the viaduct over the Solway Firth (see p. 94), 1865–69; the Cleveland Extension, Yorkshire, with the 180 ft (54·86 m) high Skelton Beck Viaduct. With Douglas Fox (1840–1921) he built the Mersey Railway Tunnel. On completion of this in 1886 Brunlees and Fox were knighted.

From 1872 to 1886 Brunlees was engineer with Hawkshaw to the original Channel Tunnel Company.

Ernst Werner von Siemens (1816–92) was born at Lenthe, Hanover. In 1834 he entered the Prussian Artillery and in 1844 took charge of the Artillery Workshops, Berlin.

He is best remembered in railway circles for having built the first practical electric railway, for the Berlin Trades Exhibition of 1879, operated from 31 May to 30 September on a track about 600 yd (549 m) long.

He was responsible for the Portrush–Giant's Causeway Tramway in Ireland, the first railway in the world to be run on hydro-electric power, opened on 28 September 1883.

John Fowler (1817–98) was born in Sheffield and trained under J. U. Rastrick on the London & Brighton Railway, as a civil engineer. Later he became resident engineer of the Stockton & Hartlepool Railway, on the completion of which in 1842 he was appointed engineer, general manager and locomotive superintendent. From 1844 he worked on the lines from Sheffield to the east coast, which became the Manchester, Sheffield & Lincolnshire Railway and from 1898 the Great Central Railway.

He designed the Pimlico Railway Bridge, the first across the Thames at London, finished in 1860. From 1860 he was engaged, with Benjamin Baker (see p. 55), on the Metropolitan Railway, London, the first section of which was opened in 1863. For this he devised the first fireless locomotive which, however, was not a success.

In 1870 he was appointed to a commission to advise on narrow-gauge railways in India and also visited Norway in this capacity.

From 1875 he entered into partnership with Baker and from 1883 to 1890 supervised the construction of the Forth Bridge in Scotland. In 1880, with Baker, he was knighted.

Werner von Siemens (The Science Museum, London)

Sir John Fowler (The Science Museum, London)

The Festiniog Railway 1 ft 11·5 in (60 cm) gauge 0–4–0 Princess *built by George England, London, in 1863. This was the first narrow-gauge steam locomotive (Festiniog Railway Company)*

Charles Easton Spooner (1818–89), the most famous name in the history of narrow-gauge railways. He was born at Maentwrog, Wales, where his father, James Spooner, had engineered the narrow-gauge tramway over the embankment to Portmadoc.

When the Act of Parliament for the Festiniog Railway was obtained in 1832 C. E. Spooner was only 14, but he assisted in the construction of this 1 ft 11½ in (600 mm) gauge railway from the slate-quarries of Blaenau Ffestiniog down to the coast at Portmadoc. When his father died in 1856, Spooner became engineer and manager.

In 1863 powers were obtained to work the line with locomotives instead of horses (ascending) and gravity (descending), and at the same time the line was improved. In 1865 it opened for passengers, becoming the world's first passenger-carrying narrow-gauge line. It was visited by engineers from all over the world.

The first 0–4–0 engines were built by George England, but in 1869 the first Fairlie double engines appeared. Some of the original engines are still at work. (See pp. 148 and 218, and colour photograph p. 179.)

Alfred Belpaire (1820–93) was the inventor of the famous firebox which bore his name. He was born in Ostend, Belgium, and in 1840 gained his engineering diploma in Paris. In that year the Belgian State Railways entrusted him with charge of the locomotive shops at Malines where his contemporary Egide Walschaert (opposite) began work. In 1850 he was appointed director of the Rolling Stock Department at Brussels.

To achieve greater efficiency from the low-grade fuel burnt on Belgian locomotives he produced his famous firebox in 1860, in a round form which was tested on the 2–4–0 No. 1. In 1864 he abandoned this type and adopted the familiar form which facilitated the use of vertical and horizontal stays. It was used on all the Belgian State Railway

engines from 1864 to 1884. At the end of 1884 he introduced new details, increasing both length and width of the grate, the area of which reached 73·8 ft² (6·8562 m²) on some express engines on the Luxemburg line.

He also invented a combined screw and lever reverse for locomotives. In 1878 he invented a steam rail-carriage, the precursor of the rail-motor. He designed large numbers of locomotives.

The Belpaire firebox was first used in Britain on the 0–6–2 tanks designed by Harry Pollitt and built in 1891 for the Manchester, Sheffield & Lincolnshire Railway. The first to be constructed in Britain were by Beyer Peacock & Company, of Manchester in 1872 for some 2–4–0s for the Malines Terneuzen Railway in Belgium, and it was through the chief draughtsman of the M.S. & L. who had been with Beyer Peacock that it was used on that railway. It was adopted as standard by G. J. Churchward on the Great Western Railway, and his designs influenced others right down to the series of standard engines built by British Railways from 1950 to 1959.

Egide Walschaert (1820–1901) inventor of one of the most efficient and widely used valve gears on steam locomotives. He was born in Belgium and started work as a mechanic on the Belgian State Railways at Malines. In 1844 he invented his famous valve gear which was fitted to an inside-

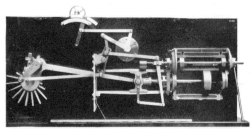

Model of Walschaert's valve gear (The Science Museum, London)

cylinder 2–2–2 at Brussels in 1848, with great success. It was used on the Crampton engines Nos. 165–70, of the Northern Railway of France, built in 1859. In Belgium it was applied to all outside-cylinder engines, but the Stephenson Link Motion was preferred for inside cylinders. The first locomotive in Britain to have the Walschaert valve gear was a 0–4–4 tank built in 1878 by the Fairlie Engine Company, London, for the Swindon, Marlborough & Andover Railway. The gear was first used in the U.S.A. in 1874 (see 'North American Locomotives', p. 128).

Thomas Bouch (1822–80) trained as a civil engineer under Larmer on the Lancaster & Carlisle Railway. In 1849 he became engineer of the Edinburgh & Northern Railway, designing the mechanism for loading and unloading wagons on the world's first train ferries, across the firths of Forth and Tay. On the South Durham & Lancashire Union Railway, later part of the North Eastern Railway, he built the great iron viaducts at Belah (highest in England), Deepdale and Barnard Castle which gave good service until dismantled in recent years. In 1877–78 he completed a bridge 2 miles (3·2 km) long across the Tay at Dundee. He was knighted in 1879, but shortly afterwards, on 28 December, the bridge blew down while a train was crossing (see p. 91). He never recovered from the shock, and died the following year.

His permanent monument remains, however, in his tremendous 150 ft (45·7 m) high Hownes Gill Viaduct, which was built in fire-bricks for the Stockton & Darlington Railway near Consett, County Durham. It was first used on 1 July 1858.

Henri Giffard (1825–82), inventor of the injector for feeding water into boilers against pressure. He began his railway career in 1841 on the Paris–Saint-Germain Railway. However, he devoted a great part of his life to the development of ballooning, on which he published two important treatises in 1851 and 1854. For his invention of the injector in 1859 he received the prize for mechanics from the Académie des Sciences, Paris. The injector eliminated the need for feed-pumps and enabled locomotives to replenish their boilers while stationary. In 1863 Giffard was created a Knight of the Legion of Honour.

David Joy (1825–1903) is best remembered for his radial valve gear for steam-engines, but he had many other inventions to his credit. He was born in Leeds and served an apprenticeship with Fenton, Murray & Jackson, the world's first loco-

The first Tay Bridge from the south in 1878

British Railways 'Q6'-type 0–8–0 No. 63455, formerly North Eastern Railway, crossing Hownes Gill Viaduct in 1964 (John Marshall)

motive-building firm. When this closed in 1843 he transferred to Shepherd & Todd, also in Leeds, and 1846 to the Railway Foundry. Here he worked on the design for the *Jenny Lind* 2–2–2 engine, forerunner of a famous type.

In 1850 he left to take charge of the Nottingham & Grantham Railway, then just opened, later becoming locomotive superintendent of the Oxford, Worcester & Wolverhampton Railway, where he remained until 1856 when he returned to the Railway Foundry.

In 1857 he patented a compound marine engine. He patented a steam reversing gear, the first in the world, and at the same time took out the first of his three patents for hydraulic organ-blowers. In 1860 he invented a pneumatic hammer.

From 1862 to 1876 he ran a business of his own at Middlesbrough. He then became secretary to the Barrow Ship Building Company and it was here,

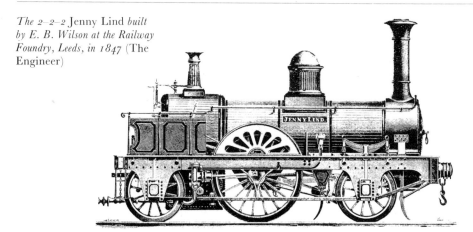

The 2–2–2 Jenny Lind *built by E. B. Wilson at the Railway Foundry, Leeds, in 1847* (The Engineer)

in 1879, that he invented his famous radial valve gear.

Its first use on a locomotive was in 1880 when F. W. Webb had it fitted to a 0–6–0 built at Crewe. The gear became standard on the London & North Western Railway and from 1886 on the Lancashire & Yorkshire Railway.

The valve gear has been criticised as mechanically unsound because it involved boring the main connecting-rod, but on all but the largest locomotives it gave excellent results.

Sandford Fleming (1827–1915), pioneer of Canadian transcontinental railways. He was born in Kirkcaldy, Scotland, and went to Canada in 1845. After gaining experience as a railway engineer under Casimir Czowski on the Northern Railway, in 1864 he was appointed chief railway engineer of Nova Scotia where in 1864–67, he built the railway from Truro to Pictou. Also in 1864 he was asked to survey a railway from Montreal to Halifax, and 1867 he was appointed chief engineer of the transcontinental railway which was a condition of the entry of British Columbia into the Confederation in 1871. On 16 July 1872 he began his great expedition across Canada, locating the route through the Yellowhead Pass and down the Thompson and Fraser river valleys to Vancouver. However, in 1880 the Government handed over construction to the Canadian Pacific Railway Company and the railway was taken through the mountains by a more southerly route. He assisted in the survey through the Kicking Horse Pass, and Fleming and his party were the first white men to cross the Rockies by this route. The Yellowhead Pass was later used by the Canadian National and Northern Railways (p. 77).

From 1879 he urged the Canadian, Australian and British governments to lay a Pacific cable. Its completion between Vancouver and Australia in 1902 was his crowning success. From 1876 he took a leading role in forcing the adoption of the first standard time zones in North America which came into operation in 1883. Fleming designed the first Canadian postage stamp and founded the Royal Canadian Institute.

Robert F. Fairlie (1831–85), the inventor of the Fairlie articulated locomotive, familiar on the Festiniog Railway in Wales. He patented the arrangements in 1863, either one or both bogies being powered, with either a single or double boiler. The first engine in 1865 had a double boiler with back to back fireboxes. In all a considerable range of varieties was produced under his patent. (See 'Articulated Locomotives', p. 137.)

David Jones (1834–1906). The name of Jones is inseparably associated with the first 4–6–0s to run on a British railway, the 'Jones Goods' of the Highland Railway (see colour illustration, p. 122). He was born in Manchester and at the age of 13 began an apprenticeship under John Ramsbottom on the London & North Western Railway, first at Longsight, Manchester and then at Crewe.

In 1855 he went to the Highland Railway and in 1870 he was appointed locomotive superintendent at Inverness. His first locomotive followed the traditional design established on the L.N.W.R. by Buddicom and Alexander Allan, with sloping cylinders set in outside framing. He continued with the spacious cabs provided by his predecessor William Stroudley.

While on the H.R. he acted also as consulting engineer for railways in Australia, South America and India and he had some influence in the design

Festiniog Railway No. 7 Little Wonder, *the first of the narrow-gauge double 'Fairlies' (Festiniog Railway Company)*

of the 'L' Class 4–6–0s built in 1880 by Dübs & Company, Glasgow, for the Indus Valley State Railway.

His 'Big Goods' 4–6–0 was clearly based on this type. The first, No. 103, appeared in 1894 (it is preserved today in the Glasgow Transport Museum) and was an immediate success. Fourteen others were built. Before he retired in 1896 he had prepared designs for a similar 4–6–0 for passenger trains. This was built by his successor, Peter Drummond, becoming the 'Castle' Class. Surprisingly, although 19 were built for the H.R., no less than 50 were built for the French State Railways in 1911.

Anatole Mallet (1837–1919) is famous as the inventor of the Mallet-type articulated engine, first patented in 1884 as a four-cylinder compound arrangement with the low-pressure cylinders on the front engine frame. It was first used in 1887 on light railways to spread the load on light rough track. In 1890 it was introduced on European main lines and in 1904 appeared in America where it developed to its greatest extent. The Virginia Railroad 2–10–10–2 of 1918 had 48 in low-pressure cylinders, the largest ever used on a locomotive. A triplex type, with a third unit under the tender, was also produced. These had two high-pressure and four low-pressure cylinders all of equal size. Three 2–8–8–8–2s were built for the Erie Railroad in 1914 and one 2–8–8–8–4 for the V.R. in 1916. Mallet opposed the introduction of simple expansion types, but none the less several types were built. Mallets developed into the world's biggest engines, examples being the Chesapeake & Ohio Railroad 2–6–6–6s, the Northern Pacific Railroad 2–8–8–4s and the Union Pacific Railroad 4–8–8–4 'Big Boys', all over 500 tons. The last, however,

being simple expansion engines are not true Mallets. (See 'Articulated Locomotives', p. 138.)

James Holden (1837–1925) was trained under Edward Fletcher (q.v.) at Gateshead, from where he took up work first in Sunderland and from 1865 on the Great Western Railway, becoming manager of the Swindon Carriage and Wagon Works. In 1885 he was appointed locomotive, carriage and wagon superintendent on the Great Eastern Railway at Stratford, London. Here he thoroughly reorganised the works and reduced the number of different locomotive types. By way of opposing an electrification scheme by a rival company in 1902, he designed and built a monster 0–10–0 tank engine, the first 'decapod' in Britain and the first three-cylinder engine since 1846 (see pp. 123 and 132). He increased the seating capacity of the suburban coaches, making possible the 'Jazz' service from London for which the G.E.R. was famous or, from the passengers' point of view, notorious. In 1891 he sportingly established a world record by having an 0–6–0 erected in 9 hours 47 minutes (see p. 149). For utilizising waste from the G.E.R. oil-gas plant he designed a liquid fuel ejector in 1887, making it possible to use oil waste as locomotive fuel (see p. 145). His most famous locomotive design was the 'Claud Hamilton' Class 4–4–0. He was a Quaker, and a philanthropist with concern for the men under him. For engine crews he provided a dormitory at Stratford which established a standard of comfort and convenience. He retired in 1907.

Thomas William Worsdell (1838–1916) the eldest son of Nathaniel Worsdell of the Liverpool & Manchester Railway, trained mainly on the London & North Western Railway at Crewe under

John Ramsbottom. In 1865 he joined the staff of
the Pennsylvania Railroad in the U.S.A. as master
mechanic at the Altoona Works. However, after
six years he returned to Crewe where he became
works manager.

In February 1882 he was appointed locomotive
superintendent of the Great Eastern Railway at
Stratford, London, and while there he patented his
two-cylinder compound locomotive in conjunction with A. von Borries of the Hanover State
Railways, Germany.

In 1885 he became locomotive superintendent
of the North Eastern Railway at Gateshead,
where many locomotives were built on his compound principle. He was succeeded by his brother
Wilson in 1890 and remained as consulting engineer until he retired in 1893.

William Arrol (1839–1913) was born near
Paisley, Scotland. At 14 he began work with a local
blacksmith and in 1863, after some years as a
journeyman smith, he obtained employment with
Blackmore & Gordon of Port Glasgow. By 1868
he had saved £85, half of which he spent on a
boiler and engine and with which he, started a
small works of his own near Glasgow. Three years
later this formed the nucleus of the great Dalmar-
nock Works.

*The Forth Bridge from the top of
the north cantilever, built by
William Arrol to designs by
Benjamin Baker and John
Fowler. The pier of Thomas
Bouch's abandoned suspension-
bridge project can be seen beside
the base of the Inchgarvie Tower,
surmounted by a lighthouse (John
Marshall)*

*Du Bousquet's masterpiece—the
4–6–4 of 1910–11 (French
Railways Limited)*

Bridge-building was added to his work and his
first contract was for bridges on the Hamilton
Branch of the Caledonian Railway, including a
long multi-span bridge over the Clyde at Bothwell.
The C.R. then entrusted him with the bridge over
the Clyde into Central Station, Glasgow, in 1875.

In 1873 he had undertaken construction of a
railway suspension bridge over the Firth of Forth to
designs by Thomas Bouch and work actually
began, but was halted after the collapse of the first
Tay Bridge in 1879. His next important contract
was the bridge carrying the North British Railway
over the South Esk on the Montrose line. On this
he gained experience which served him well when
he undertook the second Tay Bridge, to designs of
W. H. Barlow, begun in 1882 and completed in
1887. It is the longest railway bridge in Europe.

His greatest contract was the Forth Bridge of
1882–90, after which he was knighted by Queen
Victoria.

Other great works included the steelwork for the
Tower Bridge London; the first Redheugh Bridge,
Newcastle upon Tyne; three bridges over the Nile
at Cairo; the Queen Alexandra Bridge, Sunderland; the Scherzer Lifting Bridge at Barrow and
the second portion of the Clyde Bridge into Glasgow
Central Station.

Gaston du Bousquet (1839–1910) was one
of the leading French locomotive engineers. He
worked with de Glehn on the first four-cylinder
compound of 1886 and on the later 4–4–0, 4–4–2,
4–6–0 and 4–6–2 designs. From 1890 until his
death he was locomotive engineer on the Northern
Railway of France. In 1901 he introduced a class
of successful 4–6–0 tandem compound tank engines
on the Ceinture Railway of Paris. For the freight
traffic he introduced the Du Bousquet compound
tank engines of 0–6–2 + 2–6–0 type with centrally
mounted cylinders and with buffing and drawgear mounted on a separate frame. He was working
on a very advanced type of 4–6–4 express engine
when he died.

Benjamin Baker (1840–1907), civil engineer, was born in Somerset. From 1856 to 1860 he served an apprenticeship at Neath Abbey Ironworks, South Wales, and in 1860 he worked as assistant to W. Wilson on the Grosvenor Railway Bridge and Victoria Station, London. In 1861 he joined the staff of John Fowler and was his partner from 1875 until Fowler's death in 1898.

From 1861 he was engaged on the construction of the Metropolitan and District (Inner Circle) railways, London, and the extension to St. John's Wood. Later he was one of the engineers responsible for the first London 'tubes', the City & South London opened in 1890 and the Central Line opened in 1900. In these Baker adopted a method suggested to him in 1875, of making the line drop out of one station and rise into the next to assist starting and stopping. In 1896 he acted as joint engineer with W. R. Galbraith for the Bakerloo Line.

From the early years of his career Baker had made a deep study of long-span bridges, and in 1872 he evolved the cantilever system which he adopted in his designs for the Forth Bridge in Scotland, begun in 1883 and opened in 1890. For this he was knighted in 1890.

In addition, Baker was responsible for many other works in Britain, Egypt and America.

Walter Mackenzie Smith (1842–1906) British locomotive engineer. From 1874 to 1883 he was the first locomotive superintendent of the Imperial Japanese Government Railway. In 1883 he joined the North Eastern Railway under T. W. and Wilson Worsdell at Gateshead, England. In 1887 he produced his piston-valve design and in 1899 his three-cylinder compound 4–4–0 which formed the basis of the celebrated Midland Railway design of Samuel Johnson. In 1906 he produced his masterpiece, the four-cylinder compound 4–4–2.

No. 730, the first of the two four-cylinder compound 'Atlantics' built by the North Eastern Railway in 1906 to a design by W. M. Smith (British Rail)

William Cornelius Van Horne (1843–1915) was the driving force behind the construction of the Canadian Pacific Railway. He was born in Illinois, U.S.A., and at 14 he began as a telegraph operator on the Illinois Central Railroad. By 1864 he had become a train despatcher on the Chicago & Alton Railroad, and in 1870 became superintendent of transportation. Further promotion led to his appointment as general manager and later president of the Southern Minnesota Railroad which he restored to solvency. In 1881 there came his greatest opportunity when he was placed in charge of construction of the Canadian Pacific Railway. With tremendous energy he drove the vast project through to completion in 1886, becoming president in 1888 until he had to resign because of illness in 1899.

Recovering his health in 1900 he directed construction of the Cuba Railway, 350 miles (563 km) long, opened in 1902. He next completed the railway from Puerto Barrios to Guatemala, from 1903 to 1908.

He died in Montreal, following a visit to Cuba, in June 1915.

George Westinghouse (1846–1914), American engineer, inventor of the most successful compressed-air brake widely used on railways. He began working this out in 1866, first producing the non-automatic 'straight air' brake. The automatic brake (which applied itself if the train broke apart) was developed in 1872–73. Further improvements were made in 1886–87 to enable a more rapid brake application. From the beginning Westinghouse insisted on a rigorous standardisation of details so that Westinghouse-fitted stock from any railways can be coupled. The Westinghouse Electric Company was formed in 1886, other works later being established in England and Europe. The principal British railways using the Westinghouse brake were the Great Eastern, the North Eastern, the North British and Caledonian. Other companies used the vacuum-brake.

Alfred George de Glehn (1848–1936). Son of Robert von Glehn who settled in London from the Baltic Provinces. When Alfred was quite young they moved to France and changed the name to de Glehn. After training as an engineer, Alfred de Glehn became technical head of the Société Alsacienne at Belfort and here he was responsible for the design and construction of the first four-cylinder compound engine, the Northern Railway of France No. 701, in 1886. This engine had low-pressure cylinders inside driving the first crank-axle, and two high-pressure cylinders

A four-cylinder de Glehn
compound 4–6–2 No. 808 of the
Bengal-Nagpur Railway, India,
in 1943. It was built by the
North British Locomotive
Company of Glasgow in 1929
and represents the ultimate
development of the de Glehn
system (John Marshall)

outside driving the rear driving-wheels by outside cranks. The driving-wheels were not coupled. In its fully developed form as an 'Atlantic' the de Glehn compound became used throughout France. The Great Western Railway in England bought three of these compound 'Atlantics'. The de Glehn system was subsequently applied to a wide range of locomotive types. Some very large de Glehn compound 'Atlantics' and 'Pacifics' were built for the Bengal & Nagpur Railway in India.

Wilson Worsdell (1850–1920) the son of Nathaniel Worsdell, grandson of Thomas Clarke Worsdell and younger brother of T. W. Worsdell, all mentioned earlier. He was educated at the Quaker School at Ackworth and at the age of 17 began training at the Altoona Works of the Pennsylvania Railroad, where his brother was working as master mechanic. In 1871 he and his brother returned to England and after some years at Crewe, Stafford and elsewhere on the London & North Western Railway he was appointed in 1883 as assistant to Alexander McDonnell, locomotive superintendent of the North Eastern Railway at Gateshead.

From 1886 he assisted his brother T. W. Worsdell until 1890 when he became locomotive superintendent of the N.E.R., a post he held for 20 years. He was the first to introduce the 4–6–0-type engine

for passenger work in England, his 'S' Class in 1899. His 4–4–0 'M' Class achieved distinction in the Races to Edinburgh and Aberdeen in 1895. It was under Worsdell that the Tyneside electrification of the Newcastle upon Tyne suburban services was carried out in 1904, opening on 19 March 1904, and so achieving the distinction of being the first suburban electrification scheme in England by beating the Lancashire & Yorkshire Railway's Liverpool to Southport line by one week. Most of his engines were of excellent design, mechanically and aesthetically, and gave many years useful service. A particular feature was the large side-window cab clearly influenced by Worsdell's experience in the U.S.A. Examples of his 0–6–0s and 0–8–0s achieved the distinction of being the last pre-Grouping engines on British railways and are still represented on the North Yorks Moors Railway near Whitby. Worsdell was outstanding in his ability to delegate responsibility to his subordinates, giving them great freedom, while retaining absolute command.

Henry Alfred Ivatt (1851–1923) was born in Cambridgeshire and at 17 was apprenticed under John Ramsbottom and later F. W. Webb at Crewe on the London & North Western Railway. After serving in various situations on the L.N.W.R. he was appointed in 1877 as district superintendent at Cork on the Great Southern & Western Railway in Ireland. In 1882 he became works manager at Inchichore Works of the railway, at Dublin, and in 1886 he was made locomotive engineer in succession to J. A. F. Aspinall. In 1895 Ivatt was appointed chief locomotive engineer on the Great Northern Railway at Doncaster, England. The first British 'Atlantic', his No. 990, appeared in 1898 and was an immediate success (see p. 131). It was followed by 20 similar engines and in 1903 by No. 251, the first of the large-boilered 'Atlantics' which introduced the wide firebox into Britain. Ivatt's other engines included 4–4–0, 4–4–2, 0–8–0 and 0–6–0 tender engines and 4–4–2, 0–6–2 and 0–8–2 tanks.

'Atlantics' Nos. 990 and 251 are preserved at York Railway Museum.

H. A. Ivatt (British Rail)

Magnus Volk (1851–1937) was born in Brighton, the son of a German clock-maker, and was the builder of the first electric railway in Britain. In 1881 he gained a gold medal for a street fire-alarm system and the following year he equipped his house with the first telephone and the first electric light in Brighton.

In 1883 he completed the installation of electric light in the Brighton Pavilion and at the same time built a 2 ft (0·610 m) gauge railway along the beach making use of a Siemens dynamo and a 2 hp Crossley gas-engine. The first section of the railway opened on 4 August 1883, eight weeks before the Portrush–Giant's Causeway Tramway in Ireland.

In 1884 the line was extended and the gauge changed to 2 ft 9 in (838 mm) and the rebuilt line opened on 4 August 1884.

His most extraordinary venture was the Brighton & Rottingdean Seashore Electric Tramroad, with a car like a ship on long legs which ran through the sea at high water. The line was about 2¾ miles (4·426 km) long and was opened on 28 November 1896 and ran until January 1901 (see illustration, p. 176).

August von Borries (1852–1906) was the pioneer of locomotive compounding. He studied in Berlin. From 1875 to 1902 he was chief mechanical engineer of the Prussian State Railways. His first two-cylinder compound was built in 1880 and his first four-cylinder in 1899. Among his numerous innovations in German locomotives was the use of nickel steel for boilers in 1891. From 1902 until his death he was professor of transport and machinery at the Berlin Technical School. He wrote extensively on locomotive matters.

Richard von Helmholz (1854–1934), German locomotive engineer, from 1884 to 1917 chief designer at Krauss Locomotive Works, Munich. In 1884 he produced a straight-link version of the Walschaert valve gear, and in 1888 the Krauss-Helmholz truck in which the leading carrying-wheels and coupled wheels formed a bogie, as on the Flamme 2–10–0 in Belgium. He was one of the originators of the locomotive booster, or auxiliary engine.

Samuel M. Vauclain (1856–1940) American engineer, trained at the Baldwin Locomotive Works in Philadelphia from 1883. In 1889 he

Manitou & Pike's Peak 0–4–2 Vauclain compound No. 4, built by Baldwin in 1897 (replacing wrecked engine built in 1893) at Colorado Railroad Museum, Golden, near Denver (John Marshall)

Volk's Electric Railway, Brighton, the first electric railway in Great Britain (P. E. Baughan)

produced his famous compound design in which the high- and low-pressure piston-rods on both sides of the engine were connected to common crossheads, driving two cranks. Later four-crank arrangements were produced. Up to 1907 over 2000 Vauclain compounds were built.

George Jackson Churchward (1857–1933) was possibly the greatest of British locomotive engineers. At the age of 16 he was articled to John Wright, locomotive superintendent of the South Devon Railway at Newton Abbot. In 1876, when this became part of the Great Western Railway, Churchward transferred to Swindon under Joseph Armstrong. However, the following year Armstrong died and Churchward continued under William Dean. In 1895 he became assistant locomotive works manager and manager in 1896, and soon afterwards chief assistant to Dean. In this position he was given freedom to experiment with new boiler designs incorporating a high Belpaire firebox which appeared on most of the later Dean engines, including the famous *City of Truro*. In 1902 Dean retired and Churchward became chief mechanical engineer. He had already produced his first 4–6–0, named *William Dean*. It was the forerunner of the famous 'Saint' Class and later the 'Halls' and 'Granges'. Churchward adopted a system of standard components such as boilers, cylinders, etc., combinations of which could be worked into a wide range of different locomotive designs. He was so impressed by the work of the de Glehn compound 4–4–2s in France that in 1903 he persuaded the G.W.R. to buy one of these for trials. Two more were bought in 1905. For comparison Churchward designed a four-cylinder

G. J. Churchward (British Rail)

simple 4–4–2, later rebuilt into a 4–6–0, and the forerunner of the 'Stars', 'Castles' and 'Kings' and of his greatest engine *The Great Bear*, the first British 'Pacific' of 1908. From the French engines he adopted the high pressure of 225 lb/in² (15·8 kg/cm²) and the generous bearing surfaces and from American practice the front-end arrangement with long-travel valves, the tapered boiler and cylindrical smokebox. Another innovation was his superheater at a time when the merits of superheating were still doubted on other railways. He retired at the end of 1921 but continued his close association with Swindon until, on a misty morning on 19 December 1933, he was walking across the main line when he was struck and instantly killed by the 10.30 Fishguard express.

Wilhelm Schmidt (1859–1924), German engineer, the inventor of the high-degree superheater which revolutionised steam-locomotive design. The standard fire-tube design with the elements housed in a large flue-tube was first used in Belgium in 1901. It was first used in Britain in 1906 on a Great Western 4–6–0 (see p. 125) and on the Lancashire & Yorkshire Railway in a series of 0–6–0s introduced at Horwich by George Hughes.

Karl Gölsdorf (1861–1916), Austrian locomotive engineer. His father Adolf was locomotive engineer of the Austrian Southern Railways from 1885 to 1907. As locomotive engineer of the Austrian State Railways from 1893 until his death he produced over 60 designs of great elegance and ingenuity. In 1893 he introduced the two-cylinder Austrian compound and in 1901 his first four-cylinder compound. His first ten-coupled engine appeared in 1900. He designed the first 2–6–2, (1904), 2–6–4 (1908) and 2–12–0 (1911) in Europe, the last two being entirely new, and a 0–12–0 tank for the Abt rack system in 1912. He introduced a new valve gear which dispensed with the expansion link, and is remembered particularly for his conveniently arranged footplate controls and his system of locomotive numbering which was widely used.

Herbert William Garratt (1864–1913), inventor of the Garratt articulated locomotive developed in conjunction with Beyer Peacock & Company of Manchester, England. It consists of two engine units with the boiler mounted between them. The first was a 2 ft 6 in (762 mm) gauge engine built for Tasmania in 1909. South Africa became the largest user. In all some 2000 were built. (See 'Garratt Locomotives', pp. 140–4.)

Henry Greenly (1876–1947), pioneer of miniature passenger-carrying railways. He began as a jeweller's apprentice; then, after a period in a London technical school on a scholarship, he began his career as a draughtsman at the Neasden Works of the Metropolitan Railway in 1897. From 1901 to 1906 he was assistant editor of *The Model Engineer*. In 1906 he became a consulting engineer, specialising in model subjects, and for many years worked with W. J. Bassett-Lowke in preparing designs for miniature locomotives in Britain and abroad.

From 1919 he was associated with several companies engaged in the production of model locomotives and railways, and in 1922 he became engineer to the Ravenglass & Eskdale Light Railway (see p. 221) which under his guidance was converted to 15 in (381 mm) gauge. In 1926 he became chief engineer, for Captain Howey, of the 15 in (381 mm) gauge Romney, Hythe & Dymchurch Railway in Kent (see p. 221) and was responsible for all the civil engineering as well as the design of locomotives and rolling stock. In 1930 he again took up consulting practice, also contributing to model engineering journals. His books *Model Electric Locomotives and Railways* (1922), *Model Railways* (1924) and *Model Steam Locomotives* (1922) did much to establish the model-railway hobby in Great Britain.

Herbert Nigel Gresley (1876–1941) is famous as the engineer responsible for the world's fastest steam locomotive. From 1893 to 1897 he served an apprenticeship under F. W. Webb on the London & North Western Railway at Crewe, and completed his training on the Lancashire & Yorkshire Railway under J. A. F. Aspinall. In 1905 he was appointed carriage and wagon superintendent on the Great Northern Railway at Doncaster and in 1911 succeeded H. A. Ivatt as chief mechanical engineer. He was the first to introduce articulated carriages in Britain, in 1907, using one bogie to support the ends of two coaches. His bow-ended teak carriages were among the smoothest riding ever built.

He remained in charge at Doncaster until his death, becoming chief mechanical engineer of the London & North Eastern Railway at the Grouping of companies in 1923.

Most of the locomotives designed under him did good work, though some suffered from structural or mechanical defects which became prominent as maintenance standards declined during the Second World War.

His most famous achievements were the 'Silver Jubilee' and 'Coronation' streamlined trains in the mid 1930s. On 3 July 1938 his 'A4' Class 4–6–2 No. 4468 *Mallard* achieved a world record speed, for a steam locomotive, of 126 m.p.h. (202 km/h) which has never been exceeded. It was not attained without risk, and it was never established that no other locomotive could do better on the same stretch of line. *Mallard* is now in the York Railway Museum.

H. N. Gresley (British Rail)

Arturo Caprotti (1881–1938). Italian engineer, designer of a locomotive valve gear employing vertical poppet-valves operated from a rotating camshaft as in automobile practice. It was first used on a 2–6–0 goods engine on the Italian State Railways in 1921. Its first application in Britain was on the London & North Western Railway 'Claughton'-type 4–6–0 No. 5908 in 1926, resulting in a coal economy of 20·76 per cent.

London, Midland & Scottish Railway 'Class 5' 4–6–0 No. 44686 fitted with Caprotti valve gear (John Marshall)

Oliver Bulleid (1881–1970) was one of the last and in many ways the most original of steam-locomotive engineers. He was born in New Zealand and after graduating at Leeds and Sheffield Universities he was apprenticed at the Doncaster Works of the Great Northern Railway. From 1912 to 1937 he worked with H. N. Gresley, making many contributions to locomotive and carriage design.

In 1937 he became the last chief mechanical engineer of the Southern Railway for which he designed the extraordinary 'Merchant Navy'-type 'Pacific', with its numerous novel features such as chain-driven valve gear working in an oil-bath, American-type Boxpok wheels and welded boiler with steel firebox and thermic siphon. The success of this boiler greatly influenced the design of the boiler for the British Railways Standard 'Pacifics'. Bulleid's 'Pacifics' had tremendous power but poor adhesion, leakage of oil from the valve gear being the major cause of this.

The first of the 'Pacifics' came out in 1940. In 1945 a lighter version, the 'West Country' type, appeared for use on lines west of Exeter where weight restrictions ruled out the use of the 'Merchant Navy' type.

His other locomotive design for the S.R. was a 0–6–0 of unconventional appearance, but of tremendous power. At the end of his term of office on the S.R. he worked out his most revolutionary design of all, the 'Leader'-type 0–6–6–0 with six cylinders and sleeve-valves. It was produced in a hurry in a race against Nationalisation in 1948, and there was too little time to attend to the numerous snags which arose.

Following this expensive failure he went to Ireland in 1949 to become chief mechanical engineer of Coras Iompair Ereann, where he designed a locomotive to burn turf. It worked,

but with the advent of the diesel-electric locomotive it was soon eclipsed. He retired in 1958 and died in Malta. Though a century later than George Stephenson, he was no less a pioneer.

'Merchant Navy' Class 4–6–2 designed by Oliver Bulleid for the Southern Railway, England, 1944 (The Science Museum, London)

André Chapelon (b. 1892) is one of the most famous names in the history of the steam locomotive, developing the French compound engine to a high degree of efficiency. After the First World War he joined the Paris–Lyon–Méditerranée Railway; in 1925 the Paris–Orléans Railway and in 1936 he became chief experimental engineer. In co-operation with M. M. Kylala in 1926 he perfected the Kylchap double blast-pipe which gave greater freedom to the locomotive exhaust. His first 'Pacific' rebuilt in 1929 and a 4–8–0 in 1932 incorporated improvements which doubled the power output.

On the formation of the Société Nationale des Chemins de fer Français (S.N.C.F.) in 1938 he was appointed to the Department of Steam Locomotive Studies of which he became chief. He retired in 1953, but characteristically he continues to produce calculations which, could they still be applied, would result in even greater steam-locomotive efficiency.

Chapelon-rebuilt compound 4–6–2 on the Northern Railway of France (French Railways Limited)

Section 3
THE LINES

RAILWAY GAUGES
or measurement between the inner edges of the rails

Standard gauge, 4 ft 8½ in or 1·435 m, is used in Great Britain, Canada, U.S.A., Mexico, Europe (except Ireland, Spain, Portugal, Finland and the U.S.S.R.), North Africa, the Near Eastern countries, the Australian Commonwealth Railways and New South Wales, China and South Korea; also some lines in Japan, Western Australia and Victoria. In South America it is found in Paraguay, Uraguay, the North Eastern Region in Argentina, the Central and Southern Railways of Peru, Venezuela and short lines in Brazil.

Other principal gauges:

Wide gauges
5 ft 6 in (1·676 m) India, Pakistan, Sri Lanka (Ceylon), Spain, Portugal, Argentina, Chile
5 ft 3 in (1·600 m) Ireland, South Australia, Victoria, Brazil
4 ft 11⅞ in (1·520 m) U.S.S.R., Finland (The gauge was 5 ft or 1·524 m until 1 January 1972)

Sub-standard gauges
3 ft 6 in (1·067 m) Queensland, South and West Australia, Tasmania, New Zealand, South Africa, Rhodesia, Malawi, Ghana, Nigeria, Sudan, Japan, Indonesia, Newfoundland, some lines in Norway and Sweden, and in Ecuador and Chile
3 ft 5¼ in (1·05 m) Algeria, Syria, Lebanon and Jordan
1 metre (3 ft 3.375 in) Principal lines in Burma, Thailand (Siam), Vietnam, Malaysia, East Africa and Cambodia, Brazil, Argentina, Chile, Bolivia; secondary lines in Switzerland, Portugal, Greece, India, Pakistan, Iraq.

For narrow gauges, less than 1 metre, see 'Narrow gauge railways' in the section Miscellany.

At Crewe, England, there were three gauges in the early 1840s. The Grand Junction Railway (1838) was 4 ft 8½ in (1·435 m); the Crewe & Chester Railway (1840) was 4 ft 8¾ in (1·441 m); and the Manchester & Birmingham Railway (1842) was 4 ft 9 in (1·447 m).

The metre gauge holds second place in the world's route mileage. Out of about 700 000 route miles (1 126 500 km) in 1930 about 70 000 miles (112 650 km) were metre gauge. Third place is held by the 3 ft 6 in (1·067 m) gauge with a route mileage of 47 000 (75 640 km).

Australia has three different gauges. Out of over 25 000 miles (40 240 km) nearly half is 3 ft 6 in gauge (1·067 m) and the remainder is almost equally divided between 4 ft 8½ in (1·435 m) and 5 ft 3 in (1·600 m).

The 1·600 m (5 ft 3 in) was the result of employing an Irish engineer, F. W. Shields; the 1·067 m (3 ft 6 in) was adopted as an economy measure. Plans to unify the system have been discussed since 1897.

Perth to Kalgoorlie is now dual gauged, 1·435 m (4 ft 8½ in) and 1·067 m (3 ft 6 in) (see colour illustration on p. 87) and Port Pirie to Broken Hill is now 1·435 m (4 ft 8½ in).

South Australia has all three gauges. At Peterborough on the Port Pirie–Broken Hill section there is triple-gauge track, thus:

Triple-gauge at the south end of Gladstone Yard, South Australia, on wheat silo discharge tracks, in 1973; 1·067 m (3 ft 6 in), 1·435 m (4 ft 8·5 in) and 1·6 m (5 ft 3 in) (A. Grunbach)

The last of the Great Western Railway broad-gauge engines awaiting scrapping at Swindon in 1892 (British Rail)

For the Great Western Railway, England, I. K. Brunel (see p. 43) adopted a gauge of 7 ft (2·134 m). After a while a ¼ inch (6 mm) was added to give greater clearance.

The last railway to be built to the 7 ft gauge was the 4¼ mile (6·8 km) branch of the West Cornwall Railway from St Erth to St Ives, England, opened on 1 June 1877.

The last broad-gauge trains of the Great Western Railway ran on 20 May 1892. Gauge conversion was completed by 23 May.

TRACK
(For early developments see 'The Beginnings')

The first steel rails were made by Robert Forester Mushet and were laid experimentally at Derby Station on the Midland Railway, England, early in 1857, on a heavily used line. They remained in use until June 1873.

The first steel rails on the London & North Western Railway were laid at Chalk Farm, London, in 1862.

The first steel rails in the U.S.A. were laid by the Pennsylvania Railroad in 1863 at Altoona and Pittsburgh under the supervision of John Edgar Thomson (1808–74), the third president of the P.R.R. and himself an engineer.

The word 'sleeper' originated from the 'dormant timbers' placed beneath the rails and was certainly in use in England in the early eighteenth century. North Americans adopted the word 'tie', the French 'La traverse'. In German it is 'die Schwelle', simply joist.

British Rail consumes about 2 500 000 sleepers annually. Each timber sleeper measures 8 ft 6 in (2·591 m) × 10 in (254 mm) × 5 in (127 mm) in softwood or 4¾ in (120 mm) in hardwood.

The number of sleepers per mile in Britain is from 2112 to 2464 (1320 to 1540 per km) according to loadings, foundations, curves, etc. In exceptional situations as many as 2640 (1650 per km) may be used.

The maximum British axle load is 25 tons, but in the U.S.A. where loads can be up to 34 tons per axle, 3000 to 3500 ties per mile (1875 to 2188 per km) are used.

In Britain there are about 9 000 000 pre-stressed concrete sleepers in use. They measure 8 ft 3 in (2·515 m) long and weigh 588 lb (267 kg) with fastenings, compared with 237 lb (107·5 kg) for a chaired and creosoted wooden sleeper. They have an estimated life of from 44 to 50 years, more than double that of a wooden sleeper. They became popular during the wartime timber shortage and are now standard for plain line. Mechanical handling has largely overcome the weight problem. Experiments are being made with concrete beams for points and crossings.

Steel sleepers are extensively used on the continent of Europe and in other parts of the world. They can last from 40 to 50 or even 80 years and then still have scrap value. In Switzerland 70 per cent of the Federal system and the whole of the Rhaetian and other metre-gauge systems are laid with steel sleepers. Greece, Congo Republics, systems in West, East and South Africa use steel sleepers for 90–100 per cent of the track.

In Britain steel sleepers are little used, largely because of the difficulty of packing ballast beneath. Corrosion can be minimised by resilient tar coatings or by the addition of a small percentage of copper to the steel.

The latest type of track construction in Britain, known as PACT (Paved Concrete Track) is being experimented with at Radcliffe on Trent near Nottingham (1970), and at Duffield north of Derby (1972). It consists of a continuous concrete slab on which the rails are fixed. This eliminates sleepers and ballast, significantly reduces maintenance, and provides a better line for high-speed trains, giving a smoother ride. The new track is expected to be highly suitable for use in tunnels, particularly the Channel Tunnel, and for rapid transit lines. It is already in use on part of the new electric main line in Glasgow.

On French Railways (S.N.C.F.) it has been used in the new Sainte-Devote Tunnel under Monte Carlo and in an experimental cutting near Limoges. In New Zealand it is being used inside the new Kaimai Tunnel in the North Island (see p. 106).

Before it can be used extensively on main passenger lines train toilet facilities will have to be altered so that they no longer deposit waste on to the track. At present the ballast acts as an efficient filter-bed.

The simplest, most ingenious and most effective rail fastening is probably the 'Pandrol'. The principal component is a spring-steel clip quickly driven into place with a hammer, and as easily removed. Its resilience makes it unaffected by vibration, it will not work loose, and it prevents 'rail creep' (the tendency for rails to move in the direction of the traffic when a train is braking). It is suitable for wood, concrete or steel sleepers, and on the last can be insulated for track-circuiting. Rail changing is simplified and the clips can be re-used. It is eminently suitable for use with the new PACT construction. One of its greatest advantages is its low cost.

'Pandrol' rail fastenings were first used on British Railways in 1959 just south of Peterborough on the former Great Northern main line. Since then it has become standard on British Rail and the 50

The test site at Radcliffe on Trent, Nottingham, where six experimental lengths of curved concrete track are being evaluated. The point layouts are purely experimental; the section opened to passenger and freight traffic 4 June 1972. At the end of the curved sections are the three-year-old straight sections which have maintained alignment with no maintenance (British Rail)

A special freight train of steel stock hauled by a 'Class 37' diesel locomotive passing over the 1·8 km (1·1 miles) length of PACT at Duffield near Derby. Commissioned on 13 August 1972, the line will carry approximately 40 passenger and 30 freight trains each day. (British Rail)

'Pandrol' rail fastenings in use with concrete sleepers on a section of high-speed electrified main line (British Rail)

millionth clip was delivered during 1972. It has also been adopted in many other countries throughout the world.

The standard British flat-bottomed rails measure 6¼ in (159 mm) high, 5½ in (140 mm) wide across the foot, 2¾ in (70 mm) across the head and have a nominal weight of 113 lb/yd (55·79 kg/m). They are rolled in 60 ft (18·288 m) lengths. In Germany 30 m (98 ft 5 in) is common. They are then welded into continuous lengths first at the depot into 600 ft, 720 ft, 900 ft or 1320 ft (182·88 m, 219·46 m, 274·32 m or 402·3 m), and into greater lengths at the site.

London Transport use a 95 lb/yd (47·6 kg/m) 'bull-head' rails in chairs, mounted on sleepers of jarrah on underground lines.

U.S.A. railroads use rails of a standard length of 39 ft (11·887 m). Some, however, use lengths of 45 ft and 60 ft (13·716 m and 18·288 m). Rail weights on Class 1 railroads vary from 45 to 174 lb/yd (22·3 to 86·3 kg/m). On trunk lines the weights range upwards from 85 lb/yd (42 kg/m). Rail joints are generally staggered.

The longest stretch of unbroken four-track line in the world was 342·5 miles (551 km) between Castleton and Dunkirk, New York, U.S.A. Except for a 2 mile (3·2 km) break at Dunkirk the four-track line extended from Castleton to Collinwood, Cleveland, 473·75 miles (762·5 km). Today most of this length has been converted to two tracks using Centralised Traffic Control (C.T.C.).

The longest continuous four-track line in Britain is on the former Midland Railway between London and Glendon North Junction, 75 miles (120·7 km), though the two pairs of lines separate between Souldrop Box and Irchester South Junction (about 3 miles or 4·828 km), the freight lines passing through Sharnbrook Tunnel, 1 mile 100 yd (1·7 km).

Another section on the same system extends from Kilby Bridge, Wigston, to Tapton Junction, Chesterfield, 53 miles (85·295 km).

The second longest four-track line in Britain is the 60 miles (96·561 km) from London (Euston) to Roade, formerly the London & North Western Railway.

Other long sections of four-track line are: London (Paddington) to Steventon on the Great Western Railway, 56½ miles (90·93 km); London (Waterloo) to Worting Junction beyond Basingstoke, 51 miles (82·077 km). The former Great Northern Railway out of London (King's Cross) has more of its first 100 miles (161 km) quadrupled than any other similar length in Britain, but it is broken at Welwyn, Arlesey, Huntingdon and Holme.

LONGEST STRAIGHTS

The world's longest straight stretch is on the standard-gauge Transcontinental Railway of the Commonwealth Railways of Australia, across the Nullarbor Plain, 478 km (297 miles). It was

A train crossing the world's longest straight railway, across the Nullarbor Plain, Australia (Australian News & Information Bureau)

completed in 1917. In one year 712 km (442 miles 44 chains) of track was laid, with a maximum for one day of 4 km (2 miles 40 chains), unballasted at the time. This is a record in Australia. (For the world record see 'Some U.S.A. Facts and Feats', p. 107.)

The Buenos Aires & Pacific Railway, Argentina, (Central Region) is dead straight and almost level for 205 miles (330 km) between Junin and Mac-Kenna, on the 5 ft 6 in (1·676 m) gauge line from Buenos Aires to Mendoza where it connects with the metre-gauge South Transandine line.

In the U.S.A. the longest straight is the 78·86 miles (126·914 km) on the former Seaboard Air Line Railway between Wilmington and Hamlet, North Carolina. It is now part of the Seaboard Coast line which also has a 57·4 mile (92·376 km) straight between Okecchohee and West Palm Beach, Florida. Other long straights in the U.S.A. are:

Rock Island Railroad between Guymon, Oklahoma, and Dalhart, Texas, 71·94 miles (114·163 km)
Penn Central (formerly New York Central) between Air Line Junction (West of Toledo) and Butler, Indiana, 68·49 miles (110·229 km)
Monon Railroad between Brookston and Westville, Indiana, 64·52 miles (103·836 km)
Illinois Central between Edgewood and Akin Junction, Illinois, 62·96 miles (101·324 km)
Atlantic Coast line between Waycross and Kinderlou, Georgia, 60·1 miles (96·721 km)

There are, or were, five more lengths over 50 miles (80 km).

In Rhodesia is a 70 mile (112·65 km) straight between Sawmills and Dett on the Bulawayo–Waukie main line.

In Russia the Moscow & St Petersburg (Leningrad) Railway is almost straight and level for 400 miles (643·74 km). It was begun in 1843 and opened on 13 November 1851. It adopted the 5 ft (1·524 m) gauge, then standard in the Southern States of the U.S.A., and so established the Russian standard gauge of 5 ft. (See 'George Washington Whistler', p. 40.)

The longest straight in England is 18 miles (28·968 km) on the former North Eastern Railway Selby–Hull line (opened by the Hull & Selby Railway on 1 July 1840). Next is the 16 miles

(25·750 km) on the former Great Northern Railway Boston–Grimsby line between Boston and Burgh-le-Marsh, Lincolnshire, opened throughout on 1 October 1848.

The former South Eastern Railway between Tonbridge and Ashford, opened throughout on 1 December 1842, is nearly straight for 24 miles (38·624 km), but has a slight deviation at Headcorn near Staplehurst.

FLYING JUNCTIONS

The first 'flyover' was built in 1845 to carry the London & Croydon atmospheric railway (see p. 30) over the 'ordinary' lines of the Brighton and Dover railways. The Croydon and Brighton companies amalgamated on 27 July 1846 to form the London, Brighton & South Coast Railway, and on 4 May 1847 the atmospheric system was abandoned.

The first 'flying junction' was on the London & North Western Railway at Birdswood (later Weaver) Junction in Cheshire where the Runcorn line, opened on 1 April 1869, joined the former Grand Junction main line.

GRADIENTS

The steepest railway in the world is the Swiss funicular (cable-worked) incline between Piotta and Piora (Lake Ritom) in Canton Ticino, with a gradient of 1 in 1·125 (88 per cent). It is closely approached by the Châtelard-Barberine funicular south of Martigny, Switzerland, with a gradient of 1 in 1·15 (87 per cent). Both lines were built for transport of materials for hydro-electric schemes and were later adapted for passengers.

The steepest railway in the U.S.A. is the 1550 ft (472·440 m) long cable-worked incline down to the famous 'hanging bridge' at the bottom of the Royal Gorge, Colorado. It has a gradient of 64·6 per cent, or 1 in 1·55. It was opened on 14 June 1931. The engineer was George F. Cole. The journey takes five minutes. 'Of course it's safe!' states a notice at the top, for the view down into the 1000 ft (304 m) deep gorge can be quite unnerving.

The Ashley Planes on the Jersey Central Railroad near Wilkes Barre, Pennsylvania, were among the most famous railway inclines in the U.S.A. They formed part of the original main line

The famous hanging bridge on the Denver & Rio Grande Railroad in the Royal Gorge, Colorado, from the world's highest bridge, 1053 ft (321 m) above the river. The lower end of the cable railway can be seen bottom right, the steepest railway in the U.S.A. (John Marshall)

Looking up the steepest railway in the U.S.A. from the bottom of the Royal Gorge in Colorado (John Marshall)

opened in 1843, and latterly they handled millions of tons of anthracite every year. They were 2·5 miles (4·023 km) long and rose 1014 ft (309 m) in three cable-worked sections, at 5·7 per cent (1 in 17·5), 14·65 per cent (1 in 6·8) and 9·28 per cent (1 in 10·7). Because of maintenance costs they were abandoned at the end of 1948 and the trains were rerouted by the 12·5 mile (20·117 km) main-line deviation.

The world's steepest rack railway is the Pilatus Railway in Switzerland with a gradient of 50 per cent (1 in 2). (See 'Mountain and Rack Railways', p. 213.)

The steepest incline worked by adhesion is the 9 per cent (1 in 11) between Chedde and Servoz, on the electric Chamonix line of the South-Eastern Region of the French National Railways.

The steepest adhesion-worked incline in Great Britain was the 1 in 14 (7 per cent) Hopton Incline on the Cromford & High Peak Railway in

Derbyshire, opened in 1831 and closed in 1967. It was originally cable worked.

The original C. & H.P.R. included five other cable-worked inclines with gradients ranging from 1 in 7 (14·3 per cent) to 1 in 16 (6·25 per cent), and a short one at Whaley Bridge worked by a horse gin and endless chain, which continued in use until 9 April 1952.

Freight train ascending the 1 in 14 Hopton Incline on the Cromford & High Peak Railway, once the steepest adhesion-worked incline in Great Britain. Opened in 1831, closed 1967. The photograph was taken in May 1934 (H. C. Casserley)

The steepest main-line gradient in the U.S.A. is the Saluda Hill on the Southern Railway, 34 miles (54·718 km) south of Ashville, North Carolina. The grade is 4·7 per cent (1 in 21.4).

The steepest standard-gauge incline in the U.S.A. was on the north side of the Ohio River at Madison, Indiana, on the Madison & Lafayette Railroad, opened on 1 April 1839. It was 7040 ft (2·146 km) long and rose 431 ft (131·369 m) on a gradient of about 1 in 17 (5·89 per cent).

From 1866 it formed part of the Jeffersonville, Madison & Indianapolis Railroad, whose master mechanic Reuben Wells designed a massive 0–10–0 tank engine, built in 1868, to work the incline. The engine can still be seen today, in the Childrens' Museum, Indianapolis.

The world's greatest 'main-line' inclines are on the 5 ft 3 in (1·600 m) gauge São Paulo Railway in Brazil. The railway has to rise about 1700 ft (800 m) from the port of Santos to São Paulo in a distance of 49 miles (79 km). The British engineer James Brunlees (1816–92) built the first line in 1851–57. It included a single-track incline 5·28 miles (8·5 km) long on a gradient of 1 in 10 (10 per cent). It was worked by a cable on the 'tail-end' principle.

In 1900 a new double-track line was opened, 6·8 miles (11 km) long worked in four inclined sections with continuous cables. The old incline remained in use for freight.

By 1958 traffic on the inclines was nearing their limit of 9 000 000 tons per annum, so in 1968 it was decided to rebuild the original incline for rack operation, electrified at 3000 V d.c. The new incline was opened in 1974. It includes a concrete viaduct 853 ft (260 m) long at Grota Funda and a span of of 206 ft (63 m) over the River Mogi. It is operated by rack and adhesion locomotives of 3800 hp (2820 kW) and has a capacity of 21 000 000 tons per annum at only a third of the operating cost of the cable incline. The 1900 cable inclines are being retained for emergency use.

The steepest gradient over which standard-gauge passenger trains were worked in Great Britain was on the Chequerbent Incline on the Kenyon–Leigh–Bolton Branch of the London & North Western Railway in Lancashire. Mining subsidence had affected the incline making a short stretch as steep as 1 in 19·5 (5 per cent). 'Officially' the gradient was 1 in 33! At this place one end of a coach was 3 ft, or nearly 1 metre, higher than the other end.

The line was part of the original Bolton & Leigh Railway, the first railway in Lancashire, opened on 1 August 1828. Passenger services ran from 13 June 1831 to 3 March 1952.

On the 4 ft (1·219 m) gauge Glasgow Subway there are gradients of 1 in 18 (5·5 per cent) and 1 in 20 (5 per cent) on the sections under the Clyde.

The 2–8–0 No. 48178 descending the Chequerbent Incline in Lancashire. Just beyond the rear of the train the gradient is 1 in 19·5 (John Marshall)

The slightest gradient in Britain indicated on a gradient-post is 1 in 13 707 between Sturt Lane Junction and Farnborough, Hampshire, on the former London & South Western Railway.

The steepest gradient in Britain over which passenger trains work today is the 1 in 27 (3·7 per cent) on the Mersey Railway from the bottom of the Mersey Tunnel up to James Street Station, Liverpool.

Part of the double-track cable inclines opened in 1900 on the São Paulo Railway, Brazil. The earlier single-track incline, now modernised, can be seen on the left

From Middleton Junction to Oldham the branch of the Lancashire & Yorkshire Railway opened in 1842 rose for ¾ mile at 1 in 27. Passenger services ended in 1958 and the line was closed completely on 7 January 1963.

Gradient post at the summit of the 1 in 27 incline at Oldham, Lancashire (John Marshall)

In Scotland the Causewayend Incline near Manuel, about 2 miles (3·219 km) west of Linlithgow, Stirlingshire, included ½ mile (804 m) at 1 in 23 (4·4 per cent). The Commonhead Incline near Airdrie, Scotland, included a short stretch of 1 in 23. Passenger trains ran until 1 May 1930 on both these lines.

On the former Brecon & Merthyr Railway in Wales, in the 7·25 miles (11·667 km) from Talybont-on-Usk to Torpantau the line climbed 926 ft (281·94 m) on gradients of 1 in 38–40 (2·7–2·5 per cent).

The Canterbury & Whitstable Railway in Kent, opened on 3 May 1830, included 594 yd (543 m) at 1 in 28 (3·5 per cent).

The self-acting inclined plane on which descending loaded wagons pull empties up was patented by Michael Menzies, a Scottish advocate, in 1750.

The principle was first used on the Schulenberg Railway in the Harz Mountains in Germany in 1724.

The first use of a steam winding engine to draw wagons up an incline was about 1805.

The world's toughest and longest gradient is on the standard-gauge Central Railway of Peru.

In 107 miles (172 km) the line rises 15 665 ft (4775 m). This gives an *average* gradient of 1 in 36 (2·8 per cent), but this includes stations and reversing switches. The normal gradient is 1 in 25 (4 per cent), with long stretches of 1 in 20 (5 per cent) or steeper. The line was begun by Henry Meiggs (see p. 45) in 1870 and completed to Oroya in 1893, and it was opened to Huancayo, 206 miles (332 km), on 8 September 1908.

On the Burma State Railways the line between Mandalay and Lashio climbs for 12 miles (19·312 km) continuously at 1 in 25 (4 per cent). This section includes the Gokteik Viaduct (see p. 86).

The Viso zigzag at Km 112 on the Peru Central Railway. The upper level can be seen in the centre of the photograph and in the top right corner (John Marshall)

Down (westbound) goods at Woodford on part of the 1 in 33 climb to Katoomba, between Sydney and Lithgow, N.S.W., headed by 2–8–0 'standard goods' No. 5187 and three-cylinder 4–8–2 No. 5701, about 1950 (G. C. Taylor)

The steepest main line in Australia is 1 in 33 (3 per cent) up the Blue Mountains between Sydney and Lithgow, New South Wales.

The steepest adhesion-worked railway in Australia was 1 in 19 (5·3 per cent) between Campbelltown and Camden, New South Wales. It was opened as a tramway in 1879 and became a branch of the railway system in 1901. It was closed on 31 December 1962, though an enthusiasts' special was run over it the following day (see illustration). Normal trains consisted of a carriage and two wagons hauled by a '20' Class 2–6–4 tank engine. On Good Fridays up to three pilgrims' specials were run, eight or nine coaches with two '20' Class engines in front and one behind.

The author (right) at the world's highest railway summit, La Cima, on the Morococha Branch of the Peru Central Railway, 15 806 ft (4818 m). Until recently a spur branched off just beyond the right of the picture to serve a mine, reaching an altitude of 15 848 ft (4830 m) but it is now removed. This section, from Ticlio to Morococha, appeared to be out of use at the date of the photograph, 5 October 1974 (John Knowles)

Last train from Campbelltown to Camden, N.S.W., climbing the 1 in 19 up Kenny Hill. Locomotives Nos. 2010 and 2016 with No. 2029 in rear on 1 January 1963 (I. K. Winney)

Australia's steepest railway was a section of the 3 ft 6 in (1·067 m) gauge Emu Bay Railway in Tasmania where the line rose at 1 in 16 (6·2 per cent) between Queenstown and Strahan. An Abt rack was used. It was closed in 1963.

Locomotive No. 2 on the rack section between Dubbil Barril and summit on Mount Lyell Mining & Railway Company's Railway, Tasmania, in March 1963 (I. K. Winney)

The world's highest railway junction is at Ticlio, 4758 m (15 610 ft), on the Central Railway of Peru where the line divides, the main line passing beneath Mount Meiggs in the Galera Tunnel (see p. 107) and the Morococha Branch climbing to the world's highest railway summit at La Cima, to rejoin the main line at Cut-Off above Oroya.

The Central Railway of Peru is not simply the world's highest railway; it is also the most wonderfully engineered. It climbs from just above sea-level at Callao to 4783 m (15 694 ft) in Galera Tunnel in a distance of 173·5 km (107·8 miles) and

The world's highest railway junction 15 610 ft (4758 m), at Ticlio on the Peru Central Railway, on 6 October 1974. The main line passes beneath Mount Meiggs in the background in the Galera Tunnel, the world's highest tunnel. The line curving round in the foreground descends to Casapalca. The Morococha Branch can be seen climbing to the left, and above it is the Volcan Mine, until recently served by a branch from La Cima which reached a record altitude of 15 848 ft (4830 m) (John Marshall)

drops again to Oroya, 3726 m (12 224 ft) in a further 49 km (30 miles), by means of six double zigzags and one single zigzag on the main line and three double zigzags on the Morococha Branch, with 67 tunnels and 59 bridges, some of these major engineering works in themselves.

It was laid out and constructed under the direction of Henry Meiggs (see p. 45), but he died in 1877 when construction had reached Cacray, and further work was delayed by the Peru–Chile War in 1879.

Part of the condensing beam winding engine built by the Butterley Company in 1825, at the top of the Middleton Incline on the Cromford & High Peak Railway in Derbyshire (John Marshall)

A train from Cuzco to Puno on the Southern Railway of Peru at Sicuani, 11 650 ft (3551 m) above sea-level in October 1974, with two standard-gauge ALCO Co Co diesel-electric locomotives, Nos. 359 and 358 (John Marshall)

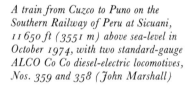

A train to Potosí at Condor, Bolivia, the world's highest railway station, 15 705 ft (4787 m). It is headed by metre-gauge Japanese 2–8–2 No. 662 (John Marshall)

The Carrion Bridge, at 252 ft (77 m) the highest on the Central Railway of Peru. It was built in 1937 to replace the 1891 Verrugas Bridge, named after the disease which attacked the workers during the construction of the first bridge in 1870 (John Marshall)

THE WORLD'S HIGHEST RAILWAY SUMMITS*

Summit	Railway	Gauge	Altitude ft	m
La Cima	Central (Peru)	standard	15 806	4818
Condor (Potosí Branch)	Antofagasta & Bolivia‡	metre	15 705	4787
Galera Tunnel	Central (Peru)†	standard	15 688	4781
Caja Real	Yauricocha (Peru)†	standard	15 100	4604
Chaucha	Yauricocha (Peru)†	standard	14 974	4564
Km 41	Yauricocha (Peru)†	standard	14 888	4538
Chorrillos	Argentine Railways (North Transandine)	metre	14 682	4475
Crucero Alto	Southern (Peru)†	standard	14 666	4470
Yuma	Antofagasta & Bolivia‡	metre	14 440	4401
Alcacocha	Cerro de Pasco (Peru)	standard	14 385	4385
Cerro	Cerro de Pasco (Peru)	standard	14 208	4331
La Raya	Southern (Peru)†	standard	14 153	4314
Pike's Peak	Manitou & Pike's Peak, Colorado, U.S.A.	standard	14 109	4302
General Lagos	Arica–La Paz (Bolivian National)	metre	13 963	4257
La Cima	Cerro de Pasco (Peru)	standard	13 822	4214
Cuesta	Bolivian National Railways	metre	13 573	4137
El Alto	Guaqui–La Paz	metre	13 471	4106
Escoriani	Bolivian National Railways	metre	13 310	4057
Between Potosí and Sucre	Bolivian National Railways	metre	13 231	4033
Comanche	Arica–La Paz (Bolivian National)	metre	13 225	4031
Kenko	Antofagasta & Bolivia	metre	13 134	4004
Muñano	Argentine Railways (North Transandine)	metre	13 120	4000
Ascotan	Antofagasta & Bolivia	metre	12 994	3960
Socompa	Antofagasta–Salta (Argentina)§	metre	12 822	3908
San Antonio de los Cobres	Argentine Railways (North Transandine)	metre	12 379	3774
Cachinal	Argentine Railways (North Transandine)	metre	12 264	3740
Oruro	Antofagasta & Bolivia	metre	12 125	3696
Tres Cruces	Argentine Railways	metre	12 116	3693
Urbina	Guyaquil–Quito (Equador)	1·067 m (3 ft 6 in)	11 841	3609
Pumahuasi	Argentine Railways	metre	11 674	3559
Incahuasi	Argentine Railways (North Transandine)	metre	11 654	3553
Climax Spur, Colorado	Colorado & Southern	standard	11 465	3450
Villazon	Villazon–Atocha (Bolivian National)	metre	11 308	3447
Iturbe	Argentine Railways	metre	10 965	3343
Diego de Almagro	Argentine Railways (North Transandine)	metre	10 840	3305
La Cumbre	Chilean Transandine	metre (rack approach)	10 466	3191
Tennessee Tunnel, Colorado	Denver & Rio Grande Western	standard	10 239	3116

* Abandoned railway summits over 10 000 ft (3048 m) in Colorado, U.S.A. are listed under 'Some U.S.A. Facts and Feats', p. 109.

† The Central and Southern of Peru and the Yauricocha railways are now part of the National Railway Company of Peru.

‡ In 1907 the Antofagasta & Bolivia Railway built a branch from Ollogue in Chile, close to the Bolivia border, to copper-mines at Collahuasi, reaching a height of 4826 m (15 835 ft) at Punto Alto. It is now disused beyond Yuma, 4401 m (14 440 ft). The Condor Summit on the Potosí Branch is now **the highest over which passenger trains are worked**. The Bolivian lines of the A. & B. were nationalised in 1962.

§ The Antofagasta–Salta Railway is divided between the Chilean National Railways and the Argentine Railways (General Belgrano Section), now North Western Region.

Summit	Railway	Gauge	Altitude ft	m
Leadville, Colorado	Colorado & Southern	standard	10200	3109
Monarch, Colorado	Denver & Rio Grande Western	standard	10148	3093
La Cima	National Railways of Mexico	standard	10020	3054
El Oro	National Railways of Mexico	standard	9977	3041
La Veta Pass, Col.	Denver & Rio Grande Western	standard	9242	2817
Timboroa	East African	metre	9131	2783
Cachinal	Taltal (Chile)	1·067 m (3 ft 6 in)	8840	2694
Nanacamilpa	National Railways of Mexico	standard	8400	2561
Acocotla	National Railways of Mexico	standard	8337	2542
Sherman, Wyoming	Union Pacific, U.S.A.	standard	8013	2443
Cerro Summit	Denver & Rio Grande Western	standard	7968	2429
Las Vigas	National Railways of Mexico	standard	7923	2415
Kikuyu	East African	metre	7857	2395
Asmara	Eritrean	metre	7854	2394
Addis Ababa	Franco Ethiopian	metre	7703	2348
Quezaltenango	Guatemalan State	standard	7650	2332
Raton Pass	Santa Fe, U.S.A.	standard	7586	2312
Ghoom	North Eastern, India (formerly Darjeeling Himalayan Railway)	2 ft (600 mm)	7407	2258
Bernina Hospice	Rhaetian, Switzerland	metre	7403	2257
Asit	Turkish State	standard	7401	2256
Nilgiri Hills	Nilgiri Railway, India	metre	7275	2217
Nurabad	Trans Persian (Southern Section)	standard	7274	2217
Furka Tunnel	Furka–Oberalp, Switzerland	metre	7098	2163
Nederhorst	South African	1·067 m (3 ft 6 in)	6871	2095
Oberalp Pass	Furka–Oberalp, Switzerland	metre	6711	2045
Belfast	South African	1·067 m (3 ft 6 in)	6463	1970
Kandapola	Sri Lanka (Ceylon) Government Railways	762 mm (2 ft 6 in)	6316	1926
Pattipola	Sri Lanka (Ceylon) Government Railways	1·676 m (5 ft 6 in)	6226	1898
Albula Tunnel	Rhaetian, Switzerland	metre	5981	1823
Between Beirut and Damascus	Beirut–Damascus	1·067 m (3 ft 6 in)	5885	1794
Kolpore, Pakistan	North Western (Mushkaf–Bolan)	1·676 m (5 ft 6 in)	5874	1791
Puerto de Navacerrada	Spanish National	1·676 m (5 ft 6 in)	5777	1761
Johannesburg	South African	1·067 m (3 ft 6 in)	5735	1748
Arosa	Rhaetian, Switzerland	metre	5715	1742
Mullar Tunnel	Northern Pacific, U.S.A.	standard	5560	1694
Bozeman Tunnel	Northern Pacific, U.S.A.	standard	5560	1694
near Marandellas	Rhodesia Railways	1·067 m (3 ft 6 in)	5538	1687
Zermatt	Brig–Visp–Zermatt, Switzerland	metre	5415	1650
Wolfgang	Rhaetian, Switzerland	metre	5358	1633
Great Divide	Canadian Pacific	standard	5332	1625
Between Peking and Suiyuan	Peking–Suiyuan, China	standard	5200	1585
Taurus	Turkish State	standard	4900	1494
La Molina	Spanish National	1·676 m (5 ft 6 in)	4659	1420
Kalaw	Burma State	metre	4610	1405
La Cañada	Spanish National	1·676 m (5 ft 6 in)	4526	1380
Brenner	Austrian Federal	standard	4496	1370
Ben Lomond	N.S.W. Govt., Australia	standard	4473	1363
Mont Cenis Tunnel	Italian State	standard	4284	1306
Arlberg Tunnel	Austrian Federal	standard	4275	1304

Summit	Railway	Gauge	Altitude ft m	
Taugevatn, near Finse	Bergen–Oslo, Norwegian State	standard	4265	1301
Tauern Tunnel	Austrian Federal	standard	3881	1183
Lone Butte	British Columbia Railway	standard	3864	1178
Connaught Tunnel	Canadian Pacific	standard	3787	1154
St Gotthard Tunnel	Swiss Federal	standard	3780	1151
Yellowhead Pass	Canadian National	standard	3717	1133
Maan	Hedjaz	1·101 m (3 ft 5¼ in)	3700	1128
Pokaka	New Zealand Railways	1·067 m (3 ft 6 in)	2671	814
Waiouru	New Zealand Railways	1·067 m (3 ft 6 in)	2670	814

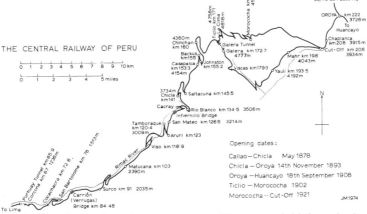

In 1893 it was completed to Oroya along the route already laid out by Meiggs. The mountain above the summit is named Mount Meiggs after the great engineer and contractor. Heights, distances and dates are shown on the adjoining map.

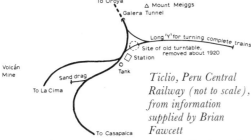

Ticlio, Peru Central Railway (not to scale), from information supplied by Brian Fawcett

During the 1950s a spur was built from the Morococha Branch at La Cima to the Volcán Mine overlooking Ticlio, reaching a world record altitude of 4830 m (15 848 ft), but it has recently been abandoned and dismantled.

The highest railway in Great Britain is the summit terminus of the 2 ft 7½ in (800 mm) gauge Snowdon Mountain Railway—3493 ft (1064 m). (See colour illustration, p. 179.)

The second highest is the summit of the 3 ft 6 in (1·067 m) gauge Snaefell Railway in the Isle of Man, 2034 ft (620 m). The Fell centre rail (see 'Mountain Railways', p. 215) is used for braking.

At the Dinorwic slate quarries in North Wales the 1 ft 10¾ in (578 mm) gauge railway reached a height of over 2200 ft (670 m). The highest engine shed in Britain was on one of the levels, at Lernion, at 1860 ft (567 m).

The highest engine-shed in the British Isles; Lernion at the Dinorwic Slate Quarry, North Wales, 1860 ft (567 m) above sea-level. The locomotive was Red Damsel, *renamed* Elidir *in 1971 (W. A. Camwell)*

The highest summit on British Rail is at Druimuachdar, 1484 ft (452 m), between Dalnaspidal and Dalwhinnie on the former Highland Railway main line from Perth to Inverness, Scotland, opened in 1863.

In 1902 a 7·25 mile (12·472 km) branch was opened from the Caledonian Railway Glasgow–Carlisle main line, at Elvanfoot, to Wanlockhead, the highest village in Scotland. The station was at a height of 1413 ft (431 m), but the line climbed to 1498 ft (456 m). It closed on 2 January 1939.

Caledonian Railway 0–4–4 tank at Wanlockhead, Scotland, on 30 July 1931, at a height of 1413 ft (431 m) (H. C. Casserley)

At Waenavon in South Wales the London & North Western Railway reached a height of 1400 ft (427 m). It was closed to passengers on 5 May 1941 and closed entirely on 23 June 1954.

On the Great Western Railway, England, the terminus of the branch to Princetown on Dartmoor was at a height of 1373 ft (418 m). It was closed on 5 March 1956.

Stainmore Summit, 1370 ft (417 m), on the former Stockton & Darlington Railway from Darlington to Kirkby Stephen (John Marshall)

Stainmore Summit on the former Stockton & Darlington–Kirkby Stephen line was 1370 ft (417 m) above sea-level. It was opened in 1861 and closed on 22 January 1962.

At Weatherhill, County Durham, on the former Stanhope & Tyne Railway, later the North Eastern Railway, the rails stood at 1378 ft (420 m). From here a private mineral branch, opened in 1846, ascended to about 1670 ft (509 m) at the top of the incline down to Rookhope. **This was the highest point reached by standard-gauge rails in Britain.** A private passenger service operated over it until about 1921. It is now abandoned, but makes an interesting walk.

The summit of the Rookhope Incline and ruins of Bolts Law Engine-house, the highest point reached by standard-gauge lines in Britain, about 1670 ft (509 m) (B. Roberts)

The lowest point on British Rail is the bottom of the Severn Tunnel, 144 ft (43·889 m) below Ordnance Datum.

The lowest point reached by any railway in the world was Jisr el Majame near Samakh (Zemach), 213·36 m (700 ft) below sea-level, where the 1·042 m (3 ft 5¼ in) gauge line from Haifa in Israel to Derraa crossed the River Jordan just south of the Sea of Galilee. At Derraa it joined the Hedjaz Railway from Damascus to Medina. It was begun in 1901 and opened through to Medina on 31 August 1908. The Haifa–Derraa section is at present out of use for political reasons.

See also 'Southern Pacific', p. 196.

TRANSCONTINENTAL RAILWAYS

The longest railway in the world is the Trans-Siberian, from Moscow to Vladivostok— 5801 miles (9336 km). It was opened in sections. By ferry across Lake Baikal and via the Chinese Eastern Railway through Manchuria, through communication was established on 3 November 1901. In 1904, while Lake Baikal was frozen over, rails were laid across the ice, but the first locomotive plunged through a gap and was lost.

The Circum–Baikal line, round the south of the lake, was opened on 25 September 1904. The 1200 mile (1931 km) Amur line, opening up through travel entirely on Russian soil, was begun in 1908 and completed in 1916.

The 'Trans-Siberian Express' covers the journey in 9 days 3 hours.

The first railway from the Atlantic to the Pacific was the 5 ft (1·524 m) gauge Panama Railroad, 48 miles (77 km) long, across the Isthmus of Panama, between Aspinwall and Panama. It was opened on 28 January 1855. Surveys were made as early as 1828.

The first big step towards an American transcontinental railroad was taken on 21 April 1856 when trains first crossed the Mississippi between Rock Island, Illinois, and Davenport, Iowa.

The first American transcontinental railroad was completed on 10 May 1869 when the last spike was driven at Promontory, north of the Great

First and Last. Two days before the driving of the Golden Spike at Promontory, Utah, one of the last westbound covered wagon trains met the first train from California. This was Governor Leland Stanford's special train, pulled by the historic engine Jupiter, *en route to the last spike ceremony a few miles east. The picture was taken on 8 May 1869, on the north shore of the Great Salt Lake, by Alfred A. Hart of Sacramento, the official photographer of the Central Pacific (now Southern Pacific) (Southern Pacific Transportation)*

Salt Lake, Utah, uniting the Central Pacific and Union Pacific railroads. Because the point of joining had not been previously established, and because the companies were receiving up to $48 000 a mile in Federal loans for track-laying, rival grading gangs passed one another and the U.P. gangs went on constructing 225 miles (362 km) of parallel grading until they were officially stopped. The section from Promontory to Ogden was taken over by the Central Pacific.

The railway ran from Omaha, Nebraska, to Sacramento, California, 1725 miles (2776 km). The old Western Pacific Railroad (no relation to the present Western Pacific) was opened from Sacramento to Oakland opposite San Francisco, a further 92 miles (148 km), on 8 November 1869. It was consolidated with the Central Pacific on 23 June 1870. Passengers crossed by ferry to San Francisco.

In its eagerness to push towards Utah in its race with the westward-building Union Pacific, Central Pacific bridged many of the High Sierra chasms with timber trestles. When the railroad was completed, they came back and the Chinese labourers that built the railroad filled them in with solid earth and embankments. This remarkable photo was taken at Secrettown Trestle, 62 miles from Sacramento on the western slope of the Sierra in 1877. Scrapers were not in use as yet for grading. Dynamite had been invented but was not in general use. The Chinese used picks and shovels, chisels and hammers, black powder, wheelbarrows and one-horse dump-carts (Southern Pacific Transportation)

Through communication between the Atlantic and Pacific coasts was finally established in 1877 when the first bridge was opened across the Missouri near Omaha. The present bridge, 1750 ft (533·44 m) long, was built in 1886.

The Central Pacific became a part of the Southern Pacific Railroad when that company was formed in 1884. It was fully absorbed in 1958.

The Lucin Cut-off across the Great Salt Lake, totalling 103 miles (166 km), was opened on

8 March 1904 and shortened the journey between Ogden and Lucin by 42 miles (67·6 km), making the original Promontory route redundant. (See 'The world's longest railway water crossing', p. 100.) The old line, however, with its curves equivalent to 11 complete circles, was not abandoned until 1942.

A short section at Promontory was relaid in 1969 for the enactment of the Centenary celebrations. For the benefit of crowds of visitors the 'last spike' suffered numerous drivings and extractions.

Donald A. Smith (later Lord Strathcona and Mount Royal) driving the last spike on the Canadian Pacific Railway at Craigellachie at 09·22 Pacific Time on 7 November 1885. It was followed by Van Horne's famous speech, here quoted in full: 'All I can say is that the work has been well done in every way.' This must be the shortest speech of its kind on record, in relation to the length of the railway: 1 word per 200 miles!

The first railway across Canada, the Canadian Pacific, was completed at a place named Craigellachie in Eagle Pass, British Columbia, when the Eastern and Western sections were

The newly built 4-4-0 No. 371 on the first through transcontinental train on the Canadian Pacific at Port Moody, British Columbia, on 4 July 1886 (Canadian Pacific Limited)

joined on 7 November 1885. Its completion within ten years was a condition of British Columbia entering the Confederation, on 20 July 1871. The first sod was cut on 1 June 1875 at Fort William, on the left bank of the Kaministiquia River. The main contract was signed on 21 October 1880 by which year 700 miles (1126 km) were under construction. The Canadian Pacific Railway Company was incorporated on 15 February 1881; construction began on 2 May 1881, and throughout 1882 2·5 miles (4 km) of track were laid every day. The Prairie Section was finished as far as Calgary on 18 August 1883 and the Great Lakes Section on 16 May 1885, thanks to the devotion and energy of William Cornelius Van Horne (see p. 55). The section through the rock and muskeg north of Lake Superior was almost as difficult as the construction through the British Columbia mountains (see pictures on pp. 2 and 77).

Transcontinental services began with the departure of the first train from Montreal on 28 June 1886. It arrived at Port Moody on 4 July. The 12 mile (19·3 km) extension to Vancouver was opened on 23 May 1887.

Three locomotives on a passenger train climbing the 'Big Hill' in the Kicking Horse Pass on the Canadian Pacific Railway, on 4·1 miles (6·6 km) of 1 in 22·25 (4·5 per cent) before the spiral tunnels were built in 1909. (Canadian Pacific Limited)

From Montreal to Vancouver, 2879 miles (4633 km), the journey takes three days on 'The Canadian' transcontinental train.

An alternative route through the Rockies at Crow's Nest Pass, through a rich coal region close to the U.S.A. border, was begun in 1897 and completed in 1930. It crosses the great Lethbridge

Viaduct over the Oldman (formerly Belly) River (see p. 98), and another 147 ft (45·8 m) high over the same river at Fort Macleod.

Old Canadian Pacific trestle on Red Sucker Cove on the North Shore of Lake Superior (Canadian Pacific Limited)

Canada's second transcontinental railway began in eastern Canada as the Grand Trunk Railway which, by 1900, owned and operated a network of lines covering Ontario and Quebec, including the former Great Western Railway with which it amalgamated in 1882, and also the Grand

Trunk Western to Chicago, and a line from Montreal to the Atlantic at Portland, Maine. After unsuccessful proposals to extend westwards through the U.S.A., the G.T.R. finally agreed that the Government should build the Eastern Division of the National Transcontinental Railway between Moncton and Winnipeg, and for the newly created Grand Trunk Pacific Railway, as a subsidiary of the G.T.R. to build from there to the Pacific Coast at Prince Rupert, 550 miles (885 km) north of Vancouver. With Government aid the G.T.P. was built to the same high standards as the Grand Trunk had been.

Both the National Transcontinental Eastern Division and the Grand Trunk Pacific were begun in 1905. The National Transcontinental was opened in stages from June to November 1915. It included the great Quebec Bridge over the St Lawrence (see p. 93), not opened until 1917. The G.T.P. was completed at a point 417 miles (671 km) east of Prince Rupert on 7 April 1914 and complete services began in September.

From Winnipeg the G.T.P. passed through Edmonton and through the Yellowhead Pass by which it made the lowest crossing of the Rockies,

A transcontinental train in the days of steam on the Canadian National Railway through the Rockies (Canadian National Railways)

with the easiest grades, of any North American transcontinental railway.

The Canadian Northern Railway,

Canada's third transcontinental line, was inspired by two men, William Mackenzie (1849–1923) and Donald Mann (1853–1934). It was made up of a number of separately incorporated railways and by 1903 had grown to 344 miles (554 km) in the east, and to 1362 miles (2192 km) in the west. By 1905 the western lines had reached Edmonton and Prince Albert, and in the east Hawkesbury was linked to Ottawa. Surveys through the Yellowhead Pass began in 1908 and on 4 October 1915 the Canadian Northern was opened to Vancouver, through the Fraser River Canyon which it shared with the Canadian Pacific. The Canadian Northern had now grown to 9362 miles (15067 km) and extended from Quebec to Vancouver.

In 1917, to aid the war effort, over 100 miles (161 km) each of the Grand Trunk Pacific and Canadian Northern tracks were removed between Lobstick Junction, Alberta, through the Yellowhead Pass, to Red Pass Junction where the Prince Rupert and Vancouver lines diverged, to make a joint line of the two competing sections.

Soon after opening the Canadian Northern was in financial difficulties and, following careful consideration by the Government, *Canadian National Railways* was formed to acquire the Canadian Northern Railway. In 1919 the Grand Trunk Pacific was allowed to go into receivership. On 21 May 1920 the Government took formal possession of the Grand Trunk Railway and in September 1920 met the debenture obligations as *de facto* proprietor of the Grand Trunk Pacific. The Grand Trunk Acquisition Act was passed on 5 November 1920. In 1923, under an Order in Council, the

A Canadian National train at Cisco in the Fraser River Canyon where it shares the valley with the Canadian Pacific Railway (Canadian National Railways)

control of all Government railways including the Grand Trunk and the Intercolonial Railways passed to the Canadian National Railways under a president and board of directors appointed by the Government. In 1949 the Newfoundland Railway was absorbed (see p. 112).

In 1923 the Canadian National Railways had 20 573 miles (33 109 km) of route, and the Canadian Pacific Railway 13 563 miles (21 828 km), making them among the world's largest railway systems.

In the U.S.A. no single railroad company operates from the Atlantic to the Pacific, with the possible exception of the Southern Pacific (see below). Following the Union Pacific–Central Pacific, the other major transcontinental routes were completed as follows:

The Atchinson, Topeka & Santa Fe from Kansas City joined the Southern Pacific from California at Deming, New Mexico, on 8 March 1881. The Santa Fe completed its own through route from Chicago to California on 1 May 1888.

The Southern Pacific from California to New Orleans on the Gulf of Mexico was formally opened on 12 January 1883. (See 'Pecos Bridge', pp. 96–7 and 'Southern Pacific', p. 196.)

The original bridge carrying the Southern Pacific Railroad over the Pecos at its confluence with the Rio Grande, Texas. It was near here that the last spike was driven to complete the 'Sunset Route' on 5 January 1883 (Southern Pacific Transportation)

The Northern Pacific, the first to the Pacific North-west, was completed at Gold Creek, Montana, on 8 September 1883.

The Oregon Short Line and the Oregon Railway & Navigation Company, forming the Union Pacific route to the Pacific Northwest, were connected at Huntingdon, Oregon, on 25 November 1884.

The Great Northern Railway between the Great Lakes and Puget Sound at Everett, Washington, was completed on 6 January 1893.

On the Pacific Coast Extension of the **Chicago, Milwaukee & St Paul** (now the Chicago, Milwaukee, St Paul & Pacific, or The Milwaukee Road) the last spike was driven at Garrison, Montana, on 19 May 1909.

The Western Pacific, the western extension of the Denver & Rio Grande main line from Denver to Salt Lake City, was opened throughout to San Francisco on 22 August 1910, making its famous passage through the Feather River Canyon and forming, with the D. & R.G.W., one of the finest scenic routes through the mountains.

The first train from the Atlantic to the Pacific was the 'Transcontinental Excursion' consisting of Pullman 'Hotel Cars', sponsored by the Boston Board of Trade in May 1870. It took eight days from Boston to San Francisco. A daily newspaper was published on the journey.

The first regular through sleeping-car service between the Atlantic and Pacific coasts of the U.S.A. did not begin until as late as 31 March 1946. Before that a change had to be made at Chicago or St Louis.

The first South African transcontinental railway linked Cape Town and Durban at Heidelberg in the Transvaal on 10 October 1895.

Another African transcontinental route was completed in 1928. It runs from Benguela, Angola, via the Congo and Rhodesia to Beira in Portuguese East Africa.

The first Trans-Australian Railway from Port Augusta to Kalgoorlie, 1693 km (1052 miles) standard gauge, was opened on 22 October 1917. Across the Nullarbor Plain it traverses the world's longest straight stretch, 478 km (297 miles) long. At Kalgoorlie it connected with the Western Australian 1·067 m (3 ft 6 in) gauge line from Perth. With the addition of standard gauge on the Kalgoorlie–Perth Section and the conversion of the section from Port Pirie to Broken Hill from 1·067 m to standard gauge, completed on 29 November 1969, a through route entirely on standard gauge was opened up from Perth to Sydney, 3960 km (2461 miles). The 'Indian Pacific Express' was inaugu-

A Trans-Australian Railway goods train on its 2461 mile (3960 km) journey from Sydney to Perth, Western Australia. As it skirts the edge of the arid and treeless Nullabor Plain the train will run for 300 miles (483 km) without bend or rise on the longest straight stretch of railway in the world (Australian News & Information Bureau)

rated on 1 March 1970 by the opening of the new standard-gauge line between Sydney, New South Wales, and Perth, Western Australia.

The Transandine Railway between Los Andes, Chile, and Mendoza, Argentina, was opened on 5 April 1910. It is metre gauge with Abt triple-rack sections, and climbs to an altitude of 3191 m (10 466 ft) at the 3·167 km (3463 yd) long La Cumbre Tunnel.

The Chile end of the summit tunnel at La Cumbre on the Transandine Railway (John Marshall)

At Mendoza it connects with the 1·676 m (5 ft 6 in) gauge line from Buenos Aires. The total distance is 1448 km (900 miles).

The Northern Transandine Railway from Antofagasta, Chile, to Salta, a distance of 904 km (562 miles) is metre gauge and was completed in 1948. It reaches a height of 4475 m (14 682 ft) at Chorrillos; 4000 m (13 120 ft) at Muñano and over 3050 m (10 000 ft) at four other summits. At Salta it connects with the metre-gauge main line from Buenos Aires.

TRANSALPINE RAILWAYS

The first transalpine railway was the line over the Brenner Pass, opened on 24 August 1867, between Austria and Italy. It is the only main line which crosses the Alps without a major tunnel, and its altitude of 1370 m (4496 ft) makes it one of the highest main lines in Europe.

The only metre-gauge transalpine route was opened on 1 July 1903 and forms part of the Rhaetian Railway in Switzerland. Between Chur and St Moritz the railway passes through the Albula Tunnel, 5·865 km (3 miles 134 yd) long, at an altitude of 1823 m (5981 ft). It is the highest of the principal Alpine tunnels.

North end of the 3 mile 1134 yd (5864·5 m) long Albula Tunnel on the Rhaetian Railway, Switzerland (John Marshall)

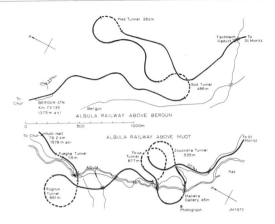

Map of spiral tunnels on the metre gauge Albula section of the Rhaetian Railway, Switzerland (John Marshall)

From St Moritz to Tirano in Italy the Bernina Railway, opened throughout on 5 July 1910, crosses the Alps in the open at an atitude of 2257 m (7403 ft). **It is the highest through railway in Europe.**

The first railway across the main range of the Alps was opened over the Mont Cenis Pass on 15 June 1868. It operated with the centre-rail friction-drive system invented in 1863–69 by John Barraclough Fell (1815–1902). It worked until 18 September 1871 when the Fréjus or Mont Cenis Tunnel was opened. This, **the first of the major Alpine tunnels**, was begun on 31 August 1857 and took 14 years to complete. It is 13·657 km (8 miles 555 yd) long and links the Italian and French railway systems, but is operated by the Italian State Railways.

The St Gotthard Railway and Tunnel were opened to goods traffic on 1 January 1882 and to passenger trains on 1 June 1882. The tunnel, 14·998 km (9 miles 662 yd), with double track, was begun on 13 September 1872. The engineer Louis Favre died of a heart attack inside the tunnel on 18 July 1879. The two bores met on 28 February 1880.

The principal railway through the Alps from east to west is the Arlberg Railway in Austria. It was completed with the opening of the Arlberg Tunnel for double track, 10·250 km (6 miles 650 yd) long, on 20 September 1884. It traverses a greater distance through magnificent mountain scenery than any other railway in Europe.

The Simplon Railway between Switzerland and Italy was completed with the opening of the first single-line Simplon Tunnel 19·803 km (12 miles 537 yd) long, on 1 June 1906. The second tunnel was opened on 16 October 1922 and is 19.823 km (12 miles 559 yd) long.

The second railway between Austria and Italy was opened by the Austrian Federal Railways on 7 July 1909 after the completion of the Tauern Tunnel, 8·551 km (5 miles 551 yd) long, under Bad Gastien. (See also 'Railway Bridges', p. 85.)

The value of the Simplon route was greatly increased by the opening of the single-track Berne–Lötschberg–Simplon Railway on 15 July 1913. It included the double-track Lötschberg Tunnel under the Bernese Oberland Mountains, 14·612 km (9 miles 140 yd) long. The tunnel deviates from a straight line to avoid a section where, on 24 July 1908, an inrush of water and rock caused the loss of 25 lives.

THE LIMITS

The most northerly railway in the world was a 2·414 km (1·5 miles) long 889 mm (2 ft 11 in) gauge line at King's Bay, Spitsbergen, on latitude 79°N only 1207 km (750 miles) from the North Pole. It connected coal-mines with the harbour, and was used in summer only. It was built in 1917 and had five German 0–4–0 tank engines. The line was closed in 1929 but was reopened from 1945 to 1949.

The most northerly 'main-line' railway in the world is at Pechenga in Murmansk Oblast, north-west Russia, 205 miles (330 km) north of

Spiral tunnels on the Albula Railway, Switzerland (Swiss National Tourist Office)

the Arctic Circle, latitude 69°33′N. The most northerly point reached is by an extension of 20 miles (32 km) to a wharf at Litsnayamari, but this carries no passenger service.

At Narvik in Norway the Lapland iron-ore

The north end of the 8 miles 555 yd (13·657 km) long Mont Cenis Tunnel (La Vie du Rail)

railway, opened in July 1903, is about 130 miles (209 km) north of the Arctic Circle.

The most northerly railroad in North America is at Fairbanks, Alaska, northern terminus of the standard-gauge Alaska Railroad, 470 miles (756 km) long from Seward, opened in June 1923. Fairbanks is just south of latitude 65°N, about 130 miles (209 km) south of the Arctic Circle. **The Alaska Railroad is also the most westerly line in North America**, at Anchorage, on longitude 150°W. It is also the only State-owned railway in the U.S.A.

The farthest west was reached by rail in Europe is at Fenit, 8 miles (13 km) west of Tralee, County Kerry, Ireland. The Great Southern & Western Railway reached Tralee in 1859, and the Tralee & Fenit Railway was opened in 1887. It was amalgamated with the G.S. & W. in 1901. The passenger service was withdrawn in 1935.

Previously the honour was shared by Valencia Harbour, Ireland, terminus of the 5 ft 3 in (1·600 m) gauge branch of the Great Southern & Western Railway from Killorglin opened on 12 September 1893, and by Dingle, terminus of the 3 ft (914 mm) gauge Tralee & Dingle Railway, opened on 31 March 1891, both in County Kerry. These are now abandoned.

The most westerly railway in Africa is at Dakar, on the metre-gauge Senegal Railways, latitude 17°24′W. The line from Dakar via Thiés to Saint-Louis was opened in 1885. The extension from Thiés to Kayes (Mali) was begun in 1907 but not completed until 1924.

The most southerly railway in the world is the Ramal Ferro Industrias Rio Turbio, an isolated 750 mm (2 ft 5½ in) gauge Argentine Coal Board line from Puerto Gallegos, about latitude 51°5′S, to the Rio Turbio coal-mines at the southern foot of the Andes in Argentina, close to the frontier with Chile. It runs due west from the South Atlantic coast for about 261 km (162 miles) and is used mainly to transport coal for shipment by sea from Puerto Gallegos. It was opened in 1958. The coal is carried in block trains of up to 1700 tons hauled by Japanese-built 2–10–2 tender engines, the largest and most powerful locomotives ever built for this gauge. Winds in this region frequently reach 100 m.p.h. (161 km/h).

At the Atlantic port of Deseado in Argentina, latitude 47°45′S, is the terminus of the 1·676 m (5 ft 6 in) gauge railway from Colonia Las Heras.

Farthest south by rail in Europe is Algeciras near Gibraltar, Spain, southern terminus of the 1·676 m (5 ft 6 in) gauge branch from Bobadilla.

The most southerly point reached by rail in Asia is Bentjulak on the island of Java on the 1·067 m (3 ft 6 in) gauge Indonesian State Railways, at latitude 8°0′S.

The farthest east in North America is operated by the Candian National Railways. The standard-gauge Cape Breton line to Sydney, Nova Scotia, longitude 60°11′W was opened on 1 January 1891, and the 3 ft 6 in (1·067 m) gauge railway to St John's, Newfoundland, longitude 52°54′W, was opened in stages from 1884 until 1897 when trains began running through to Port-aux-Basques, 547 miles (880 km). The formal opening was on 29 June 1898.

The farthest east by rail in Asia is the 1·067 m (3 ft 6 in) gauge line at Nemuro on the island of Hokkaido, Japan, longitude 145°34′E.

The new northern entrance of the St Gotthard Tunnel at Göschenen. The left-side tunnel was opened in 1959 for the car-ferry service and joins the old tunnel about 200 yd (183 m) inside. A car-ferry train can be seen entering. On the right is the Schöllenen Railway to Andermatt (John Marshall)

East end of the Arlberg Tunnel, Austria, 6 miles 650 yd (10·250 km) long (John Marshall)

Car-ferry train leaving the Italian end of the Simplon Tunnel at Iselle, propelled by a locomotive still in the tunnel and remotely driven from the front vehicle (John Marshall)

The south end of the Lötschberg Tunnel at Goppenstein, Switzerland—Berne–Lötschberg–Simplon I-C-C-I No. 206 entering (John Marshall)

A train in Valencia Harbour Station in Ireland, the farthest west ever reached by rail in Europe (National Library of Ireland)

The most southerly locomotive depot in the world, at Puerto Gallegos, Argentina, with four of the 2 ft 6 in (0·762 m) gauge 2–10–2s built by Mitsubishi, Japan; the largest engines ever built for this gauge (Ken Mills)

The limits of British Rail are:

North, at Thurso on the former Highland Railway, opened on 28 July 1874.

South, at Penzance, Great Western (West Cornwall) Railway, opened on 11 March 1852. Until 1964 it was at Helston on the G.W.R., opened on 9 May 1887.

East, at Lowestoft Central on the former Great Eastern Railway, opened on 3 May 1847.

West, the West Highland Railway between Arisaig and Morar, opened on 1 April 1901, longitude 5°53′W.

Thurso Station in Scotland, farthest north on British Rail (John Marshall)

This is almost equalled by the Highland Railway branch from Dingwall to Kyle of Lochalsh, opened on 2 November 1897, longitude 5°43′W near Kyle, and by Penzance, longitude 5°33′W.

RAILWAY BRIDGES*

The world's highest railway bridge is the Fades Viaduct over the Sioule River on the original Paris & Orleans Railway from Clermont-Ferrand to Montluçon, now the South-West Region of the French National Railways.

The central span of 144 m (473 ft) carries the rails at a height of 132·5 m (435 ft). It was completed in 1909.

The Victoria Falls Bridge over the Zambezi in Rhodesia is 420 ft (128 m) high, with a single steel span of 500 ft (152 m). It was designed by G. A. Hobson and was built in 1904 by the Cleveland

* See also 'Some North American Bridge Records', p. 95.

Bridge & Engineering Company Limited, Darlington, England.

The French engineer Gustav Eiffel (1832–1923), whose tower in Paris is world famous, built the steel Garabit Viaduct on the main line from Neussargues to Béziers on the South-West Region of the French National Railways. It is 165 m (541 ft) span and is 122 m (400 ft) high. It was completed in 1884.

The Pfaffenberg–Zwenberg Bridge on an improved alignment on the south ramp of the Tauern Railway in Austria (opened on 25 July 1909) is a great concrete arch with a span of 200 m (660 ft), **the world's longest**, and height of 120 m (394 ft). It was opened on 30 July 1971, and it eliminated two tunnels and a smaller bridge and shortened the route by over 3 km (2 miles).

Further improvements on the south ramp of the same railway include the Falkenstein Bridge, 396 m (1299 ft) long and 75 m (246 ft) high with

Fades Viaduct in France, the world's highest railway bridge, 435 ft (132·5 m) above the Sioule River (French Railways Limited)

The Pfaffenberg–Zwenberg Bridge on the Tauern Railway in Austria, 394 ft (120 m) high, with a span of 660 ft (200 m), the world's longest span concrete arch bridge, completed in 1971 (Austrian Federal Railways)

Falkenstein Bridge, also on the Tauern Railway in Austria, with spans of 394 ft (120 m) and 492 ft (150 m), 246 ft (75 m) high, completed in 1974 (Austrian Federal Railways)

Garabit Viaduct in France, 400 ft (122 m) high. It was built by Gustav Eiffel in 1884 (French Railways Limited)

one span of 120 m (394 ft) and one of 150 m (492 ft). This was begun on the day the Pfaffenberg–Zwenberg Bridge was opened, and came into use on 13 July 1974, shortening the route by 167 m (549 ft).

On the same day, 13 July 1974, work began on yet another great bridge, the Lindischgraben Bridge, with a span of 154·4 m (505 ft), expected to be finished in 1977. These new works will reduce curvature from a minimum of 250 m (820 ft) radius to 450 m (1476 ft) radius and enable speeds to be raised from 60 km/h to 90 km/h (37 to 56 m.p.h.) Work will then begin on improvements to the north ramp.

The Viaur Viaduct in France, 380 ft (115·82 m) high, built in 1896–1902 (French Railways Limited)

The steel Viaur Viaduct at Tanus between Rodez and Albi on the South-West Region of the French National Railways, built in 1896–1902 by the engineer Bodin, is 115·82 m (380 ft) high with a main cantilever span of 220 m (722 ft).

The highest bridge in South America was the Loa River Viaduct on the Antofagasta & Bolivia Railway near Chuquicamata in Chile, 102 m (336 ft) high and 244 m (800 ft) long, at an elevation of 3048 m (10 000 ft) above sea-level. The railway was completed from Antofagasta, Chile, to Uyuni, Bolivia, in 1889 and to Oruro in 1893. It was built to a gauge of 762 mm (2 ft 6 in), but in 1926–28 the gauge was changed to metre and the

Malleco Viaduct, near Collipulli, on the 5 ft 6 in (1·68 m) gauge main line from Santiago to Puerto Moutt, Chile, the highest railway bridge in South America. It is 320 ft (97·5 m) high. It was built in 1886–90

Loa Viaduct was by-passed by a 12 km (7·5 mile) deviation on easier grades.

To the best of the author's knowledge, the highest in South America is now the Malleco Viaduct just south of Collipulli, Chile, on the 1·676 m (5 ft 6 in) gauge main line from Santiago to Puerto Montt. It is a steel reinforced truss bridge of seven spans on steel towers, 347 m (1138 ft) long and 97·5 m (320 ft) high above the bed of the Rio Malleco. It was begun in 1886 and opened on 26 October 1890.

The highest railway bridge in South Africa carries the 2 ft (610 mm) gauge Port Elizabeth–Avontuur line across Van Staaden's Gorge at a height of 150 ft (45·7 m).

The longest in South Africa crosses the Orange River at Upington. It is a steel structure 2514 ft 766·2 m) long.

The highest railway bridge in Asia is the Faux-Mau-Ti Bridge on the metre-gauge Yunnan Railway in China. It is 102 m ((335 ft) high with a clear span of 55 m (180 ft 6 in). It was built in 1910.

The Faux-Mau-Ti Bridge in China, 335 ft (102 m) high, the highest railway bridge in Asia

The Gokteik Viaduct, Burma, carries the metre-gauge Lashio line 825 ft (251 m) above the River Nam Pan Hse. The tallest of the 18 steel towers stands on a natural tunnel over the river and is 320 ft (97·54 m) high. The viaduct was built in 1900 by the Pennsylvania Steel Company of the U.S.A.; it is 2260 ft (688·65 m) long, consisting of sixteen spans of 40 ft (12·192 m), seven spans of

Driving the last spike at Promontory, Utah, to complete the first North American transcontinental railway, on 10 May 1869 (Union Pacific Railroad)

The 'Western Endeavour', the first and only steam train to travel from Sydney to Perth on the newly completed standard-gauge track, in August 1970. The original 3 ft 6 in gauge (1·067 m) lines will be noted (Australian News and Information Bureau)

60 ft (18·288 m) and ten spans of 120 ft (36·58 m).

On the Hellenic State Railways, Greece, the viaduct at Assopos is 100·58 m (330 ft) high.

Gokteik Viaduct on the Lashio Branch, Burma. The nearest tower, 320 ft (97·54 m) high, stands on a natural bridge and carries the rails 825 ft (251 m) above the River Nam Pan Hse

The highest railway bridge in New Zealand is the steel trestle Mahoka Viaduct on the Napier–Gisborne extension in the North Island— 274·32 m (900 ft) long and 94·5 m (310 ft) high. It was built 1936–42.

Mohaka Viaduct, 310 ft (94·5 m) high, the highest railway bridge in New Zealand (New Zealand Railways)

The highest masonry railway bridges in Europe are both on the metre-gauge Rhaetian Railway in Switzerland. The Wiesen Bridge, built in 1908–9, crosses the Landwasser River at a

The Solis Bridge carrying the metre-gauge Albula Section of the Rhaetian Railway 292 ft (89 m) above the Albula River in Switzerland, the highest masonry railway bridge in Europe (Swiss National Tourist Office)

The Wiesen Bridge on the Rhaetian Railway in Switzerland, 289 ft (88 m) high above the Landwasser River. With a span of 180 ft (55 m) it is only 1 ft (30 cm) short of being the longest masonry arch span railway bridge in the world (John Marshall)

height of 88 m (289 ft) with a span of 55 m (180 ft). The Solis Bridge over the Albula, built in 1902, is 89 m (292 ft) high with an arch of 42 m (138 ft).

The highest railway bridge in Great Britain was the iron Crumlin Viaduct in Wales, built by T. W. Kennard for the Newport, Abergavenny & Hereford Railway and opened in June 1857. It was 200 ft (61 m) high with a total length of 1658 ft (505 m). It was demolished in 1965. The highest is now the Ballochmyle Viaduct (see below).

The highest railway bridge in England was the Belah Viaduct in Westmorland on the South Durham & Lancashire Union line of the former Stockton & Darlington Railway. It was built by Thomas Bouch (see p. 51) in 1859 and was 1040 ft (317 m) long and 196 ft (60 m) high. It was closed in 1962 and dismantled in 1963.

The world's longest span concrete arch railway bridge is the Pfaffenberg–Zwenberg Bridge in Austria (see p. 85). The second longest is the Esla Viaduct in Spain on the single-line 1·676 m (5 ft 6 in) gauge Sierra de la Culebra Railway between Zamora and Pueblo de Sanabria near Andavias. It is 481 m (1578 ft) long, with a main arch over the Rio Esla of 197 m (645 ft) span, and 84 m (275 ft 7 in) high. It was opened in 1940.

Next in order are: Plougastel Bridge at Brest, France, opened in 1929, with a span of 186·54 m (612 ft); Stockholm, Sweden, opened in 1935, with a span of 181 m (593 ft). These carry both rail and road. The bridge over the Aare at Berne, Switzerland, with a span of 151 m (495 ft) was built in 1937–41 to replace the former lattice-girder steel spans, and carries four tracks into Berne Station.

Previously the record was held by the Langwies Bridge on the metre-gauge Chur-Arosa section of the Rhaetian Railway in Switzerland, built in 1912–13. This has a span of 96 m (315 ft) and a height of 62 m (203 ft).

The world's largest masonry arch railway bridge is the central span of the Ballochmyle Viaduct over the River Ayr on the Glasgow & South Western main line from Glasgow to Carlisle in Scotland. It was begun in March 1846 and finished in March 1848. The arch has a semi-circular span of 181 ft (55 m), only 1 ft (304·8 mm) longer than the Wiesen Bridge in Switzerland. It carries the line 169 ft (51·5 m) above the river-bed. **It is now the highest railway bridge in Great Britain.**

Crumlin Viaduct, Wales, 200 ft (61 m) high, the highest railway bridge in Great Britain. It was built in 1856–7 and demolished in 1965 (John Marshall)

Belah Viaduct in Westmorland, 196 ft (60 m) high, built by Thomas Bouch in 1859 and demolished in 1963. It was the highest railway bridge in England (John Marshall)

Esla Viaduct in Spain. Its span of 645 ft (197 m) makes it the world's second longest span concrete arch railway bridge (Spanish National Railways)

Ballochmyle Viaduct, over the River Ayr on the former Glasgow & South Western Railway, is the world's longest span masonry arch railway bridge, 181 ft (55 m) and also the highest in Great Britain, 169 ft (51·5 m)

One of the world's oldest bridges still carrying a railway is that built in 1810 as an aqueduct to carry the Paisley & Johnstone Canal over the River Cart near Paisley, Scotland. It was converted to a railway in 1885, becoming part of the Glasgow & South Western system.

The first railway suspension bridge was built in 1830 to carry the Middlesbrough extension of the Stockton & Darlington Railway over the Tees. Its lack of rigidity caused its early replacement. Originally Timothy Hackworth (see p. 35) had designed a plate-girder bridge, but it was an

The world's first iron railway bridge, over the River Gaunless on the Stockton & Darlington Railway, built in 1825 and replaced in 1901 (British Rail)

untried design and the directors made the unwise choice of the suspension bridge. The type has rarely been used since for railways, except for light rapid-transit systems.

The first iron railway bridge in the world carried the Stockton & Darlington Railway over the River Gaunless at West Auckland. It was built in 1825 and was replaced in 1901. It was re-erected in York Railway Museum.

The first skew-arch masonry railway bridge in Britain, also on the Stockton & Darlington Railway, carried the Haggerleases Branch over the River Gaunless. It was built in 1829 and still stands.

The oldest iron railway bridge still in its original form and position is at Middleton on the former Cromford & High Peak Railway in Derbyshire, England. The line was opened on 29 May 1830. The incline crossing the bridge was last used on 31 May 1963 and the track was lifted in December 1964. The bridge now forms part of the 'High Peak Trail'.

The original beam winding engine, built by the Butterley Company and now beautifully restored, is preserved intact at the head of the incline (see illustration, p. 70).

Probably the world's oldest iron railway bridge still in its original form and position, at Middleton on the Cromford & High Peak Railway, Derbyshire, built in 1830 (John Marshall)

The earliest of the long railway bridges was the Victoria Bridge across the St Lawrence River at Montreal. The original bridge, begun in 1854 and opened on 17 December 1859, was a single-line tubular structure designed by Robert Stephenson. It was 1 mile 1668 yd (3·134 km) long and carried the Grand Trunk Railway, later part of the Canadian National Railways. It had a

The Victoria Jubilee Bridge, Montreal, Canada, on 18 August 1898 during reconstruction, showing the new girder bridge being built round Robert Stephenson's Tubular Bridge. The first tube has already been removed (Canadian National Railways)

central span of 350 ft (107 m) and 24 other spans of 242 to 247 ft (73·76 to 75·28 m).

The smoke nuisance and increasing traffic led to its reconstruction under engineer Joseph Hobson as an open girder bridge carrying double track and two roadways on the original piers. When reopened on 13 December 1898 it was named the 'Victoria Jubilee Bridge'.

The world's longest railway bridge is the Huey P. Long Bridge across the Mississippi above New Orleans, U.S.A., with a length of 4 miles 705 yd (7·09 km). It was opened on 16 December 1935 and belongs to the New Orleans Public Belt Railroad. It is used by the Southern Pacific, Missouri Pacific and the Texas & Pacific railroads and as a road or highway bridge. The eight river spans total 3524 ft (1074 m) with a central cantilever span of 790 ft (241 m), 135 ft (41 m) above the river.

The Lower Zambezi Bridge, Mozambique, Portuguese East Africa, is 2 miles 501 yd (3·677 km) long, made up of 33 spans of 80 m (262 ft 5 in), 7 secondary spans of 50 m (165 ft), 6 approach spans of 20 m (66 ft) at the east end and a steel trestle viaduct at the west. It was opened in 1934 and carries the 1·067 m (3 ft 6 in) gauge line from Marromeu to Tete.

The longest railway bridge in Europe is the Tay Bridge in Scotland. It is 2 miles 364 yd (3·552 km) long and it carries the Edinburgh–Aberdeen line across the Tay Estuary at Dundee. The original single-line bridge designed by Thomas Bouch (see p. 51) was opened on 1 June 1878. It was badly constructed, and on 28 December 1879 the centre spans were blown down in a gale while a train was crossing. Of the 78 passengers and crew there were no survivors.

The present double-track bridge, designed by W. H. Barlow and built by William Arrol (see pp. 46 and 54), was opened on 20 June 1887.

A Southern Pacific steam train crossing the Huey P. Long Bridge over the Mississippi near New Orleans. With its approaches, this is the world's longest railway bridge (Southern Pacific Transportation)

The Tay Bridge seen from the south. This is the longest railway bridge in Europe, 2 miles 364 yd (3·552 km). The stumps of Thomas Bouch's bridge blown down in 1879, can be seen alongside (John Marshall)

The Storstrøm Bridge, Denmark, opened on 26 September 1937, connects the islands of Zealand and Falster. It carries a single-line railway, a road and a footpath, and has a total length over water of 3200 m (10 500 ft). It consists of steel spans on concrete piers: from Zealand 21 plate-girder spans beneath the deck, alternately 57·8 m (189 ft 6 in) and 62·2 m (204 ft) span, 3 bow-string truss spans of 103·9 m (340 ft), 137·8 m (450 ft) and 103·9 m giving a clearance of 25·5 m (83 ft 8 in) above mean sea-level, and 26 more plate-girder spans. The bridge took four years to build.

The Storstrøm Bridge, Denmark, 10 500 ft (3200 m) long, the second longest railway bridge in Europe (The Engineer)

The longest railway bridge in Asia is the Upper Sone Bridge on the Grand Chord route between Calcutta and Delhi, India; opened on 27 February 1900. It is 3·063 km (1 mile 1591 yd) long.

The Hardinge Bridge over the Ganges in Bangladesh north of Calcutta was opened on 4 March 1915. It has 15 steel spans of 106·68 m (350 ft) and a length of 1·798 km (1 mile 207 yd) between abutments. The main piers are carried down to a depth of 48·77 m (160 ft) below the lowest water-level and were the deepest foundations of their kind in the world. It consumed more than 1 100 353 m³ (38 860 000 ft³) of masonry and 1 700 000 rivets. The engineer was R. R. Gales.

It carried the main line northwards from Calcutta to Siliguri at the foot of the Himalayas. It was damaged in the 1971 conflict and was temporarily repaired in 1972–74.

Other long Indian railway bridges are the Mahanadi Bridge on the South Eastern Railway, opened on 11 March 1900, 2·106 km (1 mile 544 yd) long; and the Izat Bridge over the Ganges at Allerhabad on the North Eastern Railway, 1·945 km (1 mile 367 yd) long, with 40 spans of 45·72 m (150 ft).

The longest bridge in China is the Hwang-Ho or Yellow River Bridge, of 102 spans, opened in November 1905, on the Peiping–Hankow Railway. It carries a single track and has a total length of 2·940 km (9646 ft), with a maximum span of 30 m (98 ft 6 in) and a clearance of 6·45 m (21 ft).

Other long bridges in China are: Great Bridge, Wuhan, 1·700 km (5576 ft) long, opened in 1957, and the Nanking–Pukow Bridge, 1·599 km (5249 ft) long, opened on 1 October 1969. Both carry a double-track railway with a road above.

The greatest of all railway bridges, and the oldest railway cantilever bridge is the Forth Bridge in Scotland, opened on 4 March 1890. It was designed by John Fowler and Benjamin Baker and built by William Arrol. The three cantilever towers are 361 ft (110 m) high and the double-track railway is carried 156 ft (47·55 m) above high water. The two main spans are 1710 ft (521 m) and the total length of the bridge is 8298 ft (2·528 km).

Work began in November 1882. The main columns, 12 ft (3·658 m) diameter, stand on piers 60 ft (18·3 m) diameter and rise to a height of 343 ft (104 m), leaning inwards from 120 ft (36·5 m) apart at the base to 33 ft (10 m) at the top,

The Forth Bridge viewed from the south-east (John Marshall)

The south cantilever nearing completion, with part of the suspended span built out, in 1888

361 ft (110 m) above high water. The piers of the shore towers are spaced 155 ft (47 m) apart and the Inchgarvie piers 270 ft (82·3 m).

The bridge consumed over 54 000 tons of steel, the Inchgarvie piers supporting 18 700 tons and the other piers 16 130 tons each. All this was held together by 6 500 000 rivets, themselves representing over 4000 tons. The piers consumed 740 000 ft³ (21 000 m³) of granite masonry, 46 300 yd³ (35 400 m³) of rubble masonry, 64 300 yd³ (49 000 m³) of concrete and 21 000 tons of cement. Of the 4500 workers employed on the bridge 57 were killed in accidents. Work was completed, at a cost of £3 000 000, at the end of 1889 and the first train crossed on 22 January 1890.

Britain's second largest cantilever railway bridge, and the only other besides the Forth Bridge, is across the entrance to Loch Etive, Scotland. It was designed by Sir John Wolfe Barry and erected by Sir William Arrol and opened on 21 August 1903. It carried the Ballachulish Branch of the Caledonian Railway and a road. The main span is 524 ft (159·7 m) and the total length of the 2600 tons of steelwork is 735 ft (224 m). The railway was closed on 28 March 1966 and the bridge is now used by road traffic.

The Connel Ferry Bridge which carried the Ballachulish Branch of the Caledonian Railway across Loch Etive in Scotland. It is now only a road bridge (John Marshall)

The world's largest cantilever span is the Quebec Bridge over the St Lawrence River, Canada, opened on 3 December 1917 by the Canadian National Railways. It had cost \$ Can 22 500 000 (then £4 623 000). The total length of 987 m (3238 ft) includes a main span of 548·6 m (1800 ft) and shore spans of 171·45 m (562 ft 6 in). The central suspended span of 205·74 m (675 ft) is the second one to be built. The first collapsed, causing the loss of ten lives while being hoisted into position on 11 September 1916 and now lies at the bottom of the river.

The first attempt by the Phoenix Bridge Com-

pany of Pennsylvania to erect a bridge here ended in disaster on 29 August 1907 when the south cantilever collapsed, killing 75 of the 86 men working on it.

The Quebec Bridge across the St Lawrence in Canada, the world's largest cantilever span (Canadian National Railways)

The earliest and largest 'elastic arch' railway bridge in Britain is at West Wylam on the former North Wylam Branch of the North Eastern Railway, Northumberland. It was designed by William George Laws on the principle of Leather's bridge over the Aire at Leeds, and has a span of 245 ft (74·67 m). It was built by the Scotswood, Newburn & Wylam Railway and was opened in October 1876, becoming part of the North Eastern system in 1880. It was the 'father' of the arch bridges at Newcastle upon Tyne, Sydney, the Hell Gate in New York, and others. The railway was closed on 11 March 1968, but the bridge remains.

The arch bridge at West Wylam, Northumberland which carried the former North Wylam Branch of the North Eastern Railway over the River Tyne. It was built in 1876 and was the earliest 'elastic arch' railway bridge (John Marshall)

The largest steel arch span in the world is the Sydney Harbour Bridge in New South Wales, Australia, with a main span of 503 m (1650 ft). It was opened on 19 March 1932 and carries two railway tracks, six road lanes, footway and cycle track each of 3 m (10 ft), at a height of 51·82 m (170 ft). Its total length is 1149 m (3770 ft). Originally it had four rail tracks, two of which were used by street cars until the late 1950s.

Sydney Harbour Bridge, Australia, the largest steel arch span in the world (Australian News & Information Bureau)

The largest steel arch bridge in the U.S.A. is the Hell Gate Bridge (see p. 99 for details).

Britain's longest viaduct is the original London & Greenwich Railway, the first railway in London. It is 3·75 miles (6 km) long and consists of 878 brick arches. It was designed by Lieutenant-Colonel G. T. Landmann (later engineer of the Preston & Wyre Railway) and was opened in December 1836, first to an intermediate station at Deptford, on 14 December.

Harringworth Viaduct on the former Midland Railway, Britain's longest viaduct across a valley (John Marshall)

The longest masonry viaduct across a valley in Britain is the Harringworth Viaduct in Rutland on the former Midland Railway. It is 3825 ft (1166 m) long with 82 brick arches of 40 ft (12·192 m) span and a maximum height of 60 ft (18·29 m). It was opened in 1880. It consumed about 15 000 000 bricks. The resident engineer was Crawford Barlow.

The Solway Viaduct was designed by James Brunlees (see p. 49) and was begun in March 1865 and completed in July 1868. It was part of the Solway Junction Railway between Dumfriesshire in Scotland and Cumberland in England, opened on 1 September 1869 for freight and on 8 July 1870 for passengers. Until the Tay Bridge was built it was the longest railway bridge in Europe, 5790 ft (1765 m) long. The rails were 34 ft (10·363 m) above the bed of the Solway. In January 1881 45 piers were demolished by ice-floes causing 37 spans to fall and leaving others suspended. One ice-floe was 81 ft (25 m) square and 6 ft (2 m) thick. The bridge was reopened on 1 May 1884. The last train crossed on 21 August 1921 and the viaduct was dismantled in 1934–35 after a period during which Scottish drinkers used it as a footpath to English pubs on Sundays.

The Solway viaduct, west of Carlisle, once the longest railway bridge in Europe, 5790 ft (1765 m) long. It was built in 1869 and dismantled in 1934–35 (Cumberland News)

The Severn Bridge on the Severn & Wye Railway (Great Western & Midland Joint) between Lydney and Sharpness in Gloucestershire, England, was 4162 ft (1269 m) long, with 21 iron spans of which 2 were 327 ft (100 m) long and 39 ft (11·887 m) deep. At the south end a swing span of 197 ft (60 m) crossed the Gloucester & Berkeley Canal. It was opened on 17 October 1879 and remained in use until a barge collided with a pier in fog and demolished two spans on 25 October 1960. The bridge was subsequently dismantled.

The world's first large railway embankment, or fill, was built in 1726 as part of the Tanfield Wagonway in County Durham, England. It is 100 ft (30 m) high and 300 ft (91 m) wide at the base. It remained in use until 1964.

SOME NORTH AMERICAN BRIDGES

The oldest railroad bridge in the U.S.A. still in use is at Mount Clare, Baltimore, across Gwynn's Falls. It is a stone arch of 80 ft (24.384 m) span with a clearance of 44 ft (13·411 m) above the water. It carries the double-track Baltimore & Ohio Railroad and was opened in December 1829.

The oldest railroad bridge still in use in North America, at Gwynn's Falls on the Baltimore & Ohio Railroad, opened in December 1829 (Baltimore & Ohio Railroad Company)

The oldest stone viaduct in the U.S.A. is the Thomas Viaduct of eight arches carrying the Washington Branch of the Baltimore & Ohio

An early engraving of the Thomas Viaduct carrying the Baltimore & Ohio Railroad Washington Branch over the Patapsco River in Maryland. This was completed on 4 July (Independence Day) 1835, and is the oldest stone railway viaduct in the U.S.A. (Baltimore & Ohio Railroad Company)

The Severn Bridge near Lydney, Gloucestershire, from the south. It was 4162 ft (1269 m) long and was opened in 1879. In the foreground is the swing span over the Gloucester & Berkeley Canal. In 1960 a barge collided with a pier and demolished two spans. The bridge was subsequently dismantled (British Rail)

Railroad across the Patapsco River in Maryland, completed on 4 July 1835. It was built in local granite by McCartney, contractor, who erected a monument at one end bearing his own name. The viaduct has eight elliptical arches about 58 ft (17·7 m) span and is 617 ft (188 m) long and 60 ft (18·288 m) high.

The first iron tubular bridge in the U.S.A. was built in 1847 at Bolton, Maryland, on the Baltimore & Ohio Railroad.

The first iron truss bridge, also built in 1847, was near Pittsfield, Massachussets, on the Boston & Albany Railroad.

The first all-steel bridge was opened in 1879 at Glasgow, Missouri, on the Chicago & Alton Railroad. It was 2700 ft (823 m) long.

The world's first successful railway suspension bridge was built across the Niagara Gorge below the falls by Charles Ellet in 1848. In 1855 it was strengthened by John A. Roebling (1806–69) who developed the modern suspension bridge, and an upper deck was added to carry a railway to connect the Great Western of Canada with the railways of the U.S.A. It was 821 ft 4 in (250 m) between the towers, and carried a double-track railway on the upper deck and a road beneath. It was replaced by a steel arch bridge in 1897.

The world's largest railway suspension bridge is the Benjamin Franklin Bridge over the Delaware River between Philadelphia and Camden. It was designed by Ralph Modjeski (1861–1940) in 1921 and was his last and greatest work. (See also Crooked River Bridge p. 97 and Metropolis Bridge p. 100.) When opened on 4 July 1926 it was the longest single span in the world, with an over-all length of 8291 ft (2·527 km) between the portals and with a central span of 1750 ft (533·44 m), 140 ft (42·67 m) above the river. It cost $37 078 894. A railway was opened over the bridge on 7 June 1936, operated by the Philadelphia Rapid Transit Company. The trains were underused and last ran across the bridge on 28 December 1968. A new company, the Port Authority Transit Corporation of Pennsylvania and New Jersey (PATCO) has built a fine modern rapid transit line over the bridge. It opened between Philadelphia and Camden on 15 February 1969. Trains run at 75 m.p.h. (120 km/h).

A railway which went out to sea was the 128 mile (206 km) long Key West Extension, Florida. It was built by Henry Morrison Flagler (1830–1913), was begun in 1905, partly wrecked in a 125 m.p.h. (201 km/h) hurricane in 1909, and was opened to Key West on 22 January 1912. Between the mainland and Key West there were 17¼ miles (27·8 km) of bridges and 20 miles (32 km) of embankment through shallow water. The remainder was on the 'keys'. The longest bridge was the 7 mile (11 km) long steel girder Little Duck Viaduct. The railway was closed after being damaged by a hurricane on 2 September 1935 and has been replaced by a road. The rail journey took 3¾ hours.

A train crossing the 'Seven Mile Bridge' on the Key West Extension, Florida (Florida East Coast Railway)

A PACTO rapid-transit train crossing the Benjamin Franklin Bridge over the Delaware River. With a span of 1750 ft (533 m) it is the world's longest railway suspension bridge.

The first Pecos High Bridge, the highest railroad bridge in North America, on the Southern Pacific 'Sunset Route'. It was completed in 1892 (Southern Pacific Transportation)

The highest railroad bridge in North America is the Pecos Bridge carrying the Southern Pacific Railroad over the Pecos River a few miles above its confluence with the Rio Grande, 219 miles (352 km) west of San Antonio, Texas. The original high bridge, which took 103 days to build, was completed in March 1892. It replaced the earlier line, opened on 5 January 1883, which ran down into the Rio Grande Gorge and across the Pecos by a low-level bridge in 1882.

The second Pecos High Bridge, completed in 1944, which has replaced the 1892 bridge. It has been described as the most handsome railroad bridge in the U.S.A.

The present bridge, opened on 21 December 1944, is a continuous cantilever steel structure, 1390 ft (413·784 m) long with seven spans, the longest being 374 ft 6 in (114·15 m). It carries a single line, 320 ft (97·54 m) above the river.

The Oregon Grand Trunk Railroad is carried across the Crooked River Canyon at a height of 320 ft (97·54 m) by a single steel arch span of 340 ft (103·63 m). It was designed by Ralph Modjeski (1861–1940), engineer of the Huey P. Long, San Francisco Bay, and other bridges, and was erected in 1911.

The Kinzua Viaduct, south of Bradford, Pennsylvania, is 2053 ft (626 m) long and carries the Erie Railroad across a valley at a height of 301 ft (92 m), making it the third highest railroad bridge in the U.S.A. The original iron trestle viaduct was begun on 10 May 1882 and was completed in four months at a cost of $167000. In 1900, from May to September, the viaduct was rebuilt in steel. It has 41 spans of 60 ft (18·288 m).

The world's largest reinforced-concrete viaduct carries the double-track line of the Delaware, Lackawanna & Western Railroad across Tunkhannock Creek at Nicholson, Pennsylvania. It is 2375 ft (724 m) long with 12 arches of 208 ft (63·4 m) span and an approach arch of 100 ft (30·48 m) at each end, and is 240 ft (73·15 m) high.

The highest railway bridge in Canada is the Lethbridge Viaduct carrying the Canadian Pacific Railway over the Oldman (formerly Belly) River in Alberta at a height of 314 ft (95·7 m). It was completed in 1909 and is 5327 ft (1623·63 m) long with 34 spans on steel towers. It consumed 12000 tons of steel, and it is dead straight.

The original wooden trestle built in 1886 to carry the Canadian Pacific Railway across Stoney Creek. It was the highest timber bridge in the world, about 300 ft (91 m) (Canadian Pacific Limited)

The Crooked River Canyon Bridge designed by Ralph Modjeski and built in 1911. It carries the Oregon Grand Trunk Railroad at a height of 320 ft (97·5 m)

Deep Creek Bridge on the British Columbia Railway, 331 miles (533 km) north of Vancouver, is 312 ft (95 m) high. The line was opened in August 1921.

The highest bridge on the Canadian National system carries the main transcontinental line over the Pembina River west of Edmonton, Alberta, at a height of 213 ft (64·924 m). It is a steel trestle structure 900 ft (274·32 m) long.

The Stoney Creek Bridge on the Canadian Pacific Railway 4 miles (6·5 km) east of the Connaught Tunnel was originally built in 1886 as a timber Howe-truss deck-type bridge of two spans of 200 ft (61 m) and one of 100 ft (30 m) supported on timber towers. At the time it was the highest wooden bridge in the world.

In 1893–94 it was replaced by a steel arch span of 336 ft (102·4 m) designed by H. E. Vautelet and erected by the Hamilton Bridge Company of Ontario without interruption to traffic. It was unique in being probably the only parallel double-chorded arch with its main hinge-pins in its lower chord, unlike the Garabit Viaduct in France (p. 85) in which the chords converge at the springings.

In 1929 the bridge was reinforced by an additional arch on each side, additional supports for the railway, and new deck girders. From track-level on the centre-line of the bridge to the bottom of the gorge the height is 307 ft (93·574 m). (See map on p. 113.)

The Stoney Creek Bridge of 1893 undergoing tests after reinforcement of the arch, on 21 August 1929. Span 336 ft 102 m); total length 486 ft (148 m); height from track-level above bottom of gorge 307 ft (94 m) (Canadian Pacific Limited)

Stoney Creek Bridge shown in its magnificent setting (Canadian Pacific Limited)

America's longest drawbridge span of 525 ft (160 m) forms part of the Atchison, Topeka & Santa Fe Railroad bridge over the Mississippi at Iowa, Illinois, opened in 1926.

The longest swing spans on American railroads are at Fort Madison over the Mississippi of 525 ft (160 m) completed in 1927; the Willamette River Bridge at Portland, Oregon, of 521 ft

Lethbridge Viaduct carrying the Canadian Pacific across the Oldman (formerly Belly) River in Alberta, the highest railway bridge in Canada

The largest railroad cantilever bridges in the U.S.A.

Bridge	Location	Main span		Year
		ft	m	
Baton Rouge	Mississippi	848	258	1940
Cornwall	St Lawrence	843	257	1899*
Vicksburg	Mississippi	825	251	1930
Huey P. Long	New Orleans	790	241	1935
Memphis (Harahan)	Mississippi	790	241	1916
Memphis	Mississippi	790	241	1892

* Removed when the St Lawrence Seaway was established in 1954.

The Arthur Kill vertical lift bridge, New York. It has the largest span of its kind in the world (A. Barlow)

(159 m), completed in 1908; and the East Omaha Bridge over the Missouri of 519 ft (158 m) completed in 1903.

The longest railroad vertical-lift bridge span carries the Baltimore & Ohio Railroad connection to the Staten Island Rapid Transit across Arthur Kill, New York. It was opened on 25 August 1959 and replaces the earlier swing bridge. The centre span of 558 ft (170 m) is suspended from two 215 ft (65·53 m) steel towers. It can be raised to its maximum height of 135 ft (41·14 m) or lowered to its closed position 31 ft (9·5 m) above the water in 2 minutes.

The second longest carries the New Haven & Hartford Railroad across the Cape Cod Canal, Massachusetts. It was built in 1933–35. The 544 ft (165·8 m) span can be raised from 7 ft (2·13 m) to 135 ft (41·14 m) in 2½ minutes.

The world's longest stone arch railway bridge over a river carries the former Pennsylvania Railroad over the Susquehanna at Rockville, Pennsylvania. It was built in 1902 to replace the iron truss bridge of 1877 and is 3680 ft (1122 m) long.

New York has more large bridges than any other city. Its railroad bridges include: **Williamsburg Bridge**, a suspension bridge, opened on 19 December 1903 with a channel span of 1600 ft (488 m), two side spans of 596 ft (181·66 m) and a total length of 7308 ft (2227 m). It has two decks, and carries rapid transit cars. **The Hell Gate Bridge** was built by the Pennsylvania Railroad to gain access to Long Island. The main span, a steel arch of 977 ft (297·8 m) carries four tracks at a height of nearly 140 ft (43 m) above the water, and is the largest steel arch railway bridge in the U.S.A. The long approach viaducts include a four-span bridge nearly 1200 ft (366 m) long across Little Hell Gate and two 175 ft (53·54 m) spans over Bronx Kill. The entire cost, including nearly 10 miles (16 km) of railroad, was over $27 000 000. It was opened for passengers on 1 April 1917 and for freight at the end of that year. The passenger lines were electrified early in 1918.

One of the biggest railroad bridges in the U.S.A. is the Poughkeepsie Bridge over the Hudson River about 75 miles (121 km) north of New York. The bridge company was formed in 1871 and in 1889 the bridge was completed, at a cost of $3 562 190. It is 6768 ft (2063 m) long, including two cantilever spans of 548 ft (167 m), two suspended spans of 525 ft (160 m) and two anchor spans of 201 ft (61 m). It stands on steel towers and carries the rails 212 ft (65 m) above the water which is 60 ft (18 m) deep with another 70 ft (21 m) of mud below that, so that the rails are 342 ft (104 m) above the foundations.

In 1906–7 it was strengthened at a cost of $1 534 000 to carry heavy 2–8–0 locomotives. Tracks are gauntleted over the bridge, and there is a 12 m.p.h. (19 km/h) speed limit. The bridge formed a part of the New York, New Haven & Hartford Railroad which, on 31 December 1968, became part of the Penn Central.

Poughkeepsie Bridge, completed in 1889, across the Hudson River north of New York (A. Barlow)

Metropolis Bridge carrying the Burlington Northern Railroad across the Ohio River. The near span is the longest simple truss on U.S.A. railroads, with a span of 720 ft (219·5 m)

The longest simple-truss span on U.S.A. railroads is the 720 ft (219·5 m) of the Chicago, Burlington & Quincy (now Burlington Northern) Railroad's Metropolis Bridge over the Ohio River, opened in 1917. The truss is 110 ft (33·5 m) deep. It was designed by Ralph Modjeski (see 'Crooked River Bridge', p. 97, and Benjamin Franklin Bridge' p. 96).

The longest continuous-truss railroad-bridge span in the U.S.A. is the 775 ft (236·2 m) of the Sciotville Bridge, also over the Ohio River, opened in 1918.

The world's longest railway water crossing is on the Southern Pacific Railroad, U.S.A., across the Great Salt Lake, just west of Ogden, Utah. The original Central Pacific line climbed over Promontory at a maximum height of 4907 ft (1496 m). It was on this section that the record track-laying length was laid (see p. 107) and the last spike was driven (p. 87).

The Lucin Cut-off was opened on 8 March 1904. It crossed the lake on a 20 mile (32 km) long trestle which required 38 256 piles and other timber from 4 miles² (10·36 km²) of forests in Louisiana, Texas, Oregon and California. Gradually the trestle was filled in to form an embankment until latterly 62 605 ft (19·082 km), or just under 12 miles (19·2 km), remained. As most of it was single-track, and it was several times attacked by fire, it was the most vulnerable part of the Southern Pacific system. In May 1960 650 ft (198 m) were burnt out (see illustration).

In 1955 work began on a broad embankment 12·68 miles (20·4 km) long to replace the trestle.

Part of the Great Salt Lake trestle after the fire in May 1960 (Southern Pacific Transportation)

Aerial view of the new embankment across the Great Salt Lake, Utah, looking west (Southern Pacific Transportation)

A total of 45 480 000 yd³ (34 673 000 m³) of rock, sand and gravel were consumed, mostly from quarries on Promontory Point. A maximum of 2 400 000 yd³ (1 835 000 m³) was placed in one month. For the base of the fill 15 352 000 yd³ (11 738 139 m³) was dredged from the lake to a maximum depth of 85 ft (26 m) below the water surface, to a width of 600 ft (183 m). The top of the fill, 13 ft (4 m) above water, is 53 ft (16 m) wide.

The new line was opened on 27 July 1959 (see illustration). Together with the crossing of the Bear River by the Bagley Fill, the total length of embankment in the water is 27·58 miles (44·39 km).

The total number of bridges on railroads in the U.S.A. in 1937 was 191 779 totalling 3860

miles (6212 km), in a total mileage of 235 000 (378 197 km).

TUNNELS

The world's first railway tunnel was an underground line at Newcastle upon Tyne, England, built in 1770 (see 'Underground Railways', p. 210).

Chapel Milton Tunnel on the Peak Forest Tramway in Derbyshire, England, was opened on 1 May 1800. This was a plateway with L-section

Chapel Milton Tunnel, Peak Forest Tramway, Derbyshire, built before 1800. Probably the world's oldest railway tunnel (John Marshall)

rails. At Ashby de la Zouch in Leicestershire, England, a tunnel 308 yd (282 m) long was built for the Ticknall Tramway (which also used L-section rails) in 1800–5. It was enlarged by the Midland Railway for the Ashby–Melbourne Branch opened on 1 January 1874. Passenger trains ran until 22 September 1930. Hay Hill (or Haie Hill) Tunnel on the Forest of Dean Tramroad in Gloucestershire, England, was opened in September 1809 and was 1064 yd (973 m) long. In 1854 it was enlarged by Brunel to accommodate the 7 ft (2·134 m) gauge Forest of Dean Branch from the South Wales Railway to Cinderford. It was converted to standard gauge in 1872 and was closed on 1 August 1967. Talyllyn Tunnel on the

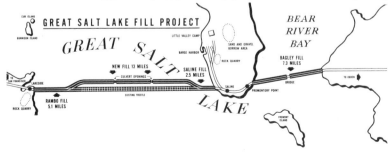

Plan of the railway across the Great Salt Lake showing the course of the new embankment (Southern Pacific Transportation)

Brecon & Hay Railway in Breconshire, Wales,
was opened on 7 May 1816 and was 674 yd (616 m)
long. In 1860 it became part of the Brecon &
Merthyr Railway and was enlarged in 1862. It was
closed on 2 May 1964.

**The first railway tunnel to be used for
passenger traffic** was Tyler Hill Tunnel on the
Canterbury & Whitstable Railway opened on
4 May 1830. It was 838 yd (757 m) long. Passenger
traffic ended on 1 January 1931 and the line closed
completely on 1 December 1952.

The Second was Glenfield Tunnel on the
Leicester & Swannington Railway opened on 17
July 1832. It was 1796 yd (1642 m) long. Passenger
trains ran until 24 September 1928 and the tunnel
was closed completely on 4 April 1966.

The first underwater railway tunnel was
the Thames Tunnel on the East London Railway.
The two parallel bores were built by Marc Brunel,
begun in 1825 and opened on 25 March 1843 for
pedestrian traffic. They were incorporated in the
East London Railway under the supervision of
the engineer Sir John Hawkshaw (see p. 45) and
opened on 7 December 1869. The railway now
forms part of the London Transport system.

*The two bores of Marc Brunel's Thames Tunnel as seen
from Wapping Station on the East London Railway. The
tunnels were begun in 1825, opened for pedestrians in 1843
and for the railway in 1869. The dome on the locomotive
is how the artist thought he saw it in the dim light (London
Transport Executive)*

**The world's longest underwater railway
tunnel** is the Severn Tunnel built by the Great
Western Railway to shorten the route between
London and South Wales. It was opened on 1
September 1886 after 14 years' work. It is 4 miles
628 yd (7·011 km) long, but of this length only
about a 1¼ miles (2 km) are actually under water
even at high tide. The engineer was again Sir
John Hawkshaw.

*The south-east portal of the Severn Tunnel at about the
time of completion in 1886 (British Rail)*

**The longest underwater tunnel in the
U.S.A.** is the Bay Area Rapid Transit (BART)
Trans Bay Tube carrying rapid transit trains
beneath the bay between San Francisco and Oakland. It is 3·6 miles (5·79 km) long, the underwater
section being the longest in the world (see 'Bay
Area Rapid Transit', p. 212). It was opened on
14 September 1974.

The 2009 yd (1837 m) long single-track St Clair
Tunnel, linking Canada and the U.S.A. under the
St Clair River between Sarnia and Port Huron
was opened on 27 October 1891 for freight and on
7 December for passengers. It cost $2 700 000. In
1908 it was electrified with single-phase a.c.
3300 V, 25 Hz. It was operated by the St Clair
Tunnel Company, a subsidiary of the Grand Trunk
Railroad of Canada which gained access to Chicago
by a series of links which became the Grand Trunk
Western. The G.T. and its subsidiaries including
1614 miles (2598 km) in the U.S.A. came into the
possession of the Canadian Government on 21
May 1920. It became part of the Canadian
National system in 1959. When the use of diesel
locomotives became universal the electrification
through the tunnel was dismantled.

The Grand Trunk's main competitor, the then
Michigan Central, also built a tunnel under the
St Clair River between Detroit and Windsor in
1906–10. This consists of two single-track tubes
2792 yd (2553 m) long of which 889 yd (813 m)
are beneath the water. This section was built by
dredging a trench and sinking the pairs of steel
tubes into it. It was originally electrically operated,
but as in the St Clair Tunnel the electrification was
abandoned with the advent of diesel-traction.

The Channel Tunnel between England and
France first came into prominence in 1874 when
the South Eastern Railway (England) obtained
Parliamentary powers to sink experimental shafts
and in 1881 to acquire lands between Dover and
Folkestone. The Submarine Continental Railway

Company Limited, incorporated on 12 December 1881, took over the S.E.R. works and drove a pilot tunnel about 2100 yd (1920 m) out under the sea. The chief engineer was Sir John Hawkshaw. Work was suspended in 1883, largely for military reasons. In 1875 a Channel Tunnel Company and a French Submarine Railway Company obtained powers to carry out works and the latter drove a 2·414 km (1½ mile) gallery under the sea from Sangatte. In 1886 the English company was absorbed by the Submarine Continental Company and in 1887 the name became the 'Channel Tunnel Company'. The original S.E.R. interests are now held by the British Railways Board.

In July 1957 the Channel Tunnel Study Group was formed to carry out extensive economic, traffic and revenue, and engineering studies. In March 1960 it submitted its report recommending a twin railway tunnel, and on 6 February 1964 the British and French Governments decided to go ahead with the project. Survey work was completed in October 1965. In 1966 it was proposed that private capital should be raised for the tunnel, being repaid through a royalty arrangement on all goods and traffic using the tunnel. It was emphasised that the tunnel would not be built at the taxpayer's expense. The estimated cost in 1973 was £468 000 000 of which the British Channel Tunnel Company and the French Channel Tunnel Company would each contribute half. Because of inflation the final cost in 1980 was expected to be between £820 000 000 and £850 000 000. Traffic forecasts prove the tunnel to be a sound economic investment. Trains would operate at a 2½ minute headway and would make possible the carriage of 4500 cars per hour in each direction, the capacity of a dual three-lane motorway, in addition to through express passenger and freight trains. On the car-trains passengers would ride in their own cars; no advance booking would be necessary, and tolls would be up to 20 per cent less than sea-ferry charges. Trains are going to operate on a 24 hour, 365 days a year basis, taking 35 minutes between tunnel terminals near Folkestone and near Calais.

The electric trains, with 6000 hp locomotives operating on the 25 kV 50 Hz system would connect the main lines of Britain and France, and would travel between London and Paris in 3 hours 40 minutes.

The Dover Strait is about 21 miles (34 km) wide with a maximum depth of water of about 200 ft (61 m). The tunnel would pass through the Lower Chalk strata at a depth of about 160 ft (49 m) below the sea-bed, with gradients of 1 in 100.

The tunnel would be about 32 miles (51·5 km) long and consist of two single-line track bores 22 ft 6 in (6·858 m) diameter inside and fully lined. A pilot tunnel bored ahead of the main tunnel would act as a probe to detect any water ingress. On completion the pilot tunnel, 14 ft 6 in (4·419 m) diameter, would be joined to the main tunnels every 273 yd (250 m) to provide an access and service tunnel.

The tunnel was expected to come into service in 1980. To connect it with London a new railway was to be built. It was proposed to site the new passenger terminal at White City where there would be good connections with the Midlands, the North and the West, and with the rest of London by the Underground Railways. Of its 80 miles (129 km), 9 miles (14·5 km) would be in tunnel and the remainder would be alongside existing railways. In November 1974 this high-speed rail link was abandoned because of expense. In January 1975 the British Government decided to abandon the entire Channel Tunnel project.

The Channel Tunnel Project
The day of breakthrough in a 312 yd (287 m) long tunnel (above, right) being driven through Shakespeare Cliff, Dover, as part of the Channel Tunnel project. The tunnel will connect a site adjoining the Old Folkestone Road, some 214 ft (65 m) above sea-level, to the site of the Old Dover Colliery on a plateau at the foot of the cliff, and will provide a road access to the lower site for men and contractors' plant and equipment. A second tunnel (centre, foreground) some 523 yd (480 m) long, is being driven under the cliff from the lower site to give contractors access to the point at which work would start on the Channel Tunnel itself. This tunnel is adjacent to the existing Folkestone–Dover railway tunnel (left). Phase II of the project, begun in November 1973, provides on the British side for the construction of approximately 1·3 miles (2 km) of service tunnel under the sea from the Kent coast, and the proving of tunnelling machines (The British Channel Tunnel Company Limited)

The Seikan undersea railway tunnel under construction in Japan will be 35·5 km (22 miles) long and will pass 100 m (330 ft) below the ocean-bed in badly faulted granite containing water-filled seams of broken rock. It will connect Yoshioka on the island of Hokkaido with Miumaya on Honshu. Work began in 1964 on shafts and pilot tunnels. It is hoped to complete it by 1975. The rails in the centre will be about 240 m (788 ft) below sea-level.

The world's longest continuous railway tunnel is on the London Underground Railway system from East Finchley to Morden via The Bank—17 miles 528 yd (27·842 km). There are, however, 24 stations and 3 junctions in the tunnel. The tunnel is 12 ft (3·7 m) diameter and the station tunnels 22 ft 2½ in (6·8 m). It was completed in 1939.

The longest ordinary railway tunnel is the 18·823 km (12 miles 559 yd) long Simplon Tunnel between Switzerland and Italy. (See 'Transalpine Railways', p. 81.)

The longest double-track railway tunnel is the Apennine Tunnel in Italy on the Diretissima line from Florence to Bologna. It was opened on 22 April 1934 and is 18·519 km (11 miles 892 yd) long.

The longest tunnel in Great Britain is the Severn Tunnel, described on p. 102. The second longest is Totley Tunnel on the former Midland Railway between Manchester and Sheffield, 3 miles 950 yd (5·697 km), opened on 6 November 1893.

Other British tunnels over 3 miles (4 km) long are:

Woodhead (New), 3 miles 66 yd (4·888 km), opened on 14 June 1954, replacing the two old single-line tunnels, 3 miles 22 yd (4·848 km), between Manchester and Sheffield on the former Great Central Railway, opened on 23 December 1845 and 2 February 1852 (see p. 25).

Standedge, 3 miles 66 yd (4·888 km), on the former London & North Western Railway between Manchester and Huddersfield, opened on 5 August 1894. The two earlier single-line tunnels, opened on 1 August 1849 and 12 February 1871, have been abandoned. (See 'Water Troughs', p. 200.)

The longest tunnel in Scotland is Greenock, on the former Caledonian Railway from Glasgow to Gourock, 1 mile 340 yd (1.92 km), opened on 1 June 1889.

Entering Scotland's longest tunnel, Greenock (1 mile 340 yd; 1·92 km) at Greenock West Station (John Marshall)

The longest tunnel in Wales is Ffestiniog, 2 miles 206 yd (3·407 km), on the Llandudno Junction to Blaenau Ffestiniog Branch of the former London & North Western Railway, opened on 22 July 1879.

South end of Ffestiniog Tunnel on the former London & North Western Railway Branch from Llandudno Junction to Blaenau Ffestiniog. It is the longest tunnel in Wales (John Marshall)

The highest tunnel in Britain was at Torpantau on the Brecon & Merthyr Railway in Wales which was 666 yd (609 m) long. The west portal was 1313 ft (400 m) above sea-level. It was opened on 1 May 1863 and closed on 2 May 1964.

Today the highest is Shot Lock Hill Tunnel on the Settle & Carlisle section of the former

Midland Railway, at an altitude of about 1153 ft (349 m). It was built in 1871–73 and is 106 yd (97 m) long. Freight traffic began on 2 August 1875 and passenger traffic on 1 May 1876.

North end of Shot Lock Hill Tunnel, 106 yd (97 m) long, on the former Midland Railway route to Carlisle. It is now the highest railway tunnel in Great Britain (John Marshall)

The total number of tunnels in Great Britain was 1049 in 1938. By then several lines had been abandoned and the total could have been about 1060. The total includes 'long bridges' classed as tunnels.

Europe's longest tunnel north of the Alps is Lieråsen between Asker and Brakerøya on the Oslo–Drammen line in Norway, begun in 1963 and opened on 3 June 1973. It is 10·7 km (6 miles 1142 yd) long, shortens the rail journey between Asker and Drammen by 12·5 km (7·767 miles) and permits speeds up to 120 km/h (74½ m.p.h.).

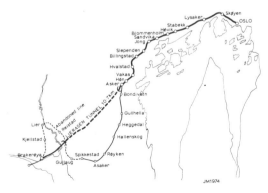

Map showing the position of the new Lieråsen Tunnel, Norway

Norway also has the three next longest tunnels in northern Europe. These are:

Kvineshei Tunnel, 9·064 km (5 miles 1112 yd)

Haegebeostad Tunnel, 8·474 km (5 miles 467 yd). These and Gyland Tunnel, 5·717 km (3 miles 972 yd) were opened under the German occupation, on 17 December 1943. Full traffic began on 1 March 1944.

Ulrikken Tunnel, 7·662 km (4 miles 1338 yd), was opened on 1 August 1964 to improve the route from Bergen to Oslo.

The longest tunnel on French Railways is the Somport Tunnel, actually between France and Spain. It is 7·874 km (4 miles 1572 yd) long, and was opened on 18 July 1928. It carries a single line, and is operated by the French National Railways (S.N.C.F.).

The longest tunnel entirely in France is the Lusse (Vosges) Tunnel, 6·870 km (4 miles 474 yd), opened on 9 August 1937.

French end of Somport Tunnel, 4·89 miles (7·874 km), opened in 1938 (La Vie du Rail)

The longest railway tunnel in Russia is the Suran Tunnel, nearly 4 km (2½ miles) long, on the Poti-Baku line in the Caucasus.

A new 8 km (5 mile) tunnel is being built through the Pambak Range on a new railway to link Yeveran, capital of Armenia, with Akstafa, a junction in Azerbaijan.

The twelve Asian tunnels over 3 miles (4 km) long are all in Japan. They are:

Hokuriku, 13·870 km (8 miles 1089 yd), opened on 10 June 1962

Shin-Shimizu, 13·500 km (8 miles 684 yd) opened in 1961

Kubiki, 11·353 (7 miles 10 yd), opened in 1970

Shimizu, 9·702 km (6 miles 50 yd), opened on 1 September 1931

New Tanna, 7·958 km (4 miles 1663 yd), opened on 1 October 1964.

Old Tanna, 7·804 km (4 miles 1493 yd), opened on 1 December 1934

Shin-Karikachi, 5·790 km (3 miles 1052 yd), opened in 1969

Senzan, 5·361 km (3 miles 583 yd), opened on 10 November 1937

Fukasaka, 5·173 km (3 miles 379 yd), opened on 1 October 1957

Nangoyama, 5·173 km (3 miles 379 yd), opened on 1 October 1964

Ohara, 5·063 km (3 miles 256 yd), opened on 11 November 1955

Otowayama, 5·045 km (3 miles 237 yd), opened on 1 October 1964

The longest tunnel in North America is the Cascade Tunnel, 7 miles 1397 yd (12·542 km) long (see 'Some U.S.A. Facts and Feats'. p. 110).

The longest tunnel in the Southern Hemisphere is the single-track Rimutaka Tunnel in the North Island, New Zealand, on the railway from Wellington to Masterton. It was opened on 3 November 1955 and is 8·798 km (5 miles 821 yd) long. It replaced the line over the Rimutaka Ranges involving the famous Fell incline of 5 km (3 miles) at 1 in 14–16 (see p. 216).

The Otira Tunnel in the South Island, New Zealand, between Christchurch and Greymouth, is 8·563 km (5 miles 564 yd) long and was opened on 4 August 1923. It has a gradient of 1 in 33 (3 per cent), rising from Otira to Arthur Pass, and at the time of building it was the longest tunnel in the British Empire and fifth longest in the world. It is electrically worked, at 1500 V d.c.

An 8·85 km (5½ mile) long tunnel through the Kaimai Hills in the North Island is being constructed as part of a 25 km (15½ mile) cut-off between Tauranga and Rotorua, to be completed in 1976. Work began in 1969. This will then be the longest in the Southern Hemisphere. PACT (Paved Concrete Track) is to be used throughout (see p. 63).

Otira Tunnel, with a train emerging from the Otira portal. The electric locomotive is an 'EA' Class 1285 hp Bo Bo (New Zealand Railways Publicity)

The longest tunnel in South America is Las Raíces Tunnel in Chile on the 1·676 m (5 ft 6 in) gauge branch from Pua to Lonquimay, about 625 km (388 miles) south of Santiago, 4·545 km (2 miles 1450 yd) long. It was opened in 1938.

The longest railway tunnel in South Africa is the twin-bore Hilton Road Tunnel between Boughton and Cedra on the Natal main line. They are 3 miles 131 yd (4·948 km) long. Next are the Hidcote Tunnels, 2 miles 84 yd (3295 m). Both are on the South African Railways system. No others are over 1 mile (1·609 km) long.

Rimutaka Tunnel—official train emerging from the eastern portal during the opening ceremony in 1955 (New Zealand Railways Publicity)

The only tunnel on the Rhodesia Railways is at Wankie. It is 278 yd (254 m) long, and was opened on 20 January 1957.

The longest tunnel in Australia is the Woy Woy Tunnel in New South Wales, double-track, 1·789 km (1 mile 197 yd) long.

The record for the most 'be-tunnelled' train in Great Britain was held in 1946 by the 10.00 London (St Pancras) to Glasgow (St Enoch) via Nottingham, Derby, Sheffield and Leeds. In all it passed through 40 tunnels totalling about 15 miles (24·14 km). Six of these were over 1 mile (1·6 km) long.

The railway with the greatest number of tunnels is the Sierra de la Culebra Railway, Spain. Between Puebla de Sanabria and Carballino, 173 km (107½ miles), there are 182 tunnels amounting to 78 km (48½ miles), the longest being the 5·949 km (3 miles 1226 yd) Padornelo Tunnel, opened in 1957–59.

The Bergen–Oslo line in Norway has 178 tunnels in 491 km (305¾ miles) amounting to 36·2 km (22½ miles). It was opened on 1 December 1909.

The highest tunnel in the world is the Galera Tunnel on the Central Railway of Peru, opened on 14 November 1893. It is 1·176 km (1287 yd) long at an altitude of 4781 m (15 688 ft). (See map on p. 73.)

SOME U.S.A. FACTS AND FEATS
(See also 'Some North American Bridge Records', p. 95.)

The railway spike with a hooked head, for holding flat-bottomed rails to sleepers, or ties, was designed in 1830 by Robert L. Stevens, first president of the Camden & Amboy Railroad (now part of Penn Central) in New Jersey. The first patent for a machine for making spikes was issued to Henry Burden of Troy, New York, in 1840. Stevens also designed the T-section iron rail and a 'fish-plate' for joining rail ends in 1830 (see p. 36). Flat-bottomed iron rails, rolled in England, became standard on the Camden & Amboy Railroad in 1832. They were 3 in (76·2 mm) wide across the base, 2 in (50·8 mm) across the top, 3½ in (88·9 mm) high, with a ½ in (12·7 mm) thick web.

Bessemer steel rails were first rolled in the U.S.A. at North Chicago Rolling Mills on 25 May 1865. By the end of the century they had almost completely replaced iron rails.

The record for laying the greatest length of track in one day was achieved during the construction of the Central Pacific Railroad in Utah on 28 April 1869 when 10 miles 56 ft (16·110 km) of single track were laid. Charles Crocker (1822–88), in charge of construction, prepared the materials and briefed his men for several days beforehand. On the great day over 4000 men,

The east portal of Galera Tunnel under the Continental Divide in the Andes, from Galera Station. It is the highest tunnel in the world, its peak being 15 688 ft (4781 m) above sea-level. It is 1287 yd (1·176 km) long on a gradient of 4 per cent, or 1 in 25 (Brian Fawcett)

Laying part of the record 10 miles (16 km) stretch, the greatest length of track laid in one day, on 28 April 1869 (Southern Pacific Transportation)

many of them Chinese, with hundreds of horses and wagons, were employed. The track advanced at almost a mile (1·609 km) an hour, 800 men laying rails at the rate of about 140 ft (73·15 m) in 1 minute 15 seconds, about as fast as a leisurely walk. Ahead of them were men preparing ties and spikes and behind them were the ballasters. The section included many curves on the western slope of Promontory Mountain where rails had to be bent. When work ended at seven o'clock that evening 25 800 ties, 3520 rails 30 ft (9·144 m) long, 55 000 lb (24 948 kg) of spikes, 14 080 bolts and great quantities of other material had been used. Each rail-handler had lifted 125 tons of iron during the day, in addition to his heavy tongs. To crown the achievement one Jim Campbell drove a locomotive back over the new line at 40 m.p.h. (64 km/h).

The whole of this section was abandoned in 1942 and the rails were removed. The original rails, of course, had been replaced long ago. (See 'The world's longest water crossing', p. 100.)

Gauges In 1871 there were 19 different gauges in use in the U.S.A., ranging from 3 ft (0·914 m) to 6 ft (1·829 m). Subsequently many 2 ft (0·610 m) gauge lines were built.

Between 1867 and 1871 it was possible to travel from New York to St Louis on 6 ft (1·829 m) gauge tracks via the present Erie route to Dayton, Ohio, and the present Baltimore & Ohio through Cincinnati to St Louis. In 1868 the Missouri Pacific Railroad was converted from 5 ft 6 in (1·676 m) to standard, and in 1871 the Ohio & Mississippi (now the Baltimore & Ohio) Railroad from 6 ft (1·829 m) to standard. These influenced other conversions, and so by 1887 nearly every important railroad in the U.S.A. was operating on standard gauge, the most outstanding exception being the Denver & Rio Grande Western Railroad which in 1888 operated a maximum of 1673 miles (2692 km) of 3 ft (0·914 m) gauge.

The world's biggest gauge conversion was carried out on the Louisville & Nashville Railroad which was built to a gauge of 5 ft (1·524 m). On 30 May 1886 about 8000 men converted over 2000 miles (3220 km) of track to a gauge of 4 ft 9 in (1·447 m). Standard gauge was adopted gradually ten years later. One section foreman and his gang converted 11 miles (17·703 km) in 4½ hours. One shop changed 19 locomotives, 18 passenger cars, 11 cabooses, 1710 revenue freight cars and several other works vehicles between dawn and dusk on 30 May. The total cost of the conversion was $195 095.69, minus $29 605 raised by the sale of redundant third rails.

Altogether about 13 000 miles (20 922 km) of route in the Southern States were converted at about the same time.

In 1920 U.S.A. railroads employed over 2 000 000 persons. In 1960 793 071 employees earned $4 956 902 360; in 1973 520 153 people earned $7 088 383 000. However, since 1916 the U.S.A. has abandoned nearly 50 000 miles (80 500 km) of railroad. This is nearly 2·5 times the maximum railway mileage in Great Britain, in 1930.

Year	U.S. railroad mileages		Great Britain	
	miles	km	miles	km
1830	23	37	c. 120	c. 190
1840	2818	4535	1484	2385
1850	9021	14 518	6084	9791
1860	30 626	49 288	9069	14 595
1870	52 922	85 170	13 563	21 828
1880	93 267	150 100	15 557	25 036
1890	163 605	263 302	17 274	27 800
1900	143 366	311 187	18 665	29 039
1910	240 313	386 744	19 979	32 154
1916	254 000	466 710 (maximum)		
1920	252 865	406 941	20 326	32 712
1930	249 619	401 721	20 445	32 903 (maximum)
1940	234 182	376 880	20 227	32 552
1950	224 331	361 030	19 790	31 849
1960	217 551	350 114	18 771	30 209
1970	209 001	336 356	11 799	18 989
1972	208 998	336 354	11 798	18 988

The largest railroad abandonment in the U.S.A. was of the Missouri & Arkansas, 335 miles (539 km) in 1948. The next largest was the Colorado Midland from Colorado Springs to Glenwood Springs, 221·3 miles (356 km) in 1919.

The State with the highest railroad mileage is Texas, with 13 381 miles (21 535 km) in 1972. Its first railroad, from Harrisburg to Alleyton, was opened in 1860. Next is Illinois with 10 686 miles (17 202 km), the earliest being Jacksonville to Meredosia opened in 1838.

The smallest mileages are in District of Columbia with 30 miles (42 km) and Rhode Island with 146 miles (235 km).

The following States had railroads open before 1835:

Alabama; Tuscumbia–Decatur, 1834
Connecticut; Northwich–Killingly, 1832
Delaware;* Newcastle–Frenchtown, 1831
Florida; Tallahassee–Port Leon, 1834
Louisiana; New Orleans–Lake Pontchartrain, 1831
Maryland; Baltimore–Ellicott's Mills, 1830
Michigan; Detroit–St Joseph, 1832
New Jersey;* Camden–South Amboy, 1834
New York; Albany–Schenectady, 1831
Pennsylvania;* Leiperville–Ridley Creek, 1809
South Carolina; Charleston–Hamburg, 1833
Virginia; Weldon, N.C.–Petersburg, Virginia, 1833
West Virginia; Baltimore–Harper Ferry, 1834

The longest continuous curve in the U.S.A. is probably the Pontchartrain curve between Ruddock and Tunity in Louisiana on the Illinois Central Railroad, skirting the western shore of Lake Pontchartrain. It is 9·45 miles (15·192 km) long with only slight changes of radius.

The Southern Railway, shortly before entering New Orleans, skirts the same lake on a curve nearly 9 miles (4·5 km) long.

The longest uniform curve is on the Texas & Pacific Railroad between Alexandria and Cheneyville, also in Louisiana. It has a radius of 6·5 miles (10·5 km) throughout its 5·7 miles (9·173 km).

SUMMITS IN COLORADO

The highest adhesion-worked summit in North America was on Mount McClellan, 13 100 ft (3992 m), on the Argentine Central (later

Argentine & Gray's Peak) Railway, from Silver Plume, Colorado, a 3 ft (0·914 m) gauge line built by Edward Wilcox in 1906. The 6 per cent, or 1 in 16·67, grades and switchbacks were worked by Shay-geared engines (see p. 144) which could pull two or three Colorado & Southern cars to the summit. Petrol cars were introduced in 1914. The 16 mile (9·6 km) long railway closed in 1917. (See also 'Manitou & Pike's Peak Railway', p. 214.)

The highest adhesion-worked standard-gauge line was the Denver & Salt Lake Railroad or 'Moffat Road' over Rollins or Corona Pass, at an altitude of 11 680 ft (3560 m). It was opened in 1907 and was used until the Moffat Tunnel was completed in 1928. It is now an exciting road.

The record was then held by the branch of the Denver & Rio Grande Western from Leadville up to Ibex, Colorado, at an altitude of 11 512 ft (3509 m). This was closed in 1944.

The Colorado Midland was a standard-gauge line from Colorado Springs to Leadville and Grand Junction, completed in 1890. At Hagerman Pass it was 11 530 ft (3515 m), but this section was abandoned in 1899, the trains then using the Busk–Ivanhoe Tunnel, over 3 miles (4·8 km) long, completed in 1893.

The highest standard-gauge summit still in use in North America on a through line is the 10 239 ft (3121 m) at Tennessee Pass north of Leadville on the Denver & Rio Grande Western Railroad. Before the summit tunnel was built the line crossed the pass at 10 424 ft (3177 m).

The highest narrow-gauge summit in North America was on the Denver, South Park & Pacific Railroad (later the Colorado & Southern), a subsidiary of the Chicago, Burlington & Quincy Railroad. This 3 ft (0·914 m) gauge line reached 11 066 ft (3538 m) at the Alpine Tunnel on the Como–Gunnison section, and 11 330 ft (3454 m) on the Fremont Pass north of Leadville. This line was opened in February 1882. The 600 yd (549 m) long Alpine Tunnel was closed in 1910.

A standard-gauge line from Leadville to Climax, 11 319 ft (3450 m), was laid in 1943.

The Silverton Northern (1906–41), 3 ft (0·914 m) gauge, reached a height of 11 180 ft (3408 m) at Animas Forks.

* The three earliest States in the Federation, admitted 1787.

The remaining summits over 10000 ft (3050 m) were on 3 ft (0·914 m) gauge lines:

Marshall Pass, 10846 ft (3306 m), on the Denver & Rio Grande main line to Gunnison, opened 1881, closed 1955.
Lizard Head, 10248 ft (3124 m) on the Rio Grande Southern Railroad, opened in 1891 and closed in December 1951.
Colorado & Southern Leadville line, 10207 ft (3111 m), opened in 1884.
Monarch, Denver & Rio Grande Western, 10148 ft (3093 m), opened in 1883. This is now standard gauge.
Cumbres Pass, 10015 ft (3053 m), on the Denver & Rio Grande Western from Antonito to Durango, opened in 1880. Today it is operated as a tourist line by the Cumbres & Toltec Scenic Railroad.

TUNNELS IN U.S.A.

On its 254000 miles (466710 km) of railroad in 1916 the U.S.A. had 1539 tunnels with a total length of 320 miles (515 km). This total number was only 50 per cent more than the total on 20445 miles (32903 km) in Great Britain in 1930.

The first American railroad tunnel was the Staple Bend Tunnel, Pennsylvania (see p. 18).

The longest tunnel in the U.S.A. is the Cascade Tunnel on the Great Northern (now Burlington Northern) main line from Spokane to Seattle in Chelan and King Counties in Washington State. It is 7 miles 1387 yd (12·542 km) long. It was opened on 12 January 1929 and replaced an earlier

Eastern portal of Cascade Tunnel, the longest in the U.S.A., opened in 1929 (Burlington Northern Incorporated)

line which climbed to a summit tunnel 2·63 miles (4·229 km) long. While this was being built trains crossed the summit by a spectacular series of zigzags in a line 12¼ miles (19·712 km) long opened in 1892 and used until the tunnel was finished in 1900 (see map and illustration).

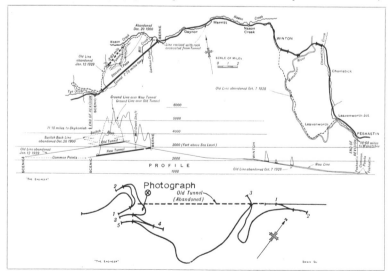

Maps and section of the Cascade Tunnels and the zigzags, showing the position of the photograph (The Engineer)

The door at the east end of Cascade Tunnel, in 1956, installed after the abandonment of the electrification. It is closed during the passage of a train and powerful fans extract the fumes from the tunnel (Burlington Northern Incorporated)

Map of Flathead Tunnel (John Marshall)

Red Indians at the dedication ceremony at the opening of Flathead Tunnel, Montana, on 7 November 1970. The photograph shows the eastern portal (Burlington Northern Incorporated)

The second longest tunnel in the U.S.A., and seventh longest in the world, is the Flathead Tunnel in north-west Montana, also on the Great Northern. It was made necessary by the Federal Government's Libby Dam project which flooded much of the former main line beneath Lake Koocanusa. It is on a new 59½ mile (96 km) diversion and passes under the Elk Mountain from Wolf Creek to Fortina Creek.

Guided by laser beam the workers holed through on 21 June 1968 after 630 days drilling from both ends. The tunnel is 36970 ft (12·479 km) or 10 ft (3·04 m) under 7 miles (11·265 km), including a 'cut and cover' section 1670 ft (509 m) long at the western end, and is 18 ft (5·486 m) wide and 23 ft 6 in (7·162 m) high above rail-level.

The tunnel was officially opened on 7 November 1970 when the photograph was taken, the special train running from Libby to Stryker via the new line and returning via the old route.

The east portal is closed by a door after the passage of a train and two 2000 hp fans, 103 in (2616 mm) diameter with a capacity of 307000 ft³ (8693 m³) per minute clear the fumes from the tunnel in 17 minutes and provide cooling air for the engines as they pull up the grade towards the east.

The third longest tunnel is the Moffat Tunnel, 6 miles 373 yd (9·997 km), under James Peak, Colorado, on the Denver & Salt Lake Railroad, the 'Moffat Road'.

In 1921 the people of Denver and near-by counties voted and passed a bond issue of $15470000 to construct the Moffat Tunnel, thus creating the 'Moffat Tunnel District'. Work began in 1921 and the tunnel was holed through on 12 February 1927. It was opened on 27 February 1928, at an altitude of 9257 ft (2822 m), replacing the original line over the Rollins, or Corona, Pass at an altitude of 11680 ft (3560 m). With the Dotsero Cut-off it shortened the route from Denver to Salt Lake City by 173 miles (278 km). The original pioneer bore carries water from the western slope of the Rockies to Denver where it is part of the main supply.

On 11 April 1947 the D. & S.L.RR. merged with the Denver & Rio Grande Western Railroad which rents the tunnel from the Moffat Tunnel District. The bonds will mature in 1982.

The most difficult tunnel in America was the Hoosac Tunnel on the Boston & Maine Railroad in Massachusetts, on the main line from Boston to Albany. It was begun in 1851 and took 14 years to complete, at a cost of $20 000 000. It was opened on 9 February 1875. It is 4 miles 1230 yd (7·562 km) long. In 1911 it was electrified at a cost of $541 000. The electrification was abandoned on 24 August 1946 when the entire operation went over to diesels.

The shortest tunnel in the U.S.A. is Bee Rock Tunnel near Appalachia, Virginia, on the Louisville & Nashville line from Corbin, Kentucky, to Norton, Virginia, opened in 1891. It is 10 yd (9 m) long.

SOME CANADIAN FACTS AND FEATS

At the time of the union of the Canadian Provinces on 1 July 1867 Canada had 15 railways totalling 2495 miles (4015 km), employing 9391 persons. There were 485 locomotives, 310 first class and 374 second class cars which carried a total of 2 920 000 passengers in the year, and 4214 freight cars which carried 2 260 000 tons.

Prince Edward Island entered the Confederation in 1873 while its railway system was under construction. The 210 miles (338 km) of line were taken over by the Federal Government and opened for traffic in April 1875.

In 1882 the Grand Trunk and the Great Western railways, which had 904 miles (1455 km) of route, were amalgamated, together with another 473 miles (761 km) of line in Western Ontario.

Twenty years after Confederation, in 1887, Canadian railway mileage was 11 691 (18 815 km), of which the Canadian Pacific system owned 4174 miles (6717 km) and the Grand Trunk system 2598 miles (4181 km). There were 1633 locomotives, 74 sleeping and parlour cars, 762 first class and 514 second class cars. By 1888 some main-line cars were electrically lit.

The first steel rails in Canada were used about 1875. In 1876 it was reported that there were 2273¾ miles (3659 km) of steel rails in Canada, about 45 per cent of the main routes.

The first train over the Sault Ste Marie Bridge entered Canada on 9 January 1888. The St Lawrence was bridged at Lachine in 1887 and at Coteau in 1890.

The first railway in Newfoundland, from St John's to Hall Bay, was begun on 9 August 1881, against much local opposition and violence. The 547 miles (870 km) of 3 ft 6 in (1·067 m) gauge line, from St John's to Port aux Basque, were completed in 1896. The first passenger trains ran on 29 June 1898.

A mixed train on the 3 ft 6 in (1·067 m) gauge Newfoundland Railway (Canadian National Railways)

The first iron railway bridge in Nova Scotia was built in 1877 at Elmsdale to replace the timber bridge. It was decided at this time to replace all Canadian wooden bridges by iron.

By the end of the nineteenth century Canadian railway mileage had grown to 17 481 (28 133 km) of which the Canadian Pacific Railway had 6873 miles (11 061 km), the Grand Trunk Railway 3138 miles (5050 km), and the Intercolonial Railway 1511 miles (2432 km).

One of the loneliest railways in Canada, the Temiskaming & Northern Ontario Railway, was completed to Moosonee on an estuary of James Bay in 1931.

The Canadian Northern and the Grand Trunk Pacific Railways were completed in 1915 by which year Canada had three transcontinental routes. The Canadian Northern ran from Quebec to Vancouver and the G.T.P.R., including the National Transcontinental Railway, extended from St John, New Brunswick, to Prince Rupert in British Columbia.

The Canadian mileage was now 35 582 (57 264 km), more than double that in 1900. In addition the Canadian Pacific Railway and the Grand Trunk Railway owned extensive mileage in the U.S.A.

The Canadian National Railways was formed in 1917. For an outline of its history see p. 77.

Newfoundland entered the Confederation in 1949 when its 705 miles (1135 km) of 3 ft 6 in

(1·067 m) gauge lines were absorbed by the Canadian National Railways. Of this, 547 miles (880 km) are on the main 'Overland Route' from St John's to Port aux Basques. In 1948 the Newfoundland lines carried 274 497 passengers and 856 560 tons of freight.

Today Canadian railways own 3311 locomotives of which 3292 are diesel and 19 electric; 2444 passenger cars and 188 770 freight cars. Each year

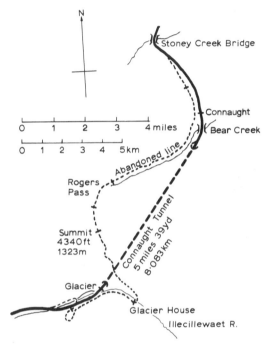

The rear of 'The Canadian' transcontinental train entering the west portal of Connaught Tunnel on the Canadian Pacific Railway. Part of the earlier route over the Rogers Pass can be seen just above the roof of the ventilation plant (Canadian Pacific Limited)

Map showing Rogers Pass, Connaught Tunnel, and Stoney Creek Bridge on the Canadian Pacific Railway

Steam train emerging from the east portal of Connaught Tunnel. Right-hand running was in force during steam days (Canadian Pacific Limited)

they operate 95 000 000 000 revenue ton-miles (153 000 000 000 ton-km) of freight service and 3 000 000 000 passenger-miles (4 900 000 000 passenger-km).

The longest tunnel in Canada is the 5 mile 39 yd (8·083 km) Connaught Tunnel in the Selkirks on the Canadian Pacific Railway. The headings met, 2·5 miles (4000 m) below the peak of Mount Macdonald, on 19 December 1915. The double-track bore, opened on 6 December 1916, replaced the difficult route over the Rogers Pass

Westbound Pacific Express on the west side of Rogers Pass, descending to Glacier in British Columbia, Canada (Canadian Pacific Limited)

which reached an altitude of 4340 ft (1323 m) and was threatened every winter with snow blockage despite 4 miles (6·5 km) of snow-sheds. It shortened the route by 4·5 miles (7·24 km), lowered the summit by 540 ft (165 m) and eliminated curves amounting to seven complete circles.

The second longest tunnel is the 3 mile 288 yd (5·073 km) Mount Royal Tunnel at Montreal on the Canadian National Railways. It was built by the Canadian Northern Railway at a cost of $3 000 000 and was opened on 21 October 1918. There are no other tunnels in Canada over 3 miles (5 km) long.

The highest railway summit in Canada is at the Great Divide on the Canadian Pacific Railway, 5332 ft (1435 m), where it crosses the boundary between Alberta and British Columbia.

Canadian railway mileage reached 44 794 (72 089 km) in 1972. Of this total Canadian National Railways owns 25 150 miles (40 474 km) in addition to 704 miles (1145 km) of 3 ft 6 in (1·067 m) gauge line in Newfoundland.

Canadian Pacific announced its new corporate identification programme on 17 June 1968, from which date its various interests became known as CP Rail, CP Air, CP Ships, CP Transport (road vehicles), CP Express, CP Hotels and CP Telecommunications. On 5 July 1971 supplementary Letters Patent were issued to the company changing its corporate name from 'Candian Pacific Railway Company' to 'Canadian Pacific Limited' in English and to 'Canadian Pacifique Limitée' in French. In 1973 CP Rail operated 16 286 miles (26 696 km) in addition to 4724 miles (8000 km) in the U.S.A., with 1181 diesel locomotives, 53 diesel railcars, 403 passenger cars and 72 501 freight cars.

CP Air operates 22 jet planes over 50 000 unduplicated route miles (80 500 km) linking five continents. CP Hotels has five city and resort hotels across Canada.

Canada's newest railway is the British Columbia Railway, with headquarters in Vancouver. It began as the Pacific Great Eastern, incorporated in 1912. Its route and dates of opening are shown on the map. The name was changed to 'British Columbia Railway' on 1 April 1972 when it was taken over by the Provincial Government. Its purpose is to tap the great natural and mineral resources of northern British Columbia. The railway extends from North Vancouver to Fort Nelson,

992·6 miles (1597·5 km), with branches of 495 miles (797 km) to Dease Lake and 61 miles (98 km) to Dawson Creek. It is proposed to extend the Dease Lake Branch into the Yukon.

Passenger services are operated by Budd diesel railcars, daily between North Vancouver and Lillooet and on alternate days from there to Prince George where there is a connection to the Canadian National line to Prince Rupert.

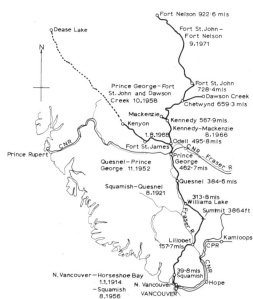

Map of British Columbia Railway (John Marshall)

Five diesel-electric locomotives in multiple unit heading a heavy southbound freight train through Cheakamus Canyon, 55 miles (88·514 km) north of Vancouver, on the British Columbia Railway (British Columbia Railway)

Section 4
MOTIVE POWER

LOCOMOTIVE TYPES

Steam locomotives are generally referred to by the system of wheel arrangements invented in 1900 by Frederic M. Whyte (1865–1941), an official of the New York Central Railroad. It can easily be worked out from the examples below. All locomotives are imagined facing to the left.

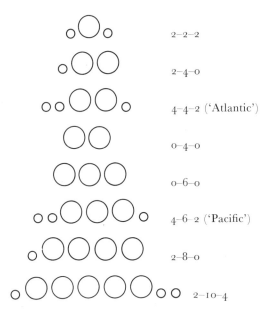

The European continental countries use an axle system, thus a 4–6–2 is a 2C1. Germany and Switzerland denote the number of driving-axles as a fraction of the total number of axles: for example, a 4–6–2 is a 3/6, a 2–8–0 a 4/5.

Electric and diesel locomotives are referred to by a letter indicating the number of driving axles: A is one, B two, C three and D four.

A locomotive on two four-wheeled bogies with a motor to each axle is a BoBo. The small 'o' indicates that the axles are not coupled. If the wheels were coupled it would be a BB. A locomotive on two six-wheeled bogies with all axles driven but not coupled is a CoCo; if the axles are coupled it is a CC; if the centre axle is not driven it is an A1A A1A. If the trucks are articulated by a connection taking buffing and drag stresses a plus sign is used; for example the locomotives of the Furka–Oberalp and Brig–Visp–Zermatt railways in Switzerland are Bo + Bo.

LOCOMOTIVE PROGRESS

The first locomotive to haul a load on rails was built by Richard Trevithick (see p. 32) in 1803–4 for the Penydarren plateway in South Wales. It had a single horizontal cylinder mounted inside the boiler and ran on unflanged wheels. Its working life was short because it was too heavy for the L-section cast-iron plates.

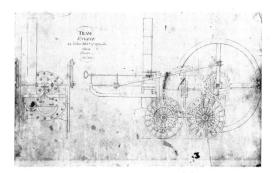

Richard Trevithick's locomotive of 1803. It is reported to have pulled a load of 10 tons and 70 passengers for a distance of 9 miles (14 km) at Penydarren in Glamorgan, South Wales on 21 February 1804 (The Science Museum, London)

The locomotive was introduced to Northumberland, England, by Christopher Blackett, proprietor of Wylam Colliery and Member of Parliament. He ordered an engine on Trevithick's principle through his engineer John Steel and it was built at Gateshead, County Durham, by John Whinfield. However, when it was tried in 1804 it was too heavy at over 5 tons and was rejected.

It was the first locomotive to have flanged wheels.

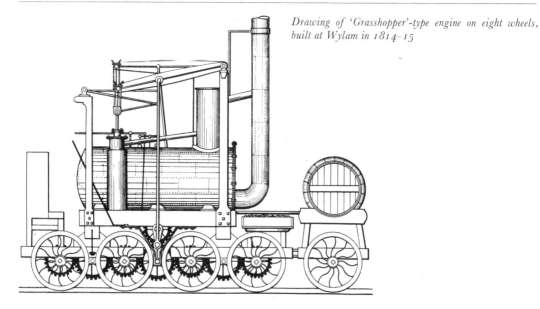

Drawing of 'Grasshopper'-type engine on eight wheels, built at Wylam in 1814–15

The short 'D'-pattern slide-valve was introduced by Matthew Murray at Leeds, England, in 1806.

The first locomotive built entirely at Wylam, Northumberland, was built in 1811 by Timothy Hackworth and Jonathan Foster assisted by William Hedley (see p. 32). It ran on four flanged wheels and had a 4 ft (1219 mm) diameter boiler 10 ft (3·048 m) long. The two vertical cylinders at the rear drove the wheels through levers and connecting-rods to a centre jack-shaft geared to the two axles. It was known as the *Grasshopper*.

The next two engines built at Wylam in 1814–15 were of the same type but ran on eight wheels to spread the load on the light track until the cast-iron rails were replaced by wrought iron in 1830. Of these, *Puffing Billy* is now in the Science Museum, London, and *Wylam Dilly* is in Edinburgh Museum.

Two more 'Grasshopper'-type engines on four wheels were built by Jonathan Foster and J. U. Rastrick (see p. 33) at Stourbridge, Worcestershire,

Puffing Billy, *built at Wylam Colliery, Northumberland, in 1814 by Hackworth, Foster & Hedley, at work at a colliery about 1859 after conversion to a four-wheeled engine (The Science Museum, London)*

as late as 1828. One, named *Agenoria* was put to work on the Shutt End Railway from Lord Dudley's Colliery at Kingswinford to the Staffordshire & Worcestershire Canal. It is now in the York Railway Museum.

The other, named *Stourbridge Lion*, was sent to the U.S.A. where it was tried on the Carbondale–Honesdale Railroad on 8 October 1829, the day before the opening (see 'Early Railroads in the U.S.A.', p. 16).

The first commercially successful locomotive was most probably that built by Matthew Murray in 1812 to an order by John Blenkinsop for the Middleton Colliery Railway, Leeds, England. It ran on four flanged wheels which were free, and was propelled by a toothed wheel which engaged in a rack on the side of one rail. The two vertical cylinders, 9 × 22 in (229 × 559 mm) drove cranks set at right angles and geared to the rack wheel. It weighed about 5 tons. (For further details see p. 11.)

The spring-loaded safety-valve was introduced in 1812 by James Fenton at Leeds, England.

The locomotive bogie was patented by William Chapman in 1813.

In May 1813 William Brunton of Butterley Ironworks in Derbyshire secured a patent for a four-wheeled engine propelled by two legs working at the rear and pushing it along. It was known as *Brunton's Mechanical Traveller* and worked between 1814 and 1815. Its boiler then exploded, killing and injuring a number of people and causing considerable damage.

George Stephenson's first locomotive, named *Blutcher*, was completed at Killingworth near Newcastle upon Tyne on 25 July 1814. It had a boiler 2 ft 10 in (863 mm) diameter and 8 ft (2·438 m) long, in which the two 8 × 24 in (203 × 610 mm) cylinders were mounted vertically along the centre. They drove the wheels through counter-shafts geared to the two driving-axles.

In February 1815 Stephenson with Ralph Dodds, viewer at Killingworth Colliery, patented an engine in which the wheels were driven directly and coupled by either rods or chains.

The first engine under this patent was built in 1815. Its wheels were coupled by rods working on cranked axles. **This was the first use of cranked axles in a locomotive**, but they were abandoned as not strong enough and for a time wheels were connected by endless chains.

The loose-eccentric valve gear was introduced by George Stephenson in 1816 with the assistance of Nicholas Wood (see p. 38), and was used on the 'Rocket'- and 'Planet'-type engines until 1835.

Carmichael's valve gear with a single fixed eccentric was introduced in 1818. The end of the eccentric rod was fixed to two V-shaped 'gabs' in the form of an X which could be raised to engage the forward valve-pin or lowered to engage the backward pin. These pins were at opposite ends of a centrally pivoted lever.

The first locomotive to have its wheels coupled by rods was *Locomotion*, No. 1 of the Stockton & Darlington Railway, built by George Stephenson in 1825. The two vertical cylinders 9·5 × 24 in (241 × 610 mm) were in line along the centre of the single-flue boiler and each drove one of the axles through rods and crank-pins on the wheels. Because these cranks were set at right angles one end of each coupling-rod had to be attached to a return crank.

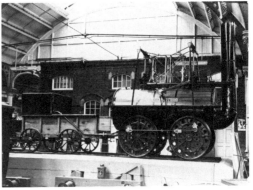

Stephenson's Locomotion, *No. 1 of the Stockton & Darlington Railway, built in 1825 (John Marshall)*

The first four-cylinder locomotive was built by Robert Wilson of Newcastle upon Tyne, England, and was sold to the Stockton & Darlington Railway at the end of 1825. The vertical cylinders were in pairs on each side of the engine and drove the rear wheels.

The multi-jet blast-pipe was introduced in 1826 by Sir Goldsworthy Gurney (1793–1875). The fusible plug (a soft metal plug in the firebox crown which melts if uncovered by water and allows steam to damp down the fire) and expansion valve gear (allowing steam to be used expansively) were also introduced by him in the same year.

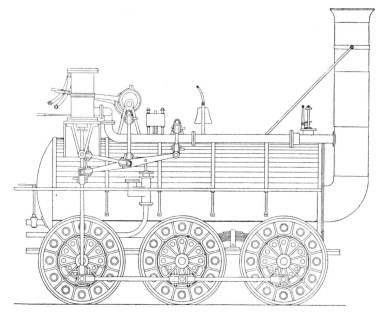

Hackworth's Royal George,
the first six-coupled locomotive,
built in 1827 (The Engineer)

The first six-coupled locomotive was Hackworth's *Royal George* built at Shildon, County Durham, in 1827. It was also the first engine in which the cylinders drove directly on to the wheels without intermediate gearing or levers. The piston-rods, however, were guided by Watt-type parallel motion, not a crosshead. Cylinders were 11 × 20 in (279 × 508 mm) and exhausted into a single blast-pipe. It weighed 8·4 tons.

The first locomotive in which the wheels were driven directly from the piston-rod working in a crosshead was Stephenson's 0–4–0 for the Bolton & Leigh Railway where it was named *Lancashire Witch* in 1828. The 9 × 24 in (229 × 610 mm) cylinders mounted on the rear of the boiler drove the front coupled wheels which were 4 ft (14630 mm) diameter. This engine also incorporated expansion valve gear in a primitive form.

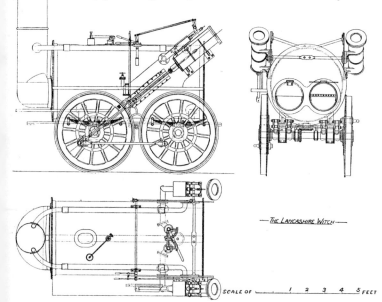

— THE LANCASHIRE WITCH —

SCALE OF ___ 1 2 3 4 5 FEET

Stephenson's Lancashire Witch *built for the Bolton & Leigh Railway, Lancashire, in 1828. It was the first locomotive in which the wheels were driven directly from the piston-rod* (The Engineer)

It was the first locomotive to be entirely suspended on leaf springs.

Stephenson's *Rocket* of 1829 incorporated the same arrangement of cylinders which, however, were only 8 × 16½ in (203 × 419 mm). It was the first engine to combine a multi-tubular boiler and a blast-pipe. Driving-wheels were 4 ft 8½ in (1·435 m) diameter and the weight of the engine was only 4 tons 5 cwt. It won the £500 prize at the Rainhill Trials. The design was mainly by Robert Stephenson.

The first inside-cylinder engine (or 'inside connected') engine, driving on to a crank-shaft, was the *Novelty* built by Braithwaite to a design by Ericsson (see pp. 39 and 42). It was also the first well-tank engine. The 6 × 12 in (152 × 305 mm) vertical cylinders drove the front axle through bell-cranks. It was entered in the Rainhill Trials in 1829, but failed.

The first locomotive powered by a horse walking on a moving platform was designed by T. S. Brandreth. In the Rainhill Trials *Cycloped* achieved a speed of 15 m.p.h. (24 km/h).

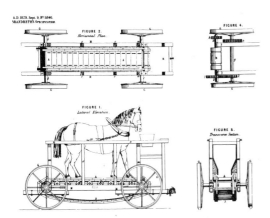

Cycloped, designed by T. S. Brandreth, the first locomotive powered by a horse. It achieved a speed of 15 m.p.h. Fig. 4 shows the two-speed arrangement (The Science Museum, London)

In the U.S.A. a similar locomotive was designed by D. C. Detmold for the South Carolina Canal & Railroad in 1830. It was named *Flying Dutchman* and won a $300 prize. On an experimental trip it pulled 12 passengers at 12 m.p.h, (19 km/h).

The bar-frame and haycock firebox first appeared in the 0–4–0 *Liverpool* built by Edward Bury (see p. 37), largely to the design of James Kennedy (1797–1886), and tried on the Liverpool & Manchester Railway in June 1830, two months before the line opened. It had 12 × 18 in (304 × 457 mm) cylinders driving on to a cranked axle. It was a highly advanced engine at the time. The inside cylinders became standard British practice and the bar-frame standard American practice. The multi-tubular boiler and smokebox were replacements soon after construction.

Edward Bury's inside-cylinder 0–4–0 Liverpool *built at Liverpool in 1830 for the Liverpool & Manchester Railway. It established the bar-frame construction for which Bury was famous (The Science Museum, London)*

The first engine to be built with a smokebox was the Stephensons' *Phoenix* built in 1830 for the Liverpool & Manchester Railway. The *Rocket* was soon afterwards rebuilt with this feature which became universal.

Stephenson's 2–2–0 engine *Planet* built in 1830 for the Liverpool & Manchester Railway had inside cylinders enclosed within the smokebox. **It was**

Stephenson's 2–2–0 Planet *built in 1830 for the Liverpool & Manchester Railway. It established the features of outside bearings and 'sandwich' frames and inside cylinders enclosed in the bottom of the smokebox (The Science Museum, London)*

**the first engine to be built with outside
sandwich frames and outside bearings**, a
feature of British practice which survived in
Stephenson's designs for many years. (The 'sandwich' frame consisted of a slab of oak or ash between
two iron plates.)

Hackworth's first inside-cylinder 0–4–0 was built
at Shildon in 1830 for the Stockton & Darlington
Railway and was named *Globe*. The 9 × 16 in
(229 × 406 mm) cylinders were mounted beneath
the driving-platform at the rear.

**The first locomotive in which the out-
side cylinders were attached to the frame**
instead of to the boiler was the *Union* built by
Rothwell, Hick & Rothwell of Bolton, Lancashire,
in 1831 for the Bolton & Leigh Railway. It was
a 2–2–0 with a vertical boiler, 9 × 18 in (229 × 457
mm) cylinders and 5 ft (1524 mm) driving-wheels.

**The first locomotive of Stephenson's
'Planet'-type** inside-cylinder 0–4–0 to be delivered to America was originally named *Stevens*
in honour of John Stevens (see 'Early Railroads in
the U.S.A.', p. 15 and 'The Pioneers', p. 31), but
was renamed *John Bull*. It went into service on the
Camden & Amboy Railroad on 12 November 1831.
Because of a tendency to leave the rails a two-
wheeled truck and pilot was fitted in front. This
was **the first locomotive pilot, or 'cowcatcher'**.
It ran until 1865 and is now preserved in the Smithsonian Institution, Washington, D.C. In 1893 it

travelled to the Chicago World's Fair under its
own steam.

The classic British 'single-wheeler' was
established by Robert Stephenson in a patent on
7 September 1833. It was a development of the
'Planet' type with a pair of wheels behind the firebox, becoming a 2–2–2, the success of the design
resulting from the outside framing which allowed
space for an adequate firebox.

The first engine, named *Patentee*, was built at
Newcastle upon Tyne in 1833 for the Liverpool &
Manchester Railway. It soon became widely
adopted in Britain and abroad and was the design
upon which the famous Gooch 'Singles' of the
Great Western Railway were based. It was developed also into the 0–4–2 and 0–6–0 goods engines.

Stephenson's 2–2–2 Patentee, *the first of the 'classic'
British single-wheelers. It was built by Robert Stephenson
& Company in 1833 for the Liverpool & Manchester
Railway (The Science Museum, London)*

Stevens, *the first engine of the
Stephenson 'Planet' type to be
delivered to the U.S.A. It was
built in 1831 by Robert
Stephenson & Company of
Newcastle upon Tyne, England,
for the Camden & Amboy
Railroad, and was assembled in
the U.S.A. It was later fitted
with a leading pony-truck and
pilot by Isaac Dripps (1810–92)
and was renamed* John Bull
(The Science Museum, London)

First experiments with piston-valves were made by Robert Stephenson in 1832. A design was prepared for a locomotive for the Liverpool & Manchester Railway, but there is no evidence of their behaviour, or that they were in fact used.

The 'petticoat' blast-pipe was also introduced by Robert Stephenson in 1832, by flaring the base of the chimney and extending it down into the smokebox to achieve a better smokebox vacuum.

The steam-whistle was introduced on the Leicester & Swannington Railway following an accident at a road crossing on 4 May 1833.

The steam-brake was introduced by Robert Stephenson in 1833, and was incorporated in his 'Patentee'-type 2–2–2.

The first inside-cylinder 0–6–0, a development of the Stephenson 'patent' type, was built by Robert Stephenson in 1833.

The bogie was first used on a British locomotive in 1833 on J. & C. Carmichael's 0–2–4 engine for the 4 ft 6 in (1·372 m) gauge Dundee & Newtyle Railway.

The 'gab motion' (valve gear) operated by four fixed eccentrics was first used by Forrester & Company, Liverpool, in 1834–36, and by R. & W. Hawthorn of Newcastle upon Tyne in 1835. Robert Stephenson & Company used the gear first on the 'patent'-type 0–4–2 *Harvey Combe* built in 1835.

The cylindrical smokebox was introduced in the U.S.A. in 1834 and was common there by the mid 1850s. It became established in Great Britain about 1900, but the old 'D' type was still being made by the London, Midland & Scottish and the Southern railways in the 1930s.

The balanced slide-valve was first patented by Hiram Strait of East Nassau, New York, on 25 June 1834. Its purpose was to eliminate the direct pressure of the steam on the top of the valve. It was first used on a railway engine by John Gray on the Liverpool & Manchester Railway in 1838. George W. Richardson patented an improved balanced slide-valve in the U.S.A. on 31 January 1872.

John Gray's expansion valve gear was first used in 1839 on the North Midland Railway. It was a complicated gear known as the 'Horse Leg'

motion. Its purpose was to cut off the steam at varying positions of the piston stroke to allow the remaining work to be done by the expansion of the steam.

The variable blast-pipe was introduced by Peter Rothwell of Bolton, Lancashire (see p. 36) in 1839. It was in the form of a hollow cone which could be raised or lowered inside the blast-pipe orifice from a lever on the footplate. It was used on Sharp's heavy goods engines of 1848–49.

The locomotive superheater was introduced by R. & W. Hawthorn of Newcastle upon Tyne in 1839.

Long-travel valves, giving greater cylinder efficiency, were first used on the Hull & Selby Railway by John Gray in 1840. They had about 6 in (152 mm) travel.

They first became established in the U.S.A. It was about 1900 before they were regularly used in England, on the Great Western Railway by G. J. Churchward (see p. 58) and in 1909 by George Hughes (1865–1945) on the Lancashire & Yorkshire Railway, but it was nearly 30 more years before they were universally adopted in Britain.

Hall's brick arch in the firebox for smokeless combustion of coal was first tried in 1841. Previously engines had burned coke or, as in North America, wood. It did not come into general use for several years but is stated to have been used on the Scottish North Eastern Railway by Thomas Yarrow from about 1857.

The Stephenson 'Long-boiler' locomotive was introduced in 1841, with the *North Star* for the 5 ft (1·524 m) gauge Northern & Eastern Railway. To obtain a large heating surface with a longer boiler, without increasing the wheelbase, the firebox was placed behind the rear axle. Mainly 2–2–0s, 2–4–0s and 0–6–0s were built to this design, but they were unsteady at speed.

The first British application of sanding gear, to sprinkle sand on the rails to help the driving-wheels to grip, was applied by Robert Stephenson in 1841.

The Stephenson (or Howe) Link Motion—valve gear with two fixed eccentrics—(see p. 46) was first used on locomotives for the North Midland Railway by Robert Stephenson in 1843.

The first 4–6–0 to run on a British railway; Highland Railway 'Jones Goods' No. 103, built in 1894 and withdrawn in 1934, photographed restored in its original livery at Keith Junction Station, Scotland, in 1961. It is now in the Glasgow Transport Museum (N. Fields)

One of the Japanese Tokaïdo expresses crossing the Fuji River, with a view of Mount Fuji (Ministry of Foreign Affairs, Japan)

The **'stationary-link' motion** was first used by Daniel Gooch (see p. 48) on the Great Western Railway and by his brother John Viret Gooch (1812–1900) on the London & South Western Railway in 1843.

Walschaert's valve gear was invented by Edige Walschaert in 1844 (see p. 50).

The pneumatic brake was invented by James Nasmyth (1808–90) in 1844.

The dial pressure gauge, replacing the mercurial gauge, was first proposed in Germany by Schinz in 1845. It was perfected in 1849 by Eugène Bourdon (1808–84) of Paris.

The first three-cylinder locomotive was built by Robert Stephenson for the Newcastle & Berwick Railway in 1846.

The compounding of locomotive cylinders (in which the steam is used twice, first at boiler pressure and then in partly expanded form at a lower pressure) was invented by John Nicholson, and in 1850 was first tried on the Eastern Counties Railway (see 'Von Borries' p. 57, 'De Glehn' p. 55, 'Du Bousquet' p. 54, and 'W. M. Smith' p. 55).

The double-beat regulator valve was introduced by John Ramsbottom on the London & North Western Railway in 1850. His famous **duplex safety-valve** was introduced in 1856 together with **screw reverser**, instead of the hand lever, and the **displacement lubricator**. It is possible that the screw reverser was used on the Aberdeen Railway a few years earlier.

The first all-steel tyres for locomotive wheels were produced by Alfred Krupp (1812–87) of Essen, Germany, in 1851 and examples were displayed at the Great Exhibition in London in that year. The first manufacturer in the U.S.A. was James Millholland (1812–75) of the Philadelphia & Reading Railroad in the early 1850s. In Great Britain they were introduced by Naylor and Vickers on the London & North Western Railway in 1859.

Steel tyres lasted for 200 000 to 300 000 miles (322 000 to 483 000 km), compared with 60 000 miles (96 500 km) for iron tyres.

The drop-grate, to facilitate fire-cleaning, was introduced by Edward Bury in 1852.

A smokebox superheater for steam locomotives was used in 1852 by J. E. McConnell (1815–83) at Wolverton on the London & North Western Railway.

Feedwater-heaters were first tried in 1854 by Joseph Hamilton Beattie (see p. 42) on the London & South Western Railway and were first applied in 1855. His double firebox and combustion-chamber to enable engines to burn coal without producing smoke were introduced in 1859.

The straight-link motion, invented by Alexander Allan (1809–91), was first used on locomotives of the Scottish Central Railway in 1854.

The firehole deflector plate to assist combustion was first applied by G. K. Douglas on the Birkenhead, Lancashire & Cheshire Junction Railway early in 1858.

The combination of brick arch and firehole deflector plate was first used by Matthew Kirtley (1813–74) in 1859 while he was locomotive superintendent of the Midland Railway at Derby. It enabled coal to be burnt without the complication of the Beattie firebox.

The steam injector (for forcing water into a locomotive boiler against pressure) was invented by Henri Giffard (see p. 51), the French balloonist, and was first used on locomotives by Sharp Stewart & Company, Manchester, England, in 1859. By 1860 nearly 30 injectors were in use on British locomotives. It was introduced in the U.S.A. by William Sellers (1824–1905) in 1860. In the first year he supplied 2800.

A steel locomotive firebox was first tried by Alexander Allan on the Scottish Central Railway in 1860. Steel fireboxes became general in American practice, but European engineers tended to continue with the copper firebox.

Steel boilers in place of wrought iron were first used by George Tosh on the Maryport & Carlisle Railway in 1862.

Steam tenders were introduced on the Great Northern Railway, England, in 1863 by Archibald Sturrock (1816–1909), the locomotive superintendent. Fifty were built, to increase the power of his 0-6-0 goods engines. Various troubles, including heavy maintenance costs, and complaints from men who were 'driving two engines and only getting paid for one' led to their withdrawal.

Some were rebuilt into small locomotives in 1870–73 by Isaac Watt Boulton (1823–99) at his famous 'siding' at Ashton-under-Lyne near Manchester.

While Sturrock was the first to use steam tenders extensively, they were first applied by the Verpilleux brothers, of Rive-de-Gier, France, who patented the invention on 26 September 1842.

The radial axlebox was invented by William Bridges Adams (see p. 39) and was first used on some 2–4–2 tanks for the St Helens Railway in Lancashire, built by Cross & Company of St Helens in 1863.

The counter-pressure brake in which the engine is reversed so that the cylinders act as compressors thereby absorbing power and avoiding wear on tyres and brake-blocks, especially on long inclines, was first used with water-injection by F. Holt on the South Staffordshire Railway in 1856. The Le Châtelier system using hot water was introduced on the London & North Western Railway in 1868.

The water-tube firebox was introduced by Johann Brotan (1843–1923) in Austria about 1870. His semi-water-tube boiler was first used in 1902 and over 1000 were built in the following 25 years.

The compressed-air brake was first used by the Caledonian Railway, Scotland, by Steel and McInnes in 1871.

The non-automatic vacuum brake was introduced by J. Y. Smith on the North Eastern Railway, England, in 1874.

The hydraulic brake was introduced by Francis William Webb (1835–1906) on the London & North Western Railway.

Gresham's automatic vacuum brake was invented by James Gresham (1836–1914) and was first used in 1878. By this system the brakes are automatically applied on both portions of the train if it breaks in two. Gresham began his work on brakes while with Sharp Stewart & Company, Manchester, where, in 1864, he began improving the Giffard injector (see p. 123) by providing means for adjusting the combining cone in relation to the steam cone.

The 'pop' safety-valve was patented in Britain by T. Adams in 1873 and was first used in 1874. A second patent in 1875 covered an annular pop chamber. In the U.S.A., however, pop safety-valves were used from about 1867 (see p. 128).

On the Lancashire & Yorkshire Railway, England, a pop safety-valve was introduced by Henry Albert Hoy (1855–1910) about 1900.

The Ross pop safety-valve was patented in 1902 and 1904 by fitter R. L. Ross of Coleraine Shed on the Belfast & Northern Counties Railway. It was first used on a locomotive by Bowman Malcolm (1854–1933), then locomotive superintendent of the B. & N.C., on his 2–4–0 No. 57 in 1908. The first new engine to be fitted was the B. & N.C. 3 ft (0·914 m) gauge compound 2–4–2 tank No. 112, also in 1908. It did not achieve extensive use in Great Britain until the 1920s.

The advantage of the 'pop' safety-valve was the small pressure difference, only about 1–2 lb/in², between opening and closing compared with 5 lb/in² or more in the Ramsbottom type.

Speed-indicators for locomotives were first used by John Ramsbottom on the London & North Western Railway in 1861. A superior pattern was devised by William Stroudley (1833–89), locomotive engineer of the London, Brighton & South Coast Railway, in 1874.

Steam reversing gear was first used by James Stirling (1800–76) on the Glasgow & South Western Railway in 1874.

The Davies & Metcalfe exhaust-steam injector, making use of exhaust steam for forcing water into the boiler, was introduced in 1876.

Steel plate frames instead of wrought iron were first used by F. W. Webb on the London & North Western Railway in 1886. The plate frame was peculiar to British and European locomotive practice. American practice used the built-up bar-frame, first used by Edward Bury at Liverpool. Later American locomotive engineers developed the cast-steel locomotive bed which finally included cylinders, valve chests and smokebox saddle, representing a triumph of the pattern-maker's and foundryman's crafts.

Steam sanding gear, devised by Gresham and Holt (Francis Holt, 1825–93, works manager, Midland Railway, Derby), was introduced on the Midland Railway in 1886. By forcing sand beneath the driving-wheels it brought about a revival of the 'single-wheeler' locomotive in Britain where it was built until about 1900 and lasted until the mid 1920s.

The British four-cylinder simple engine was introduced by James Manson (1846–1935) on the Glasgow & South Western Railway in 1897, with the 4–4–0 No. 11.

The smoke-tube superheater was introduced in Germany by Wilhelm Schmidt in 1897. It was first used in Britain in May 1906 on the Great Western Railway two-cylinder 4–6–0 No. 2901 *Lady Superior* and on the Lancashire & Yorkshire Railway in two 0–6–0s (see 'The Pioneers', p. 58).

A smokebox-type superheater was used by J. A. F. Aspinall (1851–1937), chief mechanical engineer of the Lancashire & Yorkshire Railway, on his 4–4–2 No. 737 in 1899. **This was the first British superheated locomotive**.

The Lentz poppet-valve gear was first applied in Germany by Hugo Lentz (1859–1944) in 1905. It used the type of valves familiar in internal-combustion engines. In Britain it was applied by H. N. Gresley (see p. 59) to several types of London & North Eastern Railway locomotives.

The Caprotti poppet-valve gear was first fitted to an Italian locomotive in 1920. (See **Caprotti**, p. 59 for applications).

The first British engine to be fitted with a booster was the Great Northern Railway 4–4–2 No. 1419 in 1923, No. 4419 on the London & North Eastern Railway. The booster, common in America, was tried only on the L.N.E.R. in Britain. It consisted of an auxiliary engine on the trailing truck which could be engaged and put into or out of operation as required.

The L.N.E.R. tried boosters also on two 2–8–2 freight engines, two North Eastern Railway 'Atlantics' and a Great Central Railway 0–8–4 tank. The boosters were removed after a few years' trials.

The Giesl ejector for steam locomotives was developed over a long period by the Austrian engineer Dr Giesl Gieslingen, and was finished in 1951. Multiple exhaust jets along the centre-line of the smokebox exhaust into a chimney of oblong section with a length many times its width. It provides an equal draught through the boiler tubes for less back-pressure in the cylinders compared with the conventional blast-pipe.

It was widely applied in Austria and Czechoslovakia and was tried in Australia (N.S.W. Government Railways 'C36' Class 4–6–0 No. 3616), India and East Africa. On British Railways it was tried, with obvious lack of enthusiasm, on only two engines: standard 2–10–0 No. 92250, and a rebuilt Southern 'Pacific'. The National Coal Board, however, used it quite extensively and it was claimed to be 'worth several more wagons'.

NORTH AMERICAN LOCOMOTIVES

The reason that North American steam-locomotive development was generally anything up to 20 years in advance of British was probably that workers in the U.S.A. were better paid. As long as British railways could obtain good coal for a few shillings a ton, or could employ experienced fitters at about £1 a week in well-equipped works, it was of little consequence if the typical British inside valves and motion did take days instead of hours to dismantle and assemble, or if engines were inefficient.

All the biggest advances in steam locomotive development such as superheaters, coned boilers, cylindrical smokeboxes, large bearings, outside valves and motion, long-travel valves, side-window cabs, were well established in the U.S.A. many years before they became standard practice in Britain. Inside-cylinder engines were abandoned in the U.S.A. in the 1850s and inside valve gear soon after 1905. British Railways were still building them at Swindon in the 1950s.

The first locomotive 'pilot' (or 'cow-catcher') was fitted, together with a pair of leading wheels, to the *John Bull* on the Camden & Amboy Railroad (see p. 120). The engine, originally a 'Planet'-type 0–4–0, was built by Robert Stephenson & Company, Newcastle upon Tyne, in 1831. The pilot was fitted by Isaac Dripps (1810–92) master mechanic on the C. & A.

The first American 'national type' engine was the 4–2–0, originated by John B. Jervis (1795–1885) with the *Experiment* built at West Point Foundry, New York, in 1832 for the

The Giesl Ejector as applied to 0–6–0 tank No. 24 of the National Coal Board, West Ayr Area, Scotland, at Waterside, Dalmellington in July 1969. The engine was built by Barclay in 1953 (John Marshall)

Mohawk & Hudson Railroad. It was **the first bogie locomotive in the world**. In its day it was also the fastest in the world, covering 14 miles (22·5 km) in 13 minutes. It was claimed that it reached 80 m.p.h. (128·75 km/h) over a one mile (1·609 km) stretch. The type was taken up by the Norris Brothers who redesigned it with the firebox behind the driving-axle to give more adhesive weight. Between 1835 and 1842 the 4–2–0 type formed nearly two-thirds of the total locomotives in the U.S.A.

The Norris 4–2–0 Lafayette *of 1837 (The Science Museum, London)*

Bells were first fitted on American locomotives in 1835 when the State of Massachusetts passed a law requiring this warning device.

The first locomotive to be exported from the U.S.A. was the *Columbus* built by Ross Winans (1796–1877) of Baltimore for the Leipzig & Dresden Railway in 1837.

The archetypal American 4–4–0 was first patented on 5 February 1836 by Henry R. Campbell (*c.* 1810–*c.* 1870), chief engineer of the Philadelphia, Germantown & Norristown Railroad.

The first American 4–4–0 was completed in Philadelphia on 8 May 1837. The 'classic' American 4–4–0 with 'three-point suspension' first appeared in 1839. It was a direct development of the Norris 4–2–0.

About 1870 83–85 per cent of locomotives in the U.S.A. were this type of 4–4–0. Between 1840 and 1890 about 20 000 were built.

The first steam locomotive in Canada was the *Dorchester* built by Robert Stephenson & Company, Newcastle upon Tyne, England, in 1836 and delivered to the Champlain & St Lawrence Railway (opened between St John and Laprairie, Quebec, on 21 July 1836) where it worked until it blew up in 1867 and was scrapped.

The first American locomotive whistles known to have been fitted were on two locomotives built at Lowell, Massachusetts, in 1836, appropriately under the supervision of the engineer George Washington Whistler (see p. 40). The *Hicksville* entered service at Jamaica, on the Long Island Railroad, and was reported to make 'a shrill, wild, unearthly sound, like drawing a saw flat across a bar of iron'. The *Susquehanna* was tried at Wilmington, Delaware, at 35–40 m.p.h. (56–64 km/h), and was said 'to give awful notice of its approach to any point'.

The first American 4–4–0 designed in 1836 by Henry R. Campbell. The design was superseded by the 'classic' outside-cylinder design, illustrated below (The Science Museum, London)

The first locomotive in British Columbia, Canadian Pacific 4–4–0 No. 374, now preserved at Vancouver. An example of the typical American 4–4–0 (John Marshall)

A whistle was also fitted to the first Rogers engine, 4–2–0 *Sandusky*, built in 1837 for the Paterson & Hudson River Railroad (see p. 37). It was the first locomotive in the State of Ohio. During its first trip on 6 October 1837 from Paterson, N.Y., to New Brunswick, N.J., the whistle was used so much that the engine ran short of steam.

Sandboxes were first fitted to American locomotives in 1836 following a plague of grasshoppers in Pennsylvania. On 1 August it was decided to use them on the Tuscumbia, Courtland & Decatur Railroad. The sand was sprinkled on to the rails and it prevented the engines slipping on the squashed insects.

The steam-brake was first used on a locomotive in the U.S.A. in 1848 by George S. Griggs, (1805–70), master mechanic of the Boston & Providence Railroad. But many years elapsed before it was widely used.

The first variable cut-off valve gear in the U.S.A. was produced by Eltham Rogers of the Cuyahoga Steam Furnace Company of Cleveland, Ohio, in 1849 and was first used on the *Cleveland* engine for the Cleveland, Columbus & Cincinnati Railroad in March 1850.

In Canada, as in the U.S.A., wood was the standard locomotive fuel for many years. Apart from the three locomotives of the short coal line in Nova Scotia in 1839 (see p. 20) the first experiments with coal were made about 1858–60; but it was into the 1870s before coal became generally used.

At first engines covered about 36 miles (58 km) on a cord of wood, but by 1859 this had risen to 50 miles (80 km). A 'cord' of wood was a stack 8 × 4 × 4 ft (2·438 × 1·219 × 1·219 m).

The Bissell truck, a short bogie with the pivot behind the rear axle and using inclined planes to support and to centre the front of the locomotive, was patented by Levi Bissell of Newark, NJ, on 4 August 1857. It was patented in Britain in May that year but was not used on a British locomotive until 1860. It rapidly replaced the centrally pivoted short truck. Bissell patented a two-wheeled pony truck in 1858. The most familiar application of the Bissell truck was on the 4–4–0 tanks built for the Metropolitan and District railways, London, by Beyer Peacock & Company, Manchester.

Bissell also patented an 'air spring' for locomotive suspension on 11 October 1841.

The early adoption in the U.S.A. of large numbers of driving-wheels was to obtain the necessary adhesion without excessive axle loading for the light track then in use.

The first o–8–o type was built for the Baltimore & Ohio Railroad in 1841 by Ross Winans of Baltimore. He later developed the 'Mud-Digger' type.

Buffalo, one of the Ross Winans 'Mud-Digger' o–8–os, built in 1844 (The Science Museum, London)

Baldwin's first o–8–o type appeared in 1846 when 17 were built for the Philadelphia & Reading Railroad. The two leading axles were mounted in a flexible truck.

The world's first 4–6–0, 'ten-wheeler', was the *Chesapeake*. It was ordered in October 1846 by the Philadelphia & Reading Railroad and was delivered in March 1847 by Norris Brothers. Almost at the same time another, the *New Hampshire*, was completed by Holmes Hinkley (1793–1866) for the Boston & Maine Railroad.

The first 2–6–0 was the *Pawnee*, built in 1850 by James Millholland (1812–75) for the Philadelphia & Reading Railroad. This was a rigid machine. The proper 'Mogul'-type 2–6–0 followed the invention of the two-wheeled Bissell truck in 1858. The first 'Moguls' were built in 1860 by Baldwin of Philadelphia for the Louisville & Nashville Railroad.

The first engine in North America to have a boiler made entirely of steel was the inside-cylinder o–6–o *Scotia* built at the Hamilton Works of the 5 ft 6 in (1·676 m) gauge Great Western Railway of Canada in 1860. The steel was imported from England and cost 16 cents a pound. The total weight of the boiler was 10 356 lb (4652 kg) without the copper tubes.

The first 12-coupled engine was a 'camel'-type 0–12–0 tank named *Pennsylvania* designed by James Millholland and built at the Philadelphia & Reading Railroad's shops in 1863. It was used for banking coal trains over the summit between the Schuylkill and Delaware rivers. In 1870 it was rebuilt into a 0–10–0 tender engine.

The first regular 2–8–0, named *Consolidation*, was designed by Alexander Mitchell (1832–1908) in 1865. It gave its name to the type. It was built at Baldwin Locomotive Works, Philadelphia, in 1866 for the Lehigh & Mahanoy Railroad. It soon became the most popular type in the U.S.A.

In 1867 Mitchell introduced the 2–10–0 type for the Lehigh Valley Railroad.

The first 'pop' safety-valve was patented on 25 September 1866 by George W. Richardson of the Troy & Boston Railroad. (For its introduction and use in Great Britain see p. 124.)

Walschaert's valve gear was first used in the U.S.A. on a Mason-Fairlie double-bogie tank engine built in 1874 by William Mason (1808–83) for the Boston, Clinton & Fitchburg Railroad.

The wide Wootten firebox was invented in 1877 by John E. Wootten (1822–98) when general manager of the Philadelphia & Reading Railroad. It was designed to burn waste anthracite, or 'culm', which, because of its slow-burning qualities, required a larger area to give off the same heat as bituminous coal. It was first applied on the P. & R. 4–6–0 No. 411 in 1880. The grate area was 76 ft². The cab was mounted midway along the boiler,

ahead of the firebox, so that the engines became known as 'Camelbacks' or 'Mother Hubbards'. The fireman stood on a separate platform at the rear.

The first 'Pacific' or 4–6–2 type engine was built in 1886 at the Vulcan Iron Works, Wilkes Barr, Pennsylvania, to a design by George S. Strong for the Lehigh Valley Railroad. The class name 'Pacific' did not come into use until many years later.

The first 'Atlantic' or 4–4–2 type engine appeared in 1888, also built at the Vulcan Iron Works to a Strong design for the Lehigh Valley Railroad. The class name 'Atlantic' for the 4–4–2 type was suggested in 1894 by J. K. Kenly, general manager of the Atlantic Coast Railroad, for a group of 4–4–2s built by Baldwin.

The last, largest and fastest 'Atlantics' were the four oil-fired, streamlined engines built by the American Locomotive Company (ALCO) in 1935–37 to work the *Hiawatha* between Chicago

One of the four streamlined 'Atlantics', built by ALCO in 1935, for the Hiawatha *between Chicago and the 'Twin Cities' on the Milwaukee Road. These were the first steam locomotives designed to run at speeds of over 100 m.p.h. (161 km/h) (The Milwaukee Road)*

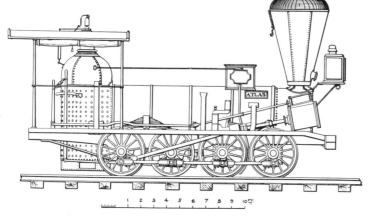

One of the early Baldwin 0–8–0s built in 1846 for the Philadelphia & Reading Railroad (Baldwin Locomotive Works)

and the 'Twin Cities' (Minneapolis and St Paul) on the Chicago, Milwaukee, St Paul & Pacific Railroad. They were the first steam locomotives in the world designed specifically to run at 100 m.p.h. (161 km/h) on every trip. They recorded speeds of over 120 m.p.h. (193 km/h).

The first 2–8–2 engines were built in 1897 by the Baldwin Locomotive Works for the 3 ft 6 in (1·067 m) gauge Japanese Railways. From these derived the class name 'Mikado'. It was introduced in the U.S.A. (where examples became affectionately known as 'Mikes') in 1903 on the Bismarck, Washburn & Great Falls Railway.

The Vanderbilt firebox, introduced by Cornelius Vanderbilt (1873–1942) in 1899 on 4–6–0 No. 947 of the New York Central & Hudson River Railroad, the railroad his great-grandfather Cornelius had established. The patent was for a boiler with a tapered barrel and a circular corrugated firebox resembling that introduced by Lentz in Germany in 1888. Although it had no stays, it gave trouble with leaks and breakages, and its limited grate area caused its early abandonment. Similar fireboxes were tried on the London & North Western and Lancashire & Yorkshire railways in England.

Vanderbilt also designed a tender with a cylindrical tank, which became popular on the Canadian National Railways from 1905 to 1930 and was widely used in the U.S.A.

Wooden lagging for boilers, to prevent loss of heat, went out of use in the U.S.A. soon after 1900. Asbestos was first tried in 1873 on the Fitchburg Railroad, but it was not until about 1900 that, with magnesium lagging, it became widely adopted.

The first 2–6–2 or 'Prairie'-type tender engine was built by Baldwin Locomotive Works in 1900. It was No. 687 on the Chicago, Burlington & Quincy Railroad. Many were built for passenger and freight work on the Mid West lines and so gained the class name 'Prairie'.

The last examples in the U.S.A. were built in 1910, but the type became popular on some eastern European lines, and in Great Britain with Gresley's famous 'V2' Class introduced on the London & North Eastern Railway in 1936. The first of these, No. 4771 *Green Arrow*, is preserved at York Railway Museum.

The 2–10–2 'Santa Fe' type was introduced by the Atchinson, Topeka & Santa Fe Railroad in 1903. These big Baldwin tandem compound machines were designed for helping heavy freight over the Raton Pass. The trailing-wheels assisted in running back down the grade.

The mechanical stoker of the Crawford plunger underfeed type was introduced on Pennsylvania Railroad 2–8–2s in 1905. From about 1915 it was gradually discarded in favour of the steam-jet overfeed system of the Street scatter type introduced about 1910, using a continuous chain belt. The Duplex stoker with screw conveyors was introduced in 1918 and replaced the Street type by 1920.

The Interstate Commerce Commission (q.v.) ruled that from 1 July 1938 the mechanical stoker should be used on all coal-burning passenger engines with over 160 000 lb (72 570 kg), and on freight engines with over 175 000 lb (79 378 kg), on the driving-wheels. As a general rule, grates of over 50 ft² (4·6 m²) merited mechanical stokers.

The Jacobs–Shupert firebox was introduced in 1908–9 on the Atchison, Topeka & Santa Fe Railroad. It dispensed with stay bolts and gave greater safety, but its numerous joints resulted in leaks and its use was not continued.

Boosters were first used in the U.S.A. on two-wheeled trailing trucks in 1915 and on four-wheeled trucks after 1925.

Baker valve gear, similar to Walschaert's but using a differently shaped link, was introduced in the U.S.A. in 1912–13.

The cast-steel one-piece engine frame, or bed, was first produced by General Steel Castings Corporation, U.S.A., in 1925. At first the cylinders were separate. Later they were cast integrally with the frame and smokebox saddle, and this became universal from 1930. The whole was a triumph of the foundryman's craft.

The four-wheeled trailing truck to carry increasingly heavy firebox loads was introduced in 1925 and with one-piece cast-steel frames in 1927. The six-wheeled truck first appeared in 1938.

The 2–8–4 'Berkshire' type originated in the U.S.A. in 1925, built by Lima Locomotive Works, Ohio, for the Illinois Central Railroad. It was the first of the Lima 'Super Power' engines.

The 2–10–4 type also originated in 1925 when Lima built some for the Texas & Pacific Railway. These gave the name 'Texas' to the type. The best-known examples were the magnificent 'Selkirks' of the Canadian Pacific Railway (see p. 134).

The popular American 4–8–4 type was introduced in 1927 on the Northern Pacific Railroad. The type represented the maximum power which could be obtained with eight coupled wheels. The type was widely adopted in the U.S.A. and Canada.

The first locomotive to be equipped with roller bearings throughout was a 4–8–4 built by ALCO in 1930 for the Timken Roller Bearing Company which numbered it 1111. Its rolling resistance was so small that on level track the 350 ton engine could be kept in motion by three girls. After demonstrations all over the country it was sold to the Northern Pacific Railroad, which numbered it 2626, in 1933.

A 'tender booster' or steam tender was fitted to the 2–10–4 'Texas'- type engines built by Baldwin for the Chicago Great Western Railroad in 1931. It added a further 18000 lb (8165 kg) tractive effort making a total of 102600 lb (46539 kg). (See 'Steam Tenders', p. 123.)

The first all-welded boiler was fitted to a Delaware & Hudson Railroad 2–8–0 in 1934, and was given several years of trials before being passed as satisfactory by the Interstate Commerce Commission.

The most powerful non-articulated passenger steam locomotive was the Pennsylvania 6–4–4–6 'duplex' No. 6100 built at the Altoona shops in 1939. It ran for only ten years. The 'duplexi' were not a success.

BRITISH AND EUROPEAN LOCOMOTIVE PROGRESS

The first British 4–4–0 was rebuilt from a Norris 4–2–0 of the Birmingham & Gloucester Railway between 1846 and 1850.

Daniel Gooch (see p. 48) built ten 7 ft (2·134 m) gauge 4–4–0s for the Great Western Railway in 1855, but with a rigid wheelbase.

The first British bogie 4–4–0s to be built new were two by Robert Stephenson & Company for the Stockton & Darlington Railway in 1860 to a design by William Bouch (1813–76; brother of Sir Thomas). Next were the London, Chatham & Dover and Great North of Scotland railways. All these engines had outside cylinders.

The typical British inside-cylinder inside-frame 4–4–0 was introduced by Thomas Wheatley on the North British Railway in June 1871. The first of these, No. 224, went down with the first Tay Bridge in 1879. It was recovered and ran until 1919.

Stockton & Darlington Railway 4–4–0 No. 160 Brougham built in 1860 by Robert Stephenson & Company at Newcastle upon Tyne to designs by William Bouch. This was the first 4–4–0 bogie engine in Britain and the first with the large American-type cab (The Science Museum, London)

The first British inside-cylinder 4–4–0, the North British Railway No. 224, as built at Cowlairs, Glasgow, in June 1871 to a design by Wheatley. This was the engine which went down with the old Tay Bridge in 1879

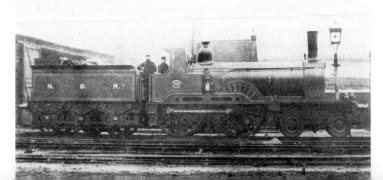

The first 2–6–0 or 'Mogul' to be built and to run in Britain appeared on the Great Eastern Railway in 1878. Fifteen were built by Neilson & Company of Glasgow to the design of William Adams (1823–1904).

The first eight-coupled main-line tender engines to run in Britain were two outside-cylinder o–8–os built in 1886 by Sharp Stewart in Manchester, originally for the Swedish & Norwegian Railway which, however, was unable to pay for them. In October 1889 they were acquired by the Barry Railway in South Wales where, in 1897, they were joined by two more of the same original order.

The first British inside-cylinder o–8–o was built in October 1892 at Crewe on the London & North Western Railway to a design by F. W. Webb. It was Webb's only eight-coupled simple engine.

The 2–8–0 type was introduced in Britain by G. J. Churchward on the Great Western Railway in 1903, nearly 40 years after the type had become well established in the U.S.A.

The first engine in service in Britain with a Belpaire firebox was the o–6–2 tank No. 7 designed by Harry Pollitt and built by the Manchester, Sheffield & Lincolnshire Railway at its Gorton Works in September 1891. It was renumbered 515 on 24 October 1893; became No. 5515, Class 'N5', on the London & North Eastern Railway in 1923; was renumbered 9250 in 1947 and was withdrawn in 1956 as British Railways No. 69250.

The first 4–6–0 to run on a British railway was Highland Railway No. 103 introduced in 1894 by David Jones (1834–1906). It ran until 1934 and, after a short spell working special trains in the early 1960s, it was placed in the Glasgow Transport Museum.

The first 4–6–0 passenger engine in Britain was the North Eastern Railway 'S' Class introduced in 1899 by Wilson Worsdell (see p. 53).

Britain's first 'Atlantic'-type locomotive was designed by H. A. Ivatt (see p. 56) and was built at Doncaster in 1898 by the Great Northern Railway. The first, No. 990, was later named *Henry Oakley* after the G.N.R. general manager.

It was closely followed by the inside-cylinder 4–4–2 of the Lancashire & Yorkshire Railway designed by J. A. F. Aspinall (1851–1937) and completed at Horwich Works in February 1899.

This was remarkable for its 7 ft 3 in (2·210 m) coupled wheels and high-pitched boiler.

Ivatt's large-boilered 'Atlantic' with wide firebox first appeared in 1900. Its appearance startled everyone at the time, but its performance was sadly inferior until it was rebuilt with superheater and piston-valves.

The first British 'Pacific' locomotive was built at Swindon in 1908 to a design by G. J. Churchward (see p. 58) on the Great Western Railway. No. 111 *The Great Bear* was a large-boilered version of his very successful four-cylinder 4–6–0. Its weight restricted it to Brunel's London–Bristol Railway, and the design was not repeated. It was withdrawn in 1923.

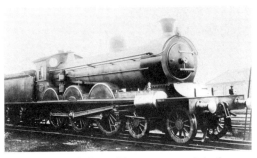

North Eastern Railway No. 2002, one of the first two 4–6–0 passenger engines in Britain, built at Gateshead in 1899 (The Science Museum, London)

The first British 'Atlantic' locomotive, Great Northern Railway No. 990, named Henry Oakley *after the general manager. Built at Doncaster in 1898, and photographed in York Railway Museum in 1964 (John Marshall)*

Britain's first 'Pacific', the Great Western Railway No. 111 The Great Bear designed by G. J. Churchward in 1908 (British Rail)

Gresley's pioneer 'Pacific' No. 1470 Great Northern *built at Doncaster in 1922. It had three cylinders, the motion of the inside valve being derived from the outside-valve spindles by a system of levers (The Science Museum, London)*

The first British 'Pacifics' to be produced as a class were designed by H. N. Gresley (see p. 59) and built by the Great Northern Railway at Doncaster. No. 1470 appeared in April 1922 and was later named *Great Northern*. The most famous, No. 1472, appeared in January 1923 and was the first engine to be completed by the newly formed London & North Eastern Railway. It was renumbered 4472 and named *Flying Scotsman*.

The first ten-coupled engine in Britain was a three-cylinder 0–10–0 tank designed by James Holden (see p. 53) and built at Stratford Works, London, on the Great Eastern Railway in 1902. Its purpose was to demonstrate that a steam train could accelerate to 30 m.p.h. (48 km/h) in 30 seconds, so defeating a proposal for a competing electric railway. It was the first three-cylinder engine in Britain since 1846 (see p. 123). Having fulfilled its purpose, it was rebuilt into a 0–8–0 in 1906.

Britain's other ten-coupled designs were the Midland Railway Lickey Banker 0–10–0 of 1919, the Ministry of Supply 2–10–0s of 1943 (see colour illustration, p. 139) and the British Railways standard 2–10–0s of 1954.

The first 12-coupled tender engine in Europe was the 2–12–0 designed by Karl Gölsdorf (see p. 58) for the Austrian State Railways. It was built in 1911 for the long 1 in 40 or 2·5 per cent grades on the Arlberg route.

The only other European 12-coupled engines were: 3 0–12–0 rack and adhesion tanks for the Austrian State Railways in 1911–12; 44 2–12–0s for the Württemburg State Railway in 1917–24; 10 0–12–0 tanks in 1922 and 20 2–12–4 tanks (12 two-cylinder in 1931 and 8 three-cylinder in 1942) for

The first ten-coupled engine in Britain, James Holden's three-cylinder 0–10–0 tank, built by the Great Eastern Railway in 1902 (The Science Museum, London)

Britain's first eight-coupled passenger engine, the London & North Eastern Railway No. 2001 Cock o' the North, *built at Doncaster in 1934 to a design by H. N. Gresley. The L.N.E.R. 2–8–2s had the highest tractive effort of any British passenger locomotives (The Science Museum, London)*

the Bulgarian State Railway; 2 2–12–2 rack and adhesion tanks for the German Reichsbahn (Austrian section) in 1941; a 2–12–0 six-cylinder compound for the French State Railways in 1947, and a metre-gauge 0–12–0 tank for the Zervanshja Mines, Yugoslavia, in 1947.

Britain's first eight-coupled passenger engine was the London & North Eastern Railway 2–8–2 No. 2001 *Cock o' the North* designed by H. N. Gresley and built at Doncaster in 1934. It was built with Lentz rotary-cam poppet-valve gear and was later rebuilt with Walschaert's valve gear and a streamlined front. With five other 2–8–2s it worked between Edinburgh and Aberdeen. Their tractive effort of 43 462 lb (19 714 kg) was the highest of any British express locomotives. They had 6 ft 2 in (1880 mm) coupled wheels.

In 1943–44 all six were rebuilt into 4–6–2s by Edward Thompson, Gresley's successor.

The only other eight-coupled engines to be regularly used on passenger trains in Britain were the Great Western Railway '4700' Class 2–8–0s with 5 ft 8 in (1727 mm) wheels.

RUSSIAN STEAM LOCOMOTIVES

The world's tallest locomotives are in Russia where the loading gauge permits engines 17 ft (5·182 m) high, 4 ft (1·219 m) higher than in Britain. They can also be up to 11 ft 6 in (3·5 m) wide.

The first Russian steam locomotive was probably a 2–2–0. It was built in 1833 at Nizhni-Tagil in the Urals by M. Cherepanov and it was run on a ½-mile (0·8 km) long 5 ft 6 in (1·676 m) gauge track.

The first locomotive in service in Russia was built by Timothy Hackworth at Shildon, County Durham, England, for the 6 ft (1·829 m) gauge 14 mile (22·5 km) long line from St Petersburg to Tsarskoe Selo in 1836. The engine cost £1885 including tender which was fitted with brakes. It was accompanied to Russia by T. Hackworth's eldest son John, then not quite 17 years old, and a group of men from Shildon. At Tsarskoe Selo John Hackworth was introduced to Tsar Nicholas. The engine was then given the blessing of the Greek Church before opening the railway, in November 1836.

In 1837 Hawthorns' of Newcastle upon Tyne built a 2–2–0 for the same railway.

The largest steam locomotives built in Russia were the two 'P38' simple expansion 2–8–8–4s built at Kolomna Works in 1954–55. They each weighed 214·9 tons and were 125 ft 6 in (38·252 m) long. They were the last main-line steam-locomotive type built in Russia.

The only 14-coupled steam locomotive was a 4–14–4 built in Russia in 1934. Its use was severely restricted by its rigidity and it saw little service before it simply 'disappeared'.

The first locomotive designed and built by the New Zealand Railways was a 2–6–2 tank, No. W192, in 1889.

THE POWER OF STEAM LOCOMOTIVES

Steam locomotive power can be represented in two ways. One is by **Tractive Effort** obtained by the formula $(D^2 \times S \times P)/W$ where D is cylinder diameter in inches, S is piston stroke in inches, P is steam pressure in lb/in² (usually 85 per cent of boiler pressure) and W is driving-wheel diameter in inches. Tractive effort is simply the force exerted at the rim of the driving-wheel. The use the engine can make of it depends entirely on its ability to grip the rails, or its adhesive weight, and the capacity of the boiler to supply the steam.

Horsepower includes a time factor (1 hp = 33 000 ft lb/minute = 746 Joules/sec or 746 Watts; in France 4500 kg m/minute = 736 Watts). In a steam-engine this depends on the rate at which fuel can be burnt and water evaporated in the boiler, as well as cylinder efficiency.

With a steam locomotive there are so many variables that a horsepower rating is only approximate and is seldom used.

THE LARGEST AND MOST POWERFUL STEAM LOCOMOTIVES

(See also 'Articulated Steam Locomotives', p. 137 and 'Garratt Locomotives', p. 140.)

The world's largest steam locomotives were the 4–8–8–4 'Big Boys' built by the American Locomotive Company in 1941–44 for the Union Pacific Railroad. Their over-all length was 130 ft 9¼ in (39·852 m), they stood 16 ft 2½ in (4·941 m) high and were 11 ft (3·353 m) wide. With tenders they weighed 1 120 000 lb (508 020 kg) and exerted a tractive effort of 135 375 lb (61 405 kg). On test they developed an indicated horsepower of 7000. The grate area was 150·3 ft² (13·96 m²); heating surface was 5755 ft² (534·6 m²) plus 2043 ft² (189·8 m²) of superheater. Working pressure was 300 lb/in² (21·1 kg/cm²). The four cylinders were 23¾ × 32 in (603 × 813 mm) and coupled wheels 68 in (1727 mm).

Twenty-five were built, for hauling heavy

One of the 'Big Boys' of the Union Pacific Railroad. These 4–8–8–4s were the world's largest locomotives, with a total weight of 344·5 tons. The four cylinders were 23¾ × 32 in (603 × 813 mm), boiler pressure 300 lb/in² (21 kg/cm²), and driving-wheels 5 ft 8 in (1727 mm) diameter (Union Pacific Railroad)

freights on the Sherman Hill section. They could run at speeds up to 80 m.p.h. (129 km/h). Seven have been preserved.

The largest locomotives in Canada were the 2–10–4 'Selkirks' of the Canadian Pacific Railway. The 'T1a' Class Nos. 5900–19 were built by the Montreal Locomotive Works in 1929; the 'T1b' Class, Nos. 5920–29 followed in 1938 and the 'T1c' Class Nos. 5930–35 in 1940. They had 5 ft 3 in (1600 mm) coupled wheels, a working pressure of 285 lb/in² (20 kg/cm²) and cylinders 25 × 32 in (635 × 813 mm). They worked passenger and freight trains through the mountain section of the C.P.R. No. 5934 is preserved at Calgary and No. 5935 at the Canadian Railway Museum near Montreal. **This was the last steam locomotive built for the C.P.R.**

Canadian Pacific 'T1b' Class 2–10–4 'Selkirk'-type locomotive No. 5421. These were the largest steam locomotives in Canada. Cylinders were 25 × 32 in (635 × 813 mm), driving-wheels 5 ft 3 in (1600 mm). They had a tractive effort of 78 000 lb (35 480 kg) and weighed 190 tons (Canadian Pacific Limited)

The largest locomotives in South America were the 216 ton 5 ft 6 in (1·676 m) gauge 4–8–2s supplied by ALCO to the Chilean State Railways in 1940.

No. 1110, one of the 4–8–2s built by ALCO in 1940 for the 5 ft 6 in (1·676 m) gauge Chilean State Railways. These were the largest steam locomotives in South America (John Marshall)

The largest metre-gauge engines in South America were the 181 ton 4–8–2 + 2–8–4 Garratts built by Beyer Peacock & Company, Manchester, in 1950 for the Antofagasta & Bolivia Railway.

The largest non-articulated locomotives in Australia were the ten '500' Class 4–8–4s Nos. 500–9 built in 1926 by Armstrong Whitworth & Company, Newcastle upon Tyne, for the 1·600 m (5 ft 3 in) gauge South Australian Government Railways. They were 25·653 m (84 ft 2 in) long with tenders and weighed 222·3 tons. They had 1·600 m (5 ft 3 in) driving-wheels. No. 504, withdrawn on 9 July 1962 with a mileage of 855 029 (1 375 993 km), was placed in the Mile End Railway Museum near Adelaide, maintained by the Australian Railway Historical Society, on 23 July 1965.

The world's most powerful steam locomotive on a tractive effort basis was a triplex articulated 2–8–8–8–4 Mallet compound tank engine built by Baldwin, Philadelphia, in 1916 for the Virginian Railroad—No. 700. It had a tractive effort of 166 300 lb (75 428 kg) working compound and 99 560 lb (90 516 kg) working simple, that is with high-pressure steam to all six cylinders. These were all 34×32 in (864 × 813 mm), coupled wheels were 4 ft 8 in (1422 mm), grate area 108·2 ft² (10·052 m²), total heating surface 8120 ft² (754 m²), total weight 377 tons.

The engine was under-boilered and quickly ran short of steam, and in 1921, following delivery of the ALCO 2–10–10–2s mentioned below, the engine was divided, the rear portion being rebuilt into a 2–8–2 tender engine and the front portion into a 2–8–8–0 Mallet, No. 610. This was later rebuilt into a 2–8–8–2 and was withdrawn in the early 1950s. It was the only Mallet to have enjoyed three wheel arrangements.

The biggest boilers and biggest cylinders ever used on a locomotive were on the ten 2–10–10–2 Mallets built by ALCO in 1918 for the Virginian Railroad, Nos. 800–809. The boilers had a maximum diameter of 9 ft 10½ in (3·009 m). The grate was 9 ft × 12 ft (2·743 × 3·658 m). Evaporative heating surface was 8600 ft² (799 m²) plus 2120 ft² (197 m²) of superheater. The low-pressure cylinders were 48 in (1219 mm) diameter × 32 in (813 mm) stroke. The engines stood 16 ft 7½ in (4·877 m) high. They worked until the railway was electrified in 1926, banking mile long coal trains weighing 10000 tons to over 15000 tons up the 11 miles (17·7 km) of 2·1 per cent grade at Clark's Gap. They were withdrawn from 1948 to 1958.

The largest three-cylinder engines ever built were the Union Pacific 4–12–2s. The first, No. 9000, was completed at Schenectady, New

Front view of Union Pacific 4–12–2 No. 9000, showing the arrangement of the three cylinders and valves (Union Pacific Railroad)

The first of the Union Pacific 4–12–2s, No. 9000, built by ALCO in 1926. These were the world's largest three-cylinder locomotives. They regularly exceeded 60 m.p.h. (97 km/h) in ordinary service. The cylinders were 27 × 31 in (685·8 × 787·4 mm), driving-wheels were 5 ft 7 in (1702 mm) diameter and they had a tractive effort of 96 600 lb (43 800 kg). The engine wheelbase was 52 ft 4 in (15·951 m) and the weight was 220 tons (Union Pacific Railroad)

York, in April 1926. A total of 88 were built, the last, No. 9087 in 1930. They were also the only 4–12–2s, and the only 12-coupled engines to exceed 60 m.p.h. (97 km/h) in normal service. Apart from the experimental Russian 4–14–4, they had the longest rigid wheelbase in the world, and they were the first non-articulated locomotives to exceed 100 ft (30·5 m) in length over drawbars. They were the first three-cylinder engines to have cast-steel cylinders.

The largest French express passenger engine was the '242A' Class three-cylinder compound 4–8–4, rebuilt by Chapelon in 1946. It had a starting tractive effort of 47 000 lb (21 319 kg) and could run up to 100 m.p.h. (161 km/h). The coupled wheels were 6 ft 4¾ in (1950 mm) diameter, and the engine weighed 145 tons.

The Great Southern Railway three-cylinder 4–6–0 No. 800 Maeve at Cork—the largest locomotive type in Ireland (John Marshall)

The largest French express passenger engine, three-cylinder compound 4–8–4 No. 242-A-1, rebuilt by Chapelon in 1946 (French Railways Limited)

The largest tank engines to run on any British railway were the ten 4–6–4 'Baltics' built by the London, Midland & Scottish Railway at the former Lancashire & Yorkshire Railway Works at Horwich to the design of George Hughes (1865–1945), then the chief mechanical engineer. Thirty were to have been built, but insufficient suitable work led to the last 20 being turned out as 4–6–0 tender engines. They had four cylinders 16½ × 26 in (419 × 660 mm) and 6 ft 3 in (1905 mm) coupled wheels.

The last of the 4–6–4 tanks was withdrawn in 1941, largely because they were a non-standard class.

The Hughes 'Baltic' tank, the London, Midland & Scottish Railway No. 11111, the largest tank locomotive type in Britain. The four cylinders were 16½ × 26 in (419 × 660 mm) and driving-wheels were 6 ft 3 in (1905 mm). The length over buffers was 49 ft 10½ in (15·2 m) and height to chimney-top 13 ft 5 in (4089 mm) (British Rail)

The largest locomotives in Ireland were the Great Southern Railway three-cylinder 4–6–0s of which three were built at Inchicore, Dublin, in 1939–40 to a design prepared under E. C. Bredin, chief mechanical engineer. The first, No. 800 Maeve, is illustrated. They were built for the Dublin–Cork expresses.

The largest driving-wheels used on any engine in Britain were 10 ft (3·048 m) diameter on the freak Great Western 2–2–2 built by Mather, Dixon & Company of Liverpool to a specification by I. K. Brunel and delivered on 12 December 1838. It 'worked' until June 1840.

The largest driving-wheels in regular use in Britain were 9 ft (2·743 m) on the eight magnificent 4–2–4 tank engines built for the 7 ft (2·134 m) gauge Bristol & Exeter Railway by Rothwell & Company of Bolton, Lancashire, to a design by James Pearson in 1854. One of these, No. 41, achieved a record speed of 81·8 m.p.h. (131·6 km/h) on Wellington Bank, Somerset, in June 1854, which remained the highest authenticated rail speed until 1890. They were replaced by new B. & E. engines of the same wheel arrangement in 1868–73.

The largest coupled wheels ever used in Britain were 7 ft 7¼ in (2·318 m) diameter on Wilson Worsdell's 'Q1' Class 4–4–0s Nos. 1869 and 1870 on the North Eastern Railway. Two were built in 1896 for taking part in the railway races to the north (see p. 176).

ARTICULATED STEAM LOCOMOTIVES

The articulated locomotive with one or two swivelling power bogies was developed to provide great power on lines with severe curvature, or to spread the weight of a large locomotive over many axles to enable it to work on light track. The principal types have been the Fairlie, Meyer, Mallet and Garratt.

The world's first articulated locomotive was a 2–2–2–2 built at West Point Foundry, New York, in 1832 for the South Carolina Railroad, U.S.A. It had a central firebox and four boilers, two at each end. It was designed by Horatio Allen (see p. 40) and formed the basis of the Fairlie type. Each engine had one central cylinder.

The next stage towards the Fairlie design was the 0–4–4–0 built by John Cockerill & Cie of Seraing, Belgium, for trials on the Semmering line in Austria, in 1851.

Robert F. Fairlie (see p. 52) was a Scotsman. He patented his articulated locomotive design on 12 May 1863 in England and on 23 November 1864 in France. The first was an 0–4–4–0 called *Progress*, built in 1865 by Cross & Company of St Helens, Lancashire, and supplied to the Neath & Brecon Railway, Wales. It had two boilers, with back to back fireboxes and a power bogie under each. Later ones had a single common central firebox.

One of three 0–6–6–0 Fairlie locomotives built by Vulcan Foundry, England in 1911 for the standard-gauge Mexican Railway, for handling 300 ton trains up gradients of 1 in 25. They weighed 138 tons

Most Fairlies were o–4–4–o and o–6–6–o, the largest being some 102 tons o–6–6–os for Mexico. The last was built in 1915 for the 60 cm (1 ft 11½ in) gauge lines on the French war front. The only survivors are on the 1 ft 11½ in gauge Festiniog Railway in Wales for which the first, *Little Wonder*, was built in 1870 (see colour illustration on p. 139).

Jean Jacques Meyer (1804–77) and his son Adolphe (1840–91) of Mulhouse, France, patented the Meyer articulated locomotive on 15 March 1861 (French Patent No. 48993). It had the cylinders at the inner ends of the power bogies. The first type, o–4–4–o, was built by Fives of Lille in 1868. The design restricted the ashpan, but the **Kitson-Meyer** type, developed at Leeds, England, overcame this by lengthening the frame and placing the firebox between the power bogies, each of which had the cylinders at the rear end.

The first Kitson-Meyer was a o–6–6–o built in 1903 for the 3 ft 6 in (1·067 m) gauge Anglo-Chilean Nitrate & Railway Company of South America. A later development, introduced in 1908, had the cylinders at the outer ends of the bogies. Some of these show the influence of the Garratt design but differ from this in having a single rigid frame mounted on the power bogies. The Garratt design gained in avoiding this duplication of framing.

The first articulated locomotives in Africa were the 3 ft 6 in (1·067 m) gauge Kitson-Meyer o–6–6–os built by Kitson for Rhodesia in 1903. At the time they were the largest and most powerful engines in southern Africa.

The largest articulated locomotives were the Mallets, patented by Anatole Mallet (see p. 53) in 1884. These were four-cylinder compounds with the high-pressure engine in the fixed rear frame and the low-pressure engine in the pivoted front frame. The first Mallet was a 60 cm (1 ft 11½ in) gauge o–4–4–o tank built in 1887 by Ateliers Métallurgiques at Tubize, Belgium.

The largest Mallet tanks (except the Virginian RR 2–8–8–8–4, p. 135) were the o–8–8–os built by Maffei in Germany for the Bavarian State Railways in 1913–14 and 1922–23. The first batch weighed 271 500 lb or 121 tons.

The first Mallet in North America was a o–6–6–o built by ALCO in 1903 for the Baltimore & Ohio Railroad. It was followed by five 2–6–6–2s built by Baldwin in 1906 for the Great Northern Railway.

The first of the Southern Pacific 'cab-in-front' Mallets was built in 1910. They were designed to enable the crews to escape the exhaust fumes in the numerous tunnels and snow-sheds in the Sierra Nevada, U.S.A., in which the line climbs nearly 7000 ft (2133 m) from Sacramento to the summit in 100 miles (161 km) and 2000 ft (610 m) from Reno in 50 miles (80 km). The engines ran 'backwards' with the tender coupled beyond the smokebox. Oil fuel was delivered to the firebox under pressure.

The greatest of all Mallets, the Union Pacific 4–8–8–4 'Big Boys' first built by ALCO in 1941, were not strictly Mallets because they were not compounds. The engines are described on p. 134.

The largest Russian locomotives, the 'P38' 2–8–8–4s of 1954–55, were likewise not true Mallets. They weighed 214·9 tons without tenders.

The last active simple-expansion Mallets are the 2–6–6–2s built by Baldwin in 1941–49 for the metre-gauge Donna Theresa Cristina Railway in Brazil, Nos. 200–5. Some were still at work in October 1974 when the photograph below was taken.

The o–4–4–o Mallet tank engine built for the Swiss Central Railway by J. A. Maffei of Munich (No. 1710) in 1893. Photographed at Lucerne Transport Museum (John Marshall)

One of the last active simple-expansion 'Mallets', a Baldwin 2–6–6–2 built in 1941 for the metre-gauge Donna Theresa Cristina Railway, Brazil, photographed at Tubarao in October 1974 (John Marshall)

No. 600 Gordon, *the second of the Ministry of Supply 2–10–0s, built by the North British Locomotive Company, Glasgow, in 1943. From then until 1969 it worked on the Longmoor Military Railway, Hampshire. It is now on the Severn Valley Railway where it was photographed at Bridgnorth, Shropshire, in July 1974 (John Marshall)*

Festiniog Railway 0–4–4–0 'Fairlie'-type locomotive No. 10 Merddin Emrys *(1879), one of the only two remaining Fairlies, at Portmadoc in 1971 (Simon Marshall)*

Former London, Brighton & South Coast Railway 'Terrier' Class 0–6–0 tank, originally No. 70 Poplar, *built in December 1872. In 1901 it was sold to the Kent & East Sussex Railway becoming No. 3* Bodiam. *It is still at work on the K. & E.S.R. (J. P. Wilson)*

The Du Bousquet 0–6–2+ 2–6–0 tank locomotive (French Railways Limited)

The world's most powerful steam locomotives on a potential horsepower basis were the 2–8–8–4 simple-expansion 'Mallets' of the Northern Pacific Railroad, U.S.A. The first, built by ALCO in 1928, was the first locomotive to weigh over 1 000 000 lb (453 600 kg) with tender. Eleven more were built by Baldwin in 1930. They had a grate area of 182 ft² (16·9 m²), **the largest ever carried by any locomotive**, a heating surface of 7666 ft² (712·3 m²) plus 3219 ft² (299 m²) of superheater and a boiler pressure of 250 lb/in² (17·6 kg/cm²). This gave them the highest potential horsepower of any steam locomotive. The large grate, however, was designed to burn anthracite, so the steaming rate was lower than could have been achieved with bituminous coal. So the maximum potential power of these engines was never fully exploited. They had a tractive effort of 145 930 lb (66 193 kg) with a booster adding 13 400 lb (6078 kg). The ALCO engine was the first Mallet to have a booster.

The heaviest train ever hauled by a single locomotive was probably one of 15 300 tons made up of 250 freight cars stretching for 1·6 miles (2·6 km) at 13·5 m.p.h. (21 km/h), by the world's then largest locomotive, Erie Railroad 2–8–8–8–2 No. 5014 *Matt H. Shay*, the first of three built in 1914–18 for banking freight trains up the 1 in 67 Susquehanna Incline in Pennsylvania. The engines were withdrawn in 1929.

One of the most interesting articulated locomotive designs was produced by Gaston Du Bousquet (see p. 54). It was a revival of the Wiener-Neustadt 0–4–4–0 tank locomotive built for the Semmering Contest, Austria, in 1851. The Du Bousquet was a four-cylinder compound 0–6–2+2–6–0 with cylinders at the inner ends of the power bogies. The first examples were built in 1905–11 for the French Nord and Est systems and the Peking–Hankow Railway, China, and in 1911 some further engines were built for the 1·672 m (5 ft 6 in) gauge Andalusian Railway, Spain.

GARRATT LOCOMOTIVES

Herbert William Garratt (see p. 58) invented the type of articulated engine named after him which was developed by the firm of Beyer Peacock & Company, Manchester, England.

The first Garratts were two tiny 0–4–0+ 0–4–0s built in 1909 for the 610 mm (2 ft) gauge North East Dundas Tramway, Tasmania. They were untypical in that they were compounds and had the cylinders at the inner ends of the engine units. They ran until 1930. In 1947 No. K1 was shipped back to England and after being stored at Beyer Peacock's in Manchester it is now on the Festiniog Railway in Wales where, however, it will have to undergo drastic alterations before it can run within the small F.R. loading gauge.

One of the first two Garratt locomotives built in 1909 for the 2 ft (610 mm) gauge North East Dundas Tramway, Tasmania. They were unusual in being compounds and in having the cylinders at the inner ends of the bogies (North Western Museum of Science & Industry, Manchester)

The first conventional Garratt with four simple-expansion cylinders at the outer ends of the engines was built in 1911 for the 2 ft (610 mm) gauge Darjeeling Himalayan Railway (see p. 224).

The first 'regular' Garratt; the 2 ft (610 mm) gauge 0–4–4–0 built in 1911 for the Darjeeling Himalayan Railway, India (North Western Museum of Science & Industry, Manchester)

The Tasmanian Government Railway 'M' Class Garratt was a 1·067 m (3 ft 6 in) gauge 4–4–2+2–4–4, and was remarkable for having eight cylinders and for running at speeds up to 88·5 km/h (55 m.p.h.). The coupled wheels were 1·524 m (5 ft) diameter. They were introduced in 1912 and ran until 1951.

The most powerful locomotives in South Africa are the South African Railways 'GL' Class Garratts—3 ft 6 in (1·676 m) gauge 4–8–2+ 2–8–4s—first built in 1929 by Beyer Peacock & Company. They weigh 211·1 tons and have a tractive effort of 78650 lb (35675 kg).

The first Garratt passenger locomotive was built by Beyer Peacock in 1915 for the 1·600 m (5 ft 3 in) gauge São Paulo Railway, Brazil. It was a 2–4–0+0–4–2 and ran until 1950.

The world's first express passenger Garratts were also built for the São Paulo Railway, as 2–6–2+2–6–2s, in 1927. In 1931–32 they were rebuilt as 4–6–2+2–6–4s. They regularly ran trains at 96·5 km/h (60 m.p.h.).

One of the Garratts built in Germany under licence from Beyer Peacock & Company for the South African Railways, in 1927–8. 'GF' Class 4–6–2+2–6–4 No. 2393 built by Hanomag, Hanover, in 1927, working a passenger train near Durban on 21 April 1943 (John Marshall)

The largest and most powerful metre-gauge steam locomotives are the 4–8–2+2–8–4 '59' Class Garratts built for the East African Railways. Thirty-four were built by Beyer Peacock and were delivered in 1955. The boiler is 7 ft 6 in diameter (2·286 m), the total weight is 251·68 tons and they produce a tractive effort of 73500 lb (33339 kg). They are now the world's largest and most powerful steam locomotives.

The largest and most powerful locomotive in Great Britain was the 2–8–0+0–8–2 Garratt built by Beyer Peacock in 1925 for the London & North Eastern Railway for banking coal trains from Wath up to Penistone in Yorkshire. It was numbered 2395 and classed 'U1'. Its two engine units were standard with H. N. Gresley's three-cylinder 2–8–0s.

East African Railways '59' Class Garratt No. 5903 built in 1955. Today these engines are the largest and most powerful steam locomotives in the world (North Western Museum of Science & Industry, Manchester)

The London & North Eastern Railway Garratt, the largest and most powerful locomotive in Great Britain. It had six cylinders and weighed 178 tons (North Western Museum of Science & Industry, Manchester)

A Budd rail-diesel-car set at Squamish on the British Columbia Railway in 1972 (John Marshall)

'Class 87' electric locomotive on a Scottish express at Preston in 1974. These 5000 hp 25 kV locomotives are the most powerful in Britain (John Marshall)

Burlington Northern commuter train of three 'gallery cars' headed by single-end diesel unit No. 9933 amid light snow at Eola, Illinois, U.S.A. (Paul Meyer)

Britain's last Garratt was a 0–4–0+0–4–0 built in 1937 for the Baddesley Colliery near Atherstone, Warwickshire, where it worked until 1965. It had a 5 ft (1·524 m) diameter boiler and weighed 61·5 tons. It is now preserved at Bressingham, Norfolk.

The largest locomotives in New Zealand were the three 4–6–2+2–6–4 Garratts built in 1920. They weighed 145·8 tons. These were the only six-cylinder Garratts exported from England and were the first locomotives in New Zealand to have mechanical stokers, exhaust steam injectors, steam reversing gear and grease lubrication to coupled axleboxes.

They were too powerful, however, for the couplings then in use, and loops were too short for the trains they could pull. After transfer from the North to the South Island in 1936, the engine units were built into six 'Pacific'-type tender engines. But their design was faulty and in 1955–56 they became the first New Zealand main-line engines to be replaced by diesels.

The largest, heaviest and most powerful steam locomotives in Australia were the 'AD60' Class 4–8–4+4–8–4 Garratts on the standard-gauge New South Wales Government Railways. They were the first Garratts to have cast-steel engine-bed frames incorporating cylinders (see p. 129). They were introduced in 1952 and weighed 264·75 tons in working order.

No. 6042, built by Beyer Peacock in 1952, was the last completed Garratt to be delivered to Australia and was the last Australian steam locomotive in regular service, being withdrawn in 1973.

The largest Garratt locomotive ever built was completed by Beyer Peacock in 1932 for the U.S.S.R. railways where it was classed 'Ya-01'. It was a 4–8–2+2–8–4 standing 17 ft (5·182 m) high, with bar-frames and a boiler 7 ft 6 in (2·286 m) diameter. It weighed 262·5 tons and had a tractive effort of 78 700 lb (35 698 kg).

The last Garratt to operate in Britain, the 0–4–0+0–4–0 William Francis at Baddesley Colliery near Atherstone, Warwickshire in April 1964 (John Marshall)

New South Wales Government Railway 'AD60' Class Garratt. These standard-gauge engines, built in 1952, were the largest, heaviest and most powerful steam locomotives in Australia (North Western Museum of Science & Industry, Manchester)

The largest Garratt locomotive ever built, the single 'Я–01' built by Beyer Peacock & Company for the Russian Railways in 1932 (North Western Museum of Science & Industry, Manchester)

The smallest Garratts ever built were the two 0–6–0+0–6–0s built in 1913 for the Arakan Flotilla Company of Burma, for 2 ft 6 in (762 mm) gauge, with a wheelbase of 24 ft 2 in (7·320 m). They weighed 23·55 tons.

GEARED STEAM LOCOMOTIVES

Geared locomotives were produced to three basic designs, principally to negotiate light temporary tracks over rough ground with steep gradients.

The 'Shay' geared locomotive was invented by Ephraim Shay (1839–1916) and was produced by the Lima Machine Works, Ohio, U.S.A. (from 1901 the Lima Locomotive & Machine Company). The first appeared in 1880. It had a three-cylinder vertical engine on one side and the two bogies were driven by a system of shafts, universal couplings and spur gears. On level track it could reach a speed of 19 m.p.h. (30·578 km/h) and on gradients of 6 to 14 per cent (1 in 16·7 to 1 in 7) it could move loads at 7·5 to 4 m.p.h. (12 to 6·5 km/h).

Standard-gauge 'Shay' No. 3 of the Mayo Lumber Company, at Cowichan Valley Museum near Victoria, Vancouver Island (John Marshall)

The Climax locomotive was built by the Climax Manufacturing Company of Corry, Pennsylvania. It had two sloping cylinders, one on each side, connected by gearing and longitudinal

shafts to the two bogies. The company operated from 1884 to 1930.

Climax *the 3 ft 6 in (1·067 m) gauge No. 9 of the Hillcrest Lumber Company, at the Cowichan Valley Museum near Victoria, Vancouver Island (John Marshall)*

Another type had a two-cylinder high-speed vertical steam-engine driving the bogies through a two-speed gear-box. A similar design was produced by the Baldwin Locomotive Works, Philadelphia.

The Heisler-type locomotive was first built by the Stearns Manufacturing Company, Erie, Pennsylvania, the first being completed on 20 August 1894 for service in Mexico. The Heisler Locomotive Works, Erie, began production of this type in 1898. It had two cylinders arranged like a V beneath the boiler, driving a longitudinal shaft geared to the bogies. This was the neatest and soundest of the three designs, but the Shay was the most popular.

Heisler-type 0–4–4–0 geared locomotive, stored at Chicago in 1972 (John Marshall)

OIL FUEL FOR STEAM LOCOMOTIVES

Some of the earliest experiments with oil fuel were made in the 1870s by a British engineer Thomas Urquhart. Similar experiments began in France in 1869. The advantage of oil fuel over coal is principally the avoidance of ash, but its use depends largely on the price and availability of fuel. An oil-fired steam-engine is still an inefficient machine producing only half of the work done by a diesel engine using the same amount of oil.

In the U.S.A. early experiments with oil fuel were abandoned because of the cost and it was not taken up again until the 1890s.

The first regular use of oil fuel was on the Russian South Eastern Railway in 1883–84, using the Urquhart system.

In the U.S.A. an oil-burning locomotive made successful test runs from Altoona to Pittsburg, Pennsylvania, and back on 17–18 June 1887.

Oil fuel was first used in Britain by the Great Eastern Railway. In 1887 James Holden, the locomotive superintendent (see p. 53), invented an arrangement for burning the waste product from the plant producing oil gas for carriage lighting. It was tried on the Johnson 0–4–4 tank No. 193 and was first regularly used on a 4–2–2 which was named *Petrolea*. About 60 engines were so fitted, but the apparatus was removed when the price of oil rose to an uneconomic level.

One of James Holden's liquid fuel burners, sectioned for demonstration purposes (The Science Museum, London)

The first oil-burning locomotive in Canada was introduced about 1910, converted from a coal-burner for work in the Rocky Mountains. The first complete class of oil-burners was built by the Canadian Pacific Railway in 1917–19.

In 1947 many British locomotives, on the Great Western, Southern and London & North Eastern railways, and on the Irish railways, were fitted up to burn oil fuel during the acute coal shortage in Britain. However, the increasing cost of oil led to its removal after very little use.

The strangest fuel ever used for steam locomotives was probably llama dung and dried moss burnt on two 60 cm (1 ft 11½ in) gauge 0–4–0 tanks on the Orenstein & Coppel Railway in Chile, a branch off the Arica–La Paz Railway.

In South Africa, during a crop surplus, coffee beans were used as fuel for steam locomotives.

STEAM-TURBINE LOCOMOTIVES

The first steam-turbine locomotive was designed by Professor Belluzzo and was built in Milan, Italy, in 1908 by S.A. Officine Mechaniche. It was a 0–4–0 side-tank engine. The four turbines were single-wheel velocity compound type with the lower part of the blades for forward drive and the upper part for backward.

A steam-turbine-electric locomotive was designed by Sir Hugh Reid and W. M. Ramsey and was built in Glasgow in 1910 by the North British Locomotive Company of which Reid (1860–1935) was chairman and chief managing director. An impulse-type turbine with condenser was coupled to a variable voltage dynamo which supplied the four d.c. traction motors at 200–600 V.

A second Ramsey-type locomotive, a 0–6–6–2 type, was completed in 1922 and was tested by George Hughes at Horwich on the Lancashire & Yorkshire Railway, and on the North Eastern Railway. Turbines and electrical equipment were by Oerlikon, Switzerland. It was built by Armstrong Whitworth & Company, Newcastle upon Tyne.

The Zoelly turbine locomotive was converted from a Swiss Federal Railways 4–6–0 in 1921 by the Swiss Locomotive & Machine Works, Winterthur. It had a 1200 hp impulse turbine across the front of the machine, driving the wheels by gearing and a jack-shaft and side-rods. A surface condenser was positioned beneath the boiler. A similar engine built by Krupp of Essen, Germany, in 1922 ran on the German State Railways.

The Ljungstrom turbine condensing locomotive was first built in 1921 at the Ljungstrom Locomotive Works near Stockholm, Sweden.

*The third Ljungstrom steam-
turbine condensing loeomotive
built by Beyer Peacock &
Company of Manchester in 1926
(North Western Museum of
Science & Industry, Manchester)*

It was rebuilt in 1922 but was withdrawn in 1924.

The second, built at Trollhattan in 1924–25 to the metre gauge for the Argentine State Railway, was capable of travelling 500 miles (805 km, without rewatering.

The third, built by Beyer Peacock & Company at Manchester, England, in 1926 was given extensive trials on the Midland section of the London, Midland & Scottish Railway. It suffered in the numerous tunnels where soot entered the condenser and caused blockages. A fourth, and last, built in 1927, was similar in design and gave good scrvice in Sweden for many years.

In 1932 some non-condensing Ljungstrom locomotives were built in Sweden and they worked iron-ore trains of 1831 tons on the Grängesberg–Oxelösund Railway from the Bergslag to the Baltic coast until displaced by electrification.

The Reid-Macleod turbine locomotive
was built by the North British Locomotive Company of Glasgow in 1923–24. It was a 4–4–4–4 with high- and low-pressure turbines and an air-cooled condenser. It had an output of 1000 b.h.p.

The London, Midland & Scottish Railway turbine 'Pacific'
No. 6202 was a non-condensing machine with one turbine for forward running and a smaller one for reverse. It was built at Crewe in 1935 to the design of William Stanier (1876–1965) and ran successfully on the London–Liverpool expresses. In 1952 it was rebuilt into a conventional engine and named *Princess Anne*, but after only a few months' service it was involved in the collision at Harrow and Wealdstone Station on 8 October 1952 and was subsequently scrapped.

The Union Pacific Railroad, U.S.A.
had a pair of steam-turbine-electric locomotives built by the General Electric Company in 1937–39. They were of the 2–Co–Co–2 type and could work either singly or together under the control of one man. They had a maximum speed of 125 m.p.h. (201 km/h). They each had high- and low-pressure

turbines and condensers, and together had an output of 5000 hp. The semi-flash-type boiler worked at a pressure of 1500 lb/in² (105·46 kg/cm²).

The first direct-drive turbine locomotive in the U.S.A.
was the Pennsylvania Railroad No. 6200, a 6–8–6 type non-condensing machine built by Baldwin in 1944 in co-operation with the Westinghouse Company. Like the L.M.S. machine of 1935, described above, it had two turbines, one forward developing 6500 hp at 70 m.p.h. (113 km/h) and a reverse developing 1500 hp at 22 m.p.h. (35·5 km/h). This magnificent looking machine ran for only five years.

The impressive Pennsylvania Railroad 6–8–6 non-condensing turbine locomotive No. 6200, built in 1944 and withdrawn in 1949 (Altoona Area Public Library)

The Chesapeake & Ohio Railroad
obtained three giant steam-turbine-electric locomotives built by Baldwin and Westinghouse in 1947–49. They were 154 ft (47 m) long 2–D+2–D–2 type with a starting tractive effort of 98000 lb (4445 kg) and a continuous of 48000 lb (2177 kg). They had a short existence because of the closure of the passenger service for which they were obtained, and also because of design faults.

The Norfolk & Western Railroad
obtained a 4500 hp turbine-electric non-condensing locomotive in 1954, built by the Baldwin-Lima-

Hamilton Corporation with the Westinghouse Company, and a boiler by Babcock & Wilcox. It measured 61 ft 1½ in (49 m) long and weighed 525 tons in working order. It could run up to 60 m.p.h. (96·5 km/h). It was numbered 2300. Although it showed marked economy in coal consumption, it was displaced in 1958 by diesels and was scrapped.

LARGE CLASSES OF LOCOMOTIVES

The largest class of locomotives to be built in Britain was the Ramsbottom 'DX' Class 0–6–0 of the London & North Western Railway, of which 943 were built between 1858 and 1874, including 86 for the Lancashire & Yorkshire Railway in 1871–74.

On the Great Western Railway a total of 863 0–6–0 pannier tanks of the '5700' Class were built between 1929 and 1950. The basic design dated back to the '645' Class of 1872 and the similar '1813', '1854' and '2721' Classes of which a total of 358 were built up to 1901. No. 5764 is still active on the Severn Valley Railway, Shropshire, and No. 5775 on the Keighley & Worth Valley Railway, Yorkshire, both built at Swindon in 1929. No. 5786 (1929) is at Hereford (Worcester Locomotive Society); the Severn Valley Railway has also preserved No. 7714 (1930), while Nos. 7752 and 7760 (1930) are in working order at Birmingham Railway Museum at Tyseley. No. 7715 (1930) is at Quainton Road, Buckinghamshire; Nos. 3738 (1937) and 3650 (1939) are preserved at Didcot, Berkshire, by the Great Western Society, and Nos. 4612 (1942), 9629 (1945) and 9681 (1949) are also earmarked for preservation. So the '5700' class can also claim to be one of the most numerous classes of preserved locomotives.

The railway with the greatest number of 0–6–0s in Britain was the Midland. In 1917 it had 1495, about 21 per cent of the total for the whole country. The '4F' 0–6–0s reached a total of 772. The next largest total of 0–6–0s was on the North Eastern Railway which had 777.

The largest class of modern locomotives in Britain was the London, Midland & Scottish Railway 'Class 5' 4–6–0 designed by William Stanier and first built in 1934. Including several variations in the design, the class eventually numbered 842 engines. A total of 13 has been preserved.

The first locomotive type to be adopted by the British Government for war service was the Great Central '8K' Class 2–8–0 designed by J. G. Robinson (1856–1943) and first built at Gorton, Manchester, in 1911. During the First World War many were built by the G.C.R. and by other locomotive-builders making a grand total of 647 engines. After the war they were dispersed, most going to the London & North Eastern Railway (as successor to the G.C.R.) where they were classed '04' and others to the Great Western Railway and to China, Australia and elsewhere. Many of them put in over 50 years' hard service. They were among the finest British freight engines.

One of the Robinson 2–8–0s of the Great Central Railway (John Marshall)

The German 'Austerity' 2–10–0, introduced in 1941, numbered more than 8000 when the last was built in 1947.

The world's largest class of locomotives was the Russian 'E' Class 0–10–0 introduced in 1912 and at length numbering about 14000 engines.

Between 1891 and 1923 9500 'o' Class 0–8–0s were built in Russia.

The largest class of steam locomotives to be built in the British Commonwealth was the Indian 5 ft 6 in (1·676 m) gauge 'WG' Class 2–8–2 first built in 1950 and eventually totalling 2450.

The largest classes in the U.S.A. were the U.S.R.A. (United States Railroad Administration) 0–8–0s numbering 1375, and the 'light' 2–8–2s numbering 1266, built 1919–20.

The Canadian Pacific Railway 'D' Class 4–6–0s totalled over 1000, but there were ten different types and variations within these, built from 1902 to 1915. The 'D10' Class, built 1905–13, totalled 502.

VETERAN LOCOMOTIVES

One of the longest lived locomotives of British Railways was the former Lancashire & Yorkshire Railway 0–6–0 saddle tank, latterly No. 11305. It was built as a 0–6–0 tender locomotive in 1877 to an order of Barton Wright, locomotive superintendent, rebuilt to a saddle tank in 1891 and withdrawn in September 1964 aged 87.

The last Lancashire & Yorkshire Railway 0–6–0 saddle tank, originally built in 1877 as a tender engine, photographed in October 1964 just after withdrawal, aged 87 (John Marshall)

Another long-lived British locomotive was former Midland Railway 2–4–0 No. 158A, built at Derby in 1866 to a design of Matthew Kirtley and, after some rebuilding, withdrawn in July 1947 as L M.S. No. 20002, aged 81. It is now preserved in Leicester Museum.

Former Midland Railway 2–4–0 No. 158A, originally built in 1866, photographed as the London, Midland & Scottish Railway No. 20002 leaving Nottingham London Road Low Level Station with a train to Northampton in April 1939 (J. P. Wilson)

The oldest locomotive still active in Britain is *Prince*, No. 2 on the 1 ft 11½ in (600 mm) gauge Festiniog Railway in Wales. It was built by George England, London, in 1863 (see illustration on p. 179) and was subsequently rebuilt in 1892, 1904, 1920, 1937 and 1955–56. (See also 'Narrow-Gauge Railways', p. 218.)

The oldest active standard-gauge engine in Britain is the former London, Brighton & South Coast Railway 'Terrier' 0–6–0 tank No. 72 *Fenchurch* which entered service in September 1872, one of the first two of its type, designed by William Stroudley (1833–89). It is now at work on the Bluebell Railway in Sussex.

The fame and esteem which this class of 50 tiny engines inspired was out of all proportion to their size. No other locomotive type has gained such warm affection. Several others are preserved in England, and one can even be seen in the Canadian Railway Historical Society's Museum near Montreal. (See colour illustration p. 139.)

As spring buffers became universal on engines of the Great Western Railway, England, during the 1850s and 1860s, the original buffers of leather stuffed with horse-hair were sold for use as music-stools.

Henry Ford's famous retort on the painting of his cars was anticipated by Richard Moon, chairman of the London & North Western Railway, who told John Ramsbottom, the locomotive superintendent: 'It is a matter of complete indifference to me what colour you paint our engines so long as they are black.' L.N.W.R. engines were first painted black, instead of green, on 17 April 1873.

LOCOMOTIVE BUILDING RECORDS

In February 1888 Francis William Webb (1835–1904), locomotive superintendent of the London & North Western Railway, had a 0–6–0 goods engine constructed in Crewe Works in 25½ hours.

The 0–4–0 Prince, No. 2 on the Festiniog Railway, Wales, the oldest active locomotive in Britain, in its present form after much rebuilding, photographed at Portmadoc in 1963 (John Marshall)

The following June this record was reduced to 16¼ hours by the Pennsylvania Railroad at the Altoona Works, U.S.A.

The all-time record was achieved by the Great Eastern Railway under James Holden (see p. 53) at Stratford, London. On 10 December 1891 0–6–0 No. 930 was completely assembled and given one coat of paint in 9 hours 57 minutes. It was steamed and tested on the line immediately afterwards. As the London & North Eastern Railway 'J15' Class No. 7930 this engine ran until 1935.

THE LAST STEAM LOCOMOTIVES

The last steam locomotive built for British Railways was the standard 2–10–0 No. 92220 *Evening Star* completed at Swindon in March 1960 (see colour illustration p. 159).

The last steam locomotives in France were the American '141R' Class 2–8–2s, a fine rugged modern design by Baldwin imported after the Second World War to help in the rehabilitation of the French railways. They were equally at home on freight and passenger trains.

The last steam locomotives built in Russia were completed in 1956. They were the 'L' Class 2–10–0s, making a class totalling about 4700; the 'LV' Class 2–10–2s and the 'P36' Class 4–8–4s.

The last steam locomotive to be built for service in North America was the Norfolk & Western 'S1a' Class 0–8–0 switcher No. 224, outshopped from Roanoke Works in December 1953. It worked only until 1960 when steam finally disappeared from the N. & W.

The last steam locomotives built by Baldwin Locomotive Works, U.S.A. were 50 'WG' Class 2–8–2s for India, 5 ft 6 in (1·676 m) gauge, in 1955. Their price was about twice that tendered by European and Japanese builders. The last built for domestic use in the U.S.A. was a 2–8–0 for the U.S. Army Transportation School at Fort Eustis, Virginia, in 1952.

The last steam locomotive on the Southern Pacific Railroad, U.S.A. made its last run, from San Francisco to Reno, in 1958.

The last steam locomotive to be built in Australia was 'B 18¼' Class 4–6–2 No. 1086 on the 3 ft 6 in (1·067 m) gauge Queensland Government Railways, built in 1958 by Walkers of Maryborough (Works No. 557). It was 60 ft 3 in (18·354 m) long and weighed 101·2 tons. It was withdrawn in 1969, one of the last to run, having covered only 247450 miles (898873 km).

The last Australian State Government Railway to make regular use of steam locomotives is Tasmania, where three 'H2' Class steam locomotives built in England in 1951, were still being used on the Hobart–Claremont–Hobart service in 1974.

The last main-line steam locomotive to be built might be 'YG' Class metre-gauge 2–8–2 built by Indian Railways at the Chittaranjan Works and completed in February 1972.

The last express passenger engine built in Britain was the 'Class 8' three-cylinder Caprotti valve-gear 4–6–2 No. 71000 *Duke of Gloucester* completed at Crewe in 1954. It was the only one of its type. It was withdrawn in 1962 and after storage with a view towards preservation the valve gear was removed and was installed in the Science Museum, London. The remaining sections are now at Loughborough, Leicestershire, being restored by the Main Line Steam Trust.

At the end of 1973 a total of 26300 useable steam locomotives remained in world stock. Of these 15000 were in Asia, 5000 in Europe, and 3700 in Africa. India had over 8300, South Africa 2365, Japan and Federal Germany each over 1000. In Great Britain there were 181 in running order of which three belonged to British Rail, on the 1 ft 11½ in (600 mm) gauge Vale of Rheidol Railway.

(See also 'Last Steam Trains', p. 191.)

DIESEL RAIL TRACTION

The 'compression ignition' system was invented by Ackroyd Stuart (1864–1927) who developed the idea between 1886 and 1890.

Dr Rudolf Diesel (1858–1913) was born in Paris and became a professor at Munich. He invented his internal-combustion engine, in 1892, to use a fairly crude oil so as to be less costly to run than a petrol engine. It was first demonstrated in 1898. Dr Diesel who, apparently, refused to allow his engine to be used for war purposes, mysteriously disappeared from a steamer to Harwich during a journey to London in 1913.

Oil burned in a diesel engine produces 1·9 times as much work as the same amount burned in an oil-fired steam locomotive. A diesel locomotive will produce less atmospheric pollution than a steam locomotive for the same amount of work.

The major problem of high-power diesel rail-traction is the transmission from engine to wheels. Mechanical and hydraulic transmissions have been used, but electric transmission is now almost universal. It should be borne in mind that a diesel-electric is simply an electric locomotive carrying its own power-station on board. It produces only about a third, and at best less than half, as much power as a modern electric locomotive of equal weight, even though the latter includes a transformer and rectifier.

The first diesel locomotive was a direct-drive 1000 hp Diesel-Klose-Sulzer unit built in Germany in 1912–13, but it ran for only a few months, as an experiment.

The first diesel railway vehicle in revenue service was an Atlas-Deva 75 bhp diesel-electric railcar built in 1913 for the Mellersta & Södermanlands Railway, Sweden. It ran until 1939.

The first 'production' diesels were five 200 hp diesel-electric railcars built by Sulzer in Switzerland in 1914 for the Prussian & Saxon State Railways.

The first diesel-electric switchers (or 'shunters' in English) were three 200 hp units built in the U.S.A. by the General Electric Company in 1918.

The first 'commercially successful' diesel-electric locomotive in America was a 300 hp unit built by ALCO in 1923, with an Inger-soll-Rand engine and General Electric Company controls and transmission. It went into service on 20 October 1925, followed by four more. The first was sold to the Jersey Central Railroad, becoming No. 1000, and worked until 1957 when it was presented to the Baltimore & Ohio Transportation Museum.

One of the most curious locomotives was the Kitson-Still steam-diesel locomotive built by Kitson & Company of Leeds, England, and tested on the London & North Eastern Railway in April 1927. It was a 2–6–2 tank engine with eight cylinders operating with internal combustion on one side of the piston and with steam on the other side. The internal-combustion engine helped in raising steam. It attempted to combine the power at slow speed of the steam-engine with the fuel-economy of the internal-combustion engine. It gave good performance on freight trains between York and Hull, but was excessively noisy, and the design was not repeated.

The first experiment with diesel-traction on British railways was in 1924 when the London & North Eastern Railway tried an Austrian-built diesel locomotive for a short period.

The first main-line use of diesel-electric traction was on the Canadian National Railways in 1925 when eight railcars were put into service. They had eight-cylinder engines made by Beardmore of Scotland. One of these covered 2930 miles (4715 km) from Montreal to Vancouver in 67 hours.

The first main-line diesel-electric locomotives were the four 1200 bhp units built for the German State Railways in 1925 to a design by the Russian engineer Professor George V. Lomonossoff (1876–1952).

The Long Island Railroad was the first in the U.S.A. to run a diesel-electric locomotive in road service, in 1926.

The first 'road' or main-line diesel-electric locomotive in Canada was introduced by the Canadian National Railways in 1928. It was a twin unit of 2660 hp, Nos. 9000–1. It was scrapped early in 1949.

The first British diesel-electric train was adapted by the London, Midland & Scottish Railway in 1928 from an ex-Lancashire & Yorkshire Railway Manchester–Bury electric train, by fitting it with a 500 hp Beardmore engine and English Electric traction equipment. It ran for a time on the Preston–Blackpool service and was later reconverted to an electric train.

The first use of diesel-traction in Ireland was in 1929 when Kerr Stuart & Company of Stoke-on-Trent tried out a 0–6–0 diesel-mechanical locomotive on the Castlederg & Victoria Bridge Tramway in County Tyrone. It ran for about six months.

The first regular use of diesel-traction in the British Isles was on the 3 ft (0·914 m) gauge County Donegal Railways in Ireland, in September 1931. The diesel railcar No. 7 was powered by a 74 hp Gardner engine. With a second, No. 8, built in November 1931, it was scrapped in 1939.

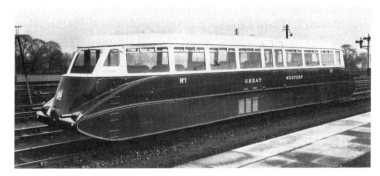

The first of the diesel railcars on the Great Western Railway, as placed in service in 1934 (British Rail)

The first diesel locomotive in regular service in Britain was rebuilt from a Midland Railway o–6–o tank engine by the London, Midland & Scottish Railway in 1931. A Paxman engine was used with Haslem & Newton hydrostatic transmission.

The first British diesel railbus was produced by Hardy Motors Limited who converted an A.E.C. 'Regal' road coach to run on rails in 1933, so beginning the long association of the Associated Equipment Company with railcars.

The first Great Western Railway diesel railcar was by Hardy Motors Limited in 1933, built by A.E.C. with Park Royal coachwork. It was fully streamlined, was 63 ft 7 in (19·379 m) long and weighed 20 tons. It seated 70 third class passengers and had a top speed of 75 m.p.h. (121 km/h). After achieving considerable attention at the International Commercial Motor Exhibition in London it was sold to the G.W.R. becoming their diesel car No. 1 and entering service in 1934.

The first high-speed diesel train, the streamlined *Flying Hamburger*, ran between Berlin and Hamburg and was introduced in the spring of 1932. It was scheduled to run at speeds of over 100 m.p.h. (161 km/h). On tests it reached over 124 m.p.h. (198·5 km/h).

The first diesel locomotives in main-line service in the U.S.A. were used on the Chicago, Burlington & Quincy and Union Pacific railroads in 1934. The first diesels on regular freight work went into service on the Santa Fe in 1940.

The 'Burlington Zephyr' of the Chicago, Burlington & Quincy Railroad entered service in 1934 as the world's first diesel-electric streamliner. On 26 May 1934 it travelled the 1015 miles (1633 km) from Denver to Chicago non-stop at an average speed of 77·6 m.p.h. (125 km/h). The train is preserved at the Museum of Science and Industry, Chicago, alongside a captured German submarine.

The first lightweight streamlined diesel passenger train went into operation between Lincoln, Nebraska, U.S.A. and Kansas City, Missouri, on 11 November 1934.

The first British streamlined diesel train was built by the London, Midland & Scottish Railway in 1938. It consisted of three articulated coaches powered by Leyland diesel engines and hydro-mechanical transmission. After successful service between Oxford and Cambridge, and Nottingham and London, it was stored throughout the war and afterwards was dismembered.

The London, Midland & Scottish Railway three-car articulated diesel train, the first British streamlined diesel train, placed in service in February 1938 and operated over various sections of the L.M.S. It was taken out of service in September 1939 and did not operate again. It was dismembered in 1945 (British Rail)

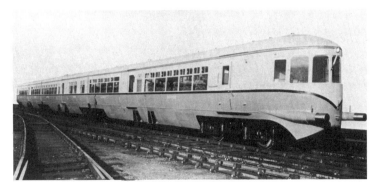

The greatest landmark in the progress of the diesel locomotive was the General Motors 'Electro Motive' No. 103, built in the U.S.A. in 1939. It was a four-unit freight machine rated at 5400 hp. In one year's trials it covered 83 000 miles on 21 roads in 37 States in temperatures from 40 degrees below zero (−40 °C) to 110 degrees (43·3 °C) at altitudes from sea-level to 10 200 ft (3109 m). Up the 25 miles of 1 in 40 (40 km of 2·5 per cent) on the Southern Pacific/Santa Fe climb to Tehachapi Pass from the west it hauled 1800 tons in one and a half hours, completely outclassing the biggest steam locomotives. From that moment the fate of the steam locomotive in America and round the world was sealed.

The first diesel-electric locomotive in road freight service in the U.S.A. was inaugurated by the Santa Fe Railroad on 4 February 1941.

The 'diesel revolution' in the U.S.A. took about 16 years. In 1945 there were 38 853 steam locomotives, 842 electric locomotives and 835 'other types'. In 1961 there were 110 steam, 480 electric and 28 150 diesel units.

The first British main-line diesel-electric locomotives were built by the London, Midland & Scottish Railway in 1947—Nos. 10000/1. They were CoCo types with English Electric Company 1600 hp engines and six nose-suspended traction motors, and weighed 128 tons each, a startling contrast to the 'Deltics' mentioned below, with a weight of 106 tons and horsepower of 3300, built only eight years later.

Rail Diesel Cars (knows as 'RDCs'), were introduced in North America by the Budd Company of Philadelphia, Pennsylvania, in 1929. They have two 300 hp General Motors diesel engines mounted under the floor, each driving one axle through a G.M. hydraulic torque converter and reverse gear. The single cars are 85 ft (25·908 m) long, weigh 113 800 lb (46·3 tons), seat 70 passengers and include a 17 ft (5·182 m) luggage compartment. For multiple-unit operation in trains, passenger-only trailer vehicles are also built with single engines.

By 1973 Budd had built about 500 RDCs. Most are in the U.S.A. and Canada. Others are at work in Australia, Saudi Arabia, Cuba and Brazil (Departamento Nacional de Estradas de Ferro— D.N.E.F., and Rède Ferroviaria Federal S.A.— R.F.F.S.A.). See colour illustration on p. 142.

Diesel multiple-unit trains first appeared in Britain in 1954, and were first put to work between Leeds and Bradford.

One of the early British Railways diesel multiple-unit trains at Hayfield in 1961. These early units have now been withdrawn and the Hayfield Branch has been abandoned (John Marshall)

Four-wheeled diesel railbuses of various designs were tried on lightly used lines in Britain for several years from 1958. Two are preserved for use on the Keighley & Worth Valley Railway, and another is on the North Yorks Moors Railway, Yorkshire, and two more are at Sheringham, Norfolk.

Multiple-unit diesel-electric trains on the Southern Region of British Railways were first used on the London to Hastings via Tunbridge Wells service on 6 May 1957. They are in six-car sets with a 500 bhp English Electric supercharged diesel engine and generator in each end car.

The first of the British Rail 'Deltic' diesels was introduced by the English Electric Company at their Vulcan Works, Lancashire, in 1955. It was then **the most powerful diesel-**

'Deltic'-type diesel-electric No. 55021 Royal Argyll Sutherlander arrived at King's Cross, London, on the 'Yorkshire Pullman', 1 July 1974 (John Marshall)

electric single-unit locomotive in the world, rated at 3300 bhp with a weight of only 106 tons. After extensive trials on the London Midland Region an order was placed for 22 units for the East Coast main line between London and Edinburgh on which they are timed at speeds of 100 m.p.h. (161 km/h). The original unit is now displayed in the Science Museum, London.

The first of the 'Deltics' to travel 2 000 000 miles (3 218 700 km) was No. 9010 *King's Own Scottish Borderer*, stationed at Edinburgh and working about 4000 miles (6437 km) a week, at speeds of 90–100 m.p.h. (145–161 km/h) between Edinburgh, London and Leeds. It is one of the class of 22 introduced in 1961, and it topped the 2 000 000 mark in the week commencing 15 January 1973. It is probably the first diesel-electric locomotive in the world to travel 2 000 000 miles in under 12 years.

By contrast the record-breaking 'A4' Class 'Pacific' *Mallard*, withdrawn for preservation in 1963, recorded only 1 426 000 miles (2 294 943 km) in its 25 years of service. The Great Western 'Star' Class 4–6–0 No. 4021 *King Edward* (renamed *The British Monarch* in 1927) took 43 years to complete its 2 034 975 miles (3 274 987 km), and the 'Saint' Class 4–6–0 No. 2920 *Saint David* took 46 years for its 2 080 754 miles (3 348 663 km).

This illustrates the tremendous availability of diesel locomotives compared with steam.

The first British main-line diesel-hydraulic locomotive, No. D600, was built by the North British Locomotive Company, Glasgow, and was delivered to the Western Region of British Railways in March 1958. It was an A1A A1A type, weighed 117·4 tons, and had an output of 2000 hp and a top speed of 90 m.p.h. (145 km/h). It was named *Active* and was the first of a class of five.

Later in 1958 the first of the 33 Western Region B B-type diesel-hydraulic locomotives was completed at Swindon, based on the successful German 'V200' Class, weighing only 78 tons and producing 2100 bhp.

The world's most powerful single-unit diesel-electric locomotive is at present the Union Pacific Railroad 'Centennial' Do Do type, introduced in 1969, a hundred years after the completion of the first transcontinental railroad. At 96 ft (29·261 m) it is also the world's longest. It is rated at 6600 hp and weighs 504 000 lb (229 000 kg). The first was numbered 6900, and a total of 47 were ordered from the Electro-Motive Division of the General Motors Corporation. They have a maximum speed of 71 m.p.h. (115 km/h). See colour illustration on p. 159.

The most powerful diesel-electric locomotives in Europe are the 20 3900 hp units, first built by Nydqvist & Holm and Frichs, Denmark, in 1972. They have General Motors (U.S.A.) 16–645–E3 engines, weigh 126 tonne and have a maximum speed of 165 km/h (103 m.p.h.). More are at present on order for Spain.

One of the Danish 3900 hp diesel-electric locomotives, the most powerful units in Europe, built in 1972. They have a top speed of 103 m.p.h. (165 km/h) (Danish State Railways)

The first British main-line diesel-hydraulic locomotive No. D600, built by the North British Locomotive Company in 1957–58 for the Western Region (British Rail)

The most powerful diesel-electric locomotives in Australia are the 'Century' 636 type built in 1968 and owned by the Hammersley Iron Pty Limited on the north coast of Western Australia. They are in two units with a total output of 3600 hp, and haul up to 240 cars each of 100 tons capacity and 120 tons gross weight, a total of 28 000 tons, at 40 m.p.h. (64.374 km/h).

The standard gauge Hammersley Railway carries a greater annual tonnage than any other single track in Australia. On a normal day six trains carry 90 000 tons of ore one way. It also uses the heaviest track in Australia, 136 lb/yd (67.5 kg/m).

The most powerful diesel-electric locomotives on an Australian Government railway are the Western Australian 'L' Class Co Co-type 3000 hp units built in 1968. They measure 19.354 m (63 ft 6 in) long, 2.946 m (9 ft 8 in) wide, and have a top speed of 134 km/h (83 m.p.h.). They are standard gauge.

GAS-TURBINE LOCOMOTIVES

The gas-turbine was first applied to rail-traction in 1941 when a 2140 hp gas-turbine-electric locomotive was built for the Swiss Federal Railways by Brown Boveri & Company of Baden. It was 16.383 m (53 ft 9 in) long, 1Bo Bo1 type and weighed 92 tons.

The Great Western Railway in England ordered a Brown Boveri gas-turbine-electric locomotive with an output of 2500 hp which was delivered in 1949 and first used in February 1950. It was numbered 18000 by British Railways Western Region.

The first British-built gas-turbine-electric locomotive was a 3000 hp unit built by the Metropolitan-Vickers Electrical Company Limited for the Western Region of British Railways in January 1952 and numbered 18100. It was 66 ft 8 in (20.320 m) long and weighed 130 tons. It was withdrawn in January 1958 and was rebuilt into an electric locomotive for the 25 kV electrification for use in training drivers, and was numbered E1000 until withdrawn finally in 1968.

The first gas-turbine-electric locomotive to be built and operated in the U.S.A. began track tests on 15 November 1948 on the Union Pacific Railroad. The first unit entered regular pool service on 1 January 1952.

The largest gas-turbine-electric locomotives are the two-unit 8500 hp machines built by the General Electric Company at Schenectady, U.S.A., for the Union Pacific Railroad. Forty-five were built, from 1957, following the success of the 25 U.P. 4500 hp gas-turbine-electrics built from 1952, which showed economies over diesels. The 1957 machines are 165 ft (50.294 m) long and weigh 408 tons.

One of the Union Pacific 8500 hp turbine-electric locomotives at Dale, Wyoming (Union Pacific Railroad)

The first British-built gas-turbine-electric locomotive, No. 18100, built by Metropolitan Vickers and put into service on the Western Region in January 1952 (British Rail)

Direct-drive gas-turbine locomotives were built by Renault in France in 1952 (1000 hp), and at Gotaverken in Sweden (1300 hp).

STEAM-LOCOMOTIVE TESTING PLANTS

The first recorded use of a stationary plant for testing locomotive performance was a small one built at Kiev in Russia in 1886 to designs by an engineer named Borodin.

The first modern testing plant was built at Perdue University, U.S.A., in 1891 to designs by Professor W. F. M. Goss. Others in the U.S.A. were built by the North Western Railway at Chicago in 1895 and by Columbia University in 1899.

The Pennsylvania Railroad Altoona plant was originally built for the St Louis Exposition in 1904.

The first European testing plant was designed by G. J. Churchward (see p. 58) and was built at Swindon by the Great Western Railway, England, in 1904.

The French testing plant at Vitry near Paris was completed in 1934. One of the first locomotives to be tested on it was the London & North Eastern Railway 2–8–2 *Cock o' the North*, Britain's first eight-coupled passenger engine (see p. 133).

The largest testing plant for steam locomotives was built at Rugby, England. It was begun jointly by the London, Midland & Scottish and the London & North Eastern railways in 1936, but work was suspended during the war, and it was completed by British Railways in 1948. It had only a brief period of use, completely out of proportion to its cost, and by assisting in the development, at vast expense, of the range of B.R. standard steam locomotives, it simply delayed the introduction of more modern motive power.

At the nationalisation of British railways on 1 January 1948 there were 20024 steam locomotives. If, on average, including all passenger, freight and shunting work and standing idle, each evaporated 5000 gallons (2273 l) of water in a day, then allowing for engines out of service British Railways were putting about 400000 tons of

water mixed with waste products of combustion into the atmosphere every day. An express engine on a 400 mile (644 km) run would evaporate about 15200 gallons (7728 l), or nearly 70 tons of water, and burn about 8 tons of coal.

With considerably less fuel consumption and atmospheric pollution an equal amount of power is produced in an electric power-station which condenses most of its water and thereby runs at far higher efficiency, besides making more efficient use of fuel in boilers.

ELECTRIC-TRACTION

The first electric railway in the world was made by Thomas Davenport, a blacksmith in Vermont, U.S.A., in 1835. It was a small railway powered by a miniature electric motor.

The first serious attempt at electric power on a railway was made by Robert Davidson in 1842 when he tried out a battery locomotive weighing 5 tons on the Edinburgh & Glasgow Railway where it ran at 4 m.p.h. (6·5 km/h).

The electric dynamo was perfected between 1860 and 1870 but its use as a motor came several years later.

The first practical electric railway was built by the German engineer Werner von Siemens (see p. 49) for the Berlin Trades Exhibition— 31 May to 30 September 1879. It was a 550 m (600 yd) long narrow-gauge line. The electric locomotive had a 3 hp motor, picking up current at 150 V from a centre third rail and returning it via the wheels and running rails. It could pull about 30 passengers on three cars at 6·5 km/h (4 m.p.h.).

The first public electric railway in the world was opened on 12 May 1881 at Lichterfelde near Berlin. It was 2·5 km (1·5 mile) long. The car ran on a 100 V supply and carried 26 passengers at 48 km/h (30 m.p.h.).

The first public electric railway in Britain was Magnus Volk's Electric Railway at Brighton, first opened on 4 August 1883 with 2 ft (610 mm) gauge. It was rebuilt to 2 ft 9 in (838 mm) gauge and extended and reopened on 4 April 1884. It was taken over by Brighton Corporation on 1 April 1940. (See 'The Pioneers' and illustration, p. 57.)

The first electric railway to run on hydro-electric power was the 6 mile (9·5 km) long 3 ft

The Giant's Causeway Tramway in Ireland before conversion to overhead wire pick-up. In the background is Dunbar Castle (National Library of Ireland)

A train on the City & South London Railway in December 1922, with one of the original electric locomotives (London Transport Executive)

(914 mm) gauge Portrush–Giant's Causeway Tramway, Ireland, formally opened on 28 September 1883. It was engineered by William Acheson Traill (1844–1933). Cars could run at 12 m.p.h. (19 km/h) on the level. At first an outside conductor rail was used, and the town section was worked by two steam-tram engines from W. Wilkinson & Company of Wigan. In 1899 the entire system was converted to overhead wire collection. It was closed in 1950.

The first electric underground railway in the world was the City & South London, opened on 18 December 1890. At first it used 14 four-wheeled electric locomotives built by Mather & Platt of Salford. By 1907 there were 52 locomotives. They ran until the line was reconstructed in 1924. One is preserved in the Science Museum, London, and a coach is in the York Railway Museum.

The first electric locomotive in the U.S.A. for use on standard gauge was designed by L. Daft for the Mount Macgregor & Lake George Railroad in 1883.

The first electric train service in the U.S.A. began on the 7 mile (11 km) Nantasket Branch of the New York, New Haven & Hartford Railroad (now part of Penn Central) on 28 June 1895.

Electric locomotives were introduced on the Baltimore & Ohio Railroad on 4 August 1895, on the Belt line from Henrietta Street, Baltimore (just south of Camden Station), to Waverley Tower—3·75 miles (6 km) through ten tunnels amounting to 48 per cent of the distance. Passenger traffic began on 1 May 1895, with coke-burning locomotives, and goods traffic began with the electrification. The first trials with electric-traction were on 27 June 1895, originally with an overhead slot pick-up, replaced in March 1902 by a third rail.

The world's first electric elevated city railway was the Liverpool Overhead Railway, England. The first section opened on 6 March 1893. The line was closed, to avoid massive renewals, on 30 December 1956.

A train on the Liverpool Overhead Railway, at Pier Head in June 1932 (H. C. Casserley)

The crossing on the Chicago Elevated Railway near Randolph and Wells station (John Marshall)

The Chicago Elevated Railway saw its first electric cars in 1895, after the system had been operated for a few years by the 'Forney'-type 0–4–4 tanks.

The Berlin Elevated Railway began as an electric line in 1902.

The world's first single-phase alternating current locomotive went into service in 1904 on the Seebach–Wettingen Railway, Switzerland. Originally it was built for a 50 Hz supply with direct current traction motors supplied by a motor generator, but in 1904 it was rebuilt for 15 000 V, 15 Hz, with a.c. motors. The railway was the pioneer of high-voltage single-phase systems. The locomotive remained in service on the Bodensee–Toggenburg Railway until 1958 when it was given a place of honour in the Swiss Transport Museum, Lucerne.

Railway electrification in North America, apart from suburban lines, has never been undertaken extensively because of the nature of the traffic.

Electrification pays off only if the equipment is used intensively, such as on the London–Birmingham and Lancashire, or the St Gotthard route in Switzerland. In North America it is more economical to assemble the traffic into one enormous train, perhaps over a mile (1·6 km) long, which can be handled by a crew of three or four men. In Europe such trains are not possible; first, because the couplings are not strong enough, and second, the track layouts are not designed for trains of such length.

Electrification was undertaken in North America where there was the difficulty of ventilation in long tunnels such as Hoosac and Cascade, and of handling heavy trains on long climbs in the days of steam locomotives. The introduction of diesel power almost eliminated these troubles and consequently the electrical equipment could be dismantled and maintenance costs thereby reduced.

The longest electrified line in the U.S.A. was on the Chicago, Milwaukee, St Paul & Pacific (The Milwaukee Road). It had a total of 656 miles (1056 km) of electrified route out of a total route length of 10 641 miles (17 125 km).

In 1973 it was decided to abandon the electrification and to convert the entire line to diesel operation.

The Milwaukee is the only system in the U.S.A. operating over its own tracks all the way from Chicago to the Pacific Northwest. It was completed to Seattle in 1908.

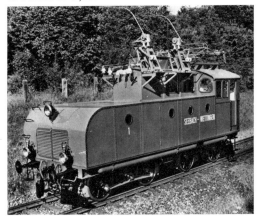

The world's first single-phase alternating current locomotive, built by Maschinenfabrik Oerlikon (M.F.O.), Zürich, for the Seebach–Wettingen Railway, Switzerland, in 1904. It ran on 15 000 V 15 Hz and had an output of 400 hp at 25 m.p.h. (40 km/h). Its maximum speed was 47 m.p.h. (60 km/h), and it weighed 40 metric tons. It is now preserved in the Swiss Museum of Transport and Communications, Lucerne, by whose courtesy this photograph is reproduced

Former North Eastern Railway 2 Co 2 electric express passenger locomotive No. 13, designed by Sir Vincent Raven for the York–Newcastle line, and built in 1923 but never used (British Rail)

The first British railway to be electrified at 1500 V d.c. with overhead catenary was the Shildon–Newport (now Tees-side) section of the North Eastern Railway. Electrically hauled coal trains with Bo Bo locomotives designed by Vincent Raven (1858–1934), the chief mechanical engineer, began running on 1 July 1915. It was proposed to adopt this system on the main line between York and Newcastle and a prototype 2–Co–2 express locomotive, No. 13, was built in 1922, but the Grouping into the London & North Eastern Railway and the severe shortage of money following the First World War prevented further progress.

With the decline of coal traffic, the Shildon–Newport section reverted to steam-haulage early in 1935. The locomotives were stored and subsequently scrapped. No. 13 survived the Second World War but was never used.

The 1500 V d.c. overhead system was recommended for adoption as a British Standard by the 1921 'Electrification Committee' Report and by the subsequent Pringle (1928) and Weir (1931) Reports.

The first British passenger railway to be electrified at 1500 V d.c. was the joint L.N.E.R. and L.M.S. line from Manchester to Altrincham where electric multiple-unit trains began running on 8 May 1931. On 3 May 1971 the line was changed to 25 kV a.c.

The first mercury-arc rectifier to be installed on a British railway was at Hendon on the Morden–Edgware line of the London Underground in 1930. It marked one of the most important technical improvements in d.c. electric-traction and made unmanned substations possible. Previously permanently manned rotary converters had to be used.

The first British suburban railway electrification was inaugurated by the North Eastern Railway between Newcastle (New Bridge Street) and Benton on 29 March 1904.

The Lancashire & Yorkshire Railway was a close runner-up when it introduced electric trains between Liverpool and Southport on 5 April 1904. In a desperate bid to beat the North Eastern Railway some trains were introduced before this, but the haste resulted in a partial breakdown and steam trains were not completely withdrawn until 13 May.

The first portion of the 'Southern Electric' was the South London line of the London, Brighton & South Coast Railway. Electric trains began on 1 December 1909 using a.c. at 6000 V with overhead collectors. It was later converted to 600 V d.c. third rail to conform to the other electrified lines south of London.

The first British main-line electrification was the Southern Railway London to Brighton and Worthing, brought into use on 1 January 1933. The system is 660 V d.c. third rail.

Electrification of the London (Liverpool Street)–Shenfield line, 20 miles (32 km), at 1500 V d.c. overhead came into operation on 26 September 1949. It was extended to Chelmsford, 9·5 miles (15·289 km), on 11 June 1956 and to Southend (Victoria), 15·5 miles (25 km), on 31 December 1956. It was converted to 25 kV a.c. in 1960.

Britain's first 'all-electric' main line (passenger and freight traffic) was the Manchester–Sheffield line of the former Great Central Railway. Through passenger services began on 14 September 1954 following the opening, on 3 June, of the new

(Above) Evening Star, *the last steam locomotive built for British Railways, at Oxenhope on the Keighley and Worth Valley Railway, Yorkshire (John Marshall)*

(Above, right) Adams 4–4–2 tank in its original L.S.W.R. livery, at Sheffield Park on the Bluebell Railway in Sussex (Simon Marshall)*

(Right) One of the Union Pacific 'Centennial' Class diesel-electric locomotives, No. 6934, the most powerful single-unit diesels in the world, heading a heavy freight up Sherman Hill, Wyoming, U.S.A. (Paul Meyer)*

(Below) The Railway Station *(1862) by W. P. Frith, showing a scene at Paddington Station, London, in the days of the 7 ft gauge (Royal Holloway College, Egham)*

Woodhead Tunnel. The 'standard' 1500 V d.c. system was used. The passenger service was withdrawn from 5 January 1970.

A Manchester–Sheffield train at Penistone in 1963, hauled by Co Co locomotive No. 27005 Minerva *(John Marshall)*

Total electrification of the Netherlands Railways, at 1500 V d.c., was completed on 7 January 1958. Following withdrawal of the Manchester–Sheffield passenger service in 1970 British Rail sold the seven Co Co locomotives, Nos. 27000–6, to the Netherlands Railways in 1972.

The 25 kV single phase system at the industrial frequency of 50 Hz was pioneered in France in 1950.

The decision to adopt 25 000 V (25 kV) 50 Hz electrification as the future British standard was made on 6 March 1956.

The first British railway to operate on 25 kV was the $24\frac{1}{2}$ mile (39.5 km) Colchester–Clacton–Walton line, on 16 March 1959.

The first British main line to operate on 25 kV was the Crewe–Manchester, on 12 September 1960. The Crewe–Liverpool line followed on 1 January 1962.

The first electric trains in Scotland (excluding the Glasgow District Subway) were the Glasgow suburban services—31 miles (50 km) of line at 25 kV. They began on 7 November 1960 but were withdrawn for alteration from 17 December 1960 to 1 October 1961.

The second stage—27 miles (43.5 km) of line south of the Clyde, was inaugurated on 27 May 1962.

The London–Manchester–Liverpool full service began on 18 April 1966. Some trains had run through from 22 November 1965. It was extended to the Birmingham area on 6 March 1967.

The extension of the electrification from London to Glasgow, covering the lines from Weaver Junction, Cheshire, to Motherwell in Lanarkshire, Scotland, was approved by the Minister of Transport in March 1970. It was opened throughout on 6 May 1974. The total cost was £75 000 000—£30 000 000 for electrification, £38 000 000 for resignalling and £7 000 000 for new electric locomotives.

The new '87' class electric locomotives, introduced in 1973 for the Scottish services, have an output of 5000 hp with a total weight of only 80 tons. They are **the most powerful locomotives on British Rail**. They have fully suspended traction motors and are designed to run at speeds of over 100 m.p.h. (161 km/h) and, unlike the other 25 kV locomotives, can be coupled and driven as multiple-units. Their output of $62\frac{1}{2}$ hp/ton is twice that of the 'Deltics', the most powerful British diesel-electric units, but their adhesion at full power on adverse grades is at the mercy of the weather.

British Railways Southern Region mainline electrification to Southampton and Bournemouth was completed on 10 July 1967, enabling through trains to run from London, using third rail at 750 V d.c. On the same day 90 m.p.h. (145 km/h) push-and-pull services were introduced, following successful tests at 100 m.p.h. (145 km/h). **The occasion marked the end of steam on B.R. Southern Region.**

Of the total British Rail network of 11 537 miles (18 988 km), 2848 miles (3570 km) are electrified with three systems: 600–750 V d.c. third rail (1100 miles; 1770 km), 1500 V d.c. (70 miles; 113 km) and 25 kV a.c. (1048 miles; 1687 km) overhead. This can be compared with the French Railways which, in a total of 21 860 miles (35 180 km), have electrified 5819 miles (9365 km), 4827 km (2999 miles) with 1500 V d.c. and 4299 km (2671 miles) with 25 kV a.c.

The first silicon-rectifier locomotive in the U.S.A., one of six, was delivered to an eastern railroad on 3 July 1962.

The world's first 50 kV electric railway is the isolated 78 mile (125.5 km) standard-gauge line linking the Black Mesa Mines near Kayenta, Arizona, U.S.A. with the giant Navajo power-station which will have an output of 2250 MW, requiring 8 000 000 tons of coal a year. The high voltage requires only one feed point at one end of the line, so reducing installation and maintenance costs. The operation of the railway is entirely automatic. It was opened on 15 March 1974.

The three 5100 hp Co Co locomotives were built by the General Electric Company. One train, powered by all three locomotives, makes three round trips daily, carrying up to 10000 tons of coal on each trip. The railway is regarded partly as a test bed for future electrification in the U.S.A.

North of Cape Town in South Africa a new 860 km (534·38 miles) 1·067 m (3 ft 6 in) gauge line from Sishen to Saldanha Bay is to be electrified at 50 kV as a direct result of the oil shortage. The line is almost straight and has easy grades. Three trains per day will each consist of 202 wagons carrying a total of 17000 tons of ore. Seventeen electric locomotives of 3000–3500 kW (about 4000–5000 hp) are on order. One year earlier diesels would have been ordered instead.

The world's most powerful electric locomotive is the Swiss Federal Railways experimental 1D2+2D1 No. 11852, built in 1939. It develops 11 100 hp at 75 km/h (46·6 m.p.h.).

The most powerful electric locomotives built as a class are the Swiss Federal Railways Re 6/6 Bo Bo Bo type. Four were built in 1972, two with articulated bodies, 11601–2, and two with rigid bodies, 11603–4, for trials on the St Gotthard line. Forty-five more are now in production, with rigid bodies. They have an output of 10 450 hp, a tractive effort of 88 600 lb (40 200 kg), weigh 120 tons, and have a maximum speed of 87 m.p.h. (140 km/h).

Two new types are being developed in Russia by CDK-Skoda, Class '55E', a Co Co type developing 8200 hp, and Class '66E'. a (Bo Bo)+(Bo Bo) developing 10900 hp for 200 km/h (125 m.p.h.) running.

Among the world's most advanced electric locomotives are the ten French four-system C C type built in 1965–66. They are designed to run on 25 kV 50 Hz single-phase a.c. and 1500 V d.c. (France); 3000 V d.c. (Belgium); or 15 kV 16⅔ Hz single-phase a.c. (Germany and Switzerland). They have an output of 4500 hp and a top speed of 400 km/h (150 m.p.h.). They are used on the Trans-Europe Express (T.E.E.) services between Paris and Brussels, 314 km (195 miles) non-stop in 2 hours 20 minutes.

In 1974 the Belgian National Railways (S.N.C.B.) obtained six four-system C C type locomotives of 5870 hp, 'Class 18'. With five three-system Bo Bos of 'Class 16' they provide a total of 19 Belgian electric locomotives for crossing frontiers. The four-system machines are equipped to run on the Belgian 3000 V d.c., Netherlands 1500 V d.c., French 25 kV a.c. 50 Hz and German 15 kV a.c. 16⅔ Hz lines.

The longest electrified railway in the world is from Moscow to Irkutsk—3240 miles (5213 km)—on the Trans-Siberian Railway, Russia.

The first electric trains in Australia began running at Melbourne, Victoria, in 1919. The first electric locomotive was introduced there in 1923. The system is 1500 V d.c.

The highest-capacity passenger trains in Australia are the double-deck electric suburban trains at Sydney, N.S.W., which carry 2500 passengers at speeds up to 96·5 km/h (60 m.p.h.). They were introduced on 12 January 1964.

In other countries outside Europe electrified railways began operating as follows:

Argentina: Buenos Aires district, 24 km (15 miles), 550 V d.c. O.H. 1909

Bolivia: Guaqui–La Paz Railway, La Paz–El Alto, 9·5 km (6 miles) 550 V d.c. O.H. 1908

Brazil: Corcovado Railway, Cosme Velho–Corcovado 3·2 km (2 miles) 750 V 3-phase a.c. O.H. 1910

Canada: C.N.R. Montreal, 2700 V d.c. O.H. 1918

Chile: Bethlehem Chile Iron Mines–Tofo, Cruz Grande, 24 km (15 miles), 2400 V d.c. O.H. 1916

Valparaiso–Los Andes and Santiago, 232 km (144 miles), 3000 V d.c. O.H. 1924

Chilean Transandine, 75·5 km (47 miles), 3000 V d.c. O.H. 1927

Costa Rica: Pacific Railroad, 124 km (77 miles), 15 kV single-phase a.c. 20 Hz O.H. 1929

Cuba: Havana–Mantanzas, 145 km (90 miles), 1200 V d.c. O.H. 1920

India: Bombay–Poona, 1500 V d.c. O.H. 1925
Bombay-Virar, 1500 V d.c. O.H. 1928

Indonesia: Djakarta district, 8 km (5 miles), 1500 V d.c. O.H. 1925

Japan: Chuo line, 1500 V d.c. O.H. 1906

New Zealand: Otira–Arthur's Pass, 14·5 km (9 miles), 1500 V d.c. O.H. 1923

South Africa: Durban area, 3000 V d.c. O.H. 1926

U.S.A.: Long Island Railroad, 700 V d.c. third rail 1905

Pennsylvania Railroad; 650 V d.c. third rail 1906 11 kV single-phase a.c. 25 Hz O.H. 1907

Reading Railroad, 11 kV single-phase a.c. 25 Hz O.H. 1906

Burlington Northern freight near Portland beside the Columbia River in the Cascade Mountains. The locomotives are Nos. 2072, 2077 and 2076.

The Inca and Ollanta at Guaqui, Bolivia, on Lake Titicaca, at a height of 12500 ft (3810 m) above sea-level (John Marshall)

Section 5
TRAINS

PASSENGER CARRIAGES

The first railway passenger carriage was a mere 'garden shed on wheels' pulled by a horse on the Stockton & Darlington Railway in England in 1825.

The first scheduled passenger service on a railway began on the Stockton & Darlington Railway on 16 October 1826. The first coach, pulled by a horse, was named 'The Union'. It was simply an ordinary horse carriage mounted on railway wheels.

In the U.S.A. the first passenger car to make a regular scheduled run was another 'shed on wheels' pulled by a horse, on the Baltimore & Ohio Railroad in 1829.

On the Liverpool & Manchester Railway in 1830 passenger carriages were similar to horse road carriages mounted on a railway-wagon chassis on four wheels.

Bogie carriages were introduced in the U.S.A. as early as 1831 by Ross Winans (1796–1877) on the Baltimore & Ohio Railroad and by 1835 they were being generally adopted. The

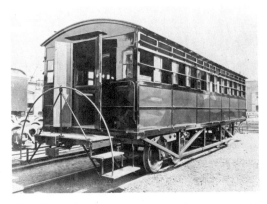

The oldest eight-wheeled passenger car in existence, built about 1836 for the Camden & Amboy Railway (Smithsonian Institution, Washington)

reason was primarily the light track to which they adapted themselves more readily than a four-wheeled vehicle. A bogie carriage built about 1836 for the Camden & Amboy Railroad, and now preserved in the Smithsonian Institution, Washington, D.C., is the **oldest eight-wheeled passenger car in existence.**

The first compartment coach was built by Nathaniel Worsdell (see p. 44) for the Liverpool & Manchester Railway in 1834. It was named *Experiment* and consisted of three horse-carriage bodies on a four-wheeled truck. From this developed the standard compartment carriage used in Britain and throughout most of Europe.

The compartment carriage was never adopted in North America where different conditions prevailed, and there the 'open' type of car was adopted. Through the influence of the Pullman Car Company this reached Europe in the 1870s and now, a century later, it is being adopted as the standard type in Britain where, however, many travellers still prefer the compartment carriage.

The first vestibule connections were provided in Connecticut, U.S.A., in June 1853 when a passenger train was fitted with covered and enclosed passageways between the cars.

Oil-lamps were introduced on U.S.A. trains in 1850; gas-lighting came in 1860; Pintsch gas in 1883; electric light in 1885 and fluorescent light in 1938.

Steam-heating was introduced in the U.S.A. in 1881. In Britain hot-water cans continued in use until the end of the nineteenth century. Steam heating was introduced here only gradually after about 1890.

The Milwaukee Road (Chicago, Milwaukee, St Paul & Pacific Railroad) was the first railway in the U.S.A. to equip all its passenger cars with steam heating, in 1887.

Electric lighting was introduced on British trains in 1881 (see 'Pullman Trains', p. 170).

The first trains in the U.S.A. to be fully equipped with electric lights ran between New York and Chicago, Boston and New York, New York and Florida and from Springfield to Northampton, Massachusetts, in 1887.

Corridor trains were introduced in Britain on the Great Western Railway on 7 March 1892. The connections between the coaches were at first locked and used only by the guards. Corridor trains next appeared on the northern lines out of London and then, in 1900, on the London & South Western Railway.

Vista-dome cars were invented and patented by T. J. McBride of Winnipeg, Canada, in 1891. The idea was simply a development of the roof-top cupola first fitted to freight-train cabooses on the Chicago & North Western Railroad in 1863 (see p. 172).

A vista-dome car was introduced on the Canadian Pacific Railway in 1902 and three more in 1906. They had a cupola at each end and a glazed centre portion with clerestory. They were withdrawn during the First World War.

The first cast-steel bogie-truck frame with integrally cast journal boxes was patented in the U.S.A. by William P. Bettendorf in 1903. Its use became standard throughout the U.S.A.

All-steel passenger cars were first placed in service in the U.S.A. on the Long Island Railroad in 1905. The L.I.RR. was also the first to operate an all-steel-car passenger fleet, in 1927.

Articulated coaches were introduced in Britain by H. N. Gresley (see p. 59) in 1907. He mounted the bodies of two old Great Northern six-wheelers on three bogies, thus improving the riding and reducing the weight and length. The idea was developed into the 'quad-arts', four-coach sets on five bogies, so familiar to a generation of long-suffering North London commuters.

Roller bearings were first used on rolling stock in 1926 on the Chicago, Milwaukee, St Paul & Pacific Railroad passenger stock because of the increased weight of the Chicago–Twin Cities (Minneapolis/St Paul) trains.

Air-conditioned cars first appeared in the U.S.A. as an experiment in 1927. They were first put into regular service in 1930. The world's first completely air-conditioned passenger train went into service on the Baltimore & Ohio Railroad

between Washington and New York on 24 May 1931. In Canada air-conditioning came into regular use in 1935 when the sleeping car *Sturgeon Falls* was so equipped.

The first air-conditioned train in Australia was the lightweight diesel-mechanical railcar named *Silver City Comet*, introduced in 1937 between Parkes and Broken Hill, 676·5 km (421 miles), in New South Wales. Times were 9 hours 45 minutes down and 9 hours 35 minutes up.

British Rail's first air-conditioned coaches were introduced on 12 July 1971 when the Mark II coaches went into service between London (King's Cross) and Newcastle and in August between King's Cross and the West Riding of Yorkshire and Scotland, following trials with an experimental train introduced on 15 June 1964. The Mark IIE coaches were introduced on the London to Birmingham, Wolverhampton and Manchester services in 1972. They provide wider entrances and better luggage storage. By the end of 1972 450 were in service. The Mark III coaches designed for 125 m.p.h. (200 km/h) went into ordinary service in 1973. Their running is remarkably smooth and, for the passenger, silent.

British Rail's 'High Speed Train' consists of seven Mark III air-conditioned passenger cars between two Bo Bo power-cars, and is designed to run at 125 m.p.h. (200 km/h). It carries 96 first class and 276 second class passengers. Each power-car has one Paxman 12RP200L 'Valenta' 12-cylinder pressure-charged and intercooled diesel engine developing 2250 bhp driving a Brush Electrical three-phase 1430 kW alternator. This supplies the four 450 hp d.c. traction motors through the rectifier and control equipment. The

The British Rail High Speed Diesel Train on the East Coast main line (British Rail)

two traction motors in each bogie are frame-mounted to reduce unsprung weight.

Features include double-glazed windows, air-conditioning, interior doors automatically operated by tread-mats, colourful upholstery, and public address system. Catering services will include a trolley service to all seats, and a full range of meals cooked in modern micro-wave ovens.

On 12 June 1973 the train reached a world record speed for diesel-traction of 143 m.p.h. between Thirsk and Tollerton while on test on the York–Darlington section. When placed in service after 1975 the high-speed trains will make possible significant reductions in journey times, for example London to Edinburgh, 393 miles (632 km), in 4 hours 30 minutes at an average speed of 87 m.p.h. (140 km/h).

The APT-E, or Advanced Passenger Train (Experimental) is a four-car articulated set designed to operate at 155 m.p.h. (250 km/h) on standard track designed and signalled for 100 m.p.h. (161 km/h) trains. The four cars are carried on five two-axle bogies of which the two end ones have electric drive to both axles. The two power-cars each contain four Leyland 300 hp gas-turbine engines driving alternators, two providing the power for each driving-axle. A fifth gas-turbine engine drives an auxiliary alternator providing power at 415 V three-phase 50 Hz for auxiliary services including air-conditioning, heating, etc.

Features of the APT are body-tilting on curves and bogie-steering to reduce friction between flange and rail. Hydraulic braking systems enable the train to be stopped within the signalling distances designed for 100 m.p.h. (161 km/h) trains.

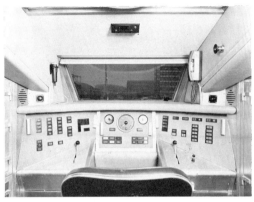

Interior view of the APT–E driving cab. Fundamental research into the dynamics of flanged wheels rolling on rails by scientists at the Railways Technical Centre, Derby, has resulted in the design and development of the Advanced Passenger Train which will run at speeds up to 155 m.p.h. (249 km/h) on existing railway lines. A four-car experimental train, APT–E, began track trials in August 1972, two prototype trains (APT–P) entering revenue-earning evaluation service in the mid 1970s (British Rail)

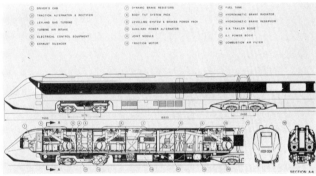

Diagram of the APT–E power car. Dimensions of power cars are 75·6 ft (23·05 m) long, 8·8 ft (2·685 m) wide, 11·9 ft (3·64 m) high (to top of exhaust cowls). The body is space-frame fabricated from steel rectangular hollow sections and clad in aluminium alloy sheet. Ergonomic studies have been made into all aspects of the driver's environment to ensure safe, efficient train operation (British Rail)

Two prototype trains, one electric and one gas turbine, are due to enter service in the second half of the 1970s.

Vista-dome cars were introduced in the U.S.A. on 23 July 1945 between Chicago and Minneapolis on the Chicago, Burlington & Quincy Railroad (now part of Burlington Northern).

APT–E (experimental) on its first main-line proving run before starting the most stringent test programme ever devised for a railway train. Information from APT–E will be used in designing two prototypes, APT–Ps.

The **Canadian** transcontinental trains on Canadian Pacific Rail, running between Montreal/Toronto and Vancouver, consisting of new stainless-steel cars was inaugurated on 24 April 1955. It is the longest vista-dome train ride in the world, 2904·8 miles (4675 km) from Montreal to Vancouver. It required the purchase of 173 new cars from the Budd Company, Philadelphia.

The vista dome car at the rear of the 'Canadian' on its run from Vancouver to Montreal, Canadian Pacific Railway, about to cross the Stoney Creek Bridge (Canadian Pacific Limited)

The 'Canadian' beside the Bow River in Alberta (Canadian Pacific Limited)

The lightest passenger cars in the U.S.A. are the air-conditioned 'Pioneer III' cars introduced by the Budd Company in July 1956. They are 85 ft (25·908 m) long, seat 88 passengers and weigh 23·4 long tons or only 595 lb (269·89 kg) per passenger. In July 1958 the 'Pioneer III MU' (multiple-unit) cars were introduced on the Pennsylvania Railroad.

The 'Tightlock' automatic coupler for passenger cars was adopted as standard in the U.S.A. in 1946.

Gallery cars, with seats on two levels, were introduced by the Chicago, Burlington & Quincy Railroad on its Chicago suburban services in 1950. Each car accommodates 148 passengers, 96 on the main (lower) floor and 52 in the single seats in the galleries (see colour illustration on p. 142).

The first 'double-decked' train in Britain, with seats at two levels, designed by O. V. Bulleid (see p. 60), went into service on the Southern Region of British Railways on 2 November 1949. Its higher capacity made longer station stops necessary and so its advantage was lost and it was withdrawn on 1 October 1971.

Canada's first gallery-car train, comprising nine air-conditioned cars built by Canadian Vickers Limited, went into operation on 27 April 1970 on the Montreal Lakeshore suburban service.

The Trans-Europ-Express (T.E.E.) service was first proposed in 1954 by Den Hollender, then president of the Netherlands Railways. Services began on 2 June 1957, and they now cover nine countries: Austria, Belgium, France, Germany, Italy, Luxembourg, Netherlands, Spain and Switzerland, by 35 trains operating over 27 routes and serving 125 stations, and carrying 500000 passengers a year in first-class accommodation with all seats reserved. The offices of T.E.E. are at the headquarters of the Netherlands Railway at Utrecht. Trains are all painted red and cream.

Motive power and rolling stock is owned by the various administrations. The first trains were diesel multiple units. In 1961 Swiss Federal Railways introduced four five-coach multi-current electric trains. In 1972 only 7 out of 35 trains were diesels.

The 'Catalan-Talgo', introduced in Spain in 1969 for running between Geneva and Barcelona, has its bogies changed at Cerebère to run on the Spanish gauge of 5 ft 6 in (1·676 m) and the European standard gauge.

The most luxurious train in the world is the title claimed by 'The Blue Train' in South Africa. It was introduced on 4 September 1972 to replace the 33-year-old former 'Blue Train' on the

Pretoria–Johannesburg–Cape Town service. It carries 108 passengers in 16 coaches and runs beautifully on air-cushioned bogies on 3 ft 6 in (1·067 m) gauge at speeds of 40–50 m.p.h. (64·5–80·5 km/h), and makes the journey in 26 hours. Accommodation is entirely in private rooms, three of them with private bathrooms complete with baths; it is fully air-conditioned and sound-proofed, and ranks as a five-star hotel. Passengers normally dress for dinner.

'The Indian Pacific' in Australia, introduced in 1970, is probably the second most luxurious train in the world, crossing from Perth to Sydney in 65 hours on standard gauge throughout. The streamlined, stainless-steel air-conditioned train provides sleeping accommodation for all passengers with showers and private toilets, a cocktail lounge, drawing-room and music-room with piano. Early morning and afternoon tea are wheeled round to all passengers.

New Zealand's 'Silver Star', introduced in 1972, runs overnight between Auckland and Wellington, covering the 462 miles in 12 hours 30 minutes, on 3 ft 6 in (1·067 m) gauge. It can claim to be the world's third most luxurious train. Mitsubishi of Japan built it in 1971. It includes the first dining car to run on N.Z.R. since 1915 and is the first all-sleeper with private toilets and showers in New Zealand.

The first modern trains with 'No Smoking' accommodation throughout began running on the Boston & Maine Railroad, U.S.A., on 1 June 1970. They carry commuters only, 90 per cent of the journeys lasting under half an hour.

BRAKES

To stop a train travelling at 60 m.p.h. (96·5 km/h) requires as much power as would lift the entire train vertically to a height of 120 ft (36·5 m).

Early trains had no continuous brakes. The only brake power was on the engine tender and the guard's van. From a speed of 30 m.p.h. (48 km/h) a train might take ½ mile (o·8 km) to stop. Hence the great height of early signals, to be seen from a distance.

The earliest practical continuous brakes were mechanical systems such as those patented by George Newall of the East Lancashire Railway in

1852 and by Charles Fay (1812–1900), carriage and wagon superintendent of the Lancashire & Yorkshire Railway, in 1856.

George Westinghouse (see p. 55) applied for an air-brake patent on 23 January 1869.

The Westinghouse continuous automatic air brake was introduced in 1872–73. 'Automatic' means that the brake applies itself on both halves of a train if it breaks apart.

The Gresham automatic vacuum brake was introduced in Britain in 1878, but it was about 1890 before all passenger trains were equipped.

Continuous automatic brakes became compulsory in Britain under the Regulation of Railways Act of 1889 (see 'Runaways', p. 188).

Most of the world's railway systems use the air brake. Countries using the vacuum brake are mainly:

Europe—British Isles (except new British Rail stock); Austrian minor railways; Spain; Portugal

Australia—Western Australia; Tasmania

Africa—South Africa; Rhodesia; United Arab Republic

Asia—most railways in India and Pakistan; Malaysia; Thailand (Siam); Burma

South America—most railways except the Trans-andine; Antofagasta & Bolivia; high-altitude lines in the Andes; Central of Brazil

PASSENGER CLASSES

Third class passengers were first carried in Britain in 1838, in open wagons without seats.

Gladstone's Railway Act of 1844 ruled that railways must carry third class passengers in closed carriages with seats at one (old) penny a mile on at least one train a day. 'Parliamentary' trains as they were known were often run at the most inconvenient times and at the slowest speeds.

The first British railway to carry third class passengers by all trains was the Midland Railway, on 1 April 1872. The Great Eastern Railway followed in the same year.

Second class was abolished on the Midland Railway and also on the joint services with the Glasgow & South Western Railway on 1 January 1875. They were the first.

Bogie carriages for first and third class
were introduced in Britain by the Midland Railway
in 1875.

The use of third class carriages by 'wearers of
kid gloves and kid shoes' was strongly condemned
by the chairman of the Lancashire & Yorkshire
Railway, Thomas Barnes, in 1880, because of the
danger of 'Americanising our institutions'!

**Third class passengers were carried on
all trains of the Great Western Railway** from
1 October 1890.

**First class was abolished on the Metro-
politan and District railways**, London, from
1 February 1940. From that date only one class
operated on all London Transport services.

**Third class was redesignated second
class on British Railways** on 3 June 1956 and
by the Ulster Transport Authority (which had
retained three classes) on 1 October 1956.

**Greece and Turkey adopted two classes
only** from 1 January 1957, leaving only Spain and
Portugal in Europe with three classes.

SLEEPING AND DINING CARS

The world's first sleeping car was designed by Philip Berlin, manager of the Cumberland Valley Railroad, now part of Penn Central,
U.S.A. It operated between Harrisburg and
Chambersburg in 1837. Sleeping arrangements
were adapted from the seating.

Similar cars were also operated between Philadelphia and Baltimore (now Penn Central) in
1838, and on the Richmond & Fredericksburg
Railroad (now Richmond, Fredericksburg & Potomac), Virginia, in 1839.

**The first provision for sleeping on British
trains** was in 1838 when a makeshift bed was
introduced. It consisted of two poles with strips of
webbing between them which were laid across the
compartment resting on the two seats.

The New York & Erie Railroad (now
Erie & Lackawanna) operated experimental sleeping cars in 1843 and a regular sleeping-car service
in 1856.

The Illinois Central introduced six state-
room sleeping cars, known as 'Gothic cars', in June
1856. Each was nearly 50 ft (15·240 m) long and
nearly 10 ft (3·048 m) wide.

Night-seat coaches, with luxurious adjust-
able reclining seats, were put into service between
Philadelphia and Baltimore in 1854.

The first sleeping-car patents were issued
to T. T. Woodruff in the U.S.A. on 2 December
1856.

The world's first proper sleeping cars
were designed by Samuel Sharp and built at
Hamilton, Ontario, by the Great Western Railway
of Canada in 1857. The design was adopted by the
Wagner and Pullman companies. The first Pullman
sleeping car appeared in 1859.

'Parlour cars' first appeared in Canada
in 1860 on the Grand Trunk, Great Western and
Buffalo & Huron railways. They were fitted out
with every possible luxury; the Grand Trunk even
had a form of air-conditioning.

**The first railway to serve meals on a
train** was the Baltimore & Ohio, U.S.A. On 10
January 1853 it ran two special trains from Baltimore to Wheeling and back to mark the completion
of the railway to that point. A caterer was engaged
to provide food.

The world's first dining cars were operated
by the Philadelphia, Wilmington & Baltimore
(now part of Penn Central) between Philadelphia
and Baltimore in 1863. Two such cars, rebuilt
from day coaches 50 ft (15·240 m) long, were fitted
with an eating bar, steam-box and 'everything
found in a first class restaurant'.

Canada's first dining cars, or 'hotel cars',
appeared in regular service on the Great Western
Railway in 1876.

**A first class sleeping car was introduced
in Britain** by the North British Railway on the
Glasgow–Edinburgh–London trains on 2 April
1873. It ran alternate nights each way, leaving
Glasgow at 21·00 and arriving in London at 9·40
via the North Eastern and Great Northern railways. There was a supplementary charge of ten
shillings (50p).

On 31 July 1873 the Great Northern Railway
introduced a similar service so that it could
operate every night.

The London & North Western and Caledonian
railways introduced sleeping-car trains on the
'West Coast Route' between London and Scotland
on 1 October 1873.

The Great Western Railway introduced sleeping-car trains in December 1877. In 1881 it built the forerunner of the modern sleeping car, with six double-berth compartments, three lavatories and an attendant's pantry. Passengers provided their own bedding. In 1890 the G.W.R. introduced the first sleeping car equipped entirely with lateral berths in compartments.

The prototype British first class sleeping car was built by the North Eastern Railway in 1894. It had four compartments with single berths, two with double berths, a smoking compartment which could be adapted to sleep two, and an attendant's pantry with gas cooker.

Dining cars were introduced on the London–Leeds trains by the Great Northern Railway on 1 November 1879.

The 'Flying Scotsman' was provided with corridor stock throughout and with dining cars on 1 August 1900. The 20-minute lunch stop at York was ended.

The first restaurant cars in Europe to use electricity for cooking were put into service on the metre-gauge Rhaetian Railway in Switzerland in 1929 by the Mitropa Company (Mitteleuropäische Schlafwagen und Speisewagen Aktiengesellschaft) of Berlin.

Third class sleeping cars were introduced in Britain by the London, Midland & Scottish, the London & North Eastern and the Great Western railways on 24 September 1928. For daytime use they had ordinary third class compartments which could be converted to four berths for sleeping. For bedding only a pillow and a rug were provided.

The first shower compartment in a British train was installed in a first class twin sleeping-car set by the London & North Eastern Railway in 1930.

A weekly through sleeping-car service between Togliattigrad in Russia and Turin in Italy was introduced on 1 June 1969. The 2486 miles (4000 km) are covered in 88 hours.

PULLMAN CARS AND TRAINS

George Mortimer Pullman (1831–97) converted two passenger coaches of the Chicago & Alton Railroad (now part of the Gulf, Mobile & Ohio Railroad) into sleeping cars at the railway company's shops at Bloomington, Illinois, in 1859. The first ran from Bloomington to Chicago on 1 September 1859. The first Pullman Car conductor was Jonathan L. Barnes. Pullman regarded these merely as experiments and in 1864 began building the first real Pullman sleeping car, named *Pioneer*, which went into service in 1865. Pullman sleeping cars were soon in common use throughout the U.S.A.

Most sleeping-car services in the U.S.A. were operated by the Pullman Company until 1 January 1969. Since then they have been taken over by the individual railroads.

Pullman 'Hotel Cars' were introduced in 1867. They were sleeping cars equipped with kitchen and dining facilities. The first Pullman-built car providing only restaurant facilities, the *Delmonico*, was operated on the Chicago & Alton Railroad in 1868.

Pullman sleeping cars were introduced on Canadian railways in 1870. The Grand Trunk Railway cars were among the best appointed of their time. The convenience could be enjoyed for an extra payment of $1.

Pullman cars were introduced in Britain on 1 June 1874 on the Midland Railway between London and Bradford. They were so popular that by the end of 1874 the M.R. had 36 in operation including 11 sleeping cars. In 1876 the services were extended to Edinburgh and Glasgow over

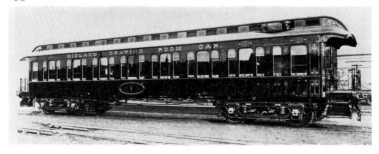

Midland Railway Pullman parlour car No. 8 built in the U.S.A. in 1876 for the London to Edinburgh and Glasgow services (The Science Museum, London)

the new Settle & Carlisle line and the Glasgow & South Western and North British railways.

The first 'restaurant car' in Britain was a Pullman named *Prince of Wales*, introduced on the Great Northern Railway between London (King's Cross) and Leeds on 1 November 1879.

The first all-Pullman train in Britain was on the London, Brighton & South Coast Railway in December 1881. It was also the first train in Britain to be electrically lit throughout. The London–Brighton 60-minute Limited Pullmans (Sundays only) began on 2 October 1898.

The Pullman Company Limited was registered in England from 1882 to 1907. It was then purchased by Mr Davison Dalziel (1854–1928), an English newspaper proprietor, until 1915 when the Pullman Car Company Limited was formed under his chairmanship to acquire the interests.

Dalziel also controlled the International Sleeping Car Company from 1927 and negotiated purchase by this company of Thomas Cook & Son (see p. 44) in 1928.

Pullman introduced the first vestibule train, in the U.S.A., in 1887.

The Pullman Car Company introduced the first two all-steel trains in England in May 1928. They formed 'The Queen of Scots' on the London & North Eastern Railway and ran between London, Leeds, Harrogate and Edinburgh.

The all-Pullman 'Southern Belle' was introduced by the London, Brighton & South Coast Railway on 1 November 1908. At the same time Buckeye couplings and drawgear were introduced into Great Britain by the Pullman Company. 'The Southern Belle' was renamed 'The Brighton Belle' on 29 June 1934, having become an electric train on 1 January 1933. It made its last run on 30 April 1972.

The first air-conditioned Pullman car went into operation between Chicago and Los Angeles on 9 September 1929, following experiments begun in 1927.

The most famous all-Pullman train, the 'Golden Arrow' service between London and Paris, was introduced on 12 September 1926 with Pullman cars between Calais and Paris. From 15

May 1929 it became all-Pullman throughout the journey.

From September 1939 to 15 October 1946 the service was withdrawn. Second class Pullmans were introduced in October 1949, but these were replaced by ordinary coaches in May 1965. It made its last run on 30 September 1972. The 4000 ton cross-Channel steamer *Invicta* which carried 'Golden Arrow' passengers to their connection with the Calais–Paris 'Flèche d'Or' from 1946 was taken out of service at the same time.

The first diesel multiple-unit Pullman train was the six-car first-class-only 'Midland Pullman' inaugurated on 4 July 1960. It ran between London (St Pancras) and Manchester (Central) and between London and Nottingham. The latter service was withdrawn on 31 December 1960. The 'Midland Pullman' was withdrawn in 1966 with the introduction, on 18 April, of the electrically hauled London to Manchester and Liverpool Pullman trains.

SLIP CARRIAGES

The earliest 'slip' carriages were on the London & Blackwall Railway during cable operation from 1840 to 1849 when coaches were detached from the moving ropes at all intermediate stations between Minories and Blackwall.

The first coaches to be slipped from moving trains were on the London, Brighton & South Coast Railway in February 1858 when a portion for Eastbourne was slipped at Hayward's Heath from the 16·00 express from London Bridge to Brighton.

Three months later the South Eastern Railway

Slip carriages on the Great Western Railway, England

slipped a portion for Canterbury off the 12·30 express from London Bridge to Ramsgate and Margate.

The first Great Western Railway slip carriages were introduced in December 1858 at Slough and Banbury.

In 1914 there were 200 slip-coach services, operated by most of the main-line companies in Great Britain and Ireland, of which the Great Western Railway operated 72. By 1918 the G.W.R. total was down to 17.

The last slip working in Britain was at Bicester off the 17·10 Paddington–Wolverhampton train on 9 September 1960, at the end of the summer service.

SPECIAL TRAINS

The first excursion train was organised by the Nottingham Mechanics Institute, England, and was run to Leicester on 20 July 1840. The second, from Leicester to Nottingham on 24 August 1840, carried 2400 passengers. (See 'Thomas Cook', p. 44.)

In the 1860s the Lancashire & Yorkshire Railway carried excursion passengers in open cattle trucks. Only after numerous complaints in the Press were temporary roofs fitted.

Queen Victoria's first railway journey, from Slough near Windsor to London (Paddington) on the Great Western Railway, was on 13 June 1842.

The first royal railway carriage was built by the London & Birmingham Railway in 1842 for Queen Adelaide.

The first 'club trains' were run by the South Eastern and London, Chatham & Dover railways between London and Dover in 1889.

The first 'railway enthusiasts' rail tour in Britain was organised by the Railway Correspondence & Travel Society (see p. 228) on 11 September 1938 when the Great Northern Railway Stirling 8 ft (2·438 m) single-wheeler No. 1 took a train of old six-wheeled carriages from London (King's Cross) to Peterborough and back. The fare was five shillings (25p).

The greatest number of passengers carried in one locomotive-hauled train in Australia was on a special run by the New South Wales Rail Transport Museum, Sydney, on 10 December 1972. It was hauled by three '38' Class diesels and carried 900 passengers (700 more were turned away).

MAIL TRAINS

Mail was first carried by train on the Liverpool & Manchester Railway on 11 November 1830.

The carriage of mails by rail in Britain was authorised by Act of Parliament in 1838.

The first travelling post office was an adapted horse-box operated by the Grand Junction Railway between Birmingham and Liverpool on 6 January 1838.

The first mail-sorting carriage to be specially constructed was designed by Nathaniel Worsdell (see p. 44) and included the first apparatus for picking up and dropping mail-bags while in motion. It was built by the Grand Junction Railway at Liverpool in 1838.

The oldest named train in the world is 'The Irish Mail' running between London and Holyhead in Anglesey, North Wales, where it connects with the sailings to Dun Laoghaire. It began on 31 July 1848 and still runs, though the name-boards have been carried only since 1927. Until the completion of the Britannia Tubular Bridge over the Menai Strait on 18 March 1850 the train ran to Bangor and passengers made part of the journey by coach.

The first railway mail traffic in the U.S.A. was on the South Carolina Railroad (now part of the Southern Railway) in November 1831 and on the Baltimore & Ohio in January 1832. Soon after the B. & O. opened between Baltimore and Washington in 1835 a car was fitted up for carrying mail between the two cities.

From 1855 the Terre Haute & Richmond Railroad (now part of Penn Central) west of Indianapolis operated Post Office cars in which mail was sorted and distributed on the journey.

A car equipped for handling overland mail for places west of St Joseph, Missouri, was introduced by the Hannibal & St Joseph Railroad (now part of Burlington Northern) on 28 July 1862.

Mail was first carried by rail in Canada on the Great Western Railway between Niagara and London in 1854, letters being sorted on the train under the supervision of P. Pardon, pioneer mail clerk of North America.

The first North American railway to use regular mail cars was the Grand Trunk Railway of Canada. In 1854 the baggage cars were replaced by specially fitted-up mail cars, at least ten years before such cars appeared elsewhere in North America.

The first permanent railway Post Office car in the U.S.A. for picking up, sorting and distributing mail on the journey was put into operation by the Chicago & North Western Railroad on 28 August 1864, between Chicago and Clinton, Iowa.

U.S. railroads carry about 50 per cent of all domestic first class mail and about 80 per cent of all domestic bulk mail.

The first special postal train in the world was inaugurated by the Great Western Railway between London and Bristol on 1 February 1855. Passengers were carried from June 1869 when one first class carriage was attached.

The first mail train between London and Aberdeen was inaugurated by the London & North Western and Caledonian railways on 1 July 1885. It did not carry passengers.

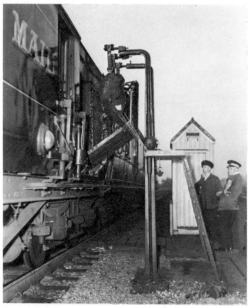

Apparatus for exchanging mail-bags, as used in Britain until 1971 (British Rail)

Travelling sorting offices and exchange apparatus were discontinued in Britain from 22 September 1940 until 1 October 1945.

Apparatus for exchanging mail-bags on British Railways was last used on 4 October 1971, just north of Penrith.

FREIGHT SERVICES

Containers were first used in the U.S.A. on the Camden & Amboy Railroad in 1849. On the Pennsylvania Railroad they were first used in 1869.

The first recorded use of refrigerators on an American railroad was on 1 July 1851 when 8 tons of butter were carried from Ogdensburg, N.Y., to Boston, Mass., in a wooden box car stocked with ice and insulated with sawdust.

In 1857 box cars with ice compartments at each end were used for carrying fresh meat from Chicago eastwards over the Michigan Central Railroad (now Penn Central).

The 'caboose' at the rear of an American freight train was originally known as a 'cabin car', 'conductor's van', 'brakeman's cab', 'accommodation car', 'train car' and 'way car'. The first recorded use of the term 'caboose' was in 1855 on the Buffalo, Corning & New York Railroad (now part of the Erie & Lackawanna). The roof-top cupola appears to have been introduced in 1863 by T. B. Watson, a freight conductor of the Chicago & North Western Railway, Iowa.

The Railway Express Agency in the U.S.A. was established on 4 March 1839 by William F. Harnden (1812–45), formerly a passenger train conductor on the Boston & Worcester Railroad (now part of Penn Central). Harnden contracted with the Boston & Providence (also now part of P.C.) and a steamship company operating between Providence and New York for the carriage of his business.

The business grew rapidly and was extended to Philadelphia and elsewhere. The Railway Express Agency Company, established on 7 December 1928, was owned and operated by U.S. railroads until 1960 when its name became 'R.E.A. Express'. It was purchased by a group of its executives in 1969. The handling of its business brings the railroads an annual income of over $40 000 000.

The first tank car specially built for transporting bulk oil in the U.S.A. went into service at Titusville, Pennsylvania, on 1 November 1865.

The first code of rules to govern the interchange of freight cars in the U.S.A. was adopted at a meeting of officials of six freight lines at Buffalo, N.Y., on 20 April 1866.

The Master Car Builders' Association was formed in the U.S.A. in 1867 to conduct tests and experiments towards the standardising of freight cars, brakes, couplers, etc. It subsequently became the Mechanical Division of the Association of American Railroads. (See p. 195.)

Containers were introduced in Britain and Europe during the early 1920s. These large boxes could be transferred bodily from train to truck or ship, so avoiding much loading and unloading.

First tests with automatic couplers in the U.S.A. were carried out by the Master Car Builders' Association beginning in 1869 and continuing for many years. Further tests from September 1885 led to the approval in 1887, by the M.C.B.A., of an automatic coupler working in a vertical plane, invented by Major Eli Hamilton Janney (1831–1912) and patented on 21 April 1868. A second patent was issued on 29 April 1873 for the basic car-coupler design in general use today. Standard, interchangeable, automatic car couplers were introduced in 1887. The Janney automatic coupler was adopted as standard on Pennsylvania Railroad passenger cars in 1884. Link-and-pin couplers on passenger cars continued until about 1888. The 'Type F' interlocking coupler for freight cars was adopted as standard in 1953.

Automatic couplers were adopted on the Imperial Japanese Government Railway on 17 July 1925, after eight years of preparation. The conversion was completed in 24 hours.

The first 'Piggy-back' service in North America was introduced in September 1855 in Nova Scotia, with horse and buggy flat-car services for farmers. Farmers' truck-wagon trains were introduced on the Long Island Railroad, N.Y., in 1884.

'Piggy-backing' was reintroduced on U.S.A. railroads in the early 1950s. It is the transport of containers and motor-truck trailers on specially equipped flat-cars. Technically it is known as 'Trailer-on-Flatcar' (T.O.F.C.) or 'Container-on-Flatcar' (C.O.F.C.). Its success resulted in an eightfold increase from 1955 to 1970 and in 1972 it handled a record number of 2 253 207 trailers.

Freight cars on U.S.A. railroads on 31 December 1973 totalled 1 710 659. This included 511 936 box cars; 365 333 hoppers; 187 347 gondolas (open wagons in England); 165 309 tank cars; 204 926 covered hoppers; 132 222 flat cars and 104 721 refrigerator cars. The average freight-car capacity is now 70·5 tons.

The average length of an American freight train over a recent ten-year period was about 70 freight cars and a caboose. In 1929 the average was only 48 cars. Experimental trains have been run with as many as 500 cars. Freight cars vary in length from 25 to 125 ft (7·620–38·104 m) and average about 45 ft (13·716 m).

Plans for an Automatic Car Identification (A.C.I.) system in the U.S.A. to facilitate prompt location of freight cars were announced in October 1967. It began in 1970 in conjunction with Tele Rail Automated Information Network (TRAIN) with a central computer at the headquarters of the Association of American Railroads in Washington.

Freightliner services on British Railways were introduced between London and Glasgow on 15 November 1965; London and Manchester on 28 February 1966; London and Liverpool on 13 June 1966; Liverpool and Glasgow on 5 September 1966; Manchester and Glasgow on 12 September 1966; London and Aberdeen on 31 October 1966. By the end of 1966 about 27 000 loaded freightliner containers had been carried.

From 1 January 1969, under provisions in the Transport Act of 1968, Freightliner Services were taken over by Freightliners Limited of which 51 per cent is owned by the National Freight Corporation (see below) and 49 per cent by British Railways Board.

The National Freight Corporation was established under the Transport Act of 1968 to promote and to provide integrated freight services by road and rail in Great Britain and to ensure that goods go by rail where this is efficient and economic.

The British Railways service for carrying new cars between Dagenham, Essex, and Halewood near Liverpool using two-tier 'Cartic' (articulated car carriers) units began on 13 July 1966.

The first British 100 ton bogie tank wagon for Shell Oil Products was completed on 21 February 1967.

The Harwich–Zeebrugge container service between England and Belgium was introduced on 18 March 1968 using special cellular container ships and wide-span transporter cranes.

The first container shipped from Japan over the Trans-Siberian Railway arrived at Harwich, England, in May 1969 after a journey of 7600 miles (12 231 km).

The longest and heaviest freight train on record was run on 15 November 1967 over the 157 miles (253 km) between Iaeger, West Virginia, and Portsmouth, Ohio. The 500 coal cars weighed 42 000 tons and stretched about 4 miles (6·5 km). The load was shifted by three 3600 hp diesels in front and three behind.

The heaviest single piece of freight ever carried by rail was a 106 ft (32 m) tall hydrocracker reactor weighing 549·2 tons, from Birmingham, Alabama, to Toledo, Ohio, U.S.A., on 12 November 1965.

The heaviest load carried by British Railways was a 122 ft (37·186 m) long boiler drum weighing 275 tons from Immingham Dock to Killinghome, Lincolnshire, in September 1968.

The record run by a 'Super C' freight in the U.S.A. was made in January 1968 on the Atchison, Topeka & Santa Fe Railroad between Corwith and Hobart yards. The 2202·1 miles (3544 km) were covered in 34 hours 35 minutes 40 seconds at an average speed of 63·6 m.p.h. (102·355 km/h).

Ton-miles on U.S.A. railroads reached a world record of 851 629 000 000 in 1973.

Canada's first remote-controlled mid-train diesel locomotives in regular freight service, using the new 'Robot' radio-command system were first tested on the Canadian Pacific on 16 November 1967. The system is now in regular use in North America.

The longest freight train on record in Canada was a Canadian Pacific train of 250 loaded grain cars, powered by seven diesel-electric locomotives, about 2·5 miles long (4 km). It ran on 22 October 1974 from west of Moose Jaw, Saskatchewan, to Thunder Bay, Ontario, where it had to be divided into three sections to be handled in the yards. It was part of experiments to increase transcontinental line capacity.

The heaviest trains in Australia are the ore trains in northern Western Australia, on the W.A.G.R. Loads up to 250 wagons each carrying 100 tons of ore are hauled by three 3000 hp diesel-electric locomotives.

In January 1974 the Public Transport Commission of Australia introduced fast container trains, the first in an interstate network. They carry 40 6 m (20 ft) long containers, and run between Sydney and Brisbane in 17 hours. (The Limited passenger trains take 15 hours 20 minutes.) The new wagons have a maximum speed of 112 km/h (70 m.p.h.).

The Trans-Europ-Express Marchandises (T.E.E.M.) services were introduced in May 1961 to provide fast international goods services at speeds of 85–100 km/h (53–62 m.p.h.) on similar lines to the T.E.E. passenger trains. They now operate 114 connections between 20 countries.

RAILCARS

The first railcar was a four-wheeled vehicle designed by James Samuel (1824–74), while resident engineer of the Eastern Counties Railway, England. It was built by W. Bridges Adams (see p. 39) at Fairfield Works, Bow, London, and was named *Express*. It first ran on 23 October 1847. It had a vertical boiler. Although it could run at 47 m.p.h. (75·5 km/h) and burned only 3·02 lb (1·45 kg) of coke a mile (1·6 km), it carried only four passengers and was hardly an economic proposition.

The first large railcar was again by J. Samuel and W. B. Adams, built in 1848 for the 7 ft (2·134 m) gauge Bristol & Exeter Railway. This vertical boilered car, named *Fairfield*, was put to work on the Tiverton Branch.

Their next, *Enfield*, built in 1849 for the Eastern Counties Railway, was the first with a horizontal boiler.

The 2–2–4 steam railcar built for the Viceroy of Egypt about 1859 (The Science Museum, London)

After a quarter of a century the railcar idea was again taken up and in 1873 Alexander McDonnell (1829–1904) of the Great Southern & Western Railway in Ireland produced a 0–4–4 tank with a staff saloon attached to the rear.

Other staff railcars were built by the Great Eastern Railway in 1874 to a design by William Adams (1823–1904); for the London, Brighton & South Coast Railway by William Stroudley in 1885 and the famous London & South Western Railway 'Cab', incorporating a single-driver engine, by Dugald Drummond (1840–1912) in 1899.

In Belgium the railcar was introduced in 1877 by M. A. Cabany of Malines. A total of 15 were built, some with six and some with eight wheels.

The next railcar phase came in 1903–11 when many railways were trying to economise on branch lines or on urban lines competing with street-cars. Most of these cars had a small 0–4–0 loco-motive forming one bogie. About 25 companies in England, Scotland, Wales and Ireland produced about as many different designs. Among the best and longest lived were the Lancashire & Yorkshire Railway cars by George Hughes.

Geared steam railcars appeared in Britain in 1905 and later were developed by the Sentinel Wagon Works at Shrewsbury and by Cammell-Laird Limited in 1923. They had a vertical high-pressure water-tube boiler, and were in use all over the world. The biggest user of these cars in Britain was the London & North Eastern Railway.

The first British internal-combustion engined railcar was the 'Petrol-Electric Autocar' built by the North Eastern Railway in 1903. Two were built and they worked between Scarborough and Filey in August 1904 and in the winter between Billingham and Port Clarence. In 1908 they were put to work on the Selby–Cawood Branch.

Direct-drive gas (petrol)-engined vehicles were being tried at the same time in North America. In 1904 a Napier car fitted with flanged wheels was

Great Western petrol-electric railcar No. 100, designed by British Thomson-Houston Company, who supplied all the electrical equipment. It entered service in 1911 and was sold in 1919 to Lever Brothers Limited at Port Sunlight, Cheshire, who used it until 1923 (British Rail)

The first of the steam railcars designed by George Hughes for the Lancashire & Yorkshire Railway. No. 3 was built in 1906 and ran until 1947 (British Rail)

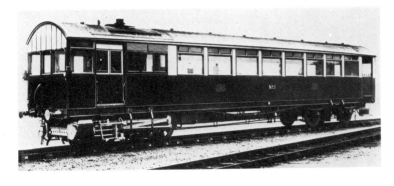

Great Western steam railcar No. 1 built at Swindon in 1903 (British Rail)

The 'daddy-long-legs' on the Brighton & Rottingdean Railway, built by Magnus Volk in 1896. At high tide the rails were covered by 15 ft (4·5 m) of water (Brighton Public Libraries)

tested over 1000 miles (1609 km) of railway in the U.S.A. and Canada.

The 'gas-electric' car was introduced in the U.S.A. by the General Electric Company in 1906 when a combined passenger and baggage car was built for the Delaware & Hudson Railroad. It was 68 ft 7 in (20·904 m) long and weighed 43·8 tons.

Many railcars for light railways, particularly in Ireland, were adapted from old buses, the first being run on the 3 ft (914 mm) gauge County Donegal Railway in Ireland in 1928.

Pneumatic-tyred railcars were introduced in France by the Michelin Tyre Company in 1931. A similar car was tried on the London, Midland & Scottish and Southern railways in England in 1932. In 1935 the L.M.S. tested the 'Coventry Pneumatic Railcar', a 16-wheeled vehicle by Armstrong Siddeley with Michelin tyres. Pneumatic-tyred cars, though much used in France, never went into public service in Britain.

(For developments in diesel railcars see 'Diesel Rail Traction', p. 149.)

The record for being the world's most extraordinary railcar must surely be held for all time by the Brighton & Rottingdean Railway, Sussex, England. The line was 2·75 miles (4·42 km) long and was built by Magnus Volk (see p. 57) on the seashore, with a total gauge of 18 ft (5·486 m). At high water the four rails were covered by about 15 ft (4·572 m) of water. The car stood on legs about 23 ft (7 m) high and had a cabin like a ship. It was the only railcar that carried a lifeboat and lifebelts as normal equipment. The railway opened on 28 November 1896 and ran until January 1901.

RAILWAY RACES

In the Great Locomotive Chase on the Nashville Chatanooga & St Louis Railroad on 12 April 1862, during the American Civil War, Captain James J. Andrews and his Yankee raiders seized the Confederate Rogers 4–4–0 *General* at Kennesaw about 25 miles (40·2 km) north of Atlanta, Georgia. They drove it 87 miles (140 km) to within 20 miles (32 km) of Chatanooga where it ran out of fuel and was caught by the Confederates in another 4–4–0, *Texas*. The chase was over light unballasted track at speeds of over 60 m.p.h. (96·5 km/h). For 50 miles (80·5 km) the *Texas* was running tender first.

Both engines are preserved; the *General* at Kennesaw Museum, Georgia, and the *Texas* at Grant Park, Atlanta.

The General *at Kennesaw Station, Georgia in February 1972, waiting to be placed in the museum building. This is the site where it was stolen in April 1862 (Louisville & Nashville Railroad)*

In the race from London to Edinburgh in 1888 the West Coast companies (London & North Western and Caledonian) on 13 August covered the 399·7 miles (643·25 km) in 7 hours 6 minutes at an average speed of 56·2 m.p.h. (90·44 km/h).

On 31 August the East Coast companies (Great Northern, North Eastern and North British) set up a record over their 393·2 mile (632·79 km) route, taking 6 hours 48 minutes at an average speed of 57·7 m.p.h. (92·86 km/h).

In the subsequent race from London to Aberdeen the West Coast companies set up a world speed record on 22 August 1895 by covering the 541 miles (870·66 km) in 512 minutes at an average speed of 63·3 m.p.h. (101·87 km/h) including three stops and the climbs over Shap and Beattock, but with only a 70 ton train.

The best East Coast time was 518 minutes for the 523·5 miles (842·5 km) on 21 August 1895, but they had reached Edinburgh in 6 hours 18 minutes, averaging 62·3 m.p.h. (100 km/h) with three stops and with a 120 ton train, thereby beating their record of 1888.

When the Atlantic liners called at Plymouth there was great rivalry between the Great Western and the London & South Western railways in getting passengers and mail to London.

The Great Western Railway 4–4–0 No. 3440 City of Truro, *photographed at Winchester Chesil Station in May 1957 while back in service on the Didcot–Southampton service (John Marshall)*

The London & North Eastern Railway 'Flying Scotsman' hauled by 'A1' Class 'Pacific' No. 4476 Royal Lancer *(British Rail)*

On 9 May 1904 the G.W.R. 'Ocean Mail' ran the 127·8 miles (205·673 km) from Millbay Crossing, Plymouth, to Pylle Hill Junction, Bristol, in 123 minutes 19 seconds with the 4–4–0 locomotive *City of Truro*. Down Wellington Bank it reached a very high speed, but the reputed maximum of 102·3 m.p.h. (164·631 km/h) has since been seriously questioned and is no longer accepted. From the recorded data, however, there is now little doubt that a speed of about 100 m.p.h. (161 km/h) was reached.

The same train, behind 4–2–2 *Duke of Connaught*, covered the 188·7 miles (191 km) from Pylle Hill Junction to Paddington, London, in 99 minutes 46 seconds, with an average speed of 80 m.p.h. (128·75 km/h) over the 70·3 miles (113·133 km) from Shrivenham to Westbourne Park, a record for sustained high speed which stood in Britain until broken by the 'Cheltenham Flyer' in 1929.

The disastrous derailment at Salisbury at 13.57 on 1 July 1906 brought the racing to an end. The London & South Western Railway boat express was wrecked taking a sharp curve at excessive speed. Twenty-four passengers and four railwaymen were killed.

The world's longest non-stop run was established by the London & North Eastern Railway in the summer time-table of 1927 with the 268·3 miles (431·788 km) between London and Newcastle.

Not to be outdone the London, Midland & Scottish Railway immediately cut out the crew-changing stop at Carnforth in the run of the 10.00 train out of London (Euston), which had just been named 'The Royal Scot', and ran the 301 miles (484·4 km) non-stop to Carlisle (Kingmoor) shed where engines were changed.

On 1 May 1928 the L.N.E.R. decided to run the 10.00 from London (King's Cross), the 'Flying Scotsman', non-stop between London and Edinburgh, 393 miles (632·5 km), thereby establishing another world record. For this purpose H. N. Gresley designed his famous corridor tender enabling the engine crew to be changed during the journey.

On the Friday before this, however, the L.M.S. stole the glory by dividing the 'Royal Scot' and running the two halves non-stop between London and Edinburgh and Glasgow.

The Edinburgh portion of six coaches was taken by the 4–4–0 compound No. 1054 whose run of 399·7 miles (643·251 km) was certainly a British record for a 4–4–0, and probably a world record.

'Royal Scot'-type 4–6–0 No. 6113 *Cameronian*

The record-breaking London, Midland & Scottish Railway 'Pacific' No. 6201 Princess Elizabeth *(British Rail)*

with the Glasgow portion achieved a world record with any locomotive by running the 401·4 miles (646 km) non-stop.

On 16 November 1936 the L.M.S. crowned this achievement by running a special 230 ton train non-stop from London to Glasgow in 5 hours 53 minutes 38 seconds at an average speed of 68·1 m.p.h. (109·6 km/h) behind the Stanier 'Pacific' No. 6201 *Princess Elizabeth*. The following day it returned with 260 tons in 5 hours 44 minutes 15 seconds at an average speed of 70 m.p.h. (112·65 km/h).

The result of this exercise was the inauguration of the L.M.S. 'Coronation Scot' streamlined train which ran between London and Glasgow in 6½ hours on 5 July 1937 stopping, however, at Carlisle for change of crew.

On the same day the L.N.E.R. introduced the 'Coronation' between London and Edinburgh, streamlined from the front of the 'A4' Class 'Pacific' to the tail of the rear observation car. It called at York and Newcastle going north and at Newcastle going south. The journey time was 6 hours.

The longest distance in Britain without an advertised stop is 565 miles (909 km) by the Night Motorail service from Kensington, Olympia, Greater London, to Inverness, Scotland, inaugurated in May 1973. It takes 13 hours 20 minutes.

RAILWAY SPEED RECORDS
(See also 'Railway Races', p. 176.)

The train that arrived seven years late left Beaumont, Texas, on the Gulf & Interstate Railway, at 11.30 on 8 September 1900 for Port Bolivar, about 70 miles (112·6 km). At High Island, 33 miles (53·1 km) on, it was caught in a tremendous flood which washed away miles of track. The passengers and crew were saved, but the train remained isolated until after the impoverished railway company had been taken over by the Atchison,

Topeka & Santa Fe Railroad which relaid the track. In September 1907 the train was overhauled and the engine steamed up and the journey, which should have taken 2 hours 25 minutes, was completed. Some of the original passengers were there to greet the train on its arrival.

The earliest rail speed records were claimed by the U.S.A. but most of these are unauthenticated and are not internationally accepted.

The first mile-a-minute run was claimed in 1848 when the locomotive *Antelope* ran from Boston to Lawrence, Massachusetts — 26 miles in 26 minutes.

The first 100 m.p.h. run (161 km/h) was claimed on 9 May 1893 when the 'Empire State Express' of the New York Central & Hudson River Railroad (introduced on 26 October 1891) running between Syracuse and Buffalo, N.Y., reached 102·8 m.p.h. (165·436 km/h) at Grimesville. On 11 May it was said to have reached 112·5 m.p.h. (181 km/h) at Crittenden West, N.Y. Experienced train-timers who were on the train, however, both recorded a maximum of 81·8 m.p.h. (131·647 km/h). The engine was the 4–4–0 No. 999 and the engineer was Charles Hogan. This engine, rebuilt with 5 ft 8 in (1727 mm) driving-wheels in place of its original 7 ft 2 in (2184 mm), is now displayed at the Museum of Science and Industry, Chicago.

On 15 June 1902 the New York Central & Hudson River Railroad inaugurated 'The Twentieth Century Limited' between New York and Chicago, covering the 961 miles (1547 km) in 20 hours. On the same day the Pennsylvania Railroad introduced the 'Pennsylvania Special' between the same places, taking 20 hours for the 897 miles (1443·5 km).

The N.Y.C. & H.R. route included a 15 m.p.h. (24 km/h) journey of a mile (1·6 km) through the main street of Syracuse which was replaced by a viaduct on 24 September 1936. The Pennsylvania Railroad

Trains at the summit of the Snowdon Mountain Railway, Wales, 3493 ft (1064 m), the highest railway in Britain (John Marshall)

A train at the upper terminus of the Gornergrat Railway, Switzerland, 3088·7 m (10 133·5 ft), the world's first electric rack railway and the highest open-air railway in Europe. Beyond is the Matterhorn (John Marshall)

Festiniog Railway 0–4–0 No. 1 Princess, *the first narrow-gauge locomotive, built in 1863 and much rebuilt since, awaiting restoration at Blaenau Ffestiniog, Wales, in April 1974 (John Marshall)*

route included 400 miles (644 km) through the Allegheny Mountains, round the famous Horseshoe Curve, and over a summit of 2194 ft (668·73 m).

The fastest long-distance train in the world was the claim made by the Pennsylvania Railroad on 11 June 1905 when the 'Pennsylvania Special' began running between New York and Chicago in 18 hours. The following day it was claimed that the train had run 3 miles (4·8 km) at 127·2 m.p.h. (204·7 km/h) at Elida, Ohio, with 'Atlantic'-type engine No. 7002, and had covered the whole journey in 16 hours 3 minutes at an average speed of 56·07 m.p.h. (91·4 km/h).

'The Twentieth Century Limited' was accelerated to 18 hours in 1908, but was later restored to 20 hours until reduced to 18 again in April 1932. On 15 June 1938 the new streamlined trains reduced the time to 16 hours. In 1929 the route had been shortened from 961 to 958·7 miles (1543 km) by the Cleveland by-pass. Steam traction with the famous New York Central 'Hudson'-type 4–6–4s ended in March 1945. 'The Twentieth Century Limited' made its last run on 13 March 1967.

The earliest speed record with electric-traction was 101 m.p.h. (162 km/h) attained by a German double-bogie locomotive built by Siemens & Halske in 1901 and operating on 1500 V d.c., but it severely damaged the track.

On 6 October 1903 a 12-wheeled electric railcar with motors by Siemens & Halske reached a speed of 126 m.p.h. (203 km/h) on the military railway between Marienfeld and Berlin. A similar car with A.E.G. (Allgemeine Elektrizitäts-Gesellschaft, Berlin) equipment reached 130·5 m.p.h. (210·2 km/h) on 23 October 1903.

This record stood in Germany until 1974 when one of the prototype luxury four-car train sets of the German Federal Railways Class 'TE403' reached a speed of 133·6 m.p.h. (215 km/h) between

Bielefeld and Hamm. These trains are designed for speeds of 200 km/h (124·3 m.p.h.) in public service and for experimental running up to 230 km/h (142·9 m.p.h.).

A new world speed record was established in Germany on 21 June 1931 when a petrol railcar driven by an airscrew maintained 143 m.p.h. (230 km/h) for 6·25 miles (10 km) between Karstädt and Dergenthin.

'The world's fastest train' was the claim made by the Great Western Railway, England, on 6 June 1932 when the 'Cheltenham Spa Express' behind 'Castle' Class 4–6–0 No. 5006 *Tregenna Castle* ran the 77·3 miles (124 km) from Swindon to London (Paddington) in 56 minutes 47 seconds at an average speed of 81·6 m.p.h. (131·3 km/h). The maximum speed was 92·3 m.p.h. (148·5 km/h). The train became known as 'The Cheltenham Flyer', but the record was held only until 1935.

Germany established a record speed for steam-traction in May 1935 when the streamlined 4–6–4 No. 05.001 reached 124½ m.p.h. (200·4 km/h) on a test run between Berlin and Hamburg. The engine was built by the Borsig Locomotive Works, Berlin, in 1935. The second engine, No. 05.002, achieved 120 m.p.h. (193 km/h) with a 200 ton train in June 1935.

The fastest speed with a steam locomotive in Canada was on a test run when one of the five Canadian Pacific 'Jubilee' Class 4–4–4s reached 112 m.p.h. (180 km/h).

A record speed with diesel-electric traction was achieved in Germany on 23 June 1939 when 133·5 m.p.h. (265·5 km/h) was reached.

The diesel-electric 'Zephyr' of the Chicago, Burlington & Quincy Railroad, on 26 May 1934, ran the 1017 miles (1637 km) from

Canadian Pacific 'Jubilee' Class 4–4–4 No. 3000. One of this type reached a speed of 112 m.p.h. (180 km/h), the fastest speed with a steam locomotive in Canada (Canadian Pacific Limited)

Denver to Chicago at an average speed of 77·6 m.p.h. (124·8 km/h) throughout.

On 23 October 1936 it ran from Chicago to Denver in 12 hours 12 minutes at an average speed of 91·6 m.p.h. (147·4 km/h); 750 miles (1270 km) were covered at 90 m.p.h. (144·8 km/h), 26·6 miles (42·8 km) at 105 m.p.h. (169 km/h) and a maximum speed of 116 m.p.h. (186·7 km/h) was reached.

The first American transcontinental speed record was made in June 1876 by the 'Jarrett and Palmer Special' when it ran the 3312 miles (5330 km) from Jersey City to San Francisco in 84 hours 20 minutes, or about 3½ days.

Edward Henry Harriman (1848–1909), while president of the Union Pacific Railroad 1903 until his death, once covered the 3344 miles (5382 km) in a special train from Oakland, California, to New York in 71 hours 27 minutes. This remained the transcontinental record until October 1934.

The Union Pacific Railroad achieved a record for diesel-traction with the first American streamlined diesel-electric express, the M10000. In October 1934 during tests it covered 60 miles (96·5 km) at 102·8 m.p.h. (165·4 km/h) and reached 120 m.p.h. (193 km/h). It crossed the continent from Los Angeles to New York—3259 miles (5245 km) in 56 hours 56 minutes, at an average speed of 62 m.p.h. (99·8 km/h). In service it ran the 2272 miles (3657 km) between Chicago and Portland in 39¼ hours. It was scrapped in 1942.

The Chicago, Milwaukee, St Paul & Pacific began experiments with high speeds in the early 1930s, and on 29 July 1934 'F6' Class 4–6–4 No. 6402, built in 1930, with a train of five roller-bearing steel cars, reached a speed of 103·5 m.p.h. (166·5 km/h) at Oakwood, Wisconsin, and averaged 92·62 m.p.h. (149 km/h) for 61·4 miles (98·8 km) between Edgebrook, Ill, and Oakwood, Wis. The

average over the 85·7 miles (137·9 km) Chicago–Milwaukee run was 76·07 m.p.h. (122·4 km/h). This was the first authentic 100 m.p.h. (161 km/h) run in the U.S.A.

The famous 'Hiawatha' service began on 29 May 1935, covering the 410 miles (660 km) Chicago–St Paul in 6 hours 30 minutes. The Chicago-Milwaukee section was covered in 75 minutes at speeds of 100 m.p.h. (161 km/h). The locomotives were the four 'Atlantics', described on p. 128, which could run up to 120 m.p.h. (193 km/h).

The success of the 'Hiawatha' created heavier loadings which led to the introduction, in 1938, of the six 'F7' Class streamlined 4–6–4s. These shared the workings with the 'Atlantics', and from 21 January 1939 worked two additional Chicago–Twin Cities trains known as the 'Morning Hiawathas'. Later that year one of them averaged 120 m.p.h. (193 km/h) for 5 miles (8 km) and maintained over 100 m.p.h. (161 km/h) for 19 miles (30·5 km).

In the course of a trial run from London to Leeds and back on 30 November 1934 the London & North Eastern Railway 'Pacific' No. 4472 *Flying Scotsman* with a load of 145 tons covered the 185·8 miles (299 km) outwards in 151 minutes 56 seconds. On the return, with 208 tons, it took 157 minutes 17 seconds. Down Stoke Bank between Grantham and Peterborough the dynamometer-car speed recorder gave a maximum of 100 m.p.h. (161 km/h) for 600 yd (548·6 m). However, this was disputed by the most experienced of all train-timers, Cecil J. Allen, who was on the train and who would accept nothing higher than 98 m.p.h. (157·72 km/h).

Bugatti railcars in France achieved some high speeds in 1935, one of them reaching 115·5 m.p.h. (185·9 km/h) near Le Mans.

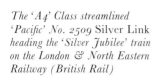

The 'A4' Class streamlined 'Pacific' No. 2509 Silver Link *heading the 'Silver Jubilee' train on the London & North Eastern Railway (British Rail)*

*A train on the former Denver &
Rio Grande Western Railway
3 ft (0·914 m) gauge branch from
Durango to Silverton heading up
the Animas Canyon behind ALCO
2–8–2 No. 478 (1923), 'K28
Class' (John Marshall)*

*A typical Colorado
narrow-gauge freight
train, with 2–8–0 No.
318 of the Golden City
& San Juan Railway,
at the Colorado Railroad
Museum, Golden near
Denver, in July 1972
(John Marshall)*

*Isle of Man Railway 3 ft (0·914
m) gauge 2–4–0 tank No. 1*
Sutherland *built by Beyer
Peacock, Manchester, in 1873,
photographed at Douglas Station
in September 1974 (Simon
Marshall)*

A world speed record for steam was achieved by the London & North Eastern Railway on 5 March 1935 when the 'Pacific' No. 2750 *Papyrus* reached 108 m.p.h. (173·8 km/h) down Stoke Bank during a round trip of 536 miles (863 km) from London to Newcastle and back at an over-all average speed of 70 m.p.h. (112·6 km/h). The outcome of this test was a new four-hour service between London and Newcastle in October 1935.

The first of the Gresley 'A4' Class 'Pacifics', No. 2509 *Silver Link*, broke the record the same year, on 27 September 1935, when it twice reached 112½ m.p.h. (181 km/h) and averaged 107½ m.p.h. (173 km/h) for 25 miles (40 km), 100 m.p.h. (161 km/h) for 43 miles (69 km) and 91·8 m.p.h. (147·7 km/h) for 70 miles (113 km) continuously, with a 230 ton train.

An attempt to break this record was made by the London, Midland & Scottish Railway during a trial of the 'Coronation Scot' with 'Pacific' No. 6220 *Coronation*. Four reliable train-timers (Cecil J. Allen, D. S. M. Barrie, S. P. W. Corbett and O. S. Nock) independently recorded a speed of 112½ m.p.h. (181 km/h) at a point only 2 miles (3·219 km) south of Crewe Station. The L.M.S., eager to beat the L.N.E.R. record, officially claimed a speed of 114 m.p.h. (183·5 km/h), but this is seriously doubted. It was followed by a hazardous entry into Crewe Station over crossovers, resulting in a heap of smashed crockery in the restaurant car.

The all-time record for steam-traction was achieved by the L.N.E.R. on 3 July 1938 when the 'A4' Class No. 4468 *Mallard* with a seven-coach train weighing 240 tons reached 126 m.p.h. (202·8 km/h) on Stoke Bank. Five miles (8 km) (mileposts 94–89) were covered at an average speed of 120·4 m.p.h. (193·76 km/h). It was done

at great risk and the engine suffered severe damage. The driver was Joseph Duddington who retired in 1944. *Mallard* is preserved in York Railway Museum.

New records were achieved in Italy by three-car electric units. On 27 July 1938 the 132·9 miles (213·9 km) from Rome to Naples were covered in 83 minutes at an average speed of 96·1 m.p.h. (154·66 km/h) and with a maximum of 125 m.p.h. (201 km/h).

On 20 July 1939 the 195·8 miles (315 km) from Florence to Milan were covered in 115·2 minutes at an average speed, start to stop, of 102 m.p.h. (164 km/h) with a maximum of 126 m.p.h. (202·8 km/h).

In Germany a record for a diesel train was made on 23 June 1939 with a speed of 133·5 m.p.h. (214·85 km/h).

The highest train speeds at the time of writing (1975) have been made in France. On 21 February 1953 Co Co electric locomotive No. 7121 with three coaches averaged 149 m.p.h. (239·8 km/h) for 3 miles (4·8 km) on the 1500 V d.c. line between Dijon and Beaune, reaching a maximum speed of 150·9 m.p.h. (242·8 km/h). The 4300 hp locomotive weighs 106 tons.

On 28 March 1955 No. 7107 of the same type reached 205·6 m.p.h. (230·9 km/h) with a three-coach train of 100 tons for 2 km (1·24 miles) between Facture and Morcenx on the Bordeaux–Hendaye line. The following day this speed was equalled by the 81 ton 4000 hp Bo Bo locomotive No. 9004, also 1500 V d.c. The drivers were H. Braghet and J. Brocca.

A rail speed record of 235 m.p.h. (378 km/h) was achieved in France on 4 December 1967 between Gometz-le-Châtel and Limours by 'L'Aérotrain' powered by jet aero engines.

The world's fastest steam locomotive, London & North Eastern Railway 'A4' Class 'Pacific' No. 4468 Mallard *(British Rail)*

The world's highest speed for a flanged-wheel vehicle on rails, of 243 m.p.h. (391 km/h) was achieved in April 1974 by the 'Linear Induction Motor Test Vehicle' of the United States Department of Transportation at its test track at Pueblo, Colorado.

A Budd diesel railcar fitted with two turbo-jet 'J-47' aircraft engines mounted on the forward end reached a speed of 183·85 m.p.h. (296 km/h) in July 1966 on the New York Central Railroad near Bryan, Ohio, between mileposts 350 and 345. The 5 miles (8 km) were covered in 1 minute 39·75 seconds at an average speed of 181 m.p.h. (291 km/h). The record was achieved near milepost 347 over a length of 300 ft (91·5 m).

The fastest train speed in the U.S.A. was 156 m.p.h. (251 km/h) recorded at Princeton Junction, N.J., on 24 May 1967 by a test train built as part of the Northeast Corridor Project.

The first regular scheduled service at over 100 m.p.h. (161 km/h) was introduced in Japan on 1 November 1965 on the new standard-gauge Tokaido line when trains began running between Tokyo and Osaka—321 miles (516 km)—in 3 hours 10 minutes at an average speed of 101·3 m.p.h. (163 km/h) with a maximum of over 130 m.p.h. (210 km/h), covering the 212·4 miles (342 km) between Tokyo and Nagoya in 120 minutes at an average speed of 106·2 m.p.h. (171 km/h). The trains, then 12 cars weighing 720 tons, are now 16 cars weighing 950 tons.

The new service between Osaka and Okayama, inaugurated on 15 March 1972, covers the 112·03 miles (180·29 km) in 1 hour, reaching a speed of 159 m.p.h. (255·9 km/h).

The fastest booked time in Britain is between Crewe and Watford Junction where trains cover the 140½ miles (226 km) in 101 minutes 30 seconds at an average speed of 83·1 m.p.h. (133·8 km/h).

The highest speed with diesel-tráction was recorded on 12 June 1973 when the British 'High Speed Train' attained a speed of 143 m.p.h. (232 km/h) over ¼ mile (0·4 km) between North-allerton and Thirsk during a test on the Darlington–York section. The previous day the H.S.T. had covered 1 mile (1·609 km) at 141 m.p.h. (226·9 km/h) between Thirsk and Tollerton. The driver was Sidney Winford of York. On 6 June the same train, driven by Ernest Cockerham of Leeds, had broken the 35-year-old British rail-speed record by

maintaining 131 m.p.h. (215 km/h) for 8 miles (12·9 km) between Northallerton and Thirsk. (See p. 164.)

The fastest metre-gauge train in Europe is operated by the Rhaetian Railway in Switzerland. The 7·12 from St Moritz to Chur covers the 55·5 miles (89·3 km) in 2 hours, over a difficult mountain route with innumerable curves and long gradients of 1 in 28·6 (3·5 per cent).

The highest recorded rail speed in New Zealand, 78 m.p.h. (125·5 km/h), was achieved on test by one of the 250 hp diesel railcars built by Vulcan Foundry Limited, Lancashire, England, in 1940. Only nine were delivered; one was lost at sea in a submarine attack. They have three-axle motor bogies and two-axle trailing bogies. Un-official speeds in the 90s (over 145 km/h) have been claimed.

The fastest steam locomotives in New Zealand were the 'Ja' Class 4–8–2s with a top speed of 75 m.p.h. (120·8 km/h).

FASTEST SCHEDULED TRAINS IN THE U.S.A. AND CANADA

The Penn Central electric 'Metroliners' were introduced between New York and Washington on 10 January 1969, covering the 224·6 miles (396 km) with five stops in 2 hours 59 minutes at an average speed of 75·3 m.p.h. (121·2 km/h). On 2 April 1969 a non-stop schedule of 2½ hours was established at an average speed of 98·8 m.p.h. (144·6 km/h), but this was discontinued.

Eight of the 'Metroliners' are booked over the 68·4 miles (110 km) from Baltimore to Wilmington in 43 minutes at an average speed of 95·4 m.p.h. (153·5 km/h). In the reverse direction nine take 44 minutes at an average speed of 93·3 m.p.h. (150 km/h).

'The Super Chief', the finest of Amtrak's (see p. 196) transcontinental trains, covers the 2222 miles (3576 km) between Chicago and Los Angeles via Kansas City and Albuquerque in 40 hours 30 minutes. It crosses the Raton Pass at 7622 ft (2323 m) and two more summits at over 7000 ft (2134 m).

The 'North Coast Hiawatha' is Amtrak's name for the former Northern Pacific 'North Coast Limited'. This streamlined train runs three times weekly taking 51 hours over the 2318 miles (3730 km) between Chicago and Seattle. It crosses the Rockies at Momestake Pass and the Cascades at Stampede Pass.

Two Canadian National diesel 'Rapidos' cover the 115·3 miles (181 km) between Dorval and Brockville in 87 minutes at an average speed of 79½ m.p.h. (128 km/h). Two other C.N.R. 'Rapidos' cover the 100½ miles (162 km) between Guildwood and Belleville in 76 minutes, again at an average speed of 79½ m.p.h.

A 'Super C' freight on the Santa Fe is booked over the 127·2 miles (202·5 km) between Winslow and Gallup in 105 minutes at an average speed of 72·7 m.p.h. (117 km/h). Another takes 175 minutes over the 205·2 miles (330 km) between Waynoka and Amarillo at an average speed of 70·3 m.p.h. (113·2 km/h).

ACCIDENTS

The first recorded fatal railway accident occurred on the opening day of the Liverpool & Manchester Railway, 15 September 1830, when William Huskisson, Member of Parliament for Liverpool, was run over by the Stephensons' *Rocket* at Parkside near Newton le Willows. His thigh was fractured and he died later at Eccles. The engine was being driven by Joseph Locke (see p. 42).

The first passenger-train accident in the U.S.A. occurred on 9 November 1833 on the Camden & Amboy Railroad between Spotswood and Hightown, New Jersey. One carriage overturned and 12 of its 24 passengers were seriously injured.

The first British railway accident to be investigated by an inspecting officer of the Board of Trade was at Howden on the Hull & Selby Railway on 7 August 1840 when a casting fell from a wagon and derailed a mixed passenger/ goods train, causing six deaths.

The first large railway accident was in France on 8 May 1842. A 15-coach express from Versailles to Paris crashed when the axle of one of the two engines broke and several coaches piled on top of it. Locked compartment doors prevented people from escaping and 48 were burned to death. This ended the locking of train doors in France.

Canada's first major railway collision occurred on the Great Western Railway west of Chatham in 1854 when a train of ballast for the

track collided with a passenger train, killing 47 people.

The worst railway accident in Canada was on the Grand Trunk Railway at Beloeil, Quebec, on 29 June 1864 when 99 people were killed. This stimulated safety-consciousness and led to the introduction of standard operating procedures on Canadian railways.

The first fatal railway accident in Australia was at Lidcombe, a suburb of Sydney, N.S.W., on 10 July 1858. A train took a curve too fast and was derailed, killing 2 and injuring 13.

Charles Dickens escaped with a shaking when he was involved in the derailment at Staplehurst, Kent, on the South Eastern Railway, on 9 June 1865, in which ten people were killed when the train ran on to a viaduct where repairs were being carried out. He never fully recovered and he died on 9 June 1870, exactly five years later.

The only major British railway disaster in which there were no survivors was on 28 December 1879 when the Tay Bridge collapsed in a gale while a train was crossing. All 75 passengers and crew of 5 were drowned. Some bodies were never recovered. (See 'Bouch', p. 51, and 'Tay Bridge', p. 91.)

Britain's worst rail disaster occurred at Quintinshill near Gretna Green, in Scotland just north of Carlisle, on 22 May 1915. Signalling irregularities led to the overlooking of a train standing on the wrong line. A military special was accepted and it collided at 68 m.p.h. (110 km/h) into the stationary train. The 213 yd (195 m) long train was telescoped to 67 yd (61 m). Fifty-three seconds later an express from the other direction ploughed into the wreckage at 60 m.p.h. (95 km/h). Fire added to the horror and destruction in which 227 lives were lost.

The world's worst railway disaster occurred at Saint-Michael-de-Maurienne in France on 12 December 1917. A packed troop train carrying 1025 soldiers in 19 Italian carriages weighing 526 tons behind a single locomotive, P.L.M. 4-6-0 No. 2592, was ordered away from Modane at the north end of the Mont Cenis Tunnel at about 22·00. The maximum permitted load for this locomotive was 144 tons. Only the first three coaches had Westinghouse continuous brake and the rest had only hand brakes. Driver Louis Girard was unwilling to proceed but was unable to act against military commands. On the

10 miles of 1 in 33 (16 km of 3 per cent) falling grade the train ran out of control, brakes became red-hot and set fire to the coaches, the engine became derailed, breaking the coupling with the train, and finally the entire train was wrecked at 91 m.p.h. (150 km/h) on a curve at Saint-Michael-de-Maurienne. Of the 560 dead which could be accounted for in the wreckage 135 could not be identified. The final death toll was estimated at over 800. The driver miraculously survived and was freed of all blame.

The first serious accident to an electric train in Britain was at Hall Road on the Liverpool–Southport line of the Lancashire & Yorkshire Railway on 27 July 1905. A signalman's error led to a collision in which 21 people were killed.

England's worst railway disaster was at Harrow & Wealdstone Station on the London Midland Region on 8 October 1952. An express from Perth, running 80 minutes late, failed to stop at signals and ran at 56–59 m.p.h. (90–95 km/h) into the rear of a crowded local train in the platform. Almost immediately a double-headed express travelling northwards at the same speed crashed into the wreckage. The death toll was 112.

This accident would almost certainly have been prevented by automatic train control such as was in use on the Western Region (see p. 206) or the type now installed on most British main lines.

The worst accident on a London 'tube' railway occurred on Friday, 28 February 1975 when the 08·37 train from Drayton Park ran unbraked through Moorgate Station on the Highbury

Branch and crashed into the end of a blind tunnel. The front 14 seats were compressed into a space of 2 ft (0·610 m). A total of 43 died and 77 were seriously injured. The rescue operation was the most difficult ever undertaken on a British railway, in temperatures often exceeding 120 °F (49 °C). The last of the bodies was not recovered until late on Tuesday, 4 March. On 15 April it was revealed at the inquiry that the driver's body contained a dangerously high level of alcohol and that he had possibly been in a trance as a result.

Previously the worst accident was at Stratford on 8 April 1953 when a train collided into the rear of another, killing 12 people. This led to modifications in signalling. Despite these accidents, London's Underground Railway has one of the finest safety records in the world.

'The Great Train Wreck' in Texas on 15 September 1896 was deliberately contrived as a public entertainment by W. G. Crush, general passenger agent of the Missouri, Kansas & Texas Railway, or the 'Katy' as the M. K. & T. was known. The event was widely advertised and drew a crowd of about 30000 to witness the event, greatly enhancing the Katy passenger receipts. At the appointed time two old empty trains were dispatched towards each other from a great distance, but the collision and boiler explosions hurled debris into the crowds of spectators lining the valley on both sides, causing a sad toll of dead and injured.

The oddest collision on record occurred in February 1913 on the Memphis branch of the Louisville & Nashville Railroad, U.S.A., during a

The hole at Lindal on the Furness Railway into which a locomotive disappeared on 22 October 1892. The engine still lies at a depth of 200 ft (61 m) (British Rail)

flood. A freight train collided in the dark with the shallow-draught packet-boat *Lochie S* which was sailing above the tracks at Cumberland, Texas. No one was injured, but the responsibility for damage was never properly settled.

A locomotive that disappeared was 0–6–0 No. 115 of the Furness Railway, England, built by Sharp Stewart & Company in 1881. On 22 October 1892 at about 8.16 it was shunting at Lindal, an area of extensive iron-ore mines, when the ground gave way beneath it and the engine began to sink in.

The crew, Driver Postlethwaite and Fireman Robinson, jumped clear and by 14.15 the engine had disappeared completely. It fell to a depth of 200 ft (61 m), beyond recovery, and the hole was filled in.

One of Britain's most curious railway disasters was at Swinton near Manchester on 28 April 1953 when the roof of Clifton Hall (Black Harry) Tunnel collapsed under a filled-in shaft. A pair of semi-detached houses above collapsed into the crater, causing five deaths. The tunnel was on the Patricroft–Clifton Branch of the London &

Worst Railway Disasters in various countries

Country	Date	Place	No. killed	Cause
France	12.12.1917	Modane	543	Runaway and derailment
Italy	2.3.1944	Balvano, nr Salerno	526	Stalled in Armi Tunnel
Spain	3.1.1944	Near Torre, Leon Province	500–800	Double collision and fire inside tunnel
Mexico	3.4.1955	Near Guadalajara	c. 300	Derailed into canyon
Pakistan	29.9.1957	Montgomery	250	Collision
Argentina	4.2.1970	Near Buenos Aires	236	Collision
Scotland	22.5.1915	Near Gretna Green	227	Double collision
Poland	22.10.1949	Nowy Dwor	c. 200	Derailment
Japan	29.1.1940	Osaka	200	Collision
Brazil	20.3.1946	Near Aracaju	185	Wreck
Jamaica	1.9.1957	Kendal	178	Derailed into ravine
New Zealand	24.12.1953	Near Waiouru	155	Bridge Collapse
Russia	13.7.1882	Near Tchery	c. 150	Derailment
Nigeria	16.2.1970	Northern Nigeria	c. 150*	
India	23.11.1956	Marudaiyar River	143	Derailment
Germany	22.12.1939	Near Magdeburg	132	Collision
England	8.10.1952	Harrow & Wealdstone	112	Double collision
Czechoslovakia	14.11.1960	Pardubice	110	Collision
U.S.A.	9.7.1918	Nashville, Tennessee	c. 101	Head-on collision
Roumania	25.12.1938	Near Kishiney	c. 100	Collision
Canada	29.6.1864	Beloeil, near St Hilaire	99	Points wrongly set
Portugal	26.7.1964	Custoias, near Oporto	94	Wreck
Indonesia	28.5.1959	Java	92	Derailed into ravine
Netherlands	8.1.1962	Woerden	91	Collision
South Africa	4.10.1965	Near Durban	81	Derailment
Northern Ireland	12.6.1889	Armagh	80	Runaway collision
Burma	9.12.1965	Near Toungoo	76	Collision
Switzerland	14.6.1891	Münchenstein	71	Birs Bridge collapse
South Korea	31.1.1954	Near Seoul	56	
Philippines	2.9.1954	Negros Island	56	
Australia	20.4.1908	Near Melbourne, Victoria	44	Brake failure
Hungary	22.12.1968	Budapest	c. 43	Collision
Yugoslavia	14.2.1971	Belgrade	34	Fire
Wales	20.8.1868	Abergele	33	Runaway collision

* A further 52 (survivors) were killed in a lorry on their way to hospital.

North Western Railway and was opened on 2 February 1850.

Grade crossing collisions cause the largest number of deaths on railroads in the U.S.A. amounting to about two-thirds of the total. There are about 180000 unguarded grade, or level, crossings in the U.S.A. where about 1500 are killed and 3700 injured annually.

The worst level (grade) crossing accident in Britain was at Hixon, Staffordshire, on the Colwich–Stone section of the elctrified main line from London to Manchester, on 6 January 1968. A transporter loaded with a 120 ton transformer was crossing at 2 m.p.h. (3·2 km/h) when the automatic barriers closed. A train arrived at 70 m.p.h. (113 km/h) before the crossing was cleared and struck the transformer, hurling it 20 ft (6 m). There were 11 deaths. The transporter was being escorted by the police who had failed to telephone the Colwich signalman for permission to cross with an exceptional load.

No passengers were killed on British Railways in 1949, 1954, 1956 and 1966 in more than 15000000000 journeys each year. In 1959 and 1963 only one passenger was killed in each year.

On the New South Wales Government Railways, Australia, during a period of 14 years there was not one fatal accident on any part of the system.

U.S.A. statistics show that railway travel is the safest of all. In terms of fatalities per 100000000 passenger miles (161000000 km) the rate for the railroads is 0.1; for internal air services 0.3; for buses 0.24; and for cars and taxis 2.39.

RUNAWAYS

The first serious passenger-train runaway in Britain was on the Oxford, Worcester & Wolverhampton Railway at Round Oak near Wolverhampton on 23 August 1858 when part of a heavy passenger train broke away and ran back into the following passenger train. Fourteen lives were lost.

A similar accident occurred at Helmshore, Lancashire, on the Lancashire & Yorkshire Railway on 4 September 1860 when 11 died.

These led to experiments with continuous brakes, and the eventual adoption by law of automatic continuous brakes (see pp. 167, 205).

The most serious runaway in British railway history occurred on the Great Northern Railway of Ireland at Armagh on 12 June 1889 when the rear half of an overloaded excursion train, which had failed on a gradient and had been divided, ran back and collided with a following train, killing 80 passengers. The train had continuous but non-automatic brakes.

This accident led to the **Regulation of Railways Act** of 1889 (see p. 205) which gave power to the Board of Trade to order absolute block working on passenger lines (only one train in a section at one time), automatic continuous brakes on passenger trains, and the interlocking of points and signals.

The British unbraked freight train has been the cause of many runaways. The worst was at Abergele on the London & North Western Railway in North Wales on 20 August 1868 when some wagons being irregularly shunted on the main line ran away and collided with a passenger train, causing 33 deaths.

On 12 December 1870, at Stairfoot near Barnsley on the Manchester, Sheffield & Lincolnshire Railway, a similar runaway killed 15 passengers.

These accidents led to the installation of trap points to derail runaways on falling gradients.

Some runaways had amusing sequels, such as at Pinwherry, south of Girvan, on the old Glasgow & South Western Stranraer line. The story is still told of the string of wagons which broke loose on Pinmore Bank one night, ran back through Pinwherry and up Barrhill Bank, then back again, repeating this five or six times before coming to rest. A permanent-way inspector named Gallacher, who was spending the night at Pinwherry Station House, said next morning that it was the busiest country station he had ever tried to sleep at—there was a train every ten minutes.

A record run of 100 miles (161 km) was made on the Chicago, Burlington & Quincy Railroad east of Denver on 26 March 1884 when a wind of tremendous force ripped off the round-house roof at Akron and set eight coal cars on the move. They ran on to the main line where the wind drove them along at speeds up to 40 m.p.h. (64 km/h). One downgrade stretch of 20 miles (32 km) was covered in 18 minutes. At Benkelman, 95 miles from Akron, a freight engine gave chase and in a few miles was coupled to the cars and they were brought under control after covering 100 miles in under 3 hours.

On the windswept Settle and Carlisle section of the former Midland Railway, England, a locomotive was once being turned at Garsdale when a freak wind caught it and kept it spinning round and round until the frantic crew managed to stop it by shovelling ballast into the turntable well. After this a stockade of old sleepers was erected round it, as shown in the photograph.

The stockaded turntable at Garsdale on the Midland Railway, Settle & Carlisle line, where a locomotive was once blown round and round by the wind. To the right is the now-abandoned M.R. branch to Hawes in Wensleydale (John Marshall)

BREAKDOWN, OR WRECKING, CRANES

'Accident cranes', known in North America as 'wrecking cranes', were originally hand-powered machines on rail trucks, with a lifting capacity of 5–10 tons. As the weight of locomotives and rolling stock increased steam-power became necessary, but many British companies were unwilling to lay out capital on such equipment. The London & North Western, one of Britain's biggest railways and the largest joint stock corporation in the world, had no steam accident cranes until 1910.

The term 'breakdown crane' came into use in Great Britain during the First World War.

The first steam accident cranes on a British railway were some self-propelling machines of 5 tons capacity on four-wheeled trucks built for the Midland Railway by Appleby Brothers, London, in 1874–75.

Five years later the same firm built some of 10 tons capacity for the London & South Western Railway.

For many years the world's most powerful wrecking crane was one built for the Norfolk & Western Railroad, U.S.A., by Industrial Works (later Industrial Brownhoist) of Bay City, Michigan, in 1912. It could lift a load of 134 tons (150 short tons) at a radius of 17 ft (5·182 m).

The most powerful British steam breakdown cranes are ten of 75 tons capacity built by Cowans Sheldon & Company Limited, Carlisle, and completed in 1962. Two more were built with diesel-power.

Wrecking crane on the Canadian Pacific Railway at Vancouver, built in 1913 by Industrial Works, Bay City, Michigan, U.S.A. (John Marshall)

The world's most powerful railway breakdown, or wrecking, crane has a lifting capacity of 500 000 lb, or 223·2 tons, at a radius of 17 ft 6 in (5·33 m). It was built by Cowans Sheldon & Company Limited, Carlisle, England, in 1960 for the Quebec Cartier Mining Company of Canada. It is powered by a Rolls-Royce 255 bhp supercharged oil engine through a hydraulic torque converter. It is carried on two three-axle trucks on standard gauge, and is designed to operate in temperatures down to 60 °F below zero (−51 °C).

In 1961 Cowans Sheldon supplied the same Canadian Company with a wrecking crane of 300 000 lb or 134 tons capacity at 17 ft 6 in (5·33 m) radius. Both cranes can negotiate curves of 150 ft or 45·7 m radius.

Cranes of similar though not greater capacity have been built in the U.S.A.

TRAIN FERRIES

The first wagon ferry was operated by the Monkland & Kirkintilloch Railway, Scotland, on the Forth & Clyde Canal in 1833. It was simply a barge fitted with rails and a turnplate.

The first railroad car ferry in the U.S.A., the *Susquehanna*, went into operation on the Susquehanna River between Havre de Grace and Perryville, Maryland, in April 1836. In the winter of 1854 the river froze so solidly that rails were laid on the ice, and between 15 January and 24 February 1378 freight and other cars were hauled across.

The world's first 'train ferry' was designed by Thomas Grainger and was built in 1849 by Robert Napier & Sons on the Clyde. Named *Leviathan*, it ferried goods wagons across the Firth of Forth, Scotland, between Granton and Burntisland.

In 1858 a similar vessel, named *Carries*, was put on the Tayport–Broughty Ferry crossing near Dundee.

Thomas Bouch (see p. 51) is sometimes credited with the design of these; actually he designed only the loading mechanism.

The Harwich–Zebrugge train ferry between England and Belgium began operating under Great Eastern Train Ferries Limited on 24 April 1924.

The Dover–Dunkirk train ferry was inaugurated on 14 October 1936. Through trains between London and Paris were operated by the Southern Railway of England, the Northern Railway of France, the Société Anonyme de Navigation Angleterre–Lorraine–Alsace, and the International Sleeping Car Company.

One of the most famous train ferries was the *Baikal* which operated across Lake Baikal in Siberia as a link in the Trans-Siberian Railway. It was launched on 29 July 1899 and entered service in April 1900, combining the duties of train ferry and ice-breaker. It remained in use as a ferry until

Danish train ferry Prins Henrik *(Danish State Railways)*

The Contra Costa, *operating between San Francisco and Oakland, California, had the distinction of being the largest train ferry in the world*

the Circum–Baikal Railway round the south of the lake was completed in 1904, and it was destroyed in the civil war of 1918–20.

The largest fleet of train and automobile ferries is operated by Danish State Railways (Danske Statsbaner). There are six train ferries and three car ferries, and in addition train ferries operated jointly with the German Federal Railway, German State Railway and Swedish State Railways. The total distance covered is 208 km (129 miles). The speed with which the Danes handle the trains on to and off the ferries is almost unbelievable.

LAST STEAM TRAINS

The last steam-worked transcontinental trains on the Canadian Pacific Railway, after 67 years, ran in October 1954.

The last steam locomotive to pull a train on the C.P.R. was 'A–1–e' Class 4–4–0 No. 29, built in 1887. It hauled a special from Montreal to St Lin and back on 6 November 1960.

The last regularly scheduled steam train in the U.S.A. ran on 27 March 1960 on the Grand Trunk Western system, operated by the Canadian National Railways.

Steam locomotives were finally withdrawn on the Canadian National Railways on 25 April 1960.

The last steam-worked branch line on British Railways was the Brockenhurst–Lymington Branch in Hampshire. It was opened on 12 July 1858 and was steam-worked until 30 March 1967. Electric trains began on 1 April.

Steam-traction was eliminated from British Railways on 8 August 1968, except for the summer-only service on the Vale of Rheidol narrow-gauge railway in Wales.

A commemorative 'Farewell to Steam' tour was operated by B.R. on 11 August 1968 from Liverpool to Carlisle and back. The fare was £15 15s (£15·75).

The last express worked by the famous French compound 'Pacifics' ran between Calais and Amiens on 26 May 1971.

The last regular steam passenger train in Australia ran from Newcastle to Singleton, N.S.W., in July 1971. It was hauled by 'C32' Class 4–6–0 No. 3246, built in 1893, which ran a total of 2 270 000 miles (3 653 500 km). No. 3242 of this type achieved **the record mileage for an Australian steam locomotive**, of 2 370 000 miles (3 814 460 km).

The last steam-powered goods train in Australia ran in N.S.W. on 22 December 1972.

The last steam-hauled expresses in New Zealand ran between Christchurch and Dunedin in October 1971. However, two 'Ab' Class 'Pacifics' were returned to service for use on summer tourist trains between Lumsden and the Kingston railhead on the shore of Lake Wakatipu in Southland.

Section 6
MISCELLANY

BRITISH AND IRISH RAILWAYS

Under the Railways Act of 19 August 1921, a total of 123 separate British railway companies were amalgamated into four groups; the London, Midland & Scottish, the London & North Eastern, the Great Western and the Southern. Certain inter-group joint companies continued to operate separately. The Grouping came into effect on 1 January 1923.

All Irish railways wholly in the 'Free State' (Eire), both 5 ft 3 in (1·600 m) and 3 ft (0·914 m) gauge, were grouped into the Great Southern Railways on 1 January 1925.

The London Transport Executive was formed under the Transport (London) Act of 1969 which transferred the operation of the Underground Railways and the red buses from the former London Transport Board to the Executive, and financial and policy control to Greater London Council from 1 January 1970. The Executive owns 237 miles (382 km) of railway of which 235 miles (378 km) is electrified with third rail at 600 V d.c., and operates over 154 miles (409 km) of route. The red buses run over 1695 miles (2728 km) of roads.

The background history goes back to the Act of 13 April 1933 when the London Passenger Transport Board was established to take over the Metropolitan Railway, the Metropolitan District Railway, the London Electric Railway, the Central London Railway, all the London street tramways (now abandoned) and nearly all bus and coach undertakings in its area. It became part of the British Transport Commission on 1 January 1948 and was renamed the London Transport Executive. On 1 January 1963 it was again renamed, becoming the London Transport Board when the British Transport Commission was dissolved under the 1962 Transport Act.

The Irish Transport Company (Coras Iompair Eireann), formed under the Eire Transport Act of 19 November 1944, began operation on 1 January 1945. Under it the Great Southern

Railways and the Dublin United Transport Company Limited were merged.

The proposal to nationalise British Railways was first announced by the Government on 19 November 1945. Canals and long-distance haulage were included.

The Transport Act received the Royal Assent on 6 August 1947, nationalising British railways and canals from 1 January 1948.

At Nationalisation British Railways operated about 20000 miles (32 190 km) of route with 20024 steam, 55 diesel and diesel-electric and 16 electric locomotives. There were 6701 stations of which 4815 handled freight.

Under the guidance of Dr Richard Beeching B.R. went through a period of amputation mania during which the mileage dropped from 18771 miles (30209 km) in 1960 to 13261 miles (21342 km) in 1969.

At the end of 1972 there were 11537 miles (18988 km) of route, 3 steam locomotives (2 ft (610 mm) gauge), 3683 diesel and diesel-electric locomotives (of which 50 were on hire from manufacturers) and 317 electric locomotives. These totals do not include diesel, diesel-electric and electric multiple-unit sets. The number of stations had dropped to 2362 of which only 182 handled freight.

In 1972 B.R. train-miles amounted to 196000000 (315500000 km) with coaching stock and 53000000 (85400000 km) with freight stock. The system was divided into regions: Scottish, North Eastern, London Midland, Eastern, Western and Southern. On 1 January 1967 the Eastern and North Eastern Regions were combined.

Now the Regions are being replaced by eight Territories: 1 Scotland (Glasgow); 2 North East (Newcastle); 3 North West (Manchester); 4 Yorkshire (York); 5 Midlands (Birmingham); 6 Anglia (London); 7 Western (Cardiff); and 8 Southern (London and Croydon).

The Transport Act (Northern Ireland) received the Royal Assent on 10 August 1948, incorporating the Ulster Transport Authority. The Northern Ireland Road Transport Board, the Belfast & County Down and the Northern Counties railways and other transport services were acquired by 1 April 1949.

The abbreviated title 'British Rail' and its new totem, two horizontal lines and two arrowheads, were adopted in the summer of 1964. The totem began to appear on rolling stock in February 1965.

The largest British railway scheme ever approved by Parliament in one Act was the Lancashire, Derbyshire & East Coast Railway, Warrington to Sutton on Sea, with branches, amounting to 170 miles (274 km) of railway on 5 August 1891. Only the section from Chesterfield to Lincoln, 39 miles (63 km) was built, and was opened throughout on 8 March 1897. It was amalgamated with the Great Central Railway (see below) by an Act of 1906.

Eleven Acts of Parliament were obtained for the Uxbridge & Rickmansworth Railway. It was incorporated by Act of 1861, then abandoned after four more Acts, reincorporated in 1881 and abandoned again, after three more Acts, in 1888. In 1895 a third company was incorporated and in 1899 a further Act was obtained. Construction was never even started.

The last main line into London, the Great Central Railway (formerly the Manchester, Sheffield & Lincolnshire Railway) was opened to passengers on 15 March 1899. Coal traffic had begun on 25 July 1898 and general freight began on 11 April 1899. The railway was pioneered by Edward Watkin when he was chairman of the M.S.&L., the Metropolitan and the South Eastern railways and of the Channel Tunnel Company. He saw the London Extension as part of a main line linking Manchester, London and Paris. The name 'Great Central' was adopted on 1 August 1897.

The G.C.R. became part of the London & North Eastern Railway on 1 January 1923, and was run down and finally closed by British Rail in the late 1960s.

The shortest independent standard-gauge railway in Great Britain was the Easingwold Railway from the East Coast main line at Alne, Yorkshire, 2½ miles (4 km) long. It was opened for goods on 1 July and for passenger traffic on 27 July 1891 and ran passenger trains until 29 November 1948. It was closed completely on 30 December 1957. It possessed only two engines, and only one at a time.

The last 'early-morning' (workmen's) tickets on British Railways were issued at the end of 1961.

RAILROADS, OR RAILWAYS, IN THE U.S.A.

Early railroads in the U.S.A. were given land grants, or loans, by the Federal Government under an Act passed by President Millard Fillmore on 20 September 1850. By 1871 the Government had granted 131 000 000 acres (53 000 000 ha) of land, then worth about $125 000 000, to over 80 railroads, for the construction of about 19 000 miles (30 600 km) of route. This amounts to less than a thirteenth of the total mileage built. Yet in exchange all American railroads were required to carry Government freight at half price and mail at a 20 per cent reduction. When Congress repealed this provision in 1945, from 1 October 1946, it was calculated that the railroads had saved the Government about $1 250 000 000, or ten times the value of the original land grants.

Some early railroads, however, were dishonest or ruthless. In the 1860s a group of railroad tycoons in North Carolina received $6 000 000 in bonds from the Federal Government for building 93 miles (150 km) of railroad worth under $1 000 000.

In 1867 Cornelius Vanderbilt, having gained control of two New York City lines, cut off rail access to Manhattan, thereby forcing the New York Central into his net, afterwards voting himself a personal bonus of $6 000 000 in stock. When his successor, his son William, was asked if he ran the N.Y.C. for the public benefit he replied 'The public be damned!' By the 1870s the Americans regarded their railroads as 'Public enemy No. 1'. Some of the legislation against which the railroads are fighting today originated in this period. They brought much of it upon themselves.

The Interstate Commerce Commission (I.C.C.) was created by Act of Congress signed by President Grover Cleveland on 4 February 1887. It regulates rates, services and abandonments of services among railroads, motor carriers, pipelines, inland water-carriers and freight forwarders engaged in interstate commerce. While it regulates 100 per cent of railroad traffic, it regulates only 39 per cent of inter-city road haulage, 14·6 per cent of river and canal traffic, 4·4 per cent of coastal sea traffic and 1·1 per cent of Great Lakes traffic.

In the early 1900s the Interstate Commerce Commission encouraged road and water traffic to compete with the railroads (understandably in view of their over-exercised monopoly) by providing generous Federal assistance in the form of highways and waterways.

This pattern continues today. While the U.S.A. railroads pay 24 per cent of their profits in taxes, road operators pay 5 per cent, air lines 4 per cent, and water-carriers o per cent. In addition the competing carriers have received Federal assistance amounting to $246 000 000 000 in the period from 1955 to 1970.

The railroads of California, with 7385 miles (11 885 km), payed the highest taxes, $36 762 622, in 1973, followed by Illinois with 10 822 miles (17 417 km) which payed $35 592 897. Hawaii, with no railroads, received $24 034 in railroad taxes.

Class I railroads pay over $900 000 000 in taxes per year, but receive meagre Federal assistance totally out of proportion to the contribution they make to the nation's economy.

Class 1 railroads are those with an operating revenue exceeding $5 000 000. All others are Class II railroads. Class I railroads operate about 95 per cent of the total mileage and employ about 92 per cent of the railroad workers. 'Line-haul' railroads are those operating between terminals. 'Switching' or 'Terminal' railroads operate between local yards or terminals.

There are about 560 operating railroads in the U.S.A., of which 74 are Class I line-haul railroads and 486 are switching or terminal companies or Class II railroads. Amalgamations reduce these numbers, for example between 1916 and 1969 the number of line-haul railroads dropped from 1243 to under 375 of which only 74 are Class I railroads.

Standard Time was introduced in North America on 18 November 1883 when nearly 100 'local times' observed by the railroads were abolished. There are four time zones: Eastern, Central, Mountain, and Pacific, all one hour apart. Standard Time was sponsored and put into effect by the General Time Convention of Railway Managers, now part of the Association of American Railroads (see below), but it was not until 19 March 1918 that Congress passed the Standard Time Act, making this the official time.

The General Time Convention of Railway Managers, a predecessor of the Association of American Railroads, adopted the first standard code of train rules on 14 April 1887.

The Association of American Railroads, with headquarters in Washington, was formed on 12 October 1934 by amalgamation of the American Railway Association, The Association of Railway Executives, Railway Accounting Officers' Association, Railway Treasury Officers' Association, and the Bureau of Railway Economics. It acts as joint agency in research, operation, traffic, accounting and finance. Membership is open to all Class I railroads. In March 1971 there were 232 full-member companies including 116 line-haul railroads, 22 switching and terminal companies, and 1 leased line in the U.S.A., 5 Canadian and 5 Mexican railroads.

The Department of Transportation, with headquarters in Washington, was established on 15 October 1966 by Public Law 89–670, and began operation on 1 April 1967. Eleven offices were transferred to it from other Federal agencies. It develops national transport at the lowest costs consistent with safety and efficiency, co-ordinates transport policies of the Federal Government, and administers the Uniform Time Act.

Railroads can move an item of freight for a fifth of the fuel, a sixth of the accidents and a tenth of the land that road haulage requires for the same load, and carry seven times as much freight per employee. They carry 70 per cent of the coal in the U.S.A., 74 per cent of canned and frozen foods, 46 per cent of the meat and dairy products, 71 per cent of household appliances, 76 per cent of automobiles and parts, 86 per cent of pulp and paper, 78 per cent of timber, 63 per cent of chemicals and 68 per cent of primary metal products.

If the railroads in the U.S.A. were to shut down for one week the national income for the year would be reduced by nearly 6 per cent. An eight-week shut-down would reduce the gross national product for the year by 24 per cent and increase unemployment by 22 per cent.

U.S.A. railroads operate about 15 000 passenger-train cars. Of these about 8200 are passenger cars, and the others are dining cars, parlour cars, lounge cars, mail cars and baggage cars.

In 1968 U.S.A. railroads carried 296 000 000 passengers travelling 13 200 000 000 passenger miles (21 243 000 000 km). This is less than 10 per cent of the total number of passengers on public or hire transport. This total itself is only about 10 per cent of the total passenger miles. The other 90 per cent travels by private car.

The National Railroad Passenger Corporation, known as 'Amtrak', was formed under the Rail Passenger Service Act of 1971, and took over the passenger services of 22 of the leading railroads of the U.S.A. The principal companies remaining outside were the Southern and the Denver & Rio Grande Western. Amtrak bought up 1200 passenger cars including sleepers, diners, dome-cars and chair-cars, and now operates about 200 trains daily over about 27 125 route miles connecting 440 cities in the U.S.A. and into Canada. Its claim is 'To make the trains worth travelling again'. **It operates the world's longest non-stop run**, by the 'Silver Meteor', New York City to Miami, Florida, between Richmond, Virginia, and Jacksonville, Florida, 1377 miles (2216 km) at an average speed of 61·3 m.p.h. (98·5 km/h).

The Penn Central Company was formed on 1 February 1968 by the merging of the Pennsylvania and New York Central railroads. On 31 December 1968 the New York, New Haven & Hartford Railroad became part of the P.C., which now owns 19 853 miles (31 935 km) and operates nearly 22 000 miles (35 400 km) of railroad of which 727 miles (1170 km) are electrified in 16 States, two Canadian provinces and the District of Columbia. It carries nearly 300 000 passengers a day and operates nearly 3000 freight trains every 24 hours with 4041 locomotives (174 electric and 3867 diesel-electric), 3109 passenger cars (including 766 multiple-unit electric cars) and 165 495 freight cars and other vehicles, and 2270 cabooses.

The Burlington Northern Railroad was formed on 2 March 1970 by the merging of the Chicago, Burlington & Quincy, the Great Northern, the Northern Pacific and the Spokane, Portland & Seattle railroads. It operates 25 536 miles (41 096 km) of route with 2036 diesel and diesel-electric units including railcars, 114 975 freight cars, 587 passenger cars, and extends from Chicago to Vancouver and Seattle.

One of the largest railroad systems in the U.S.A. is the Southern Pacific Transportation Company, with headquarters at San Francisco, California. It operates 11 514 miles (18 525 km) of route (more than the entire British Rail network) serving 12 States by about 750 freight trains every day, representing more than 9 per cent of all the rail freight in the U.S.A. Its trains cross the longest railroad bridge (Huey P. Long, New Orleans) and the highest (Pecos, Texas) and make the longest water crossing (Great Salt Lake, Utah) in the U.S.A. (See 'Some American Bridge Records', pp. 95–101.)

It owns nearly 88 000 freight cars and 2300 diesel locomotives. Its main line from Oakland, opposite San Francisco to Los Angeles and New Orleans, the 'Sunset Route', 2513 miles (4024 km), reaches an altitude of 5074 ft (1547 m) at Paisano, Texas, and a depth of −200 ft (−61 m) at Salton, California. From a height of 42 ft (12·8 m) at Sacramento its main line to Ogden climbs through the Sierra Nevada Mountains to a summit of 7043 ft (2147 m) in 100 miles with long grades of about 1 in 40 or 2·5 per cent. (See 'Articulated Steam Locomotives', p. 138.) Besides rail traffic it operates trucks over 26 000 miles of highway, and more than 2300 miles of pipe-line.

Other U.S.A. systems operating over 10 000 miles (16 000 km) are: Atchison, Topeka & Santa Fe, 12 569 miles (20 228 km); Missouri Pacific 11 819 miles (19 021 km); Chicago & North Western 11 401 miles (18 357 km); Chicago, Milwaukee, St Paul & Pacific 10 479 miles (17 992 km) and the Southern Railway System 10 022 miles (16 126 km).

The shortest and most exclusive railroad in the U.S.A. is a 600 ft (183 m) long subway connecting the Senate Office buildings with the Capitol at Washington, D.C. It is used solely by Government officials. Trains shuttle to and fro 40 to 50 times an hour. New 20 m.p.h. (32 km/h) cars were installed in 1959, covering the journey from the old Senate Office Building in 41 seconds and from the new in 55 seconds. A new subway was completed in 1962.

LARGE NATIONALISED RAILWAYS

The U.S.S.R. railways By 1913 the Russian railway network comprised 25 State and 13 private lines. The entire system was nationalised after the Revolution of 1917. The total mileage on 1 January 1973 was 84 700 (136 300 km) of 4 ft 11⅞ in gauge (1·520 m) of which 22 475 miles (36 170 km) were electrified; 1108 miles (1783 km) of 1 ft 11 in (889 mm) to metre-gauge lines; 473 miles (761 km) of 3 ft 6 in (1·067 m) gauge in South Sakhalin formerly controlled by Japan, and 54 miles (87 km) of standard gauge. The Russian gauge was 5 ft (1·524 m) until 1 January 1972 when the standard was narrowed by 4 mm.

Canadian National Railways, operating 24 575 miles (39 550 km) of standard gauge and 704 miles (1133 km) of 3 ft 6 in (1·067 m) gauge, is dealt with on pp. 76 and 112.

Chinese People's Republic railways: The Chinese Government took over control of railways from 1908. The mileage open in 1973 was about 23 900 (38 500 km), mostly standard gauge.

South African Railways was formed in 1910 on the unification of the Cape, Orange River, Transvaal and Natal Colonies. The administration runs 13 352 miles (21 488 km) of 3 ft 6 in (1·067 m) gauge lines, of which 2791 miles (4492 km) or 21 per cent are electrified, and 439 miles (706 km) of 2 ft gauge (610 mm).

The Indian Railway Board was constituted in its present form in 1951. It owns 18 667 miles (30 041 km) of 5 ft 6 in gauge (1·676 m), 15 876 miles (25 550 km) of metre gauge, 2 310 miles (3718 km) of 2 ft 6 in (762 mm) gauge and 383 miles (616 km) of 2 ft (610 mm) gauge.

Argentine Railways were built largely with foreign capital. The railways were nationalised in 1948 and **Argentine State Railways** was established in 1956. The system is divided into seven separate railways with gauges of 1 metre, standard, and 5 ft 6 in (1·676 m). The total route mileage is 25 074 (40 355 km) of which 76 miles (123 km) are electrified.

Brazilian Federal Railways (Rede Ferroviaria Federal S.A. or R.F.F.S.A.) was established on 30 September 1957. It is divided into four regions and operates a total of 15 252 miles (24 546 km) of route, mostly metre, but including 125 miles (202 km) of 2 ft 6 in (0·762 m) gauge and 1039 miles (1673 km) of 5 ft 3 in (1·6 m) gauge.

Japanese National Railways was formed under the Railway Nationalisation Law of 1906. In 1973 12 976 miles (20 883 km) of 3 ft 6 in (1·067 m) gauge and 455 miles (733 km) of standard gauge were open. Railways are still under construction. The electrified mileage in 1973 was 3877 (6240 km) of 3 ft 6 in (1·067 m) gauge and all of the standard gauge.

National Railways of Mexico was formed by mergers and acquisitions beginning in 1908. It operates 8436 miles (13 577 km) of standard gauge of which 64 miles (103 km) are electrified, and 248 miles (400 km) of 3 ft (914 mm) gauge including 29 miles (47 km) of mixed gauge.

EUROPE

Belgian National Railways is the world's oldest nationalised system. The present administration, formed on 23 July 1926 took over the system operated by the Belgian State Railways. The system is one of the densest in the world for railway mileage per square mile of country. Mileage at the end of 1972 was 2536 (4081 km) of which 767 miles (1232 km) were electrified, all standard gauge.

In addition Belgian National Light Railways operates 178 miles (287 km) of narrow gauge and other light railways and 6615 miles (10 646 km) of bus route.

Czechoslovak State Railways was first established in 1919 and was re-established in May 1945. It operates 13 053 miles (21 007 km) of standard gauge of which 1521 miles (2448 km) are electrified, 110 miles (177 km) of metre and 1 ft 11⅝ in (600 mm) gauge and 63 miles (101 km) of the Russian 4 ft 11⅞ in (1·520 m) gauge.

French National Railways (Société National des Chemins de fer Français; S.N.C.F.) was formed on 31 August 1937. On 31 December 1972 it operated 21 860 miles (35 180 km) of standard gauge of which 5819 miles (9365 km) were electrified.

The German State Railway (Deutsche Reichsbahn) was established on 1 April 1920, but on 11 October 1924 by the Railway Act of 30 August, amended by the Act of 13 March 1930, the system was made independent of the Government. It was placed once more under State control on 30 January 1937. After the Second World War the name denoted only the system in East Germany. Today it operates 8938 miles (14 384 km) of standard gauge of which 860 miles (1384 km) are electrified, and 629 miles (1012 km) of narrow gauge.

The German Federal Railway (Deutsche Bundesbahn; D.B.) was formed by the State Railways Act of 13 December 1951 to operate the lines in Western Germany. On 31 December 1972 it consisted of 18 318 miles (29 479 km) of standard gauge of which 5338 miles (8590 km) were electrified.

Italian State Railways was formed in 1905–7. It operates 9950 miles (16 014 km) of standard gauge, of which 4919 miles (7905 km) are electrified.

Spanish National Railways (Red Nacional de los Ferrocarriles Españoles; R.E.N.F.E.) was formed under the Law of 27 February 1943. It operates 8403 miles (13 524 km) of 5 ft 6 in (1·676 m) gauge, of which 1953 miles (3143 m) are electrified.

Switzerland has 3210 miles (5166 km) of railways of which 1764 miles (2839 km) form the Swiss Federal Railways system, known in German as Schweizerische Bundesbahnen (S.B.B.); in French as Chemins de Fer Fédéraux (C.F.F.) and in Italian as Ferrovie Federali Svizzere (F.F.S.). A total of 877 miles (1411 km) are narrower gauge, mainly metre. There are 14 rack and pinion railways (excluding mixed rack and adhesion lines) totalling 59 miles (95 km), and 50 funicular or rope-worked railways totalling 31 miles (49·5 km).

Switzerland leads the whole of Europe in the frequency of its trains in relation to its area and in the world is second only to Japan. Of the private railways, the largest is the metre-gauge Rhaetian system, in Graubünden, with 244 miles (392·5 km) of route which, with the Furka–Oberalp and Brig–Visp–Zermatt railways form one of the largest metre-gauge networks in Europe. Second in size is the standard-gauge Berne–Lötschberg–Simplon Railway with 155 miles (249·5 km).

The standard-gauge South Eastern Railway, between Pfäffikon and Arth Goldau, includes gradients of 1 in 20 (5 per cent). Bridges on the Swiss Federal Railway number 5455 with a total length of 53 miles (85 km). The 670 tunnels include three of the world's longest, the Simplon, the Lötschberg and the St Gotthard (see p. 81). The St Gotthard Tunnel handles 244 trains daily including freight trains carrying about 100 000 tons every day.

Eleven, or nearly a third, of the fast and luxurious 'Trans'-Europ-Express' or T.E.E. trains serving all the principal cities in western Europe begin or end their journeys in Switzerland, or pass through it.

There are about 1800 electric locomotives and motor coaches, and a few diesels for special duties. The most powerful electric locomotive is 11 100 hp. The average annual electricity consumption on Swiss Railways is 2 000 000 000 000 kWh.

The largest metre-gauge system in Europe is the Greek Pireus–Athens–Peloponnesus Railway (S.P.A.P.) with a route length of 497 miles (800 km). In September 1962 it was amalgamated with the Hellenic State Railways which now operates 597 miles (960 km) of metre-gauge lines and 969 miles (1560 km) of standard gauge.

The 24-hour time system was introduced on Italian Railways in 1898. Between then and 1912 it was adopted by Belgium, France, Portugal and Spain. Thomas Cook & Son first used it in the Cooks' Continental Timetable in December 1919. It was adopted by British Railways in its time-tables in summer 1964.

LOADING GAUGES

Britain pays a penalty for being first with railways by suffering a restricted loading gauge with universal dimensions of only 12 ft 8 in (3860 mm) high by 8 ft 10 in (2692 mm) wide. Some sections, however, such as the Great Northern, Great Central, Lancashire & Yorkshire and Great Western considerably exceed this. For most lines it is 13 ft (3962 mm) high by 9 ft (2743 mm) wide. The greatest is 13 ft 9 in (4189 mm) × 9 ft 8 in (2946 mm). On the Liverpool–Southport electric line the coaches were built 10 ft (3·048 m) wide.

The world's largest loading gauge for standard-gauge lines is in the U.S.A., 15 ft 6 in (4724 mm) × 10 ft 9 in (3277 mm).

The Indian loading gauge for 5 ft 6 in (1·676 m) gauge lines is 14 ft 8 in (4470 mm) × 10 ft 6 in (3200 mm). In 1961 it was decided to increase it to 15 ft 6 in (4725 mm) × 13 ft 6 in (4110 mm).

The standard for European lines, as recommended by the Berne Conference, is 14 ft 0½ in (4279 mm) × 10 ft 4 in (3150 mm). **Australian standard-gauge** lines are about the same —14 ft (4267 mm) × 10 ft 6 in (3200 mm).

The world's biggest loading gauge is the Russian standard for the 4 ft 11⅞ in (1·520 m) gauge—17 ft 4¾ in (5302 mm) × 11 ft 2 in (3413 mm).

The South African loading gauge for its 3 ft 6 in (1·067 m) gauge lines is larger than the British standard—13 ft (3962 mm) × 10 ft (3048 mm).

The biggest loading gauge on metre-gauge lines is on the East African Railways— 13 ft 6 in (4115 mm) × 10 ft 6 in (3200 mm).

DIRECTION OF RUNNING ON DOUBLE LINES

The first railway to be planned and built as a double line was the Liverpool & Manchester Railway, opened on 15 September 1830. Left-hand running was adopted from the start.

A train on the 15 in (381 mm) gauge Ravenglass & Eskdale Railway, Cumbria, headed by 2–8–2 No. 9 River Mite, built by Clarkson, York, in 1966, at Irton Road in August 1974 (John Marshall)

Thyrister controlled electric railcar on the metre-gauge Rhaetian Railway at Pontresina, Switzerland (John Marshall)

Romney, Hythe & Dymchurch Railway 15 in (381 mm) gauge 'Pacific' Northern Chief on a train at Hythe, Kent, in August 1973 (Simon Marshall)

Sections of the Stockton & Darlington Railway had been doubled previously, but in the form of extended passing loops. Doubling between Brusselton Incline and Darlington was not undertaken until 1831–32.

The following British railways adopted right-hand running from the beginning:

The Clarence Railway in County Durham of which the first portion opened in 1833. It became part of the Stockton & Hartlepool Railway on 1 January 1851 and of the West Hartlepool Harbour & Railway Company on 17 May 1853. The right-hand running continued until its absorption by the North Eastern Railway on 1 July 1865.

The London & Greenwich Railway, the first railway in London, opened in 1836–38. Right-hand running was adopted very early in the line's history and it continued until changed to left-hand running on 26 May 1901.

The Manchester & Bolton Railway, opened on 29 May 1838, changed from right- to left-hand running when it was joined at Clifton by the East Lancashire Railway which opened on 28 September 1846.

The Newcastle & Carlisle Railway, opened on 18 June 1838, changed from right- to left-hand running on 7 March 1864, after its absorption by the North Eastern Railway in 1862.

Right-hand running operates on the following railways:

Europe: Austria (some sections), Bulgaria, Czechoslovakia, Denmark, Finland, Germany, Hungary, the Netherlands, Norway, Poland, Spain (the former Madrid, Zaragoza & Atlantic Railway only), Turkey, the U.S.S.R. and Yugoslavia.
Asia: China (some sections) and the U.S.S.R.
North America: Canada and the U.S.A. (except the Chicago & North Western Railroad).

Other countries use left-hand running or have no double line sections.

Using modern signalling methods, several railways in the U.S.A. are now equipped for either-direction running on both lines, with complete safety, so allowing one train to overtake another and so increasing line capacity.

WATER-TROUGHS

Water-troughs ('track-pans' in the U.S.A.) were invented by John Ramsbottom (1814–92) while locomotive superintendent of the London & North Western Railway in 1859 and were patented in 1860.

The first water-troughs were installed in 1860 at Mochdre on the Chester–Holyhead section of the London & North Western Railway and were transferred to Aber on the same line in 1871.

The highest water-troughs in the world were at Garsdale on the Midland Railway Settle–Carlisle line, England, at 1100 ft (335 m) above sea-level, installed in 1907. Only 27 miles away, on the London & North Western Railway at Hest Bank near Lancaster, the water-troughs were almost at sea-level.

The only water-troughs inside a tunnel were in the Diggle end of the three 3 mile 66 yd (4·888 km) bores of the Standedge Tunnels on the London & North Western Railway between Manchester and Huddersfield. The tunnels are the only level stretch on the whole route.

Water-trough in the south end of the up-line Standedge Tunnel between Manchester and Huddersfield on the former London & North Western Railway. Overflow water drained into the canal tunnel alongside (John Clarke)

The total number of water-troughs in Britain was 141. Some, for example on the Lancashire & Yorkshire Railway, were steam heated in frosty weather.

Track-pans were used in the U.S.A. from 1870 to 1956. Britain and the U.S.A. were the only countries to make extensive use of water-troughs.

LOCOMOTIVE DEPOTS

The oldest locomotive 'roundhouse' shed is the old No. 1 Shed of the former Midland Railway at Derby, England, built in 1839. It is now used as a crane repair shop.

The first mechanical locomotive coaling plants in Britain were installed at Crewe (North) Shed in 1913 and at Hull (Dairycoats) shortly afterwards. Only one now remains, 'preserved' at Steamtown, Carnforth, Lancashire.

SNOW-PLOUGHS

The rotary snow-plough was invented by J. W. Elliott, a dentist of Toronto, Canada, who patented a 'compound revolving snow shovel' in 1867. The idea was not taken up, however.

The first rotary snow-plough was built by Leslie Brothers of Orangeville, Ontario, Canada, in 1883–84 and was tested by the Canadian Pacific Railway. Its success led to an improved design constructed in 1887 by the Dunforth Cooke Company (which became part of the American Locomotive Company in 1901) and which was put into operation on the Union Pacific Railroad.

Denver & Rio Grande Western Railroad 3 ft (914 mm) gauge snow-plough at Antonito, Colorado, U.S.A. on the Cumbres & Toltec Scenic Railroad, 1 August 1972 (John Marshall)

RAILWAY AIR SERVICES

The first air service operated by a British railway was by the Great Western Railway linking Cardiff, Torquay and Plymouth on 12 April 1933, in conjunction with Imperial Airways, using a three-engined Westland 'Wessex' plane.

Railway Air Services Limited was incorporated on 21 March 1934, in Great Britain. De Havilland 'Dragon'-type eight seater two-engined planes were used. In 1939 it became 'Great Western & Southern Air Lines'. It was suspended at the outbreak of war in September 1939 and was resumed afterwards by Imperial Airways, later British European Airways, now part of British Airways.

Four De Havilland planes of Railway Air Services Limited, operating in conjunction with the Great Western Railway, England (British Rail)

The railway with the most extensive air services is the Canadian Pacific (see p. 114).

DOCKS AND SHIPS

The first three Canadian Pacific ships, *Empress of India, Empress of Japan* and *Empress of China*, built at Barrow-in-Furness, England, in 1889–90, began operation in spring 1891. The C.P.R. then advertised tours 'Around the World in 80 days', for $610! The name 'Canadian Pacific Steamships Limited' was adopted on 8 September 1921, and on 17 June 1968 it became 'CP Ships' (see p. 114).

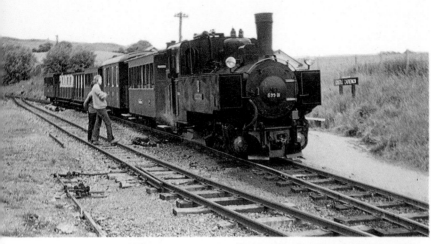

A train on the 2 ft 6 in (762 mm) gauge Welshpool & Llanfair Railway in Wales at Castle Caerineon in June 1972, headed by 0–8–0 tank No. 699.01. This locomotive was built as a 0–8–0 tender engine with short side tanks in 1944 by the Société Franco-Belge, Raismes, France, for the German military railways. On 6 January 1946 it was lent to the Salzkammergutlokalbahn, Austria, which bought it on 1 April 1950. In 1955 it was resold to the Styrian Provincial Railways, Austria, which rebuilt it in 1957 with full-length side tanks and bunker. In 1965 it was put into store until 1969 when it was bought by the W. & L. (Simon Marshall)

A scene on the 2 ft 3 in (0·686 m) gauge Talyllyn Railway, Wales, at the Dolgoch Viaduct, with 0–4–0 tank No. 6 Douglas of 1918 (Simon Marshall)

No. 7 Owain Glyndwr (1923), one of the three 2–6–2 tanks on the 1 ft 11½ in (600 mm) gauge Vale of Rheidol Railway, Wales, photographed at Devil's Bridge in August 1971 (Simon Marshall)

The Lancashire & Yorkshire Railway operated more ships than any other British railway. Twenty-nine (including some owned jointly with the London & North Western Railway) were handed over to the London, Midland & Scottish Railway at the Grouping on 1 January 1923.

BRITISH RAIL WORKSHOPS

British Rail are the world's largest dock-owners with docks, harbours and wharves in 76 places, with a total quay length of 501 402 ft (156 668 m), or about 95 miles. At the end of 1972 B.R. used 44 350 ft (13 518 m) of quays in its own harbours. It also owns the world's largest graving dock, at Southampton.

British Rail 'Seaspeed' Hovercraft service between Southampton and Cowes, Isle of Wight, began operation on 5 July 1966, and a further service between Portsmouth and Ryde began on 26 March 1968. The first international car-carrying service went into operation between Dover and Boulogne on 1 August 1968. At the end of 1972 B.R. operated 4 Hovercraft and 49 ships.

The last paddle-steamers operated by British Rail were engaged on the New Holland Pier–Hull ferry across the Humber. *Wingfield Castle,* withdrawn on 15 March 1974 (see illustration) was built by W. Gray & Company of West Hartlepool in 1934, and was 200 ft (61 m) long. It had coal-fired boilers and a triple-expansion three-cylinder engine. *Tattershall Castle* (Gray 1934) was withdrawn in June 1973. *Lincoln Castle* is similar, built by A. & J. Inglis of Glasgow in 1940. The steamers had a draught of only 4 ft 6 in (1·372 m) to clear sandbanks at low tide. The service is expected to end when the Humber Bridge is opened, possibly 1977.

P.S. Wingfield Castle *(W. Gray & Company, West Hartlepool, 1934) at Hull on the crossing from New Holland. One of the last paddle-steamers operated by British Rail. It was withdrawn in March 1974 (John Marshall)*

The world's highest railway-owned ships are operated by the Southern Railway of Peru, now part of the National Railways of Peru, on Lake Titicaca in the Andes at a height of 12 500 ft (3810 m). The first ship, *Yavari* of 170 tons, was built in 1861 and was carried up from the coastal port of Mollendo in sections on the backs of mules and Indians to Puno on the lake. With the original steam-engine replaced by a diesel it is still in use.

Another ship, the 650 ton *Inca*—228 ft (69 m) long and 50 ft (15·2 m) beam—was built at Hull, England, in 1905, sailed out round Cape Horn to Mollendo, was dismantled and transported up the Southern Railway (completed to Puno in 1876) and reassembled on the lake (see colour illustration on p. 162). The flagship of the Titicaca fleet is the *Ollanta* of 850 tons, built in 1929. There are five ships at work on an itinerary of 1350 miles (2173 km). The longest voyage, Puno to Guaqui, takes 12-hours for the 120 miles (193 m). Lake Titicaca is the highest navigable water in the world.

BRITISH RAIL WORKSHOPS

British Rail Engineering Limited, formed in January 1970 to enable B.R. workshops to compete with private engineering firms by tendering for outside work, is a wholly owned subsidiary of the British Rail Board. It manages the 13 main railway works and carries out all types of railway engineering for B.R. and for other companies. Export work is handled jointly by B.R.E. and Metro-Cammel Limited. The works are at Ashford, Kent; Crewe, Cheshire; Derby; Doncaster; Eastleigh, Hampshire; Glasgow; Horwich, Lancashire; Shildon, County Durham; Swindon, Wiltshire; Temple Mills, London; Wolverton, Buckinghamshire; and York.

RAILWAY ROAD SERVICES

The first railway-operated buses in Britain began on Monday, 17 August 1903, when the Great Western Railway inaugurated a service between Helston and the Lizard in Cornwall with Milnes Daimler buses that had originally been used in connection with the Lynton & Barnstaple narrow-gauge railway, where they were owned and operated by the railway chairman, Sir George Newnes.

Another service began on 31 October between Penzance and Marazion; meanwhile the North Eastern Railway introduced buses on 7 September 1903.

The London & South Western Railway began operating buses on 1 June 1904.

One of the Great Western Railway Milnes-Daimler buses at Helston Station, Cornwall, about to depart for the Lizard (British Rail)

The first railway buses in Scotland were operated by the Great North of Scotland Railway between Ballater and Braemar on 2 May 1904. By 1911 the company operated six services.

By 1928 the Great Western Railway operated 330 buses on 154 routes. In the early 1930s, however, along with other railway companies, the road interests were sold to other bus companies operating in the area and a great opportunity for developing a unified transport system was lost.

ROAD-RAIL VEHICLES

The first 'Road-railer' was placed in service by the London, Midland & Scottish Railway in 1931. Designed by J. Shearman of the L.M.S., it was a Karrier chassis with a Craven body and could be quickly adapted for rail or road use. It was used between Blisworth and Stratford-upon-Avon, being used on the road in Stratford. It could

run at 70 m.p.h. (113 km/h) on rails and at 60 m.p.h. (96·5 km/h) on roads. It was scrapped after only a few years.

The London, Midland & Scottish Railway 'Road-railer' bus, introduced in 1931 (British Rail)

A road-rail truck was used by the London & North Eastern Railway on the West Highland section in Scotland for several years from 1934. It was a Karrier 2 ton truck on which the road wheels could be raised or lowered as on the bus just described. It was used in track maintenance.

The most modern application of the road-rail principle is the German Daimler-Benz 'Unimog 406' shown in the illustration. This runs on the rails on its rubber-tyred wheels, guided by small rail wheels which can be raised or lowered by hydraulic jacks in front and behind. With a 2 ton ballast weight on the platform making a total weight of only 6·5 tons the 'Unimog' can pull a load of 300 tons on a gradient up to 1 in 200 or 150 tons up 1 in 100. It has high adhesion, even on wet rails. No special ramps are needed for transfer between rail and ground. When required only for rail running the guide wheels can be removed and the road wheels changed for Michelin pneumatic-tyred rail wheels with steel flanges. The operation takes 40 minutes and reduces the weight to 5 tons.

Daimler-Benz 'Unimog' road-rail truck. The guide-wheels in front and behind are raised and lowered hydraulically and the road tyres provide good rail adhesion (John Marshall)

The first use of a 'steam navvy' or excavator on railway construction in England was on the West Lancashire Railway from Southport to Preston. One was purchased from Ruston, Proctor & Company of Lincoln for £1150 on 12 June 1877.

The first extensive use of these machines was on the construction of the Great Central main line to London, but this was 12 years later.

SIGNALLING

The first use of the electric telegraph on a railway was on the Great Western Railway in England, in 1839. William Fothergill Cooke (1806-

79) and Charles Wheatstone (1802-75), both subsequently knighted, had been experimenting on the London & Birmingham Railway, and they installed it between London (Paddington) and West Drayton. It was extended to Slough in 1843.

In 1845 it was instrumental in the arrest at Paddington Station of a murderer named Tawell who had boarded a train at Slough. From that moment the telegraph was established. (See Frith's *The Railway Station* p. 159.)

It was introduced in the U.S.A. on 24 May 1844. The first use of the telegraph for train dispatching in the U.S.A. was at Turner (now Harriman), New York, on 22 September 1851.

The block system with Cooke and Wheatstone's electric telegraph was first used at Clay Cross Tunnel on the North Midland Railway near Chesterfield in Derbyshire in 1841. In the U.S.A. it was introduced by Ashbel Welch in 1865.

Semaphore signals were first used for railways at New Cross, Kent in 1841, on the South Eastern Railway, England.

The first railway to use the block system from the opening was the Norwich & Yarmouth Railway, opened on 1 May 1844.

Automatic block signals were introduced in the U.S.A. in 1866.

Staff-working on single lines was introduced on the London & North Western Railway in 1853.

Interlocking of signals and points was patented by John Saxby in England in 1856.

Somersault signals, pivoted in the centre, were adopted by the Great Northern Railway, England, in 1876 following the double collision at Abbott's Ripton on 21 January 1876 caused by a signal being put out of order by frozen snow. They were also used on the Barry, Brecon & Merthyr and Rhymney railways in Wales and on the Northern Counties Railway in Ireland.

The first use of telephone communication on U.S.A. railroads followed tests on 21 May 1877 at Altoona, Pennsylvania.

The Regulation of Railways Act, enforcing the block system, interlocking of signals and points, and the provision of continuous automatic brakes on passenger trains on British railways, came into operation on 30 August 1889.

The 'K3' Class 2–6–0 No. 61823 passing a somersault signal near Daybrook, Nottingham, on a section of the old Great Northern Railway on 14 August 1959 (John Marshall)

Automatic signalling was installed on the London & South Western Railway between Andover and Grately, Hampshire, and was brought into use on 20 April 1902.

Audible cab signalling was introduced by the Great Western Railway, England, on the double-track Henley Branch on 1 January 1906 and on the single-line Fairford Branch on 1 December when the ordinary distant signals were removed.

The Great Western Railway audible cab signalling was first installed on a main line in 1908, on the four-track section between Slough and Reading, Berkshire, and was extended to London (Paddington) in 1912. About this time the automatic brake application was added, becoming known then as the 'Automatic Train Control' (A.T.C.) Between 1931 and 1937 2850 miles (4587 km) of route were equipped.

The first electro-pneumatic signalling installation in Britain was on the Lancashire & Yorkshire Railway at Bolton in 1904.

Centralised Traffic Control (C.T.C.) was introduced in the U.S.A. on a 40-mile route at Berwick, Ohio, on 25 July 1927. It has since been installed on over 40000 miles (64300 km) of track.

The Hudd Intermittent Inductive A.T.C. Apparatus was installed at 112 distant signal locations on the London–Southend line in 1938. On the London & North Eastern Railway Edinburgh–Glasgow line the system came into use on 13 August 1939.

Train to land radio telephones were first used on the Canadian National Railways in 1930.

Radio channels for exclusive railway use were allocated by the Federal Communications Commission, U.S.A., on 17 May 1945 and the first construction permit was granted on 27 February 1946.

The first train to land telephones in the U.S.A. were installed in 1947 on the Baltimore & Ohio *Royal Blue*, New York Central *Twentieth Century Limited* and the Pennsylvania *Congressional*, *Potomac* and *Legislator*.

In Europe telephones are installed on many trains used by business executives in France and Germany.

The first push-button route-selecting signalling control system in Britain was brought into operation by London Transport at Ealing Broadway on 29 November 1952. London Transport's last electro-pneumatic semaphore signal was removed from service on 21 November 1953.

British Railways system of A.T.C. for use with non-electric traction was approved by the Minister of Transport on 30 November 1956.

The first automatic level-crossing barriers on British Railways were installed at Spath Level Crossing near Uttoxeter, Staffordshire, on the now-abandoned Churnet Valley line, and came into use on 6 February 1961.

STATIONS

The world's oldest railway station is the Mount Clare Station in Baltimore, Maryland,

Mount Clare Station, Baltimore, on the Baltimore & Ohio Railroad, completed on 24 May 1830. This is the oldest surviving railway station in the world (Baltimore & Ohio Railroad Company)

U.S.A., opened on 24 May 1830 by the Baltimore & Ohio Railroad. The first trains were drawn by horses. See p. 16.

The World's oldest station building is at Cuautla, Mexico. It was built in 1657 and was used as a convent until 1812. It became part of the railway station about 1860.

The oldest station built for a 'modern' steam-powered railway is at Liverpool Road, Manchester, England; the original terminus of the Liverpool & Manchester Railway, opened on 15 September 1830. Its passenger services ended, however, when Manchester (Victoria) was connected to the L. & M. on 5 May 1844 and since then it has been a goods station.

The world's highest railway station is at Condor, Bolivia, on the metre-gauge line from Rio Mulato to Potosí, at an altitude of 15 705 ft (4787 m). (See colour illustration on p. 70.) The railway was completed in 1908.

The highest station on standard gauge is Galera on the Peru Central, 15 673 ft (4777 m). It was opened on 14 November 1893.

The World's largest station is the Grand Central Terminal, New York. It has 44 platforms, all below ground, on two levels, with 41 tracks on the upper and 26 on the lower level, and covers 48 acres (19·4 ha). It was built in 1903–13. It is used by 550 trains and 180 000 people daily.

Other large stations are:

Pennsylvania Terminal, New York	32 platforms
Union Station, Washington	32 platforms
Saint-Lazare, Paris	27 platforms

Liverpool Road Station, Manchester, the world's second oldest station (John Marshall)

Clapham Junction, besides being the largest station in Britain, in area, is also the busiest junction, with over 2070 trains passing through every 24 hours.

Carlisle Station was used by more railway companies than any other British station. Until the Grouping on 1 January 1923 it was used by the North British, North Eastern, Midland, London & North Western, Maryport & Carlisle, Glasgow & South Western, and Caledonian railways. Carlisle Station was administered by the Carlisle Citadel Station Joint Committee, established under an Act of 22 July 1861.

The largest span station roof ever built was the 300 ft (91·44 m) span of the second Broad Street Station, Philadelphia, U.S.A., built in 1892 by the Philadelphia & Reading Railroad.

Largest British stations

	Platforms	Total length		Area	
		ft	m	acres	hectares
Clapham Junction	17	11 185	3409	27·75	11·229
Waterloo, London	23*	15 352	4679	24·5	9·813
Victoria, London	17	18 412	5611	21·75	8·8
Crewe	16	11 394	3473	23	9·307
Waverley, Edinburgh	19	14 305	4360	18	7·28
London Bridge	21	13 574	4157		
Liverpool Street, London	18	11 410	3478	16	6·475
Paddington, London	16	15 025	4580	14·75	5·968

*Including two Waterloo & City Railway platforms below ground.

One of the two Vauclain compound 4–2–2s built by Baldwin for the Philadelphia & Reading Railroad, U.S.A., in 1896, leaving Broad Street Station, Philadelphia, with a three-car express for New York. The photograph shows part of the world's largest-span station roof

The Pennsylvania Railroad Station at Jersey City, built in 1888, had a roof span of 252 ft (76·810 m).

The largest station roof in Great Britain is at London (St Pancras), built by the Midland Railway, with a span of 240 ft (73·15 m) and 100 ft (30·48 m) high above rail-level. It was designed by William Henry Barlow (see p. 46), and the station was opened on 1 October 1868.

Manchester Central, owned originally by the Cheshire Lines Railway, had a roof span of

210 ft (64 m) and was 90 ft (27·432 m) high. It was opened in 1880 and closed on 5 May 1969. It formed the terminus of the Midland Railway trains from London St Pancras and from Liverpool Central and Chester.

Milan Central Station, designed by Ulisse Stacchini and completed in 1930, has a central roof span of 236 ft (70·283 m). The main building is one of the most grandiose in existence.

The largest station roof in South America is at the Retiro terminal at Buenos Aires. It is

St Pancras Station, London, the largest station roof span in Britain (British Rail)

Longest railway station platforms	ft	m
Chicago, Illinois (State Street Centre subway)	3500	1066
Kharagpur, Bihar, India (formerly Bengal & Nagpur Railway)	2733	833
Perth, Western Australia (standard gauge)	2500	762
Sonepur, India (formerly Bengal & North Western Railway)	2415	736
Bulawayo, Rhodesia	2302	702
New Lucknow, India (formerly East India Railway)	2250	685
Bezwada, India (formerly Madras & Southern Mahratta Railway)	2100	640
Jhansi, India (formerly Great Indian Peninsula Railway)	2025	617
Colchester, England	1981	603·8
Kotri, India (formerly North Western Railway)	1896	578
Mandalay, Burma	1788	545
Bournemouth, England	1748	533
Perth, Scotland	1714	522
York, England	1692 and 1575	516, 480
Edinburgh (Waverley), Scotland	1596	486
Trichinopoly, India (formerly South India Railway)	1546	471
Ranaghat, India (formerly Eastern Bengal Railway)	1522	464
Crewe, England	1509	460
London (Victoria), England	1500	457
Dakor, India (formerly Bombay, Baroda & Central India Railway)	1470	448
Newcastle upon Tyne, England	1389	423
Cambridge, England	1254	382

The largest station roof in South America, at Retiro Station, Buenos Aires, Argentina, on the 5 ft 6 in (1·676 m) gauge General Mitre System. A four-car diesel multiple-unit train is leaving (John Marshall)

820 ft (250 m) long with two spans totalling 328 ft (100 m) wide and each 82 ft (25 m) high. It was built in the late 1920s by the former Central Argentine Railway.

The largest station waiting-room in the British Isles, and the most elegant, was the Great Hall at Euston, London. It was designed by Philip

The Great Hall at Euston Station, London, designed by P. C. Hardwick and opened in 1849. It was demolished in 1962. In the foreground can be seen the statue of George Stephenson (British Rail)

Charles Hardwick (1822–92) when he was only in his mid twenties and was opened to the public on 27 May 1849. It measured 126 ft (38·4 m) long, 61 ft (18·6 m) wide and 64 ft (19·5 m) high. The flat panelled ceiling was the largest of its kind in the world. It was one of London's architectural treasures, but it was demolished, along with the great Doric Arch, in the rebuilding of Euston Station in 1962.

The world's largest waiting-rooms are those in Peking Station, China, opened in September 1959, with a total capacity of 14000 persons.

Smoking was not permitted at stations on the London, Brighton & South Coast Railway. This rule continued until 1923, when the company became part of the Southern Railway.

At Dartmouth, Devon, is a station which has never had any trains. It was opened on 16 August 1864 and is connected by a ferry with Kingswear Station across the Dart Estuary. Since 30 October 1972 the section from Paignton to Kingswear has been owned by the Dart Valley Railway and operated by the Torbay Steam Railway.

A similar arrangement existed at Hull Corporation Pier where the Great Central Railway had a booking office connected by the Humber Ferry (see 'Last paddle-steamers of B.R., p. 203) with New Holland Pier Station.

The station with the longest name is Llanfairpwllgwyngyllgogerychwyrndrobwllllantysiliogogogoch in Anglesey, North Wales. Translated this means 'Mary's church by the white hazel pool near the fierce whirlpool with the church of Tysilio by the red cave'. The station was closed on 14 February 1966, but was brought back into use after the Britannia Bridge was damaged by fire on 23 May 1970 until the bridge was re-opened on 31 January 1972. After a further period of closure it was reopened on 7 May 1973.

The longest station seat in Britain was at Kirkby in Furness, on the former Furness Railway north of Barrow. It was 135 ft (41 m) long and could seat 100 persons. It was removed soon after the Second World War to make space for a footbridge, following a fatal accident to a passenger crossing the line.

At Grange-over-Sands on the same railway is a seat 76 ft 3 in (23·25 m) long which will seat about 55 persons under cover.

The world's longest station name, on probably the largest platform ticket—it measures 6 × 2 in (152 × 51 mm)

At Chester Station trains to London via the former London & North Western Railway and Great Western Railway routes left in opposite directions. It is still possible to travel from Chester to Paddington by the former G.W.R. route—provided the passenger is not in a hurry.

Similar situations could be seen at Plymouth (North Road), Exeter (St David's), Nottingham (Midland), and Trent now demolished, between Nottingham and Derby. Also at Trent, trains to and from London could call at the same platform going in the same direction.

The first station escalator was installed at Seaforth Sands Station on the Liverpool Overhead Railway in 1901.

UNDERGROUND RAILWAYS

The earliest recorded 'underground railway' and probably the first in the world was a 3 mile (4·8 km) line from East Kenton Colliery near Newcastle upon Tyne to the River Tyne. It was begun about 1770 by Christopher Bedlington. Wooden rails were used. It could also claim to be the **world's first railway tunnel.** It closed with the colliery in 1810.

The first underground passenger railway in the world was the Metropolitan Railway, London. It was opened, with mixed 7 ft (2·134 m) and standard gauge, from Bishop's Road to Farringdon Street on 10 January 1863 and extended to Moorgate on 23 December 1865. The broad-gauge outer rails were removed on 1 March 1869. Trains were lit by gas.

With the Metropolitan District Railway, the first section of which was opened from Kensington to Westminster on 24 December 1868, the Metropolitan formed a circular route known as the 'Inner Circle' which was completed on 6 October 1884, together with the opening of the connection with the East London Railway through Marc Brunel's Thames Tunnel. It was electrified from

12 September 1905 and the last steam trains ran on 22 September.

The world's first 'tube' railway was the Tower Subway beneath the River Thames in London. It was opened, using cable-traction, on 2 August 1870, though it had worked experimentally since April. From 24 December 1870 it closed as a railway and was used as a footway until March 1896. It now carries a water-pipe.

The Mersey Railway between Liverpool and Birkenhead was opened on 1 February 1886.

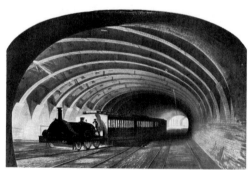

An early scene on the Metropolitan Railway, London; a 7 ft (2·134 m) gauge train at Bellmouth, Praed Street, in 1863 (London Transport Executive)

Baker Street Station on the Metropolitan Railway, London, about 1866 (London Transport Executive)

The former Mersey Railway o–6–4 tank No. 5 Cecil Raikes at Shipley Colliery, Derbyshire, in 1940 (John Marshall)

It includes 1 in 27 (3·7 per cent) gradients under the River Mersey, and at its lowest point it is 128·6 ft (39·2 m) below Ordnance Datum. At first it was worked by steam locomotives, one of which, Beyer Peacock o–6–4 tank No. 5 *Cecil Raikes* (1885), is preserved at Liverpool awaiting restoration. The photograph shows it at work at Shipley Colliery near Nottingham on 20 April 1940. On 3 May 1903 the Mersey Railway became the first steam underground railway to be electrified.

The first electric underground railway in the world was the City & South London, opened on 18 December 1890 (see under 'Electric Railways', p. 156).

The Glasgow District Subway was opened on 14 December 1896. It was 4 ft (1·219 m) gauge, cable operated, and consisted of two parallel tunnels, for either direction, forming a loop round the city centre, twice crossing beneath the River Clyde. It was electrified at 600 V d.c. in 1935, the 'inner circle' coming into operation on 28 March and the 'outer circle' on 5 December. It was the first electric passenger railway in Scotland.

The first section of the Paris Underground (the Métro) from Port-Vincennes to Porte-Maillot was opened on 10 July 1900.

The first driverless underground railway was the Post Office Subway in London. It was begun in 1914 and fully opened in December 1927. It is 2 ft (610 mm) gauge and 6·5 miles (10·5 km) long, from Paddington Station to the Eastern District Post Office. The main double-track tunnels are 9 ft (2·743 m) diameter. It carries about 30 000 mail-bags a day.

Underground Railways were first opened in other towns as follows: Boston, U.S.A., 1898; New York, 1900; Berlin, 1902; Philadelphia, 1908; Hamburg, 1912; Buenos Aires, 1914; Madrid, 1919; Barcelona, 1924; Sydney, 1926; Tokyo, 1927; Moscow, 1933; Osaka, 1933; Chicago, 1943; Stockholm, 1950; Toronto, 1954; Rome, 1954; Leningrad, 1955; Cleveland, Ohio, 1956; Nagoya, 1957; Lisbon, 1959; Haifa, 1959; Kiev, 1960; Milan, 1964; Montreal, 1966; Rotterdam, 1968; Munich, 1971, San Francisco 1972.

Pneumatic-tyred trains were introduced on the Paris Métro on 8 November 1956.

London's newest underground railway, the Victoria Line, was completed throughout from Walthamstow Central to Brixton on 23 July 1971. The Fleet Line is at present under construction.

The first train on the Victoria Line, London, at Seven Sisters on 3 January 1969 (London Transport Executive)

The longest escalator on the London Underground, at Leicester Square Station (London Transport Executive)

The first London Transport train with automatic driving equipment entered experimental service on the District Line on 8 April 1963. Full-scale trials on the 4 mile (6·5 km) Woodford–Hainault shuttle service on the Central Line began on 5 April 1964. The entire service on the Victoria Line is operated by automatic trains.

The first escalators on the London Underground were at Earl's Court between the District and Piccadilly line platforms, brought into operation on 4 October 1911. The last lifts, or elevators, on the London Underground were installed at Broad Street, Central London Railway, in 1913.

The longest escalator on the London Underground is that serving the Piccadilly Line at Leicester Square Station. The shaft is 161 ft 6 in (49·3 m) long with a vertical rise of 80 ft 9 in (24·6 m).

The world's longest station escalator is on the Leningrad Underground with a vertical rise of 195 ft (59·5 m). On the Moscow Underground is one with a rise of 164 ft (50 m).

The greatest depth below ground-level on the London Underground is 194 ft (59·2 m) at Hampstead.

LONDON COMMUTERS

Of 1 250 000 journeys to work in Central London, London Transport carries 34 per cent by Underground and 14 per cent by bus. British Rail carries 460 000, or nearly 40 per cent, and two-thirds of this on the Southern Region. Thus the private cars which choke London's streets represent less than 12 per cent of the people travelling.

RAPID TRANSIT RAILWAYS

Rapid Transit Railways are being planned, built or opened in numerous cities where it is realised that they are a better investment than ever more roads and bigger car-parks which simply create more traffic.

To attract the car-owner, particularly where railways are regarded as outmoded, trains must be fast and comfortable. Even in London, where habitual rail-users have become inured to overcrowding, there may be a limit to the toleration of discomfort, though at times this seems almost impossible. **Free parking of cars and bicycles**, as provided on the San Francisco system described below as an example of what can be achieved by an enlightened authority, is a step in the right direction. Niggling parking fees which barely cover attendants' wages merely antagonise the motorist and repel traffic.

The Bay Area Rapid Transit (BART) linking San Francisco and Oakland in California is one of the most advanced systems in the world. For greater stability, a gauge of 5 ft 6 in (1·676 m) was chosen. It passes under the Bay in twin concrete tunnels 3·6 miles (5·8 km) long built in 57 sections from 315 to 350 ft (96–107 m) long, 48 ft (14·630 m) wide and 24 ft (7·315 m) high, laid in a trench on the sea-bed. The joints were designed to withstand displacement in earthquakes without

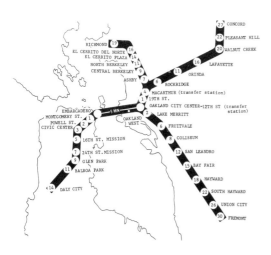

BAY AREA RAPID TRANSIT SYSTEM

PEAK-HOUR TRAVEL TIMES IN MINUTES

Diagram of the Bay Area Rapid Transit System showing peak-hour travel time in minutes.

The Trans-Bay Tube between Oakland and San Francisco, passing beneath the Bay Bridge (B.A.R.T.)

Bay Area Rapid Transit System train at Bay Fair Station, Oakland (B.A.R.T.)

leakage. The 1000 V d.c. third-rail system totals 75 miles (120 km). Comfortable, remotely controlled trains, running silently at 50–80 m.p.h. (80–130 km/h) cross from Oakland to San Francisco in 9 minutes, start to stop. Tickets are issued, inspected and collected by electronically controlled machines. Everything is designed to the highest aesthetic standards.

The first section, Fremont to MacArthur in Oakland, 28 miles (45 km), was opened on 11 September 1972. The remainder was opened during 1973, except the trans-Bay tubes which were opened on 14 September 1974. No smoking is allowed either in stations or trains.

MOUNTAIN AND RACK RAILWAYS

The world's first rack railway was the Middleton Railway near Leeds, England. John Blenkinsop (see p. 34) took out a patent in 1811 for a rack-rail system, for which the first engine was built by Matthew Murray in 1812. The 'rack' teeth were cast in the outside of one rail. The engine was propelled entirely by the rack mechanism; the carrying-wheels were idle. (See 'The Beginnings', p. 11.)

The first railway with a central rack was the Jefferson Incline on the north bank of the Ohio River near Madison, Indiana, built in 1847. The eight-coupled engines had a separate vertical-cylindered engine for driving the rack mechanism.

The first mountain rack railway was opened on 3 July 1869. It was built by Sylvester Marsh (see p. 42) to carry passengers to the 6293 ft (1918 m) summit of Mount Washington in New Hampshire, U.S.A. The railway is standard gauge, 3 miles (4·8 km) long, and has a maximum gradient of 1 in 3·1 (32·26 per cent). A wrought-iron ladder-type rack was used.

Nicholas Riggenbach (1817–99) designed a similar rack, patented in 1863, and first used on the 4·5 mile (7·25 km) standard-gauge line from Vitznau to the summit of the Rigi, Switzerland, opened on 23 May 1871. The last 2 miles (3·2 km) were opened on 27 June 1873 to a summit level of 5741 ft (1750 m). It was electrified on 3 October 1937.

The Riggenbach rack is used also on the metre-gauge Brünig and Bernese Oberland railways in Switzerland.

Old Peppersass, *the first locomotive on the Mount Washington Cog Railway, New Hampshire, U.S.A. (John Marshall)*

Roman Abt (1850–1933) invented his rack system in 1882. It was first used in 1885 on a railway at Blankenburg in the Harz Mountains.

Three-quarters of the world's rack railways use the Abt system in which two or sometimes three flat steel bars having teeth in their upper edge are fixed side by side so that the gap in one comes opposite the tooth of the next or, in the triple rack, a third of the space of one tooth.

The steepest rack railway in the world is the Mount Pilatus Railway in Switzerland, with a gradient of 1 in 2 (50 per cent). A special rack was

devised by Edward Locher (1840–1910). It has horizontal teeth on each side which prevent any possibility of slipping or derailment. The railway was opened on 4 June 1889 with steam and was electrified on 15 May 1937.

For this railway a gauge of 800 mm (2 ft 7½ in) was chosen. Roman Abt adopted this as his standard and it was used for 11 mountain railways in Switzerland, and others elsewhere.

The Snowdon Mountain Railway in Wales, 2 ft 7½ in (800 mm) gauge, uses the Abt double rack and Swiss-built steam locomotives. It was opened on 6 April 1896. In its 4·5 miles (7·25 km) it climbs from Llanberis to the summit at 3493 ft (1064 m) on gradients of 1 in 5·5 (18 per cent). (See colour illustration on p. 179.)

The Abt system is used on 'main lines' on the Furka–Oberalp and Brig–Visp–Zermatt railways in Switzerland.

The world's first electric mountain rack railway was the Gornergrat Railway at Zermatt, Switzerland, opened on 20 August 1898. It is metre gauge with Abt rack and operates on three-phase a.c. at 725 V. With a summit at 10 134 ft (3088 m) it is the second highest railway in Europe and the highest in the open. (See colour illustration on p. 179.)

The highest railway in North America is the Manitou & Pike's Peak Railway in Colorado. This standard-gauge line is 8·9 miles (14·3 km) long with an average gradient of 1 in 6 (16·66 per cent). The lower terminus is at 7538 ft (2298 m)

An early scene on the Rigi Railway during steam days. It was opened in 1871, the first mountain railway in Europe (Swiss National Tourist Office, London)

The Mount Pilatus Railway in steam days. This is the steepest rack railway in the world (Swiss Federal Railways)

and the summit is 14 109 ft (4300 m). On Windy Point Hill it climbs for 2 miles (3·219 km) at 1 in 4 (25 per cent). It was opened on 1 June 1891 with steam-power. Diesel-electric cars, built in Switzerland, were introduced in 1963. One of the Vauclain compound steam locomotives is preserved at Manitou and another at the Colorado Railroad Museum at Golden near Denver.

The highest railway in Europe is the metre-gauge Jungfrau Railway in Switzerland, opened on 1 August 1912. At Jungfraujoch it is 11 332 ft (3454 m). The upper section is entirely in a tunnel 7·123 km (4 miles 750 yd) long. The Strub rack is used.

Switzerland's only steam mountain railway is now the Brienzer Rothorn Railway, 800 mm (2 ft 7½ in) gauge with Abt rack. It was opened on 17 June 1892. The summit is at 7707 ft (2349 m).

John Barraclough Fell (1815–1902) invented the centre-rail friction-drive system named after him in 1863–69. It was devised for the railway

A train at the Jungfraujoch Station, the highest in Europe (Swiss National Tourist Office, London)

A Masterton–Upperhutt excursion train powered by four 'H' Class 0–4–2 Fell tank locomotives passing the windbreaks on 'Siberia' Curve while ascending the 1 in 15 Rimutuka Incline between Cross Creek and Summit Stations (New Zealand Railways Publicity)

over the Mont Cenis Pass, opened in 1868 and used until the Mont Cenis Tunnel was completed in 1871.

The most famous Fell centre-rail railway was the Rimutaka Incline in New Zealand on the line from Wellington to Masterton, opened on 12 October 1878. Gradients were 1 in 14–16 (7–6 per cent) for 3 miles (4·8 km). It was closed when the Rimutaka Tunnel was opened in 1955 (see p. 106).

The Fell centre-rail is used on the 3 ft 6 in (1·067 m) gauge Snaefell Mountain Railway in the Isle of Man, but for braking purposes only. The electric cars climb to the top, 2034 ft (620 m), by adhesion.

The first and only railway to the top of a volcano was built by Thomas Cook & Son, the travel agents, to the top of Vesuvius in Italy. The funicular railway, with gradients as steep as 1 in 1·9, was opened in 1880 to the summit station at 4012 ft (1213 m) just below the crater.

The composer Luigi Denza (1846–1922) wrote a popular song 'Funiculi-Funicular' to celebrate the occasion. Richard Strauss thought this was a Neapolitan folk-song and incorporated it in the Finale of his symphonic fantasy *Aus Italien* (1886).

The railway was destroyed in the eruption on 20 March 1944. It has been replaced by a bus between Pugliano and Lower Station and a chair lift from there to the crater.

MONO RAILWAYS OR MONORAILS

The first recorded mono railway was built by Henry Palmer in 1821 for transporting foodstuffs from warehouses to wharves at London Docks. It consisted of boards supported on posts straddled by the cars which were pulled by horses.

The first passenger-carrying monorail was built in 1876 by General Roy Stone in Fairmont Park, Philadelphia, as part of the city centenary exhibition.

One of the twin-boilered locomotives—complete with headlamp—on the Listowel & Ballybunion Railway in Ireland (National Library of Ireland)

The first commercial monorail was also American, built in 1880 to connect Brooklyn and Coney Island, New York. It ran for a few months but failed for lack of revenue.

Only two types of monorail have achieved success. The type invented by Charles Lartigue in 1883 was used for the Listowel & Ballybunion Railway in County Kerry, Ireland. This 9 mile (14·5 km) line was opened on 1 March 1888. The twin-boilered locomotives and cars straddled the rail which was supported on trestles, as shown in the photograph. The most comical pieces of the equipment were the mobile steps which were marshalled into the train to enable passengers to cross the line. Loads had to be balanced. Once when a piano had to be transported it was balanced by a cow. The cow had to be returned by balancing it with two calves which were then sent back one on each side. The railway was closed in October 1924.

Lartigue-type monorails were also built in North Africa, central France, Russia, Guatemala and Peru.

The Tokyo–Haneda Monorail in Japan is a modern version of the Lartigue system. It was opened in October 1964 to connect Tokyo with the international airport at Haneda. Trains cover the 8 miles (13 km) in 15 minutes.

A similar monorail was opened in Seattle, U.S.A., in 1962 in connection with the World's Fair. It is about a mile (1·6 km) long.

The second type of monorail, still in operation, is the 9·3 mile (15 km) long Wuppertalbahn from Elberfeld to Barmen in Germany.

This is the Langen suspended type, much of it straddling the Wupper River. It was opened on 1 March 1901. By 1960 it had carried 1 000 000 000 passengers. It was this system which inspired the Swiss engineer Feldmann to build the first mountain aerial ropeway, up the Wetterhorn, opened in July 1908 and closed in 1914.

The Tokyo–Haneda Monorail, opened in October 1964 (Ministry of Foreign Affairs, Japan)

NARROW-GAUGE RAILWAYS
(less than 1 m gauge)

The current fascination with narrow-gauge railways is largely because, while other railways have progressed continuously, narrow-gauge railways stopped progressing about 1900–10 and so represent steam railways of that period or earlier. Many people find in them a relief from the rush of modern travel, *provided the journeys are not too long*.

Many such lines were built to open up backward areas and their ultimate closure in the face of road competition can be seen more as a measure of their success than of their failure.

GAUGES

3 ft 0 in (0·914 m) Formerly extensively used in Colorado, U.S.A., and in Ireland, and the Isle of Man. Still in use in Central America, Colombia, Peru, Mexico, Newfoundland, Canada and Alaska

2 ft 11 in (0·891 m) Some lines in Sweden

2 ft 7½ in (0·8 m) Mountain and rack railways

2 ft 6 in (0·762 m) Austria, Yugoslavia, Czechoslovakia, India, Sri Lanka (Ceylon), Wales (Welshpool & Llanfair Railway), and on the former Leek & Manifold Valley Railway in England

2 ft 5½ in (0·750 m) Argentina, Brazil

2 ft 0 in (0·610 m) and 1 ft 11·6 in (0·600 m) Sierra Leone and secondary lines in Wales, South Africa, India, Pakistan, southern Chile, northwest Argentina. Also the Lynton & Barnstaple and Ashover Light railways in England, both abandoned.

The world's first public narrow-gauge railway was the 1 ft 11·6 in (0·600 m) gauge Festiniog Railway in Wales, engineered by James Spooner (1789–1856) and opened for slate traffic on 20 April 1836. Trains ran by gravity from Blaenau Ffestiniog to Portmadoc and empties were pulled back by horses which rode down on the trains. Steam locomotives were introduced, for the first time on a narrow-gauge railway, in 1863 by Charles Easton Spooner (see p. 50), son of James. Passenger traffic officially began on 6 January 1865, but passengers had been carried unofficially for years before that. Traffic declined during the Second World War and the railway was closed in 1946. In 1954 the Festiniog Railway Society Limited was formed and passenger services were resumed on 23 July 1955. A magnificent piece of restoration work has been achieved and work is still going ahead on a completely new section of line.

James Spooner was also engineer to the 2 ft 3 in (0·686 m) gauge Talyllyn and Corris railways in Wales, mentioned below.

The Corris Railway, from Aberllefeni and Corris to Machynlleth, was opened for horse-drawn slate traffic in 1859. Steam-traction began in February 1879. Passengers were carried from 4 July 1883 to 1 January 1931 and the line closed on 23 August 1948. It was 6·5 miles (10·5 km) long.

The Talyllyn Railway, from Towyn to Abergynolwyn—6·75 miles (10·87 km)—was opened in December 1865. Passengers were carried from October 1866. In 1950 it became **the world's first privately preserved railway.**

The first narrow-gauge railroad in the U.S.A. was the 3 ft (0·914 m) gauge Denver &

The oldest narrow-gauge engine in Colorado; the Denver & Rio Grande Western 3 ft (914 mm) gauge 2–8–0 No. 346 built in 1881, photographed at the Colorado Railroad Museum, Golden, near Denver (John Marshall)

The 2–8–2 No. 45 at Fort Bragg on the standard-gauge Californian Western Railroad in August 1972 (John Marshall)

American-type 5 ft 6 in (1·676 m) gauge 4–4–0 No. 306 (Caleta, 1912) preserved at the San Bernardo Shops near Santiago, Chilean State Railways, with a glimpse of the Andes beyond (John Marshall)

The Ruinacci Bridge, with a main span of 86·52 m (284 ft) at a height of 65 m (213 ft), on the metre-gauge Centovalli Railway (Locarno–Domodossola) in Ticino, Switzerland (John Marshall)

Rio Grande Railway from Denver to Colorado Springs, opened on 26 October 1871. The locomotive *Montezuma* which was used was the first narrow-gauge passenger engine built or operated in the U.S.A.

After attaining a maximum of about 3000 miles (4800 km) the 3 ft gauge in Colorado was finally abandoned in the late 1960s except for the 45 mile (72 km) long Durango–Silverton Branch and the Alamosa–Durango line between Antonito and Chama, 65 miles (105 km), over the Cumbres Pass, 10015 ft (3053 m), both now preserved as tourist attractions. At present the Cumbres & Toltec Scenic Railroad (C.A.T.S.) is the **longest preserved railway in the world**, and the highest, and to many the most scenic.

Typical of the Colorado 3 ft lines was the Uintah Railroad which, in 13 miles (21 km), had 233 curves from 1425 ft (434 m) to 72 ft (22 m) radius, including 27 sharper than 114 ft (34·7 m) radius. It had 5 miles (8 km) at a record 7·5 per cent or 1 in 13·3 and crossed into Utah at 8437 ft (2572 m) at Baxter Pass. It was abandoned in 1938.

In contrast, the Denver & Rio Grande Western between Villa Grove and Alamosa, Colorado, in the heart of the Rockies, was dead straight for 52·82 miles (85 km), falling from 7900 ft (2408 m) to 7550 ft (2301 m) at Alamosa.

The 3 ft gauge is still used on the White Pass & Yukon Railway, 111 miles (178·5 km) long, of which 20 miles (32 km) are in Alaska and the rest in Canada. It was **the first railway in Alaska**, opened in stages from 21 July 1898 and completely from Skagway to Whitehorse on 8 June 1900.

The first 2 ft (0·610 m) gauge line in the U.S.A. was the Bedford & Billerica Railroad which opened on 28 November 1877. There were 14 systems operating 2 ft gauge in the U.S.A. 10 of which were in Maine. The last to close was the Monson Railroad in December 1944.

Two feet gauge steam may still be enjoyed in the U.S.A. on the 5·5 mile (8·85 km) Edaville Railroad at South Carver, Massachusetts; Silver Dollar City, Missouri; Cripple Creek, Colorado and a few short lines elsewhere.

The total mileage of narrow-gauge railroad in the U.S.A. in 1890 was about 10000 (16000 km), operated by about 500 independent companies.

The 2 ft (0·610 m) gauge 0–4–4 tank No. 3 (formerly belonging to the Monson Railroad) on the Edaville Railroad, Massachusetts, U.S.A. (John Marshall)

Ennis train at Ennistynion on the 3 ft (0·914 m) gauge West Clare Railway, Ireland (N. Fields)

In the Isle of Man, between England and Ireland, the 3 ft (0·914 m) gauge railway system began operation on 1 May 1873 when the Douglas–Peel section opened. The system grew to 46·75 miles (75·2 km) (see colour illustration on p. 182). It is now all closed except the Castletown–Port Erin section which has been preserved.

Ireland's first 3 ft gauge line opened in 1873. Over 500 miles (805 km) were built. The last, the West Clare, closed on 1 February 1961.

The Ravenglass & Eskdale Railway in England's Lake District, was opened as a 3 ft gauge line on 24 May 1875, carrying passengers from November 1876, for 7·5 miles (12 km) into the Cumbrian Fells. It was rebuilt into a 15 in (381 mm) gauge line in 1915–17 (see 'Henry Greenly', p. 59). Today it is operated by a preservation company formed on 30 March 1961 (see colour illustration on p. 199).

The world's smallest public railway is the 15 in (381 mm) gauge Romney, Hythe & Dymchurch Railway in Kent, England. It was authorized in 1925 under the Light Railways Act of 1896 and was opened on 16 July 1927. It is 13·8 miles (21 km) long and from Hythe to New Romney, 8·3 miles (13·5 km), is double-track. It is the only double-track 15 in gauge railway in the world on which passenger trains pass each other many times daily at speeds of 20–25 m.p.h. (32–40 km/h). The railway possesses ten steam locomotives designed by Henry Greenly (see p. 59) and built in 1925–31 (see colour illustration on p. 199).

The Fairbourne Railway on the Welsh coast began as a 2 mile (3·2 km) 2 ft (610 mm) gauge horse tramway in 1890. It was rebuilt to 15 in (381 mm) gauge in 1916 and ran until 1940. In 1947 it was reopened and in 1954 and 1963 obtained the 2–4–2s No. 14 *Katie* and No. 18 *Sian*, **the largest engines on a British 15 in gauge railway**, and the only ones which make no pretence at being scale models.

The 2–4–2 No. 18 Sian *on the Fairbourne Railway, Wales. This and its sister No. 14* Katie *are the largest 15 in (381 mm) gauge locomotives in Britain (John Marshall)*

The Welshpool & Llanfair Railway opened on 4 April 1903. Passenger services ended on 7 February 1931 and the railway closed on 31 October 1956. A preservation company was formed on 4 January 1960 and part of the line was reopened on 6 April 1963. Some of its stock is from the Zillertalbahn in Austria (see colour illustration p. 202).

An Illinois Central Railroad
express leaving Chicago in July
1972 headed by three diesel-
electric units, two single-ended
and one centre unit (John
Marshall)

Baldwin 2–6–0 No. 14
at Duran near Guayaquil
on the Guayaquil &
Quito Railway, Ecuador,
in 1974 (John
Marshall)

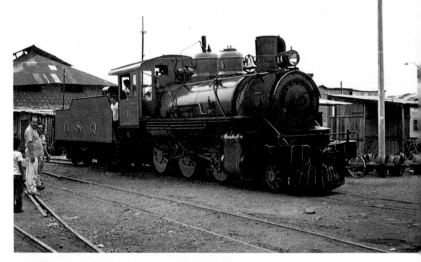

A train on the Bern–Lötschberg–
Simplon Railway, Switzerland,
crossing the viaduct at Hohten in
the Rhône Valley, in July 1972,
behind Bo Bo locomotive No. 167
(John Marshall)

The Leek & Manifold Valley Light Railway 2 ft 6 in (0·762 m) gauge 2–6–4 tank E. R. Calthrop *at Hulme End, Staffordshire*

Scotland's only narrow-gauge passenger railway was the Campbeltown & Machrihanish Light Railway across the Mull of Kintyre. It was 2 ft 3 in (0·686 m) gauge and 6 miles (9·6 km) long. It was opened on 17 August 1906 and closed in the autumn of 1932. There were four 0–6–2 tanks and six carriages.

Britain's longest narrow-gauge railway was the 1 ft 11·6 in (0·600 m) gauge 21·25 mile (34·2 km) long Welsh Highland Railway from Dinas, on the London & North Western Railway Caernarvon–Afon Wen line, to Portmadoc where it connected with the Festiniog Railway. It was built in three portions, the oldest being the Croeser Tramway built in 1863 from Croeser Quarries to Portmadoc. On 14 May 1881 the North Wales Narrow Gauge Railway, engineered by C. E. Spooner, was opened from Dinas Junction to South Snowdon. The final link, from South Snowdon to Croeser Junction was opened on 1 June 1923 and the connection to the Festiniog Railway on 8 June. The entire railway closed on 19 September 1936.

The longest narrow-gauge railway in England was the 1 ft 11·6 in (0·600 m) gauge 19·75 miles (31·8 km) long Lynton & Barnstaple Railway in Devon which opened on 11 May 1898 and closed on 29 September 1935.

The first narrow-gauge railway to carry standard-gauge wagons on transporter trucks was the 2 ft 6 in (0·762 m) gauge 8·25 miles (16·8 km) long Leek & Manifold Valley Light Railway in Staffordshire, England. It opened on 27 June 1904 and closed on 10 March 1934. The transporters were designed by the engineer, Everard Richard Calthrop (1857–1927), for the Barsi Light Railway, India, of which he was also engineer, but they were first used on the Manifold Valley line. They are now widely used in several countries, on different gauges.

British Rail's only steam railway is the 2 ft (0·610 m) gauge Vale of Rheidol Railway, Wales, opened on 22 December 1902 from Aberystwyth to Devil's Bridge (see colour illustration on p. 202). It is 12 miles (19 km) long.

One of the oldest working narrow-gauge engines in Britain is the vertical-boilered 0–4–0 *Chaloner*, No. 1, built by De Winton & Company of Caernarvon in 1877. It worked in Penybryn

Quarry until 1897, then Pen-yr-Orsedd Quarry until 1952, both in the Nanttle Valley, Wales. It now runs on the 3·5 miles (5·6 km) long 2 ft (0·610 m) gauge Leighton Buzzard Narrow Gauge Railway in Bedfordshire.

Austria's best-loved narrow-gauge railway was probably the 2 ft 6 in (0·762 m) gauge 36 miles (61 km) long Salzkammergutlokalbahn from Salzburg to Bad Ischl, opened throughout on 3 July 1893 and closed on 14 October 1957.

The Zillertalbahn from Jenbach to Mayrhofen in Austria, 21 miles (34 km) long, 2 ft 6 in (0·762 m) gauge, was opened on 2 January 1900. Today it is one of the most popular narrow-gauge railways in Europe. Its oldest locomotive is the 0–6–2 tank No. 2 *Zillertal* built at Linz in 1900.

The 0–6–2 tank No. 2 Zillertal *on the 2 ft 6 in (0·762 m) gauge Zillertalbahn, Austria*

One of the most interesting industrial narrow-gauge railways was the 1 ft 10 in (0·559 m) gauge system operated by Arthur Guinness, Son & Company (Dublin) Limited, the famous brewers, in Ireland. It was built in 1874–78 and was on two levels connected by an 864 ft (26·35 m) long spiral tunnel with 2·65 turns on a radius of 61 ft 3 in (18·7 m) and a gradient of 1 in 40 (2·5 per cent). The first of the 0–4–0 steam locomotives was supplied by Sharp Stewart & Company of Manchester in 1875 and it ran until 1913. Various other locomotives were obtained but none was absolutely satisfactory until a special design was prepared by Samuel Geoghegan (1845–1928), the brewery engineer. The first of these 'Geoghegan Patent' engines was built by the Avonside Engine Company of Bristol in 1882. It had two cylinders mounted above the boiler to keep working parts away from ground dirt. Eighteen more were built from 1887 to 1921 by William Spence of Dublin. Diesels were introduced in 1947 and the last steam-engines ran in 1957.

The company also had a 5 ft 3 in (1·600 m) gauge connecting line. For working this Geoghegan designed a special 'haulage truck' into which a narrow-gauge engine could be fitted, propelling it by a friction drive from its wheels. Two were built in 1888, another in 1893 and the fourth in 1903. Broad-gauge working ended in 1965.

One of the narrow-gauge steam-engines is preserved at the Narrow Gauge Railway Museum at Towyn, Wales.

One of the world's most spectacular narrow-gauge railways is the 2 ft (0·610 m) gauge Darjeeling Himalayan Railway in India. It was opened from Siliguri, then the northern

One of the Guinness Railway locomotives at work (N. Fields)

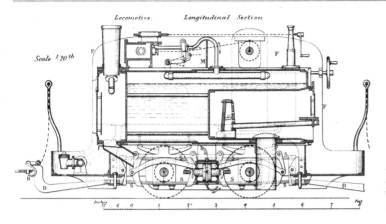

Longitudinal section of Geoghegan Patent Locomotive (Journal of the Irish Railway Record Society)

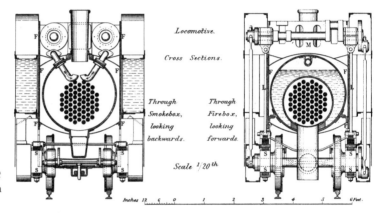

Cross-section of Geoghegan Patent Locomotive (Journal of the Irish Railway Record Society)

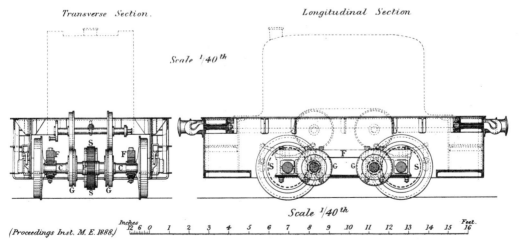

Diagram of haulage truck (Journal of the Irish Railway Record Society)

terminus of the Eastern Bengal Railway from Calcutta, to Darjeeling in the Himalayan foothills, in July 1881. From Sukna, 533 ft (162 m) above sea-level, and about 350 miles. (563 km) from the sea, 7 miles (11 km) beyond Siliguri, the railway climbs for 40 miles (64 km) mostly at 1 in 25 (4 per cent) to a height of 7407 ft (2557 m) at Ghoom from where it drops to 6812 ft (2076 m) at Darjeeling. The total length is 51 miles (82 km). The line includes five spiral loops and three reversing zigzags to gain height. One of the loops includes the sharpest curve on the line, only 59·5 ft (18 m) radius.

Darjeeling train at Sukna on the 2 ft (610 mm) gauge Darjeeling Himalayan Railway, now part of the North Eastern Railway, India, 22 April 1944 (John Marshall)

A branch of 28 miles (45 km) along the magnificent Teesta River Valley to a station below Kalimpong was opened in 1915. This is now closed.

Throughout most of its existence the railway has been worked by 0–4–0 saddle tanks of a type first built in 1888 by Sharp Stewart in Glasgow. For a time a 0–4–0 + 0–4–0 Garratt was used, built by

A train at Kalijora on the now-abandoned Teesta Valley Branch of the Darjeeling Himalayan Railway in April 1944 (John Marshall)

Beyer Peacock, Manchester, in 1910. It was their second design (see p. 141) and the first normal simple-expansion Garratt with the cylinders at the outer ends.

The greatest narrow-gauge engineering in India is found on the 2 ft 6 in (0·762 m) gauge Kalka–Simla Railway in the north-west Himalayan foothills. It was built in 1899–1903 to give access to Simla where the Indian Government made its summer headquarters. From a height of 2143 ft (653 m) at Kalka where it connects with the 5 ft 6 in (1·676 m) gauge line from Delhi, it climbs by gradients of 1 in 33 to a height of 6808 ft (2075 m) at Simla in 59 miles (95 km). There are 103 tunnels, the longest being Barogh, 1251 yd (1144 m). The track is of 'main-line' standard with 60 lb/yd (29·76 kg/m) rails.

The principal steam locomotives were the 'K' Class 2–6–2 tanks first built in 1908 by the North British Locomotive Company, Glasgow.

A train on the 2 ft 6 in (0·762 m) gauge Kalka–Simla Railway headed by a 2–6–2 tank locomotive (Dr H. E. Vickers)

The heaviest narrow-gauge trains in the world run on the 2 ft 6 in (762 mm) gauge Rio Turbio Railway in Argentina, also the world's most southerly railway. This photograph shows a 1700 ton train of empty coal cars, nearly a kilometre (0·6 mile) long, behind a Japanese 2–10–2 , No. 113 (Ken Mills)

Section 7
RAILWAYS IN HUMAN AFFAIRS AND THE ARTS

RAILWAY WORKERS

The railroads of the U.S.A. employed 1 660 850 persons in 1929 earning an average rate of $1743 per annum. In 1972 the number had fallen to 526 091 earning an average of $12 213. Railroads of Illinois employed the highest number, 53 530, followed by Pennsylvania with 46 700, New York with 31 685 and Texas with 26 250.

The first railroad in the U.S.A. to institute a formal pension plan for all ranks of employees was the Pennsylvania, on 1 January 1900. It applied to all employees from the age of 70 which from that date became the compulsory retiring age.

The Federal Railroad Retirement Act (U.S.A.) came into effect for all railroads on 1 July 1937, replacing voluntary retirement and disability benefits on about 80 major railroads.

In 1972 British Rail employed 196 635 persons, an average of about 17 per mile of route, compared with about 2·5 in the U.S.A. This comparison, however, does not take into account the density of population and traffic.

The first woman railroad employee in the U.S.A. was Susan Morningstar who was hired to help to clean the Baltimore & Ohio terminus at Baltimore, Maryland, in February 1855.

The first 'train hostess', Miss Kathryn Sullivan, began her work in 1935 on 'The Rebel', one of the first American streamlined trains, on the 751 miles (1209 km) run between St Louis and New Orleans on the Gulf, Mobile & Ohio Railroad.

The youngest locomotive engineer ever appointed was probably Richard Peacock (1820–99). He was appointed locomotive superintendent of the Leeds & Selby Railway in 1838 at the age of 18. In 1841 he became locomotive superintendent of the Manchester, Sheffield & Lincolnshire Railway and founded its works at Gorton, Manchester.

In 1854, when aged 34, he joined Charles Beyer (1813–76) to found the famous locomotive works of Beyer Peacock, also at Gorton.

Daniel Gooch (see p. 48) was just 21 when he was appointed first locomotive superintendent of the Great Western Railway, under I. K. Brunel in 1837. He founded the famous works at Swindon in 1841–43.

Bowman Malcolm (1854–1933) was appointed locomotive engineer at the age of 21 on the Belfast & Northern Counties Railway in 1876. He remained in that position until his retirement 46 years later in 1922 at the age of 68. He had served the railway for 52 years. He died on 3 January 1933 aged 79.

In the workshops at Guadalupe on the Central Railway of Peru in 1926 were three workers whose combined ages were 298 years. The labourer in the castings store was 104, his foreman was his junior by six years, aged 98. The pattern-store keeper was a mere youngster of 96. The senior member of the trio exasperated his two junior colleagues by addressing them as 'sonny'. Two of them died shortly afterwards, still in harness.

RAILWAY SOCIETIES AND ENTHUSIASTS

The oldest British society for railway enthusiasts is the Railway Club, London (112 High Holborn, London WC1 V6JS), founded in 1899. Its *Journal* has been issued since 1902.

The Stephenson Locomotive Society with members throughout Britain and all over the world (34 Durley Avenue, Pinner, Middlesex HA5 1JQ) was formed in 1909. It maintains a lively monthly *Journal*, catering for the serious enthusiast with an interest in technical matters and in railways generally, first published in 1924.

The Newcomen Society for the study of the history of engineering and technology was founded on 4 June 1920 and incorporated on 3 May 1961. The *Transactions* contain many articles of great interest to railway historians. (The Science Museum, London SW7 2DD.)

The Railway Correspondence & Travel Society, like the Stephenson Locomotive Society with a widely dispersed membership, was founded in Cheltenham in 1928. Its monthly journal, *The Railway Observer*, first published on 1 May 1928 as the *Railway News*, first appeared in March 1929.

One of the last Stanier 'Pacifics', No. 46251 City of Nottingham leaving Preston with a Railway Correspondence & Travel Society special on 5 October 1963 (John Marshall)

It keeps members up to date with locomotive stock changes and allocations.

All the above societies organise programmes of lectures, the Railway Club in London and the others in centres throughout Britain. Other activities include rail tours and visits.

The Irish Railway Record Society was founded on 24 October 1946. (24 Avondale Lawn, Blackrock, Co Dublin.) The *Journal* is published twice yearly.

The Railway & Locomotive Historical Society of the U.S.A. was founded in 1921 and incorporated in 1926. (Baker Library, Harvard Business School, Boston (63), Mass.)

The National Railway Historical Society, U.S.A., was founded in 1935 and incorporated in 1937 to further the preservation of historical railway material. It publishes *The Bulletin* bi-monthly. (Suite 312–14, Empire Building, 13th and Walnut Streets, Philadelphia, Pa. 19107.)

The Canadian Railroad Historical Association was founded on 15 March 1932 at the Château de Ramezay Museum, Montreal. The

Bulletin was first published in 1938, but ceased in 1941. In August 1941 the Association obtained a Charter. The *News Report*, now *Canadian Rail* has been published monthly since October 1947. The Association operates an extensive railroad museum at Delson near Montreal. (Box 22, Station B, Montreal 110, Quebec.)

The Upper Canada Railway Society was founded in 1941 and incorporated in 1952. It serves enthusiasts of both steam and electric railways. (P.O. Box 122, Terminal A, Toronto.)

The Railway & Canal Historical Society was founded on 4 September 1954. Besides an interesting journal members enjoy lectures in various centres and a comprehensive programme of outdoor visits to railways and canals. (Littlemoor, Puddington, Near Tiverton, Devon EX16 8LN.)

The Association Française des amis des Chemins de Fer was founded in 1929. It publishes a monthly journal *Chemins de Fer*. (Gare de l'Est, Paris 10.)

The Swedish Railway Club (Svenska Järnvägsklubben) was founded in March 1958. Its main interests are in railway history. (Box 124, 10121 Stockholm 7, Sweden.)

The Australian Railway Historical Society was founded in 1933 as the Australian Railway & Locomotive Historical Society. The name was changed in November 1951. It publishes the *Bulletin* monthly. (P.O. Box E 129, St James, N.S.W. 2000.)

The New Zealand Railway & Locomotive Society was founded in 1944. It publishes the **New Zealand Railway Observer** monthly. (P.O. Box 5134, Wellington C1.)

The Transport Trust, of Great Britain, is a charitable organisation concerned chiefly with the safeguarding of all forms of transport relics, documents, books, photographs, films and other historical material, and with co-ordinating the preservation of all forms of historic transport objects throughout the nation. It was constituted in 1965 and registered as a charity in 1967. Membership is open to all. (18 Ramillies Place, London W1V 2BA.)

The above addresses were correct at the time of writing. They are mostly of honorary secretaries, and it is well to check addresses in the current *Directory of Railway Officials and Year Book* or recent railway periodicals.

One of the world's most distinguished railway enthusiasts was King Frederick IX of Denmark. He was born on 11 March 1899 and succeeded to the throne on 20 April 1947. He had an encyclopaedic knowledge of Danish railways and was a competent engine-driver. He died on 14 January 1972 and, in accordance with his wish, his funeral train on 24 January made the 20 mile (32 km) journey from Copenhagen to the ancient capital of Roskilde behind two 'E' Class 'Pacifics', Nos. 978 and 994.

The earliest record of an elopement by train was in 1842 when Hercules Macdonnell abducted Emily Moylan. They travelled from London to Gretna Green, partly by train and were married. The railway north of Lancaster was not opened until 1846.

RAILWAY PUBLICATIONS

The first periodical devoted to railways was *The Railway Magazine* which first appeared in London in May 1835 and ran weekly until December 1840 when it became *Herapath's Railway Magazine* (later *Journal*) until December 1903 when it merged with *The Railway Times*.

The longest running railway periodical is *The Railway Magazine* (London) first published in July 1897 and monthly ever since except from May 1942 to December 1949 when it was issued every other month.

Until March 1974 the record for the longest run was held by *The Railway Times*, first published in London on 29 October 1837 and issued weekly until 28 March 1914, 76 years 7 months.

The oldest American railroad periodical was the *American Railroad Journal*, first published on 2 January 1832. From 1887 to 1892 it became *The Railroad and Engineering Journal*, then *The American Engineer and Railroad Journal* until 1911. Subsequent changes were: January 1912–May 1913 *The Railway Mechanical Monthly*, June 1913–December 1915 merged with *Railway Age Gazette* (1909); 1916–49 *Railway Mechanical Engineer*; 1950–52 *Railway Mechanical and Electrical Engineer*; from 1953 *Railway Locomotives and Cars*.

The oldest American magazine for enthusiasts is the *Railroad Magazine*, founded in 1906 and published monthly in New York.

The popular American monthly magazine *Trains* was first published in 1940 in Milwaukee, Wisconsin.

The author of the record number of railway books is O. S. Nock. His first, *The Locomotives of Sir Nigel Gresley*, was published in 1945 since when he has produced between 70 and 80 books, besides innumerable articles.

The record for longevity as a railway writer must have been held by the late Cecil J. Allen. His first article 'Great Eastern Expresses' appeared in *The Railway Magazine* in 1906 when he was 20. He contributed 535 articles in the series 'British Locomotive Practice and Performance'. In all he wrote 45 books. He died on 5 February 1973 aged 87. He was active to the end. His last book, *Salute to the Southern*, was published in 1974.

RAILWAYS IN LITERATURE

The earliest English poem about railways by an important writer is 'Steamboats, Viaducts and Railways' by William Wordsworth (1770–1850), No. 42 of his *Itinerary Poems* (1833). Three of his poems are anti-railway: 'On the projected Kendal and Windermere Railway', and 'Proud were ye, Mountains', Nos. 45 and 46 of his *Miscellaneous Sonnets* (1844); and 'At Furness Abbey', No. 48 (1845).

Robert Louis Stevenson (1850–94) wrote two railway poems, 'From a Railway Carriage' from *A Child's Garden of Verses*, and 'The Iron Steed'. In conjunction with his stepson, **Lloyd Osbourne**, he wrote a novel *The Wrong Box* in which a railway accident and a joker changing the labels on packages in a guard's van result in some exquisite situations.

Thomas Hardy (1840–1928) left us two railway poems: 'Midnight on the Great Western' and 'Faintheart in a Railway Train', as also did **Siegfried Sassoon** (1886–1967), 'A Local Train of Thought', a homely picture of a branch-line train, and 'Morning Express', a vivid account of a train's arrival and departure.

Other railway poems were written by **Edmund Blunden** (1896–1974) and **Rupert Brooke** (1867–1915). The most prolific writer of railway poems and essays is **John Betjeman** (b. 1906).

Hans Christian Andersen (1805–75), the Danish fairy-tale author, wrote a remarkable piece in *Le Figaro* describing trains and train journeys. This was in 1840, seven years before the first railway was opened in Denmark, and was one of the earliest pieces of railway writing by a fiction author.

Railway fiction is mainly in the form of the short story. In 1845 'Tilbury Tramp' (C. J. Lever) (1806–72) published *Tales of the Trains*, five short stories based on train journeys.

William Makepeace Thackeray (1811–63) has left us *Jeames on the Gauge Question*, a short story of a journey from London to Cheltenham with changes of carriage at Swindon and Gloucester and the confusion arising from the transfer of 93 packages and a baby.

Mark Twain (Samuel Langhorne Clemens) (1835–1910) wrote a comic short story *Punch, Brothers, Punch* based on the noise of wheels on rails.
Arthur Quiller Couch (1863–1944) produced several works containing references to railways: *Delectable Duchy* (1893) in his native Cornwall, *The Destruction of Didcot* (1908) and *Pipes in Arcady* on a Cornish branch line, reprinted in *Sixteen On* edited by Charles Irving (1957).

One of the 'Reginald' stories, *The Mouse* (1930) by **H. H. Munro** (Saki) (1870–1916), takes place in a railway carriage. D. H. Lawrence (1885–1930) wrote a short story called *Tickets please*, based on a journey on the Nottingham–Ripley street tramway, and L.A.G. Strong (1896–1958) wrote two, *Departure* (1929) at a country station, and *The Gates* (1931) about a crossing keeper.

Railways and crime have often been linked in authors' minds. Although railway journeys are frequently mentioned in the 'Sherlock Holmes' stories of **Arthur Conan Doyle** (1859–1930), in only one, *The Adventures of the Bruce Partington Plans* (1924), do railways feature, in this the Metropolitan Railway, forms an important part of the story. 'The Lost Special' from his *Round the Fire Stories* (1908) describes the events leading to the total disappearance of a train.
Three of the 'Dr Thorndike' stories by **R. Austin Freeman** (1862–1943) have railway settings, or railway incidents form an essential part of the plot: *The Moabite Cipher*, *The Blue Sequin* and *The Case of Arthur Brodski* (1928).
The Mysterious Death on the Underground Railway by **Baroness Orczy** (1865–1947) is another example of a crime story where the railway setting is an important ingredient. F. W. Crofts (1879–1957) wrote several crime stories with railway

settings: *Crime on the Footplate, Death of a Train, Death on the Way, The Level Crossing, The Mystery of the Sleeping Car Express* and *Sir John Magill's Last Journey*.

Three of the well-known crime books by Dame Agatha Christie (b. 1890) have railway settings: *Mystery of the Blue Train* (1928); *Murder on the Orient Express* (1934) and *4.50 from Paddington* (1957). *Murder on the Orient Express* has recently been filmed by EMI Films, using French National Railways '230G' Class 4-6-0 No. 353 and four coaches restored by the Wagon Lits Company to conform to the 1930s period.

Novels with railway settings tend to be written mainly by authors with particular interest in railways. However, in his novel of the 'Hungry Forties', *Sybil* (1845), **Benjamin Disraeli** (1804–81) makes considerable references to railways.

Charles Dickens (1812–70) was fascinated by railways and they figure prominently in many of his works. In *Dombey and Son* (1848) Chapters 6 and 15 contain accounts of the London & Birmingham Railway; *Our Mutual Friend* (1864–65) refers to the London & Greenwich and the Great Western railways and Paddington Station, not entirely accurately, and in a postscript Dickens describes his experiences in the Staplehurst accident in 1865 (see 'Accidents', p. 185). *The Uncommercial Traveller* refers to railways in Kent. *The Mystery of Edwin Drood* (unfinished at his death in 1870) makes reference to the South Eastern Railway. Of his other works, his story *A Flight* is based on a journey from London Bridge to Folkestone. Four of the 'Mugby Junction' stories (1866) are by Dickens: *Barbox Brothers, Barbox Brothers & Co.*; *Main Line: the Boy at Mugby*; and *No. 1 Branch Line: the Signalman*. These stories came to be written as a result of an enforced stop at Rugby Junction on the London & North Western Railway, following a fire in the coach in which Dickens was travelling. Finally, *Lazy Tour of Two Idle Apprentices* contains references to the L.N.W.R. in the Chester district.
Besides his terrible experience in the Staplehurst disaster, Dickens had other railway adventures. During a journey to Holyhead, *en route* for Ireland, his train was snowed up near Bangor for four hours, with no train heating. On one of his American journeys, between Rochester and Albany, he was caught in one of the worst floods on record when nearly 300 miles (482 km) of line were inundated. After he had spent an enforced night at Utica the railway company got him to Albany through floods

and floating blocks of ice, taking ten hours for a journey normally taking three.

The great American writer of Western thrillers, Zane Grey (1872–1939) gave a vivid picture of the construction of the Union Pacific Railroad in *The U.P. Trail* (1918) describing the experiences of a young engineer and a girl.

An even better story on the same subject is *The Mountain Divide* (1912) by **Frank Hamilton Spearman** (1859–1937). Another U.P. book is *Building the Pacific Railway* (1919) by **Edwin L. Sabin.**

Probably the best railroad novel written in the U.S.A. is *The Big Ivy* (1955) by **James McCague.**

Edith Nesbit (Bland) (1858–1924) produced one of the best loved of all railway stories, *The Railway Children* (1906) in which three children prevent a train from running into a landslip. A very successful film version was made on the Keighley & Worth Valley Railway in Yorkshire. In *Hatter's Castle* (1931) by **A. J. Cronin** (b. 1896) the villain, Denis, perishes in the Tay Bridge disaster after the deceived heroine has left the train at a signal stop. This made a dramatic sequence in the film version.

Bhowani Junction (1954) by **John Masters** (b. 1914) is a vivid portrayal of the Indian railway scene and of the Anglo-Indian community during the Second World War. Some readers, however, may find the sensuous aspect somewhat overdrawn. This also has been made into a film.

Hamilton Ellis (b. 1909), the well-known railway writer and artist, has produced two novels about railways: *The Grey Men* (1939), a mystery story on the West Highland Railway, and *Dandy Hart* (1947) set in southern England in the period 1830–60. In *The Engineer Corporal* (1940) he gives a vivid account of 'The Great Locomotive Chase' during the American Civil War. This story is also told in 'The Railway Raid in Georgia' from *A Book of Escapes and Hurried Journeys* (1925) by John Buchan (1875–1940).

L. T. C. Rolt (1910–74), best known for his biographies of Telford, the Stephensons and Brunel, wrote a novel *Winterstoke* (1954) set in an imaginary Midlands town in the nineteenth century during the financing and construction of rival railway projects.

It is in the form of the essay that railway literature achieves its greatest profusion. Many, written as articles for periodicals, of an amusing, light-hearted or ephemeral nature, can hardly be classed as 'literature', but there are some by **Paul**

Jennings (b. 1918), **Hamilton Ellis** and others which can be read repeatedly with enjoyment. Among well-known writers who have given the railway consideration in essays are **Robert Lynd** (1879–1949) who wrote three: *In the Train, Railway Stations I have loved*, and *Trains*; **A. A. Milne** (1882–1956) who gave us *A Train of Thought* (1921); and **J. B. Priestley** (b. 1894), *Man Underground* (1932) in which he philosophises on travelling beneath London.

An example of factual literature on railways is *Across the Plains* (1892) by Robert Louis Stevenson. **Pierre Berton** of Canada (b. 1920) has written two volumes on the building of the Canadian Pacific Railway which contain fine historical writing and deserve consideration as literature: *The National Dream, The Great Railway, 1871–1881* (1970) and *The Last Spike, The Great Railway 1881–1885* (1971).

The railway does not figure prominently in drama. John Galsworthy (1867–1933) wrote a one-act comedy in three scenes, *The Little Man* (1915) set on railway platforms and in a railway carriage compartment. Perhaps the best-known play is *The Ghost Train* (1925) by Arnold Ridley (b. 1896) which has been made into a film on several occasions (see p. 232). In *Brief Encounter* by **Noel Coward** (1899–1973) part of the action is set in a railway station. The most completely 'railway' play is probably *The Knotty*, first produced by the Victoria Theatre, Stoke-on-Trent, in 1966, a musical documentary outlining the history of the North Staffordshire Railway. Extracts are now available on a gramophone recording.

RAILWAYS IN THE CINEMA*

The first cinema show by the French brothers Louis and Auguste Lumière, on 28 December 1895, included a scene entitled 'Arrival of a train at La Ciotat Station'. Members of the audience leapt from their seats as the train came towards them 'out of the screen'.

The first railway film was a single scene called 'Black Diamond Express' on 43 ft (13·106 m) of film produced in the U.S.A. by Thomas Edison (1847–1931) on a device known as the 'Kinetescope', in 1896. It showed Locomotive No. 665 of the Lehigh Valley Railroad passing on a train to Buffalo.

* This section is not intended to be a catalogue, or 'screenography'.

The first British film taken from the front of an engine was made in 1896 between Exeter Central and St David's stations, down the incline and through the tunnel. It was followed in 1897 by a similar film 'Railway Ride over the Tay Bridge'.

The first railway film to tell a dramatic story was 'The Great Train Robbery', produced in the U.S.A. by Edwin S. Porter (1870–1941), a collaborator with Edison, on the Delaware, Lackawanna & Western Railroad in 1903. It was one of the most important landmarks in the first 15 years of the cinema industry.

Train wrecks made exciting film scenes. In 1897, 1898 and 1908 some excellent shots were made using models. In 1914 Vitagraph of the U.S.A. produced *The Wreck*, the first film of a train wreck using actual old locomotives and stock on a specially rented track. Its success led to a spate of films and even public events of deliberately contrived crashes (see p. 186).

The Great Locomotive Chase (see p. 176) provided a perfect story for an exciting film. It was first filmed in 1911 in *Railroad Raiders of '62*. In 1927 Joseph M. Shenck, using replicas of the locomotives *General* and *Texas*, produced *The General* running for 90 minutes.

One of the last of the silent railway films, *The Wrecker*, a British production by Gainsborough Studios in 1929, was based on a stage play by Arnold Ridley and Bernard Merivale. It was filmed principally on the Southern Railway, partly on the Basingstoke & Alton Light Railway, which still had passenger trains until 12 September 1932.

One of the most popular stories for a film was *The Ghost Train* based on the play by Arnold Ridley. It was first produced by C. Bolvary as a silent film in 1927, running for 108 minutes. A second version, produced by Walter Forde with sound in 1931, ran for 72 minutes. In 1937 a third version was produced with sound for B.B.C. Television, transmitted on 20 December. Gainsborough produced a fourth version, running for 84 minutes, in 1941, and a further television presentation was made by the B.B.C. on 20 December 1948.

The first British sound film on a railway subject was *The Flying Scotsman* produced by British International Pictures in 1930. Three reels had been shot as a silent film then, after half an hour, it suddenly became 'talkie'. For the film the London & North Eastern Railway 'Pacific' No. 4472 *Flying Scotsman* was used for six weeks followed by running rights on ten successive Sundays between London (King's Cross) and Edinburgh.

The three best loved of British railway films are probably '*Oh! Mr Porter* (Gainsborough 1937), filmed on the Basingstoke & Alton Light Railway in Hampshire (closed to all traffic on 30 May 1936); *The Titfield Thunderbolt* (Ealing Studios 1952), inspired by the preservation of the Tal-y-llyn Railway in Wales, filmed in colour on the Limpley Stoke–Camerton Branch of the Great Western Railway in Somerset; and *The Railway Children* based on the story by Edith Nesbit (1858–1924) and filmed in 1969, also in colour, on the Keighley & Worth Valley Railway in Yorkshire. All three films provide entertainment of a high order and an abundance of universal human interest, but *The Titfield Thunderbolt* is marred by two impossible scenes, one a battle between a locomotive and a steam-roller and the other in which a locomotive is driven along roads. Both, however, are highly amusing.

RAILWAYS AND ART

The earliest railway pictures of any value are those produced as series of prints made during the construction or soon after the opening of some of England's earliest main lines. Chief among these are:

The Liverpool & Manchester Railway, a series of coloured aquatints by **Thomas Talbot Bury** (1811–77), published by Ackermann & Company in 1830. Rudolf Ackermann lived from 1764 to 1834. See p. 15.

The Newcastle & Carlisle Railway, a series of drawings by **James Wilson Carmichael**, a marine artist (1800–68), published in Newcastle in 1837 and reprinted in 1970.

The London & Birmingham Railway and **The Great Western Railway**, two series of hand-coloured lithographs by **John Cooke Bourne** (1814–96), produced in 1837–39. The G.W.R. pictures were reprinted in 1969 and the L. & B. in 1970. Bourne's view of Camden Shed is shown on p. 24.

The Manchester & Leeds Railway, a series of lithographs by **Arthur Fitzwilliam Tait**

(1819–1905), published in both black and white and colour in 1845. They were reprinted in 1972. Tait's view of Summit Tunnel is shown below. Tait was primarily a landscape and animal painter. He emigrated to the U.S.A. in 1850.

A. F. Tait's lithograph of Summit Tunnel on the Manchester & Leeds Railway (1845)

All these pictures, besides being works of art in themselves, possessed the additional advantage of technical accuracy and are valuable historical documents.

The first great artist to be inspired by the railway was Joseph Mallard William Turner (1775–1851) whose famous painting *Rain Steam and Speed, the Great Western Railway* (1844) shows a 'Firefly' Class locomotive on a train crossing Brunel's Maidenhead Bridge towards Reading. (National Gallery, London.)

David Cox (1783–1859), an English landscape-painter and one of the greatest English water-colourists, was inspired by Turner's painting to paint his *Wind, Rain and Sunshine* (1845) which recaptures some of the atmospheric effects but is really a landscape with a small train in the background. He also painted *The Night Train* about 1857, another landscape with a small train motif. (Both Birmingham City Art Gallery.)

Adolf Friedrich Erdmann von Menzel (1815–1905), a German historical and genre painter and illustrator, produced *Die Berlin–Potsdamer Bahn* in 1847. The curve of the railway is an important element in the composition, and a train is shown. (Berlin Nationalgallerie.)

Gustave Doré (1832–83) in his sketches of London published in 1872 (reprinted 1971) included two showing railways. *Ludgate Hill* shows a street scene which makes modern traffic appear insignificant. Over the bridge above a train of the London, Chatham & Dover Railway is entering the Ludgate Hill terminus. In *Over London by Rail* we look through an arch of a railway viaduct along a row of cramped, overcrowded tenements to another viaduct over which a train is passing.

In 1871 the French landscape-painter **Camille Pissarro** (1830–1903), on a visit to London with Claude Monet (see below), by way of escaping from the Franco-Prussian War, painted *Penge Station, Upper Norwood* (Courtauld Institute Galleries, University of London). The picture shows an early signal, and a train approaching through a cutting, in a bright, spring-like setting.

Penge Station, Upper Norwood *by C. Pissarro (Courtauld Institute Galleries, London)*

Claude Monet (1840–1926), French landscape artist and one of the greatest of the Impressionists, was greatly inspired by Turner's work during his London visit in 1871. His earliest known railway picture is *Train dans la Champagne*, probably before 1870 (Louvre, Paris). In 1875 he painted his *Le Train dans la Neige* (Marmottan Museum, Paris) and *Railway Bridge at Argenteuil* with a train passing over (Philadelphia Museum of Art). His best-known railway paintings are his series of ten of the Gare Saint Lazare, Paris, in 1877. At the time he was still an unknown and impecunious artist. He put on his best clothes and introduced himself to the station superintendent as 'Claude Monet, the painter'. The superintendent, knowing nothing of art, believed he was a world-famous artist and had trains stopped and arranged specially for his benefit, and when Monet had finished he was graciously bowed out by uniformed officials. Today the series is scattered. One is in New York, one in Harvard University, and one in the Marmottan Museum, Paris.

Perhaps the best loved of all railway pictures is *The Railway Station* (1862) **by William Powell Frith** (1819–1909) showing a bustling scene at Paddington Station, London, with one of Gooch's broad-gauge engines, the *Great Britain* of 1847, on the left, and on the right the arrest of a criminal. Above all are the leaping arches of Brunel's great station roof. (See colour illustration on p. 159.)

The railway carriage compartment was a popu-lar setting for some Mid-Victorian paintings. **Abraham Solomon** (1824–62) produced a pair of paintings in 1854 entitled *First Class — The Meeting* and *Second Class — The Parting*. In the first a girl is fascinated by a young officer while her father talks animatedly between them. (In the original version the father was asleep in the corner, but this did not accord with Victorian decorum!) The second shows the sad parting of a mother and her son who is emigrating.

Honoré Daumier (1808–79) produced a vivid impression of travelling conditions in the mid nineteenth century in *The Third Class Carriage* about 1862 (Metropolitan Museum, New York).

August Leopold Egg (1816–63) left us *The Travelling Companions* (1862), now in Birmingham City Art Gallery, showing two extravagantly attired women, one asleep and the other reading, in a first class compartment, totally oblivious of the beautiful coastal scenery near Menton on the French Riviera.

To Brighton and back for 3s 6d by **Charles Rossiter** (1827–97) is a colourful painting of a group of mid-nineteenth-century excursionists, in a third class carriage with wooden seats and roof but no windows and with the rain driving in from the left (Birmingham Museum and Art Gallery).

To Brighton and back for 3s. 6d. *by Charles Rossiter (1827–97) (Birmingham Museum and Art Gallery)*

Most of the increasing number of railway artists today are ardent railway enthusiasts. Hamilton Ellis is mentioned in 'Railways and Literature' on p. 231. His numerous paintings are distinguished for their technical accuracy. The paintings of **Terence Cuneo** (b. 1907) are remarkable for their animated life and energy. An outstanding example is his reconstruction of the opening of the Stockton & Darlington Railway.

Nathaniel Currier (1813–88) and James Ives (1824–95) formed a partnership in the U.S.A. in 1857 and for over 50 years mass produced about three lithographs every week, hand-coloured by one girl per colour. They depicted accurately every aspect of American life, and a great many were pictures of railways.

One of the leading American artists is Howard Fogg of Boulder, Colorado, whose vivid portrayal of railway scenes in Colorado are among the most colourful of railway pictures. In Fogg's pictures the pioneering days of the 3 ft (0·914 m) gauge are brought once more to life.

RAILWAY ARCHITECTURE

In Victorian England the railway was almost alone in maintaining a high standard of architectural design. The most outstanding examples of fine design were the great viaducts and tunnel entrances, displaying a simplicity of form unique at the time. Some of the leading architects applied their skills to railway stations, but for these they often chose exotic and extravagant styles.

Famous examples were:

London, Euston Station, the Doric Arch and Great Hall designed by Philip Charles Hardwick (see p. 209).
Newcastle upon Tyne Station built in 1846–55 in the Classical style, by John Dobson (1787–1865).
London King's Cross Station, 1851–52, in a style of the utmost dignity and simplicity by Lewis Cubitt (1799–1883).
Huddersfield Station designed by J. P. Pritchett & Son has a magnificent central edifice flanked by Corinthian Colonnades. It was built in 1847–48.
London St Pancras Station. 1866–75, is one of the greatest pieces of Victorian Gothic, by Sir Gilbert Scott (1811–78). To pass through this building and to emerge beneath Barlow's tremendous arched roof is a startling experience.
York Station on the former North Eastern Railway is one of the finest examples in England,

constructed in 1871–77 with three great arched roofs laid out in a long curve. The architects were Thomas Prosser, Benjamin Burley and William Peachy.

Huddersfield Station Yorkshire (John Marshall)

Sir George Gilbert Scott's St Pancras Station Hotel, London; a superb example of Victorian Gothic architecture. It was designed in 1865, begun in March 1866, and was opened on 5 May 1873. The west wing was completed in 1875. The total cost was £1 000 000. The building consumed 60 000 000 Nottingham bricks, 80 000 ft³ (2265 m³) of 14 varieties of stone, and 9000 tons of wrought iron. The hotel was closed in 1935 (British Rail)

Outstanding examples in Europe and America are:
Paris, Gare du Nord, 1861–65, by Jacques Ignace Hittorf (1793–1867), and **Gare de l'Est**, 1847–52, by François Duquesney (1800–49).
Boston, Massachusetts, Kneeland Street Station by Gridley J. F. Bryant (1816–97) was the most completely equipped station in America when it was completed in 1847.
Philadelphia, Broad Street Station on the Reading Railroad, designed by F. H. Kimball (1849–1919) and built in 1891–93, has a distinguished building displaying Renaissance features, and the greatest of all arched roofs, of 300 ft (91·44 m) span, by Wilson Brothers & Company, Engineers.
Helsinki Station, designed in 1905 by the Finnish architect Eliel Saarinen (1873–1950) was not completed until 1914. It is one of the finest in Europe.
Stuttgart Station, the work of the German architect Paul Bonats (1877–1951), is a leading example of modern station architecture. It was built in 1928.

Some of the finest examples of modern station design are to be found on the London Underground system, mostly built in the 1920s and 1930s, by Adams, Holden and Pearson, largely inspired by Frank Pick.

The original station at Thornaby, Teesside, Yorkshire, exhibited a notice asking passengers: 'Have you observed the varied carvings on the string cornices of the station buildings?'

RAILWAYS AND STAMPS

The first postage stamps with a railway subject were three issued in New Brunswick, Canada, in 1860. They were of 1 cent value, coloured brown-purple, purple and dull claret, and showed an inside-cylinder 4–4–0 with spark-arresting chimney.

The United States depicted the opening of its first transcontinental line in 1869 with a blue 3 cent stamp showing a Norris-type 4–4–0 with inclined cylinders and spark-arresting chimney. In 1944 the 75th anniversary of the transcontinental railway was marked by the issue of another blue 3 cent stamp showing the famous last spike ceremony.
The Pan American Exhibition at Buffalo in 1901 was marked by the issue of special stamps, one, a red 2 cent, showing the 'Empire State Express' headed by New York Central & Hudson River Railroad 4–4–0 No. 999.

Peru issued three stamps in 1871 showing arms and an early 2–2–2 locomotive. By 1962 Peru had issued 34 different stamps carrying railway subjects.

Belgium was the first country to issue rail parcel stamps, when the railway-operated parcel service began in 1879. The first issues, 1879–82, carried a winged wheel emblem. Issues from 1882–1894 showed an early locomotive in the background. By 1964 a total of 387 different stamps had been issued.

The United States issued a set of parcel-post stamps in 1912–13. One of these, a rose-carmine 5 cent, showed a mail train headed by a 2–6–2 'Prairie' locomotive.

The Central American States, Mexico and West Indies have issued many stamps carrying railway subjects. **Guatemala** introduced railway tax stamps in 1886. **Nicaragua** produced ten stamps in 1890 bearing arms and a train, and by 1937 had issued a total of 113 stamps carrying railway subjects. **Salvador** issued 16 stamps in 1891 showing a train and a mountain. **Mexico** made ten issues in 1895–98 illustrating an early mail train. **Honduras** followed in 1898 with eight issues showing an early steam train.

The first Asian country to issue stamps of railway subjects was North Borneo, in 1912, with two showing an early train.

China issued its first stamp with a railway subject in 1913. By 1966 a total of 156 had been issued.

Russia produced a stamp showing a train in 1922, and by 1966 had issued a total of 111.

A century of friendship between the U.S.A. and Canada, 1848–1948, was celebrated by the issue of a U.S.A. blue 3 cent stamp showing the Niagara gorge suspension bridge of 1848 as strengthened by Roebling to carry trains in 1855. (See 'Some American Bridge Records', p. 95.)

Belgium was the first country to issue railway centenary stamps, in 1935, with a set of over 20 railway parcel stamps from 1 Fr to 100 Fr, of 15 different colours, showing the first locomotive built in Belgium, State Railways 2–2–2 No. 6 *Le Belge*, built by John Cockerill at Seraing to a Stephenson design. They marked the centenary of the opening of the Brussels–Malines line on 5 May

One of the largest railway bridges in Switzerland, the Bietschtal Bridge on the Bern–Lötschberg–Simplon Railway. Locomotive No. 201 is crossing with a train to Brig. (John Marshall)

1835. In 1949–52 there appeared a set of 18 railway parcel stamps featuring famous Belgian locomotives, the first again showing *Le Belge*. An extra 300 Fr stamp (purple) issued in 1952 showed an electric train of 1951.

Germany celebrated the opening of the Nuremberg–Fürth line on 7 December 1835 by the issue of a set of stamps in 1935 showing the Robert Stephenson 2–2–2 *Der Adler* (The Eagle)

Switzerland's first locomotive *Limmat* appeared on a 5 cent stamp in 1947 to celebrate the centenary of the opening of the Zürich–Baden line on 9 August 1847. In addition there were three other stamps showing railway scenes and four showing Swiss stations.

Other countries which marked their railway centenaries on stamps included: Austria, 1937; Italy, 1939; Hungary, 1946; Denmark, 1947; Yugoslavia, 1949; Chile, 1951; India, 1953; Australia, Brazil, Norway, 1954; Sweden, 1956; Argentina, Egypt, 1957.

The U.S.A. missed its railway centenary, but made up by celebrating the 125th anniversary of the Baltimore & Ohio Railroad Charter of 1827 with a blue 3 cent stamp in 1952, showing a horse passenger-carriage, an inaccurate replica of the first steam locomotive, *Tom Thumb*, and a diesel-electric locomotive.

Similarly Australia's 125th anniversary in 1962 and Jamaica's in 1970 were celebrated by stamp issues.

The only British stamp having any connection with railways was a multi-coloured 9d stamp in 1967 to commemorate the European Free Trade Association. It showed three railway wagons in front of a ship.

The opening of the Forth road bridge in 1964 was marked by the issue of a black, light blue and carmine-red 6d stamp showing the new bridge and the railway bridge in the background.

For Christmas 1968 Great Britain issued a special multi-coloured 1s 6d stamp showing a boy playing with a train set. **This was the first British stamp showing any kind of locomotive.**

125th ANNIVERSARY of the RAILWAY
THE PROJECTOR - 1845
JAMAICA 3c

125th ANNIVERSARY of the RAILWAY
ENGINE 54 - 1944
JAMAICA 15c

125th ANNIVERSARY of the RAILWAY
ENGINE 102 - 1967
JAMAICA 50c

MALAWI 4d
SADDLEBACK

MALAWI 9d
'S' CLASS

1'6 MALAWI
ZAMBESI

3'- MALAWI
DIESEL RAIL CAR

New Zealand 3c
CLASS "W"

New Zealand 4c
CLASS "X"

New Zealand 5c
CLASS "Ab"

1873-1973
Steam Railway Centenary
Sutherland 2-4-0
ISLE of MAN 9½p
J. H. NICHOLSON R.I. 1973 HARRISON & SONS LTD

New Zealand 10c
CLASS "Ja"

1873-1973
Steam Railway Centenary
Caledonia 0-6-0
ISLE of MAN 3p
J. H. NICHOLSON R.I. 1973 HARRISON & SONS LTD

1873-1973
Steam Railway Centenary
Kissack 2-4-0
ISLE of MAN 7½p
J. H. NICHOLSON R.I. 1973 HARRISON & SONS LTD

1964 日本郵便
東海道新幹線開通記念 10

1873-1973
Steam Railway Centenary
Pender 2-4-0
ISLE of MAN 9p
J. H. NICHOLSON R.I. 1973 HARRISON & SONS LTD

The Isle of Man and Jersey both issued their own railway centenary stamps in 1973, of 2½p, 3p, 7½p and 9p values. They carried pictures of locomotives.

The Railway Philatelic Group makes a special study of Railway Stamps. Honorary Secretary: Peter Johnson, 20 Rockley Road, Leicester LE4 0GJ.

The carriage of letters by rail was legalised in Britain by agreement with the Postmaster-General in 1891. The additional rate was 2d (two old pence). On 15 January 1920 it was increased to 3d when the Post Office letter rate was 1½d. It was again increased to 4d on 1 September 1920 when postage became 2d. (The Post Office rate was later reduced, again to 1½d.) The stamps were green and identical except for the name of the railway company. The last stamps were issued in 1920.

RAILWAYS AND MUSIC

One of the earliest composers to be influenced by the railway was the Dane, Hans Christian Lumbye (1810–74), whose *Københauns Jernbane Damp-Galop* or *Jernbane Galop* (Railway Galop) is an exhilarating orchestral item.

Johann Strauss junior (1825–99) wrote a fast polka *Vergnügungszug* (Excursion Train), opus 281.

His brother Eduard Strauss (1835–1916) composed an entertaining polka, *Bahn Frei*; a musical train ride complete with guard's whistle and engine hooter.

Tablet on the building at Stockton on Tees commemorating the place where the first passenger was booked. This was on 10 October, just 150 years ago at the time this book is published. (British Railways)

The Czech composer Antonin Dvořák (1841–1904) was a keen railway enthusiast and made daily visits to the main station in Prague where he was friendly with many engine crews. On one occasion he was too busy to go, so he sent his servant to note the number of the engine on a particular train. When the man returned he was severely reprimanded for having noted the tender number by mistake!

The French composer Arthur Honegger (1892–1955) was fascinated by the steam locomotive and in 1924 wrote his famous locomotive tone-poem for orchestra *Pacific 231*.

The Brazilian composer Hector Villa-Lobos (1887–1959) gave us a delightful musical picture of a Brazilian narrow-gauge train in 'The Little Train of the Caipira' which forms the final toccata section of his second *Bachianas Brasilieras* (Brazilian Bach pieces), composed in 1930.

Vivian Ellis (b 1904) wrote a short orchestral piece (about 4 minutes) entitled 'Coronation Scot' about 1937–38.

The British composer and conductor Eugene Goossens (1893–1962) was a very knowledgeable railway enthusiast as was **Constant Lambert (1905–51)**. There are many other examples of organists, conductors, composers and instrumentalists with a keen interest in railways.

The most evocative of all 'musical train rides' was written in 1826 or 1828 by a composer who had never heard of a railway—Frans Schubert (1797–1828). It is the fourth movement (Finale) of the Great C Major Symphony, No. 9, which has all the rhythm and energy of an express train behind a big steam-engine. In the opinion of the author it captures the atmosphere of a journey in a way that deliberate attempts have failed to achieve.

Index

M